PROGRESS IN
NEURAL NETWORKS

Volume 2

edited by

Omid M. Omidvar

 ABLEX PUBLISHING CORPORATION
NORWOOD, NEW JERSEY

ISSN: 89-696306
ISBN: 0-89381-735-4

Ablex Publishing Corporation
355 Chestnut Street
Norwood, New Jersey 07648

To my parents
who taught me love and respect

Table of Contents

Preface

Progress in Neural Networks is a series concerned with the advances in neural networks—natural and synthetic. This series reviews state-of-the-art research in modeling, analysis, design, and development of neural networks in software and hardware areas. This series is intended to serve as a platform for detailed and expanded discussion of topics of interest to the neural network and cognitive information-processing communities. We hope the series will help to shape and define academic and professional progress in this area. This series seeks contributions from leading researchers and practitioners to provide its audience with a wide variety of in-depth discussion of active research and presentation of complex ideas in the neural networks field. The second volume consists of chapters that are self-contained and tutorial in nature; however, one must have a background in general information about neural networks to appreciate the depth and complexity of the research presented here. This series is intended for a wide audience, those professionally involved in neural networks research, such as lecturers and primary investigators in neural computing, neural modeling, neural learning, neural memory, and neurocomputers.

The first chapter in this volume focuses on self-organizing neural classifier for complex imagery. The second chapter deals with constraint satisfaction networks for vision. The third chapter is devoted to neural networks for position, scale, and rotation invariant pattern recognition. Chapter 4 is on generalization of back propagation networks. Chapter 5 deals with optical implementation of closest vector selection in neural networks. Chapters 6 and 7 are devoted to the study of the biological basis for artificial neural networks and analysis of neuronal spike trains. Chapter 8 is of interest to scientists in the area of unsupervised learning. Chapter 9 focuses on neural modeling of complex systems. Chapter 10 discusses neural systems for computation and decision making. Chapter 11 details neural feature analysis and is of interest to scientists in neural character recognition. Chapter 12 deals with research in graph theory aspects of neural networks and its relation to cellular automata. Chapter 13 discusses neural networks pattern processing and logical reasoning capabilities. The last chapter is devoted to primacy and recency effects in back propagation learning.

This is an attempt to provide the readers with an in-depth presentation of a specific subject without limitation on the size, shape, and content of the presented work. We adhere to all the valuable principles of integrity in research while pursuing this endeavor. This series is the result of the hard work of about more than 50 reviewers who have done a great deal of work for which I am grateful for their frank and valuable suggestions and recommendations. I would like to thank the president of Ablex, Mr. Walter Johnson, who trusted my judgment to start a series in neural networks back in the late 1980s; Ms. Carol Davidson for her invaluable advice every step of the way; and Ms. Roxanne Guidice for her constant work on the production of the series. Also, I would like to thank Ms. Sylvia C. Neuman for keeping my correspondence up to date, my wife for her continuous encouragement, and my children for their understanding of the fact that my work has as much importance as their computer games. Last but not least I am grateful to all the authors for their valuable contributions to this volume and the series. The third volume is also available now, and Volumes 4 to 10 will be available in the near future.

Omid M. Omidvar, Ph.D.
Series Editor
Computer Science Department
University of the District of Columbia

1

Prospects for Classifying Complex Imagery Using a Self-Organizing Neural Network

Murali M. Menon
Karl G. Heinemann
Massachusetts Institute of Technology Lincoln Laboratory
Lexington, MA

1. INTRODUCTION

The Neocognitron of Fukushima [1] is a massively parallel multilevel neural network system which performs visual pattern recognition. Its architecture models the anatomy of the human retina in a qualitative way. This system also resembles the Adaptive Resonance model of Carpenter and Grossberg [2] in that it is self organizing and operates without a "teacher." The Neocognitron has a demonstrated capability to discriminate alphabetical characters stored in a matrix of 16 × 16 pixels. Performance on handwritten characters in a 19 × 19 matrix was demonstrated by Fukushima [3]. A more recent study by Stoner and Schilke [4] has confirmed the model's ability to classify dot-matrix characters. While many accurate character recognition algorithms already exist, the Neocognitron is noteworthy because it handles positional shifts and moderate deformations in the shapes of input characters. These properties suggest that Fukushima's model might be very useful in solving more demanding machine vision problems. Work at the Massachusetts Institute of Technology Lincoln Laboratory has produced a simulation of the Neocognitron on a serial machine. This program has operated successfully on wire-frame images embedded in a matrix of 128 × 128 pixels. The model was able to classify images by extracting features from the input images and retaining only those whose response was above the average. Results from different Neocognitron systems showed that its shift tolerance depends on the number of levels used. A four-level system was unable to classify patterns uniquely and tolerate shifts with an input plane of 128 × 128 pixels. However, a single-level version was found that did classify properly and provide shift invariance at the same time. The shift-tolerance property can be exploited to cope with other kinds of variation by submitting appropriate transforms of the imagery as input. This approach has been investigated by applying a polar transform to achieve automatic recognition of rotated images.

2. MODEL DESCRIPTION

The Neocognitron is a structured network of analog processing units which receive and transmit zero or positive valued analog signals. This network contains four distinct kinds of computational elements called S-cells, C-cells, V_s-cells, and V_c-cells. Each class of processor is defined by the types of cells which provide its input and a specific mathematical operation which determines the strength of its output.

The output from an individual processor generates input signals for certain other nodes after passing through a set of weighted connections. Each of these communication channels multiplies the transmitting unit's output by a specific connection strength (weight) and presents that product as an input for the receiving unit. The weight for a given connection can take on any positive value, so the effect of a specific unit's output may vary considerably from one node to the next.

Cells in the Neocognitron generally receive inputs from a number of different nodes and respond to the total received signal, but signals from the different types of processors are summed separately, because they affect the response in different ways. For a given unit, different patterns of output at the source nodes will produce varying levels of total input. This behavior arises, because the specific pattern of connection weights will amplify some of the individual source signals more than others. The total input will be particularly high when the source nodes send strong signals along paths with large weights, and it will decrease as strong signals are shifted to paths with smaller weights or the paths with large weights carry smaller signals. Thus, communication through the weighted connections enables the processors to detect differences in the pattern of transmitted signals. An analog transfer function then produces corresponding variations in the response level.

The Neocognitron's processing elements are organized into a hierarchical series of levels, where units of each type appear at every level. All these levels share a common structure wherein the different types of cells are segregated into distinct layers, and signals traverse these layers in the same order. A schematic representation of this architecture is shown in Figure 1.1, where an image comes in at the left and data flow to the right. A layer of V_s-cells and a layer of V_c-cells also exists at each level, but these have been omitted in order to simplify the diagram. Output from any given level serves as input for the next one, until a layer representing the final classification categories is reached.

The system is strictly a feed-forward network where signals originate at an initial input layer and propagate towards the final output layer. A hierarchical structure is produced by connecting the cells in a "fan-out" pattern, so that the

LEVELS AND LAYERS IN THE NEOCOGNITRON

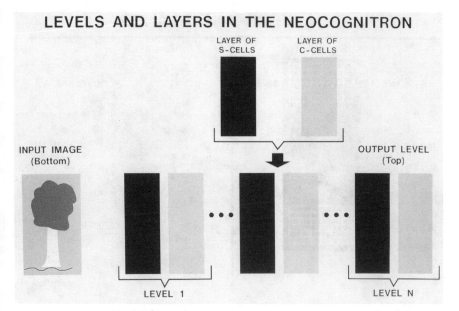

Figure 1.1.   Multilevel feed-forward architecture of the Neocognitron.

number of units gradually decreases as signals propagate into deeper levels of the system. Under this connection scheme, each unit receives input signals from specific small regions on the layers which immediately precede it. However, the number of indirect connections between a processor and more distant predecessors grows significantly as the number of intervening layers increases. For any particular cell, the complete set of input sources on an earlier layer will be referred to as the cell's "receptive field" on that layer. Since processors at deeper levels gain access to progressively larger portions of the input patterns, they can respond to progressively more complicated features, and simpler features will be detected over a progressively larger receptive field. The final output layer consists of cells whose receptive field covers the entire input layer. This hierarchical structure contributes to the Neocognitron's capacity for shift invariant pattern recognition.

In order to completely explain the property of shift invariance, one must consider the structure of an individual level. The S-cells and the C-cells on any given level are organized into a number of subgroups which will be called "S-planes" or "C-planes" according to the type of processor which is involved. V_s-cells and V_c-cells also are grouped into planes, but there is only one V_s-plane and one V_c-plane on any level. These cell planes are treated as two-dimensional matrices where the location of an individual element is specified by a pair of column and row coordinates.

The relationships between planes, layers, and individual cells are illustrated in Figure 1.2. All the elements in a given plane share a single pattern of connection

LAYERS AND PLANES

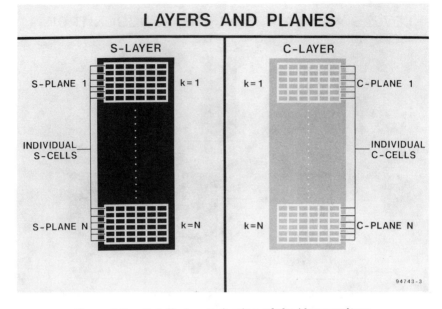

Figure 1.2.   Detailed organization of the Neocognitron.

weights on their input channels. Consequently, a specific pattern of transmitted signals will elicit the same response from any element which observes that pattern exactly. While the input field of an individual processor covers only a small portion of the source layer, the fields of adjacent cells can be positioned in a way which insures that the entire source layer is covered. If the number of cells in the plane, the size of their input fields, and the offset between these fields are correctly matched, one can guarantee that some cell will show the optimum response when a specific pattern appears anywhere in the source layer. Hence, the behavior of these cell planes provides a massively parallel technique for shift invariant feature detection. This architectural feature is the fundamental mechanism responsible for the Neocognitron's tolerance of positional shifts.

The Neocognitron acquires its ability to classify patterns because each level contains a number of separate S-planes and C-planes. These two structures must always be paired with one another, so a given level has the same number of each type. However, the number of paired cell planes can vary from one level to the next. Each of the S-planes has a distinct pattern of input connection weights, but the C-planes on any particular level share one pattern in common.

The weights which feed into the S-planes have a special role, because they change as the system learns. All the other connection weights are built into the design of a specific Neocognitron architecture, and they cannot be modified. As the system learns to discriminate between diverse input images, the S-planes become sensitive to different spatial arrangements of the source signals. However, units in any given plane will receive small input signals from almost any pattern that happens to occur. Difficulties could arise if all these signals were allowed to propagate deeper into the system. Some of the very weak signals could be greatly amplified when they pass through connections with large weights, and the results might convey some very misleading information.

In order to avoid this problem, the Neocognitron incorporates mechanisms which suppress the transmission of insignificant input signals. Interactions between the different types of processors work in concert with their particular response functions to provide a form of adaptive filtering. This design prevents the S-cells and C-cells from responding unless the pattern dependent input signal exceeds an independent estimate of the "typical" incoming signal strength.

A brief discussion of the different processors' actual operating characteristics and their interconnections will help to illustrate and clarify these general principles.

2.1. Cells in the S-layer and the V_c-layer

The S-cells in a given level obtain information about the previous one through two separate input mechanisms. Units in the first S-layer respond to the initial input signals, while those on subsequent levels receive input from C-planes on the preceding level. Direct connections from C-cells to S-cells carry excitatory signals which act to increase the S-cell's output. The S-cells also receive an inhibitory input which reduces the output signal through a shunting effect. This inhibitory signal ultimately comes from the same C-cells which produce the excitatory ones, but a layer of V_c-cells intervenes to perform some additional processing.

Any given level contains a number of S-planes and a single V_c-plane which all share the same geometric structure. The units at a given position in any of these planes share the same input fields, which extend over a specific set of adjacent coordinates in the preceding C-planes. Figure 1.3 illustrates the configuration of direct connections going from a C-layer to a particular S-plane. As a result of this connection scheme, S-cells and V_c-cells receive input from small regions on all of the C-planes. This arrangement enables the S-cells to recognize groupings of features that might have been detected in earlier stages of processing. If k refers to the kth S-plane in level l and n refers to a specific position in that S-plane, the response of the corresponding S-cell is given by:

$$Us_l(k_l, n) = r_l \times f(A) \tag{2.1}$$

where:

$$A = \left[\frac{1 + \sum_{k_{l-1}=1}^{K_{l-1}} \sum_{veS_l} a_l(k_{l-1}, v, k_l) \times Uc_{l-1}(k_{l-1}, n + v)}{1 + \frac{r_l}{l + r_l} \times b_l(k_l) \times Vc_l(n)} - 1 \right]. \tag{2.2}$$

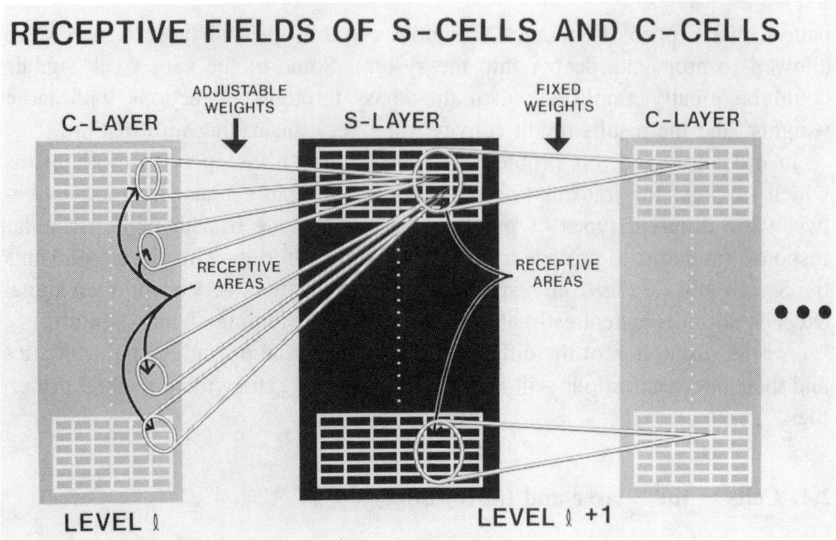

RECEPTIVE FIELDS OF S-CELLS AND C-CELLS

Figure 1.3. Interconnection architecture of the Neocognitron.

Expression $Uc_{l-1}(k_{l-1}, n + v)$ represents an excitatory signal coming from the unit at position $n + v$ on C-plane k_{l-1}, and $Vc_l(n)$ represents the inhibitory input. In Equation 2.2, $a_l(k_{l-1}, v, k_l)$ are the connection weights for excitatory input, and v designates a relative position inside the region of input. Positional variations of the weight values give rise to the "weight patterns" which were discussed earlier. These weight distributions differ from one source plane (k_{l-1}) to the next, so that the S-cells can recognize combinations of different source patterns. Note that $a_l(k_{l-1}, v, k_l)$ does not depend on the S-cell position, n, because all members of a given plane k_l have the same distribution of input weights. In the Equation 2.2, the inner sum computes the total excitatory input from a specific C-plane, and the outer sum adds together the contributions from different planes.

The inhibitory effect works through this expression's denominator, where the connection weight $b_l(k_l)$ multiplies the output from a single node on the V_c plane. This inhibitory signal comes from the V_c cell at location n, which corresponds to the S-cell's position in its own plane. The V_c-cell at those coordinates receives input from the same C-cells which are exciting the S-cell, and it responds by computing a weighted root-mean-square:

$$V c_l(n) = \sqrt{\sum_{k_{l-1}=1}^{K_{l-1}} \sum_{v \in S_l} c_l(v) \times U c_{l-1}^2 (k_{l-1}, n + v)} \qquad (2.3)$$

where $c_i(v)$ represents the input connection strength for a particular position v in that cell's input field. These weights can follow any distribution which decreases monotonically as the magnitude of v increases, and they must be normalized so that their sum is exactly equal to unity, that is:

$$\sum_{k_{l-1}=1}^{K_{l-1}} \sum_{v \in S_l} c_l(\dot{v}) = 1. \qquad (2.4)$$

In the present study, the $c_l(v)$ were defined by a decaying exponential distribution:

$$c_l(v) = \frac{1}{C(l)} \alpha_l^{r'(v)} \qquad (2.5)$$

where $r'(v)$ is the normalized distance between location v and the center of the input region ($0 \le r' \le 1$). The parameter α_l is a small constant ($\alpha_l < 1$) which determines how quickly these weights fall off as $r'(v)$ increases. Consequently, weights at the edge of $S_l(r' = 1)$ are equal to a fraction of α_l of the value at the center ($r' = 0$). The expression $C(l)$ is a normalizing constant:

$$C(l) = \sum_{k_{l-1}=1}^{K_{l-1}} \sum_{v \in S_l} \alpha_l^{r'(v)} \qquad (2.6)$$

which insures that Equation 2.4 will be satisfied. All the V_c-cells in a given plane (and level) use the same pattern of input connections, but α_l is free to assume a different value for each level.

The weighted root-mean-square signal from a V_c-cell propagates to all S-cells at the same coordinates n. However, the weights on these connections, $b_l(k_l)$, are all independent, so the actual inhibitory effect will differ from one S-plane to the next. In addition, the denominator of the S-cell response function contains a factor $r_l/1 + r_l$, which further modulates the inhibition. This factor can provide any degree of attenuation as the parameter r_l goes from 0 to ∞, and it has great sensitivity at the low end of its dynamic range. Note that r_l also appears as a multiplicative factor in the S-cell response function. It is given this additional role to curb growth in the final output when high attenuation (low r_l) makes the inhibition ineffective. The values for r_l are set by the system designer, and the subscript indicates that these values can be different at each level. Hence, the action of these parameters enables the system designer to control the overall influence of the weighted root-mean-square input at each level of the system. In order to prevent division by zero when inhibitory input is totally absent, the attenuated signal is incremented by one. This solution conveniently neutralizes the denominator when there is no inhibitory input.

As discussed previously, an S-cell's excitatory input measures the degree of similarity between a particular arrangement of source signals and a feature represented by the distribution of input weights a_l. The quotient in Equation 2.2 compares the actual excitatory input with some fraction of the weighted root-mean-square source signal. The resulting ratio is decreased by one to determine which of the two input signals is greater. A positive difference indicates that the excitatory signal is greater, because the previous ratio exceeded unity, and a negative difference indicates that the inhibitory signal was greater. The function "f" which operates on this result is the linear threshold function:

$$f(x) = \begin{cases} x(x \geq 0) \\ 0(x < 0). \end{cases} \tag{2.7}$$

Consequently, an S-cell responds only if the excitatory input exceeds the inhibitory input, and the transmitted signal is proportional to the relative difference. The double sum in the numerator is incremented by one to produce proper behavior (zero response) when excitatory input is absent.

The Neocognitron learns to discriminate between different patterns of input by updating the adjustable weights $a_l(k_{l-1}, v, k_l)$ and $b_l(k_l)$ in Equation 2.2. Weights for the excitatory connections (a_l) start off with small values that allow different S-planes to produce distinct responses to an arbitrary input pattern. The inhibitory weights (b_l) are set to zero initially. Increments for both types of weight are determined by finding those S-cells which show the greatest response with respect to a certain set of the others. These units are selected by imagining that all S-planes on a given level are stacked vertically.

Many overlapping columns are defined in this stack, where a column goes through the same set of spatial positions in each S-plane. The learning procedure examines each column and records the position and plane where the S-cell response is strongest. This analysis is carried out for all possible columns, so that the entire S-layer is considered. If two or more maxima occur in one S-plane, the strongest one of those is retained and the others are discarded. Hence, this selection procedure locates the strongest response in each S-plane, but the maximum for a given plane can be rejected if it is overshadowed by the output from a nearby cell in some other plane. If this procedure selects a representative for S-plane $\hat{k}_l$ at position $\hat{n}$, then the input weights for that plane are reinforced according to the rules:

$$\Delta a_l(k_{l-1}), v, \hat{k}_l) = q_l \times c_{l-1}(v) \times Uc_{l-1}(k_{l-1}, \hat{n} + v) \tag{2.8}$$

$$\Delta b_l(\hat{k}_l) = q_l \times Vc_{l-1}(\hat{n}). \tag{2.9}$$

None of the weights are reinforced if all the columns produce the same response. The parameter q_l is a gain factor that controls the rate of learning at each level, and it usually becomes larger as one progresses to higher levels. Since the increment for a given excitatory weight is proportional to input from the C-cell, only those connections carrying strong input signals are substantially reinforced. Consequently, the most significant modifications occur for connections where the input and the output are both relatively strong. This behavior is similar to Hebbian learning without a decay term. Note that the Neocognitron could be operated in a supervised learning ("with a teacher") mode by specifying the plane $\hat{k}_l$, and location $\hat{n}$ to be used at each level for a given input image. Further refinements are possible by including decay terms in the learning rule, but only Equations (2.8) and (2.9) were implemented in the present work.

2.2. Cells in the C-layer and the V_s-layer

The interactions and operational characteristics of the C-cells and the V_s-cells function in a manner that is very similar to the subsystem of S-cells and V_c-cells. These processors also take a given collection of source features and perform a comparison of two metrics. The result again determines whether information about that feature set will be passed on to higher-level classifiers. Units in the C-layers and the V_s-layer have input fields on the preceding S-planes. The exact locations covered by a specific field are related to the position of the receiving unit, just as before. However, elements in a given C-plane receive excitatory inputs from only one particular S-plane, and each S-plane communicates with only one C-plane. This design principle is depicted in Figure 1.3, and it is responsible for the pairing of cell planes that was mentioned above. V_s-cells receive input from all the preceding S-planes and generate an inhibitory signal. The C-cells compare these excitatory and inhibitory inputs by applying the same shunting mechanism which an S-cell uses:

$$Uc_l(k_l,\ n) = g\left[\ \frac{1 + \Sigma_{v \in D_l}\ d_l(v) \times U\ s_l(k_l,\ n + v)}{1 + V\ s_l(n)} - 1\ \right] \qquad (2.10)$$

where D_l is the region of input on the S-layer, Us is the S-cell output from position $n + v$ on S-plane k_l, and d_l is the input connection weight at relative position v in the region of input. This expression is quite similar to the S-cell response function given in Equations (2.1) and (2.2), but the excitatory component in the numerator includes contributions from only one S-plane, and the connection weights for inhibitory input are set to unity. The excitatory connection weights d_l have fixed values that are determined according to the same general principles used for the weights $c_l(v)$ in Equation 2.3. In practice, setting the d_l to be uniform across the receptive field has proven to be adequate.

Cells in the V_s plane produce the inhibitory signal, Vs_l, which is a weighted arithmetic mean of the S-cell outputs:

$$V s_l(n) = \frac{1}{K_{l_{k_{l=1}}}} \sum^{K_l} \sum_{v \in D_l} d_l(v) \times U s_l(k_l, n + v).$$ (2.11)

This V_s-cell response function computes the average S-cell output over the regions of input (D_l) for position n on all of the S-planes (K_l).

Since the numerator and the denominator in Equation (2.10) both contain the same set of connection weights $d_l(v)$, the essential effect of equations (2.10) and (2.11) is to compare particular features on the S-layer with an average for all the S-planes. The C-cell response function in Equation (2.10) computes an adjusted signal ratio and passes it through the nonlinear saturation function:

$$g(x) = \begin{cases} \dfrac{x}{\beta + x} & (x \geq 0) \\ 0 & (x < 0) \end{cases}$$ (2.12)

where β defines the degree of saturation. This parameter is typically chosen to be 0.5 for all levels. As a result of this processing, the C-cells select only those features which have a stronger response than the overall average. If every S-plane contained identical features, then none of the C-cells would respond. However, similar behavior ensues from the processing which occurs in S-cells (i.e., neither type of unit responds unless the input from a particular pattern is stronger than a measure of the "typical" source signal). In addition, both types of cells monotonically increase the strength of their response as the relative difference between the two inputs becomes greater.

2.3. Overall Structure and Function

Most implementations of the Neocognitron are multilevel systems with an S-layer and a C-layer at each level. An example of the complete architecture is given in Figure 1.4, where l refers to the level, k refers a specific plane on a given layer, n refers to the absolute cell position within a plane, and v refers to the relative position within a receptive field. When the system operates, different patterns of connectivity decompose the input image into distinct spatial features. A learning rule then reinforces those patterns which produce the greatest response. As this type of system learns, different S-cells become sensitive to distinct combinations of features in the input plane.

The C-layer examines all feature groupings and rejects those that yield weak or mediocre output. Successive levels act to recognize increasingly complex

NEOCOGNITRON
(Fukushima)

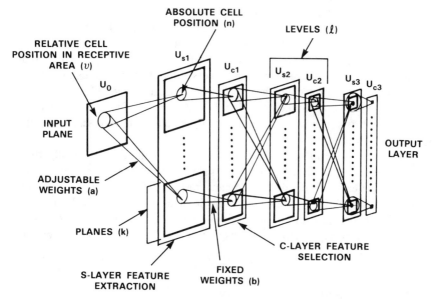

Figure 1.4.   Architecture of the Neocognitron.

feature groupings. On the top C-layer, each cell comprises an entire plane. Each C-cell in this final layer produces its maximum response only when a specific input image is presented.

3. RESULTS AND DISCUSSION

The Neocognitron's functional description contains many parameters which can be adjusted independently at each level. Cell planes in successive layers contain progressively fewer units as signals travel from the initial input layer to the top C-layer. The best sizes for input regions depend on the type of features in the input. Input images with few internal features need an initial region of input which covers the entire object so that the overall shape can be discerned. Smaller regions of input can be used for imagery containing many distinct features. Typically, the regions of input range in size from about 11×11 to 3×3 for wire-frame objects in a 128×128 image plane, and the first S-layer's region of input on the initial image plane is largest. The acuity of discrimination is controlled by the selectivity parameter, r_l, in Equations (2.1) and (2.2). Large values of r_l in the lower levels causes the Neocognitron to extract subtle features that can differentiate highly similar images. Smaller values of r_l result in the assignment of those same images to one class. When the value of r_l is too large, all patterns will be classified together, because the number of extracted features is too small. Typically, a successful scheme chooses the first level's r_l so that each input image produces a unique set of features, and subsequent levels then have decreasing values of r_l. The input weights for the V_c-plane Equations (2.5) and (2.6) also play a role in the feature extraction process. More features are extracted as the distribution of these weights becomes steeper, because fewer C-cells make substantial contributions to the inhibition. Finally, the rate of learning, q_l, increases from lower to higher levels in a manner which allows feature sensitive cells to develop slowly at all levels.

The input weights were initialized with small values that vary slightly between different S- and C-planes. A slight dependence on the plane number insures that each plane will have a unique response. This variation is necessary, because C-cells will not respond if all the S-planes produce identical features. As an alternative, one could initialize the weights with biases towards certain expected features (e.g., set the weights so that the system responds to horizontal and vertical edges).

3.1. Classification

A four-level Neocognitron structure was trained to classify three different wireframe objects. The training set, shown in Figure 1.5, consists of binary images which are stored in matrices of 128 × 128 pixels. Structural parameters for the different levels are listed in Table 1.1. A four-level configuration with six planes per layer was used, providing a theoretical storage capacity of six different patterns. Only three different images actually were presented to this system, because the ability to uniquely classify inputs degrades (very sensitive to the choice of parameters) when the number of input patterns exceeds 50% of the

Input Image 1   Input Image 2   Input Image 3

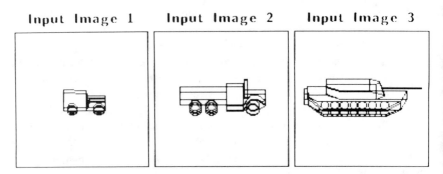

Figure 1.5. Input images used to train the four-level Neocognitron.

Table 1.1. Parameters for training on three input images.

Level	No. Planes	S-plane Size	C-plane Size	S-rec. Area	C-rec. Area	r_l	q_l	S-col. Size
1	6	121 × 121	62 × 62	7 × 7	5 × 5	4	1	4 × 4
2	6	57 × 57	30 × 30	5 × 5	5 × 5	4	4	4 × 4
3	6	25 × 25	13 × 13	5 × 5	5 × 5	3	6	4 × 4
4	6	8 × 8	1 × 1	5 × 5	5 × 5	2	20	4 × 4

number of planes. Training was conducted by presenting each of the images in turn ($1 \Rightarrow 2 \Rightarrow 3$), and 20 iterations were required to stabilize the weights. The category of classification corresponds to the top (level 4) C-cell with the maximum response. Results for the images in Figure 1.5 are recorded in Table 1.2. The results show that the first input image (jeep) produced a maximum response in the sixth top C-layer cell, while images 2 (truck) and 3 (tank) produced a maximum response in cells 2 and 3, respectively. As discussed above, the Neocognitron classifies input patterns by choosing unique features to characterize each one. Figures 1.6 through 1.8 show the features extracted by all six planes in the first S-layer for each of the input images in Figure 1.5. These features are simply the output from the cells in S-planes of the first level, represented on an 8-bit grey scale to aid in visualization. The output strengths are coded with intensity (i.e., the maximum response is black and zero response is white). In Figure 1.6, each S-plane is extracting different sets of features from the first input image. Plane 4 in Figure 1.6 seems to emphasize horizontal features, while plane 6 responds mostly to vertical features. The response in planes 4 and 6 for the other input images (Figure 1.7 and 1.8), shows that these planes concentrate mostly on horizontal and vertical features. Note that in the other planes, the system has selected many common features such as lines, corners, and circles, and there also is overlap between the different planes. The key point is that the S-cell outputs in these planes represent a set of features that uniquely classifies all the inputs. The features are not necessarily the ones that a human observer would choose as a basis for classification. The response patterns in the feature planes bear a close resemblance to the input images because the two phenomena occur on adjacent levels. Features on higher levels generally are

Table 1.2. Trained results (using parameters in Table 1.1).

Input Image	C-plane with Max Response
1	6
2	2
3	3

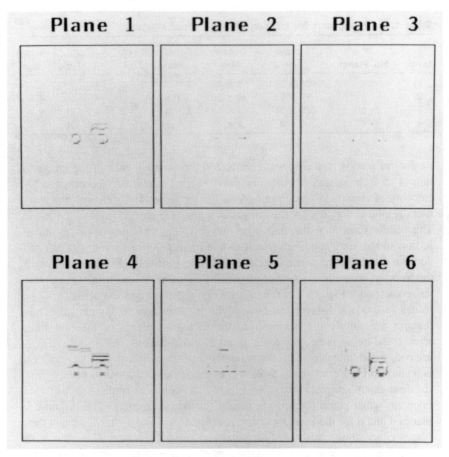

Figure 1.6.   Extracted features for S-planes on the first level for image 1.

less similar to the input patterns, since they represent combinations of simpler features from the preceding planes. Though a human observer would have difficulty in interpreting features on higher levels, they act as abstract signatures that characterize particular input patterns. The selection of features is controlled by parameter r_l in Equations (2.1) and (2.2). Increasing this parameter from a value of 4 to a value of 12 on the first level causes the system to become more critical and choose fewer features (Figure 1.9). The classification procedure also is influenced by the distribution of inhibitory connection weights c_l over an S-cell's region of input. A large value of α_l in Equation (2.5) results in a small inhibitory radius where very few of the C-cells make substantial contributions to the inhibition. Small values of α_l increase the inhibitory radius so that a densely populated region of input will produce significant inhibition to counter the excitation.

The order of pattern presentation influences the actual mapping between individual input images and specific output C-cells, but the system reaches a

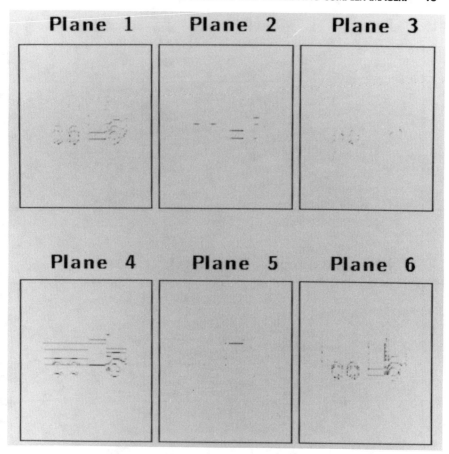

Figure 1.7.   Extracted features for S-planes on the first level for image 2.

stable configuration in all cases. In a self-organizing system, the details of the final mapping are not important as long as it is stable. All the simulations performed here exhibited this behavior. A wide range of system parameters have been used, and the model has always settled into a state where the top-level C-cells produce consistent outputs on every iteration.

3.2. Learned Primitives

In the previous section, the extracted features represent the S-cell output responses, and are determined by the excitatory connections $a_l(k_{l-1}, v, k_l)$. These excitatory connections represent the primitives learned by the system that were sufficient to separate the input images. By examining the patterns formed by the connections it may be possible to identify the primitives that uniquely character-

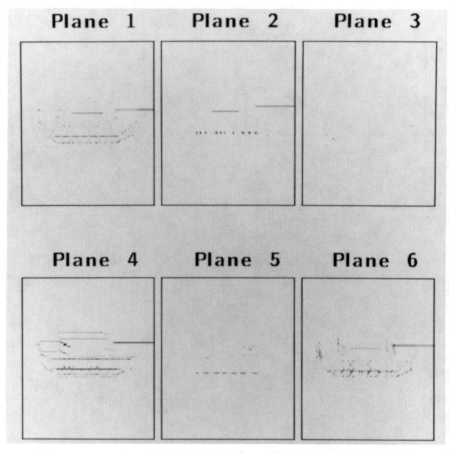

Figure 1.8.   Extracted features for S-planes on the first level for image 3.

ize a given set of images. The excitatory connection strengths used by the first S-layer are shown in Figure 1.10. The results were not very encouraging in terms of primitives that are obviously present in the original images. The hope had been to produce a set of primitives for wire-frame images such as corners and lines; instead, a complicated set of analog patterns was obtained. The pattern in S-plane 3 shows a strong response for a centrally located cross shape. The other S-planes, however, seem to indicate a maximum response at a single pixel.

The conclusion is that the model will learn primitives that are sufficient to separate the input patterns, and these primitives in general will not be the visually obvious ones. A further implication is that preloading the excitatory weights before training would be very difficult to implement, because it is not apparent what constitutes a separable set of primitives (especially for higher levels).

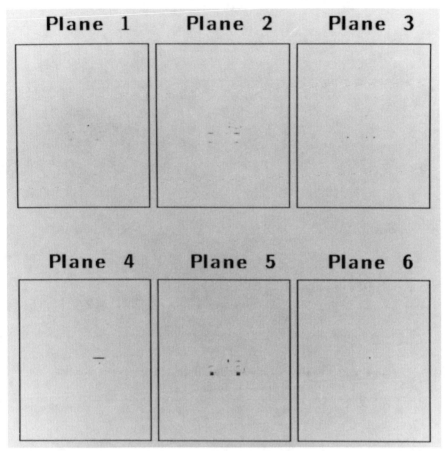

Figure 1.9.   Extracted features for S-planes on the first level for image 1 with higher selectivity.

3.3. Shift Invariance

The Neocognitron's shift invariance property was studied by presenting a set of images showing each vehicle at four different positions in the 128×128 matrix. Figure 1.11 shows the shifted versions of image 1; note that large displacements are used (100% of the object width). Initial results indicated that the system described in Table 1.1 was not shift invariant for all three patterns. Several of the shifted images were misclassified. Further testing of the model showed that the rate of decay for the C-cells' input weights has a major effect. There seems to be a tradeoff between the ability to classify and shift invariance where the actual point of compromise depends on certain properties of the C-cells' weighting function. Uniform weights (no weighting) make the system shift invariant, but

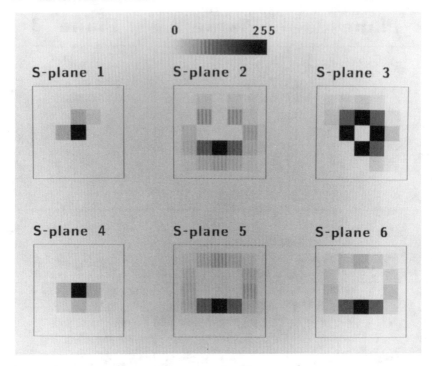

Figure 1.10. Excitatory connection strengths for level 1 S-cells.

patterns cannot be classified consistently. In general, reliable classification requires a very steep weighting function.

The degree of shift tolerance also varies with the amount of overlap that exists between adjacent regions of input. It is essential that the regions of input for S-cells have a great deal of overlap, because these cells respond to very precise features. Actual occurrences of a selected feature can be missed if they fail to coincide with the available regions of input. A high degree of overlap is less important for the input regions of C-cells. However, copious overlap at any layer increases the number of levels which are needed before the cell population falls

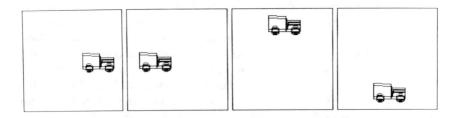

Figure 1.11. Shifted versions of image 1.

to one per plane in the final C-layer. For the case of a 128 × 128 input, the Neocognitron must have at least 15 levels to allow adequate overlap. In the examples that Fukushima has published, alphabetic characters from a 16 × 16 input layer were used, so only three to four levels were required. The processing time for a 15-level simulation on serial hardware is prohibitive (about 10 hours on a VAX-8600 computer to classify three patterns). Hence, implementation in parallel hardware seems to be the only viable solution for processing large input images.

One simple architecture has been found which classifies patterns reliably and maintains shift invariance: a single-level system with one S-layer and one C-layer. Planes on the S-layer are made identical in size to the input plane (128 × 128), and the C-planes contain a single cell each. Input regions for the C-cells cover 128 × 128 pixels, and uniform weighting is used within this field. The selectivity parameter r_l in Equations (2.1) and (2.2) is made sufficiently large to uniquely classify all the patterns. Using this scheme, the Neocognitron could classify the three images in Figure 1.5 in a completely shift invariant manner. This design has a drawback, because the C-layer's selection of features may be based on the sheer number of pixels in an object, rather than their detailed arrangement. In a multilevel system, the features are gradually extracted and selected, so that more subtle variations in the imagery can be resolved.

3.4. Performance with Noise

The effect of noise was investigated by submitting corrupted images to a system that had been trained on a noise-free data set. Uniform noise was introduced into the input images by replacing a certain portion of the pixels with random values. For the system described in Table 1.1, the ability to recognize patterns becomes unreliable when more than 30% of the pixels are corrupted. In general, this threshold will depend on the value used for the sensitivity parameter, r_l, during training; tolerance to noise is increased with lower sensitivity. Essentially, the Neocognitron calculates the inner product of a specific subpattern and the excitatory weights for an S-cell. The result is compared to a threshold determined by the selectivity parameter (r_l) and the inhibitory weights. Hence, the response with noise should be similar to that of a matched filter. In many systems, the distribution of raw pixel values is modified by some form of preprocessing, such as a median filter. Under these circumstances, the noise will no longer be distributed uniformly across the image. Further study is needed to evaluate the effect of such preprocessing on the model's performance with noisy imagery.

3.5. Sensitivity to Parameters

Our simulations were performed using 32-bit floating point numbers to represent and update all system variables. From a hardware implementation point of view it was of interest to change the resolution used during the simulations. We attempted to reproduce the previously described classification results by simulating the model on a supercomputer using 64-bit resolution, but were unsuccessful. Further investigation revealed that the problem was in choosing an S-cell with maximum response, which is used to update the associated set of excitatory weights. The computation of the S-cell output response in Equation (2.2) depends on forming a ratio between two large values (since the weights do not decay) and testing whether this ratio is below or above unity. This leads to many S-cells across many S-planes having approximately the same value. Hence, small errors introduced by rounding off and truncation, or small changes in the choice of the selectivity parameter (r_l) can lead to differences in which S-cell is chosen as the maximum. If an S-cell in a different S-plane is chosen, then an entirely different set of excitatory connections will be reinforced in Equation (2.8), which will change the entire training history for weights located at higher levels. Results from various simulations has shown that the ability of the model to separate input images depends on the exact choice of the selectivity parameter to better than one part in a thousand, and on the compuational resolution.

3.6. Object Rotation

Another form of preprocessing might enable the Neocognitron to recognize a particular type of scene variation by transforming the differences between images into positional shifts. This concept has been successfully applied to the problem of recognizing rotated objects. A simple one-level Neocognitron was trained on polar transforms of the images in Figure 1.5. The three vehicles were then rotated through various angles, and polar transforms of the resulting images were submitted as input. Since the polar transform operation converts angular orientations into a linear coordinate, the different orientations for a given object were mapped into a positional shift with wrap-around. Use of a 128 × 128 input plane provides an angular resolution of about three degrees. The system successfully discriminated three images with no rotation, 7-degree rotation, and 15-degree rotation. Polar transforms of the input patterns are shown in Figure 1.12, while Figure 1.13 show features which the system extracted for the first image. Note that plane 4 in Figure 1.13 has no response at all, indicating that no features were extracted. Self-organizing systems offer the advantage that they can identify the significant features in any representation of the image "without a teacher."

The preprocessing stage should locate the object's center of mass and perform the transform with respect to that position. This step minimizes distortions in the transformed image (e.g., truncation of the image due to edge effects). A difference in scale between the stored and presented patterns would present another problem. This difficulty can be overcome by using a combination log-polar transform which translates scale change to a shift on one axis and rotation to a shift on the other.

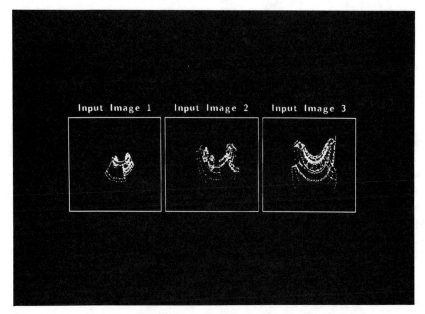

Figure 1.12. Polar transforms.

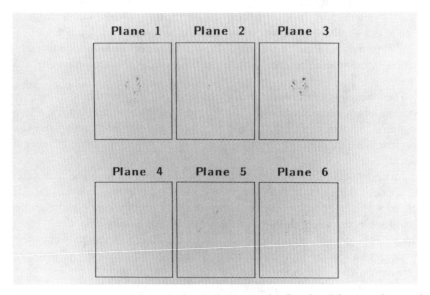

Figure 1.13. Extracted features for S-planes on the first level for transforms of image 1.

4. CONCLUSIONS

The Neocognitron model has been adapted to operate on complex wire-frame imagery and the performance of this implementation was evaluated. This study found that a four-level system with six S-planes and six C-planes per level can classify three different wire-frame images. The model works in two stages which are associated with S- and C-layers. Cells in different S-planes extract distinct features, and weights for each plane are reinforced according to the pattern of input which produces the strongest response. The C-layer compares the response of individual S-planes with an overall average and rejects those features whose response falls below this average. This procedure is repeated across many levels until a single cell at the top C-layer responds to a specific input pattern. The first S-layer decomposes the input image into many small features and increasingly complex feature groupings are recognized in subsequent levels until the entire image has been characterized. Since the regions of input typically overlap, a number of cells respond to each group of features, and slightly deformed or shifted versions still produce significant responses.

Our results indicate that in order to achieve full shift-tolerance, the Neocognitron must be designed with a high degree of overlap between adjacent regions of input. As a consequence, the cell layers should be thinned quite gradually. A four-level system is not sufficient to provide shift invariance for 128×128 imagery. We estimate that an input plane of this size will require a system of at least 15 levels, and a system of this magnitude is best implemented in parallel hardware. A one-level system with a 128×128 region of input was found to classify patterns in a shift tolerant manner for the three-image training sequence used in our simulations. However, this is not an acceptable solution when a large number of patterns must be classified. In general, pattern classification using the Neocognitron will be practical with a multilevel architecture on a parallel machine.

The robustness of the model was tested by degrading the original training set with uniformly distributed noise. The degraded inputs were tested using a Neocognitron that was previously trained on th original noise-free training set. Correct classification could be maintained with up to 30% of the input pixels corrupted.

Analog input images with a resolution of 8-bits per pixel were also used to test the model. The classification performance of the model was considerably degraded with analog inputs. We could not identify a set of model parameters that would separate analog intensity images. The main difficulty with using analog images is a greatly increased sensitivity to the choice of model parameters. Analog input images should undergo some type of preprocessing step such as edge extraction before being used as input to the Neocognitron.

Further work is needed to develop a systematic method for parameter selection. One promising approach is to incorporate a global feedback mechanism which would adjust the gain (q_l), and selectivity (r_l) at each level. The Neocognitrons's sensitivity to parameter changes also needs to be studied more extensively. This analysis would identify the set of parameters values which provides correct classification for the widest possible variety of input imagery. It is important to recognize that investigation of global feedback mechanisms and model sensitivity for large images (128×128 pixels and larger) can only be realized in a parallel hardware implementation.

REFERENCES

[1] K. Fukushima. "Neocognitron: A Self-organizing Neural Network Model for a Mechanism of Pattern Recognition Unaffected by Shift in Position," *Biological Cybernetics*, Vol. 36, 1980, pp. 193–202.

[2] G.A. Carpenter and S. Grossberg. "Brain Structure, Learning and Memory," J. Davis, R. Newburgh, and E. Wegman (Eds.), *AAAS Symposium Series*, 1985, pp. 1–45.

[3] K. Fukushima, S. Miyake, and T. Ito. "Neocognitron: A Neural Network Model for a Mechanism of Visual Pattern Recognition," *IEEE Transactions on Systems, Man and Cybernetics*, Vol. SMC–13, 1983, pp. 826–834.

[4] W. Stoner, and T.M. Schilke. "Pattern Recognition with a Neural Net," *Real Time Signal Processing IX (SPIE)*, Vol. 698, 1986, pp. 171–181.

2
Constraint Satisfaction Networks for Vision

Rakesh Mohan
Exploratory Computer Vision Group
IBM Thomas J. Watson Research Center
Yorktown Heights, NY

1. INTRODUCTION

A common problem faced in computer vision is, given a set of related hypotheses and a set of constraints on them, to select the best subset of hypotheses that satisfy the constraints. The relationships between the hypotheses are either cooperative, where one hypothesis supports others, or competitive, where one hypothesis is in conflict with others. This problem is often called the *constraint satisfaction problem* [1,2].

In vision, the constraint satisfaction problem arises in various areas. Some important examples are correspondence, feature labeling, and early vision. In stereo and motion correspondence, features from one image are matched to features in another image. The various possible matches are hypotheses which are related by physical constraints such as continuity, proximity, and disparity continuity [3]. In model matching, image tokens are matched to object models, with the constraints on the hypothesized matches arising from geometrical considerations or description hierarchies [4]. In labeling, the hypotheses are the possible labels for image tokens [5].

The relationship of *conflict* arises from alternate hypotheses being proposed for the same token; in correspondence, the various potential matches for a given feature are in conflict, as are the alternate labels for a feature in labeling. The relationship of *support* arises from part-of relationships (i.e., for tokens linked by part-of relationships in a description hierarchy, the hypotheses which preserve the part-of relationships are mutually supportive).

Consider correspondence between curves and edges of the left and right stereo images of Figure 2.1. If we match an edge **e,** which is a part-of a contour **c,** to an edge **e',** which belongs to contour **c',** then a match between **c** and **c'** supports, and is supported by, the match between **e** and **e'.** A match between **c** and c_1 is in conflict with the match between **e** and **e'.** Consider the problem of labeling the

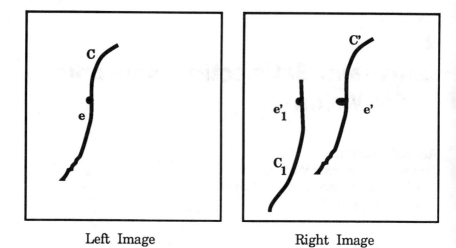

Left Image   Right Image

Figure 2.1.   Stereo matching.

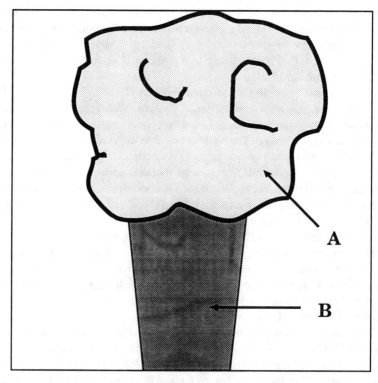

Figure 2.2.   The labeling problem. Adapted from [6].

regions A and B in Figure 2.2. Let us assume that the object in the scene can be interpreted as either a cone with ice cream or a tree. The label of "ice cream" to region A and "cone" to region B are mutually supportive as both ice cream and cone are parts-of the same object. The labels of ice cream and foliage for region A are mutually conflicting as they are alternate hypotheses for the same token, namely region A.

2. CONSTRAINT SATISFACTION

A visual process generates a set of *hypotheses* as a result of processing *data*. For example, in stereo correspondence, the stereo image pair is the data and the proposed matches between features are the hypotheses. For each hypothesis, certain *measurements* are made on the data which either support or contradict this hypothesis. In stereo matching, the difference in orientation of two matched edges could be such a measurement. There are relationships of *support* and *conflict* among the hypotheses. These relationships are represented as real numbers and their value is in proportion to the strength of the relationship between the hypotheses. The *constraint satisfaction problem* is to select the subset of hypotheses which have maximal support from the data and the selected hypotheses, and minimal conflict from the data and the selected hypotheses. We term this subset the *best consistent* set of hypotheses, where the hypotheses have the highest support from the data and are most consistent with each other. Given:

- A set of **Hypotheses** $\mathbf{H} = \{h_i | h_i \text{ is a hypothesis}\}$, $|\mathbf{H}| = N$.
- A binary function **Support** $S(h_i, h_j) = T_{ij}$, $T_{ij} > 0$.
- A binary function **Conflict** $C(h_i, h_j) = T_{ij}$, $T_{ij} < 0$.
  The entries of the matrix $T_{N \times N}$ not specified by S or C are set to zero.
- A unary function **Measurement** $I\ (h_i) = I_i$.
  I_i is a weighted sum of the measurements on the data for the hypothesis h_i. Measurements that support the hypothesis are positive and measurements that contradict a hypothesis are negative.

We have to find:

- An **Assignment** $V\ (h_i) = V_i$, $V_i \in \{0,1\}$ for all $h_i \in \mathbf{H}$.
  $V_i = 1$ indicates that hypothesis h_i is selected and $V_j = 0$ indicates that hypothesis h_j is rejected.

such that:

$$E = \sum_i \sum_j S(h_i, h_j)\, V(h_i)\, V(h_j) + \sum_i \sum_j C(h_t, h_j)\, V_i\, V_j + \sum_i I(h_i)\, V(h_i) \qquad (2.1)$$

is maximized. Rewriting Equation (2.1):

$$E = \Sigma\Sigma T_{ij}V_iV_j + \Sigma I_iV_i \qquad (2.2)$$

The constraint satisfaction problem has been converted into an *optimization* problem. We will call $-E$ the cost or energy function (to be minimized) associated with the constraint satisfaction problem.

The problem of labeling Figure 2.2 can be formulated in the above terminology.

- $h_1 = A$ is ice-cream
- $h_2 = A$ is foliage
- $h_3 = B$ is cone.
- $h_4 = B$ is trunk.
- $\mathbf{H} = \{h_1, h_2, h_3, h_4\}$.
- $C(h_1, h_2) = T_{12}$. Since h_1 and h_2 are in conflict, T_{12} is negative. Let us choose $T_{12} = -1$ for convenience. Let $C(h_2, h_1) = C(h_1, h_2)$.
- $C(h_3, h_4) = T_{34}$, Let $T_{34} = -1$ and $C(h_4, h_3) = C(h_3, h_4)$.
- $S(h_1, h_3) = T_{13}$, Let $T_{13} = 1$ and $S(h_3, h_1) = S(h_1, h_3)$.
- $S(h_2, h_4) = T_{24}$, Let $T_{24} = 1$ and $S(h_4, h_2) = S(h_2, h_4)$.
- Let $I_1 = -0.1$, $I_2 = 0.2$, $I_3 = 0.9$, $I_4 = 0.3$. Let us assume that we have measures like color, texture, temperature (if we have infrared images), etc., to measure if region A is an ice cream and so on.

Then:

$$E = \Sigma S + \Sigma C + \Sigma I = 2\,V_1V_3 + 2\,V_2V_4 - 2\,V_1V_2 - 2\,V_3V_4 - 0.1\,V_1 + 0.2\,V_2 + 0.9\,V_3 + 0.3\,V_4.$$

If we try all possible combinations of values for V_i (i = 1, . . . ,4), we find that the term above is maximized for $V_1 = 1$, $V_2 = 0$, $V_3 = 1$, $V_4 = 0$ (i.e., the optimal labeling of Figure 2.2 is that of an ice cream cone). Note also, that in general we have to consider all possible combinations for the values V_i, therefore, the constraint satisfaction problem is combinatorial in the number of distinct hypotheses (i.e., it is in NP).

3. CONSTRAINT SATISFACTION NETWORKS

The cost function in Equation (2.2) has been formulated such that the optimal solution of the constraint satisfaction problem corresponds to the minima of the cost function. Parallel optimization techniques such as simulated annealing [7], Hopfield networks [8,9], Boltzman machines [1,10,11], and connectionist methods [12] have been proposed for such problems.

Hopfield networks have been selected as the optimization technique as:

- Constraint satisfaction problems map directly and naturally to Hopfield networks, or their simple modifications.
- Hopfield networks exhibit fast convergence, usually in the order of $5 \sim 10$ time constants.
- The neurons in the Hopfield networks are simple and can be implemented in hardware.

3.1. Hopfield Networks

A Hopfield network [13,14] is composed of nodes, termed neurons, whose behavior is specified by:

$$C_i \frac{du_i}{dt} = -\frac{u_t}{R_i} + \sum_{j=1}^{N} T_{ij} V_i + I_i - h_i \tag{3.1}$$

where:

$$V_i = g(u_i) = \frac{1}{2} [1 + \tanh(u_i)]$$

N Total number of nodes.
T_{ij} Weight on link from node j to node i.
I_i Total input to node i.
V_i Output of node i.
u_i Membrane potential, or activation level, of node i.
g Gain function. It is sigmoidal.
C_i Capacitance.
R_i Resistance.

The addition of h_i, the resting potential or bias, which is not present in the equations proposed by Hopfield, is useful in adjusting the sensitivity of a neuron by shifting its gain curve. For purposes of analysis of the network, the resting potential may be combined with the input.

When the network has symmetric connections (i.e., $T_{ij} = T_{ji}$), where each element has the above equation of motion, the network converges to a stable state. This property has also been shown for more general networks [15]. When the gain function g is high (width of the gain curve is narrow), the stable states of the N elements are the local minima of the cost function:

$$E = -\frac{1}{2} \sum_i \sum_j T_{ij} V_i V_j - \sum_i V_i I_i \tag{3.2}$$

with the outputs V_i of the nodes at 0 or 1 [14].

Note that minimizing E in Equation (3.2) is equivalent to maximizing E in Equation (2.1), after replacing T_{ij} by half its value. The signs in the above cost function suggest that if we wish to select mutually supporting hypotheses and reject mutually conflicting hypotheses, the weights T_{ij} between supporting hypotheses should be positive and that between conflicting hypotheses should be negative. Also, the signs in Equation (3.1) and (3.2) show that supporting evidence should be included as positive input and contradicting evidence as negative input.

3.2. Neural Constraint Satisfaction Networks

Hypotheses, and the relationships of support and conflict among them, naturally define a network, with the hypotheses represented by nodes and their relationships modeled by arcs. The Hopfield network is used to implement this network, which we call a *constraint satisfaction network* [2,16]. Each hypothesis is directly mapped onto a neuron, a weight is assigned to each type of relationship between the hypotheses and measurements on the hypotheses are fed as inputs to the neurons. The network is relaxed, following Equation (3.1), and after a sufficient number of iterations, the hypotheses corresponding to nodes with high outputs are selected. The CSN for the problem of labeling Figure 2.2 is shown in Figure 2.3.

There are two basic ways of using neural CSN to solve constraint satisfaction problems:

1. Assign, compute, or learn[1] numerical weights T_{ij} for the relationships of support and conflict. Sum the various measurements for each hypothesis as a real number. Implement a Hopfield network where each hypothesis is represent by a unique node, the T_{ij} specify the interconnection weights, and the measurements are fed as input to the nodes.

2. Convert the energy (or cost) function describing the problem into a form that corresponds to Equation (3.2). From this correspondence, determine the various interconnection weights (T_{ij}) and inputs (I_i). Finally form the Hopfield network given these interconnection weights and inputs.

Techniques 1 and 2 are equivalent and the use of a particular technique is largely a matter of taste and convenience. Technique 1 is more useful where the problem is naturally phrased in terms of networks, such as in connectionist systems [12], semantic networks [17], and description hierarchies [18,19]. For these problems, writing the associated cost function may not add extra clarity or insight to the problem, and may be omitted. On the other hand, for problems that

---

[1] In our work, we have assigned weights (see Sections 4 and 5 for details). Learning weights may not be simple, specially in multilayered CSN. Computing weights or parameters for optimization processes is an open area of research.

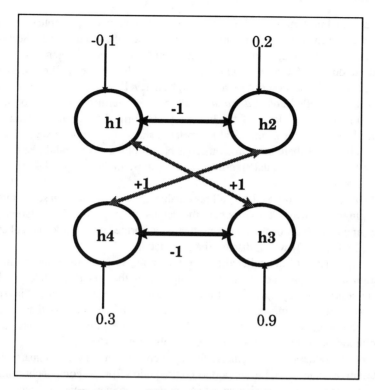

Figure 2.3.   CSN for labeling Figure 2.2.

are usually specified in terms of cost functions, such as various problems in early vision (Section 8), Technique 2 may be simpler to use.

The behavior of each node in the Hopfield network is specified with a differential equation. One way of simulating the behavior of the neurons is to approximate the differential Equation (3.1) by a difference equation:

$$u_i\,(t + \Delta t) = u_i(t) + \Delta u_i(t) = u_i + \Delta t \left(\frac{1}{C_i} \left(-\frac{u_i}{R_i} + \sum_{j=1}^{N} T_{ij}V_i + I_i - h_i \right) \right) \quad (3.3)$$

For simplicity, we have used $C_i = 1$ and $R_i = 1$ in our simulations. To simulate hard connections, and to allow the changes at each neuron to be integrated over the network, we have cut up each time constant, $\tau = C_i R_i$, into 10 slices (i.e., $\Delta t = 0.1\tau$). Thus, each iteration is implemented as 10 subiterations.

4. A SIMPLE CSN

Perceptual organization [20] is the ability of the human visual system to group image tokens on geometrical relationships such as co-curvilinearity, symmetry, closure, and proximity [21][2]. Computer implementations of perceptual organization are presented for the domains of indoor scenes of curved objects (Section 3) and that of aerial images of buildings (Section 4). The goal is to generate for each of these domains, a *description hierarchy* where the features at the lowest level are edges and the descriptors at the highest level correspond to object parts. Descriptors, called *collated features* (alternatively termed collations or simply groupings), at each level of the hierarchy are formed by grouping features at lower levels on their geometrical interrelationships. The problem we face is that for each feature there are numerous possible groupings; we would like to select those that have perceptual significance (i.e., those that correspond to objects or object parts).

Our strategy is to first detect all reasonable groupings, and then select the best groupings. We will not discuss here the details of the geometrical relations, the grouping processes, or the reasoning that is performed on the selected collations (see [16,18,19,22] which discuss these in detail).

At each level of the collated feature hierarchy, various collations are in contention as they provide alternative groupings of the underlying tokens. Also, some collations may have been formed on weak evidence; evidence that seems too weak when compared to that for other collated features at that level. A selection process has to choose "good" collations (i.e., those which have a high likelihood of corresponding to individual object parts).

The "goodness" of a collated feature depends on how it compares to its alternatives in terms of the support or contradiction from its component primitive features and other related image features (measurements on the image data).

For the domain of curved objects, the description hierarchy is comprised of curves, symmetries, and ribbons. A *ribbon* is an area bounded by two symmetric curves and by contours closing the ends between the symmetric curves [22,28]. The goal is to detect ribbons which correspond to the visible object surfaces. Figure 2.4 is a schematic representation of the different levels of the hierarchy, the collated feature for each level, and the geometrical relationships used.

Symmetry is a specific geometrical relationship between two curves [22]. This relationship defines an *axis,* which is the locus of the midpoints of the lines joining points on one curve to their mapping in the other. Since the axis represents the symmetry relationship, we will use the axis to denote the symmetry (which consists of the two curves and the axis). For each curve in an image, possible symmetry relationships with every other curve in the image are considered. Thus, with n curves, there are n^2 possible symmetries. This number is limited by the use of heuristics. However, ideally only one symmetry should be

---

[2] Perceptual organization is sensitive to more relationships, such as similarity, and to more modalities than visual, such as audio. In the work reported in Sections 4 and 5, we have limited ourselves to perceptual organization on certain geometrical relationships on 2-D images. For more information on perceptual organization, consult [16,18,21,22,23,24,25,26,27].

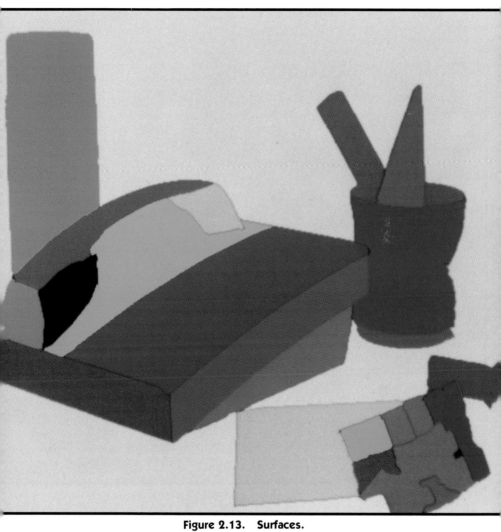

Figure 2.13.   Surfaces.

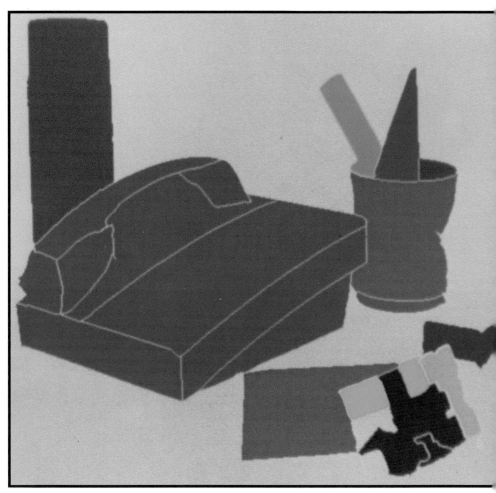

Figure 2.14. Objects.

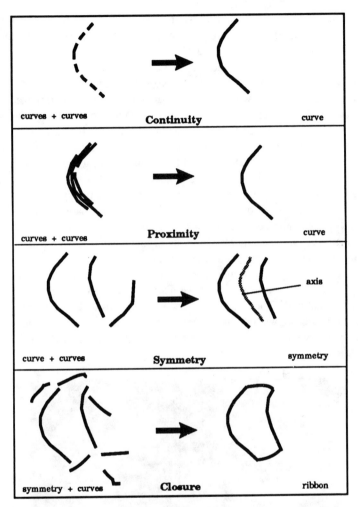

Figure 2.4. The grouping process and various levels of collations in the description hierarchy.

selected for each side of a curve, as each side of a curve may bound one surface at the most. Some curves may have no symmetry relationship, while for others we may wish to entertain more than one symmetry.

To select the best symmetries, a simple, *single-layered* constraint satisfaction network is generated. In this network, each axis is represented by a node (or a neuron). Each of its competitors is connected to it by a negatively weighted link. For each axis, the input is computed as a weighted sum of a numerical representation of measures of cover, aspect ratio, length-similarity, skew, and parallelism, on the symmetry axes and the symmetric curves. The network converges after a few iterations (about five iterations; each iteration represents one time constant and is itself implemented as 10 subiterations), and the nodes with high output (> 0.8) are considered selected while the rest are rejected.

The value for an axis is computed as ($8.0 \times$ aspect $- 15.0 \times$ (angular difference between the two curves in radians) $- 4.0 \times$ (normalized length difference) $- 3.0 \times$ (angular difference between the ends) $- 5.0 \times$ skew-angle $+ 2.0 \times$ length) and is fed to its node as input. The numbers used in the linear combination of the measures are chosen to normalize the different units used for the different geometrical measures and to assign relative weighting to the different measures in accordance with their subjective importance. Some tuning of the numbers was done to get acceptable results—the same numbers were used unchanged for a number of different images. The constraint satisfaction network is used to prune the number of collations. Structural evidence, from the monocular reasoning phase of the segmentation process, finally decides whether a given pair of symmetric curves does bound a surface.

Figures 2.5–2.8 show an indoor image and the features detected in it. Figures 2.10(a)–11(d) show "snapshots" of the axes selection process by the constraint satisfaction network. The axes that correspond to nodes with high output after the subiteration are shown by thick lines. The symmetry axes that get selected earliest are those for which there are no competing alternates (Figure 2.10(a)).

Figure 2.5. Intensity image.

Figure 2.6.   Edges detected.

Figure 2.7.   Curves.

Figure 2.8.   All the axes hypothesized.

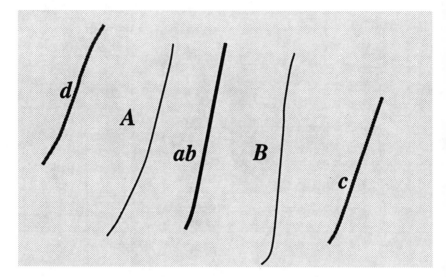

Figure 2.9. Competition between symmetry axes. For curve A, the symmetry axis *c* is in competition with axis *ab*. For curve B, the axis *d* is in competition with axis *ab*. Note that axis *c* is not an axis for curve *B* and could, therefore, be in competition with axes other than *ab* and *d*.

Next, those axes with high evaluation, especially those with high aspect ratios, get selected (Figure 2.10(b)). Some axes, which get selected during the early stages of the relaxation process (Figure 2.10(c)), get suppressed later (Figure 2.10(d)). While some of these axes are subsequently selected (Figures 2.11(a), 2.11(b)), some of them may not get selected at the end (Figure 2.11(d)). The network stabilizes after the twenty fifth subiteration (Figure 2.11(d)) and there are no new axes selected (or rejected) in subsequent iterations.

In addition to the axes selected by the constraint satisfaction network, axes where the symmetric curves are joined, at least at one end, by a single curve, were also selected. This structural relationship ensures that symmetry axes which have low input (due to low aspect-ratios or high skew) but high chances of corresponding to surfaces (due to simple closure at one end) also get considered for forming ribbons. Most of these axes also get selected by the constraint satisfaction network.

Figure 2.12 shows the axes selected from Figure 2.8. Ribbons are formed using the selected symmetries. Reasoning on the ribbons yields ribbons which most likely correspond to the significant visible surfaces in the scene (Figure 2.13). These ribbons can then be combined, on the basis of their geometrical relationships, into the likely objects (Figure 2.14).

Table 2.1 shows the variation in performance of the single-layered CSN with changes in the weights. The last column indicates if any symmetry, which corre-

Figure 2.10.   Behavior of the CSN during relaxation. Axes shown in bold lines correspond to nodes with high output.

Table 2.1.   Change in network performance with change in weight.

Change in weights	Number of symmetries selected	Number of correct symmetries missed
0%	55	none
+100%	55	none
+200%	59	none
−50%	54	none
−75%	54	none

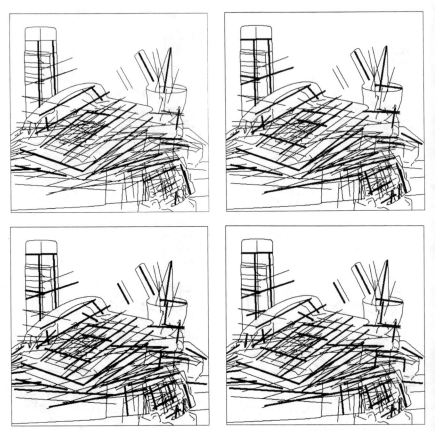

Figure 2.11.   Behavior of the CSN during relaxation. Axes shown in bold correspond to nodes with high output.

Figure 2.12.   Selected symmetry axes.

sponds to a surface ribbon detected with the original weight settings, has been missed. As can be seen from Table 2.1, the network is robust to changes in weights, indicating that an exact choice of weights is not necessary for proper functioning of the constraint satisfaction network.

5. MULTILAYERED CSN

In the previous section we had a simple case where all the hypotheses were at the same level and the resulting network had a single layer. For the case of aerial images of buildings (Figures 2.15, 2.16) we used a multilayered CSN [16]. The roofs of the buildings are modeled as combinations of rectangles. The description hierarchy consists of the line, parallel, U-contour (parallels with one end closed), and rectangle-collated features. First edges are grouped into lines, the lines into parallels and so on. The objective is the selection of rectangles which have the greatest likelihood of corresponding to roofs. We wish to achieve this by evaluating the collations *at all hierarchy levels simultaneously*. The resulting constraint satisfaction network is multilayered; each layer is dedicated to groupings from one level of the hierarchy, and connections between the layers arise from part-of relationships.

The "goodness" of a collated feature depends on how it compares to its alternatives in terms of the support it has from related collations at other levels, and the support or contradiction from its component primitive features and other

Figure 2.15.   Aerial image.

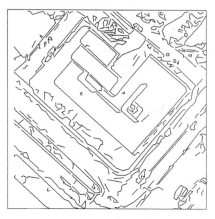

Figure 2.16.   Edges detected.

related image features. A collated feature is not supported just by its component collations, but also by the collations it is a component of. The later relationship is due to the fact that the percept of a larger structure strengthens that of a smaller component structure. In general terms, collated features which are linked by part-of relationships are mutually supportive and those that share component collations are mutually competitive. The goal is to find the optimal feature groupings consistent with the known optical and geometrical constraints [1,29]. Note that all the constraints must be simultaneously satisfied to reach global consistency across all levels of the hierarchy.

To construct the CSN, each collation detected is represented as a node or neuron. The relationships between the collations define the links between the nodes. In the network in Figure 2.17, nodes for collated features which support each other are connected via positively weighted links (thin lines) while mutually conflicting collations are linked via negatively weighted links (bold lines).

Supporting links are between those collated features at *different* levels of the feature hierarchy which group the same underlying edges (i.e., collations that are connected by *part-of* relationships). For example, there is a supporting link between a parallel and each of the two lines that form the parallel. If the parallel is part of a rectangle, then there is a supporting link between the parallel and the rectangle. The relationship of support is also inherited, for example when a rectangle is formed from two U-contours, it also forms supporting links with the parts of the U-contours (i.e., the parallels and the lines). The supporting links are generated automatically as a by-product of the collation detection process: once a collation is detected, links of support between it, and the collations it groups, are formed. For example, when a U-contour is detected, a node for it is generated and is linked to the nodes of the parallel and the line (base of the U) that were grouped to form it.

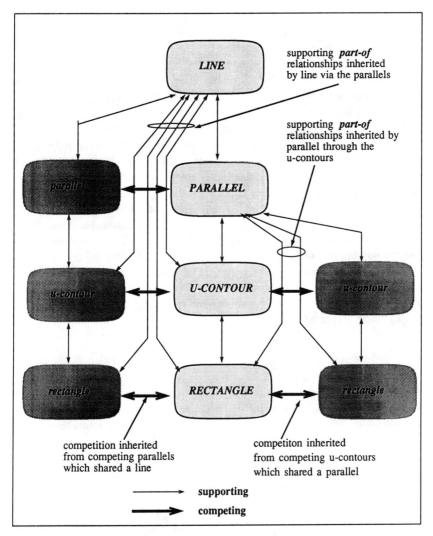

Figure 2.17. Multilayered CSN.

Conflicting links are formed between collated features at the *same* level of hierarchy, which are alternate groupings of the same edges. For example, when two lines of dissimilar length are found to be parallel, two parallel-collations are formed: one corresponding to the shorter line and the other to the longer line. These two parallel collations are in conflict and would be connected by a conflicting link. Relationships of conflict are also inherited. If two rectangles are formed from two conflicting parallels, then the two rectangles are also in conflict. The conflicting links are formed after all the collations are formed. The relationship of conflict is first found between collations at the lowest level of the hierarchy (i.e., lines) and then we progress up the hierarchy, with each level inheriting conflicts from its components in the lower levels.

The input to each node is a weighted sum of measurements on the collation represented by that node. To insure the selection of perceptually significant feature groupings in the scene, the choice of weights should reflect the perceptual importance placed on the optical and geometric constraints between the various collated features. The perceptual significance of a collated feature lies in its indication of actual object structure in the scene. The input to a node representing a *line* collation is the weighted sum of the percentage of its length actually covered by edges, the numbers of corners detected at its ends and the number of lines crossing through sections of it that are gaps (I_{line} = % edge-coverage + 0.4 $\times$ # of corners − # of crossings). The relevant measures on *parallels* are the amount of overlap between the lines, and the width of the parallels, on *U-contours* are the number of actual corners between the base and the parallel sides and the number of lines crossing the base, and on *rectangles* are the number of corners between its sides, and the amount of texture inside the rectangle. The number of lines lying inside a rectangle, which do not belong to any rectangle, are used as a measure of the texture on the rectangle, with less textured rectangles being preferred.

5.1. Performance of the Network

The network is started with all nodes at rest (i.e., membrane potential and output at zero and the network is relaxed). The network converges in a few iterations and the nodes with high output (> 0.8) are selected. We have found the network

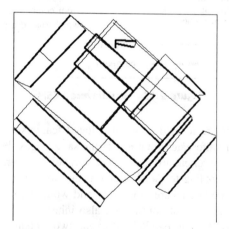

Figure 2.18.   Lines.

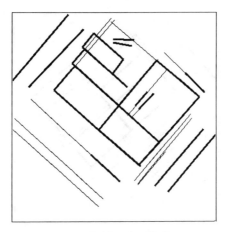

Figure 2.19.   Parallels.

to converge within ten iterations for all of our test scenes. Feature groupings at all levels of complexity get selected simultaneously, the ones selected have been indicated in the figures by bold lines. Only the selected rectangles are used further for stereo matching and structural reasoning to obtain 3-D models of the buildings.

The weights on the links range from -1.0 to 1.0. We chose the weights in proportion to the perceived importance of the source collation as supporting or conflicting evidence to the destination collation. The weights that were used are as shown in Table 2.1 (the table is to be read as T_{ij} being the weight on the link *from* node j to node i). The input to each node is also represented as a real number. The evaluation of the input as a real number depends on the type of

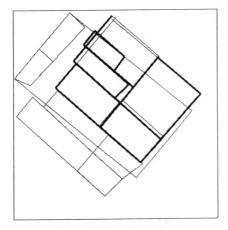

Figure 2.20.   U-contours.

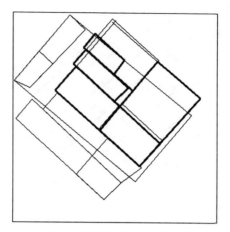

Figure 2.21. Rectangles.

measurements made for each collation, and the relevance of the measurement to the collation. For example, each corner contributes 0.7 to the input to the rectangle, indicating that the presence of a corner (a corner can be interpreted as two lines in the specific geometric relationship of orthogonality) is considered to be of the same order of significance as a parallel.

In our implementation, the weights on the links are not symmetric, so the convergence results for Hopfield networks cannot be used. However there is support that the networks can converge under nonsymmetric weights [30]. We have found our networks to converge on all our selection of weights within ten iterations.

In the beginning, some tuning of the weights, and the bias on the the nodes,

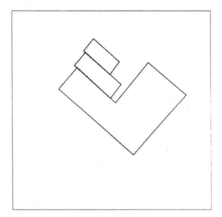

Figure 2.22. Roofs.

Figure 2.23.   Building.

was done on one image so that the nodes that fired corresponded to the collations that we visually perceived as "good." After this initial setting of weights, no further tuning was done, the same set of weights (shown in Table 2.2) have been used successfully for all the images we processed. We have found that the network is not sensitive to even large changes in the weights if the total amount of evidence ($\sum_{j=1}^{N} T_{ij}V_j + I_i$) arriving at the nodes does not change drastically. Table 2.3 shows the performance of the network in selecting rectangle collations, from those displayed in Figure 2.21, against percentage change, from the values in Table 2.2, in the weights. The last row of the table may indicate that when the weights are too low some of the nodes, which may fire with higher weights, may not be able to rise above their threshold to fire. The sensitivity of the nodes can be controlled by using the bias h_i, which is similar to the resting potential of neurons. By controlling the bias we control the amount of positive evidence required by a node to fire it. The network, in its present form, does not have the ability to "self calibrate" (i.e., to automatically adjust the sensitivity of a node on the basis of the total amount of information arriving at it).

Table 2.2.   Interconnection weights for the layered CSN.

Weights	Line	Parallel	U-contour	Rectangle
Line	—	0.5	0.5	0.6
Parallel	0.6	—	0.3	0.8
U-contour	0.7	0.6	—	0.7
Rectangle	0.7	0.7	0.8	—

Table 2.3.   Effect of change in weights on the selection.

Change in weights	Number of rectangles selected	Number of correct rectangles missed
+200%	9	none
+100%	9	none
0%	10	none
−50%	8	none
−75%	5	none

This scheme, since it is based on competition between alternate collations for the same underlying edges, may lead to a situation where a collation, which is not comparable to the other selected collations of its hierarchy class in the scene (in terms of its related measurements or evidence), is selected solely because it is the only grouping of its component edges and has no competing collations. To avoid this situation, a "winner-take-all" [6,12] type of network is superimposed on the Hopfield network. In this network, each node has self excitation (+1) and competes (−1) with all the other collations of the same hierarchy class. While stability results for such "winner-take-all" type of networks are known [31], the stability results for the resulting "hybrid" network are not known.

6. CORRESPONDENCE

Correspondence involves the matching of features detected in one image to features in another image or set of images. In stereo correspondence, features obtained in the left and right images of a stereo pair are matched to compute disparity, or the displacement in the position of the features. Depth can be computed from the disparity and the camera model [5]. In motion correspondence, features from one image are matched to features from a set of images forming the motion sequence. The matches can be used for tracking moving objects, for computing the motion of the observer and objects, and for computing the 3-D structure of the objects in motion [32]. In scene matching, features from one image are matched to those obtained in other images. The matches are useful in detecting change, when the images have been shot at different times, or for building descriptions of objects when the images have been shot from different viewpoints. In model matching, features from an image are matched against a database of stored models of known objects in order to identify the objects in the scene.

In all correspondence tasks, the primary problem is the ambiguity of the matches arising from the following:

- Primitive features typically do not contain enough information to be matched unambiguously, especially as the images are shot from different viewpoints or at different times.
- Some features present in one image may not be present in another due to causes like occlusion.
- In images containing repetitive patterns, it is difficult to match features equal to or smaller than the largest repeated pattern.

There are two standard (nonexclusive) approaches to alleviating the problem of ambiguous matches:

- Use of high-level features which contain sufficient information for judging a match [16,20] (also see Section 6.1).
- Exploit physical constraints such as: depth varies smoothly at most places [3], moving objects are rigid [33], disparity along smooth contours varies smoothly [34].

These techniques provide the constraints which can then be exploited to cast the correspondence problem into the following constraint satisfaction problem. Given as a set of possible matches, where each match can be evaluated by some measure based on the features matched, choose the best consistent set of matches given the physical constraints.

6.1. Stereo Correspondence

In stereo matching, one of the problems is the ambiguity involved in matching edges or intensity windows. Since these features carry little information on which the quality of each match can be independently decided, optimization techniques have to be used to obtain the best global match. The number of features matched is extremely large, making both the matching and the optimization computationally expensive. Some of these problems can be alleviated by using more abstract features such as linear segments and contours for the matching [35]. Further gains in reducing the cost of the matching, decreasing the number of ambiguous matches, and handling large changes in disparity, can be made by employing yet more abstract features.

Ribbons (Section 4) are high-level features that can be used for stereo correspondence, and work well even for unregistered stereo pairs with large vertical disparities [18]. First ribbons are detected in each image of the stereo pair. For each ribbon we define an epipolar window in the other image which accounts for the possible horizontal and vertical disparity. Ribbons are matched on the basis of

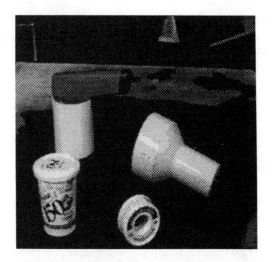

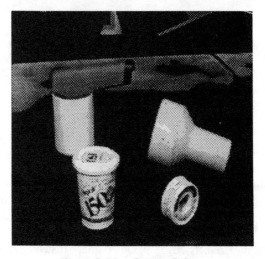

Figure 2.24.   Stereo Pair.

matches between their axes, the corresponding symmetric curves, and their widths and lengths. These two constraints, epipolar overlap and shape similarity, are sufficient to assign unique matches to many ribbons in the stereo pair. In the cases of ambiguous matching (i.e., if some ribbons in the left and/or right image have multiple matches) we pick the best match using a constraint satisfaction network.

Each node $n_{L^i R^i}$ of the constraint satisfaction network is a matched pair of ribbons L^i and R^i. If the ribbon L^i has a potential match with any ribbon R^j, which

Figure 2.25.   Edges detected in stereo pair.

is not the same ribbon as R^i, and the ribbon R^i has a potential match with any ribbon L^k then the node $n_{L^iR^i}$ is in competition with nodes $n_{L^iR^j}$ and $n_{L^kR^i}$. Thus, each node in the network is in competition with any other node in the network which has in its match pair either the same left ribbon or the same right ribbon. The competing nodes are connected with negatively weighted links. Each match has an input which is a numerical value assigned by an evaluation of the match. A match is evaluated on the basis of the similarity of shapes of the matched ribbons. The factors considered in evaluating a match are the difference in widths of the ribbons, the difference in the lengths and orientations of the corresponding contours and axes, and the amount of epipolar overlap [18].

Figure 2.24 displays a stereo image pair. Figure 2.25 shows the detected edges which were used to find the ribbons shown in Figure 2.26. Figure 2.27

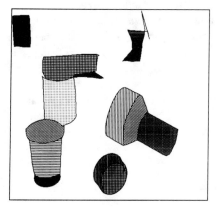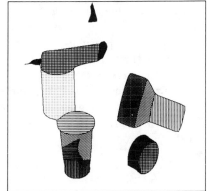

Figure 2.26.   Ribbons detected in stereo pair.

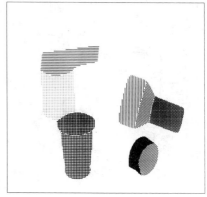

Figure 2.27. Matched ribbons in stereo pair.

displays the matches obtained after constraint satisfaction. The matches are indicated by the texture patterns.

6.2. Motion Correspondence

Motion perception is a rich source of information about the observer and his environment [36,37]. It is believed to be mediated by two distinct processes [32,38], namely the short-range [39,40] and long-range processes. The long-range process deals with larger displacements and is based on correspondence between features detected in sucessive images of a motion sequence [32]. Various visual cues can be used to guide the correspondence process, such as similarity in the shape, size, color, contrast [32], and topological properties [41] of the features. However, motion perception is vivid when observing moving dot patterns [32] where all the features are similar, and motion is readily perceived between very different features [42]. Another strong visual clue for correspondence is the spatial proximity in terms of retinal distance (i.e., distance between the 2-D projected features, and not the actual 3-D distance) of the features in sucessive frames [32,42,43]. In this section, we consider only geometrical cues for motion correspondence.

Ullman proposed [32] that the preferred correspondence between two sucessive frames is one that gives the minimal distance between the matched features. This *minimal distance mapping* scheme can be formulated as a constraint-satisfaction problem:

$$E = \frac{A}{2} \sum_i \sum_j \sum_{k \neq j} V_{ij} V_{ik} + \frac{B}{2} \sum_i \sum_j \sum_{k \neq i} V_{ij} V_{kj} + C \sum_i \sum_j V_{ij} d_{ij}$$

$$+ D \sum_i \sum_j (V_{ij} - n)^2 \tag{6.1}$$

V_{ij} is the match between feature i in image obtained at time t, j a feature obtained at time $t + 1$, and d_{ij} is the disparity between i and j. The first two terms insure unique matches, the third term enforces the minimal distance mapping by penalizing matches with large disparities, and the last term is a bias to insure exactly n matches. A similar solution to the minimal-distance mapping by Hopfield networks can be found in [44].

However, many of the matches have near optimum values (see Figure 2.28), and the network is likely to get stuck in local minima. One solution is to use optimization schemes which guarantee locating the global minimum (such as simulated annealing [7]), but these schemes are computationally expensive. Another technique is to add information, in the form of additional constraints, to reduce the number of local minima. The use of additional information in optimization problems, in this case perceptual organization constraints, is similar to the use of regularization for ill-posed problems [45] and adding prior expectations in Bayesian formulations [46]. We use perceptual organization to provide these additional constraints [47].

The minimal distance mapping scheme is a minimal formulation in that it is the minimum amount of information required to form the correct correspondences (see [32] for details). However, it ignores other sources of information such as the structure of the scene and the coherence of motion across several frames. The geometrical relationship of *proximity* encodes information about

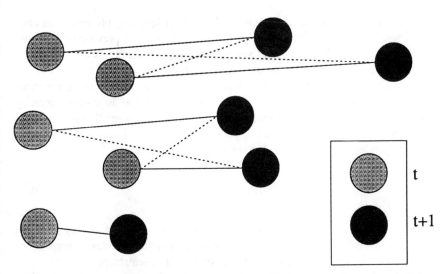

Figure 2.28.   Presence of local minima. The bold lines show the correct correspondences. Consider the dashed lines indicating wrong match. Locally, wrong matches can be formed such that the differences in displacement, as compared to the correct match, is small. These wrong matches cause the motion paths to cross locally.

scene structure as proximate features in the image are likely to be projections of proximate features in the scene and thus have a high likelihood of belonging to the same object. Thus, nearby features have a similar direction of motion, except at object boundaries. The addition of:

$$\frac{F}{2} \sum_i \sum_j \sum_{k \neq i} \sum_{l \neq j} V_{ij} V_{kl} \frac{\cos \theta_{ijkl}}{q_{ik} q_{jl}} \tag{6.2}$$

where θ is the angle between the directions of match ij and match kl, and q_{ik} is the distance between the features i and k (which are on the same frame) to Equation (6.1), favors the selection of matches which enforce a similar direction of motion in proximate features [47]. This is implemented by positively weighted links. Links are formed only between matches for features less than q_{thrsh} apart and for $\theta < \pi/3$. Enforcing a similar motion for proximate features has the potential drawback of favoring wrong matches near object boundaries.

The motion of objects is smooth (unless there is sudden impact) and thus their projection on the retina traces a smooth curve. This coherence of motion across several frames can be exploited by detecting *co-curvilinearity* in the successive positions of features in the motion sequence (this phenomenon has also been termed temporal coherence [44,48]. It has been found that in humans, perceptual organization on co-curvilinearity can be reasonably modeled by locally colinear relationships [49].

In motion correspondence, co-curvilinearity is enforced by preferring matches for a feature which have the most colinear direction to the previously observed direction of motion for that feature. If a feature i in frame t was matched to feature k in frame $t - 1$, then the preferred match for i in frame $t + 1$ is the feature j such that the angle between ki and ij is the minimum among the other possible matches for i. Proximity also plays a strong role in co-curvilinearity [18,49]. However, as the minimal distance mapping favors small displacements, it already accounts for the effect of proximity in co-curvilinearity and we have only to model the colinearity. The term:

$$G \sum_i \sum_j V_{ij} \cos \varphi_{kij} \tag{6.3}$$

where k is the previous match of i and φ is less than $\pi/3$, is added to Equation (6.1). Term (6.3) above is implemented as positive input to nodes corresponding to matches obtained after the first frame of a motion sequence.

The constraint satisfaction based motion correspondence system was tested on motion sequences (7 to 10 frames) of random dot patterns (20 to 500 random dots per image) with object translation and rotation [47]. It was found that the minimal distance mapping criterion, when used alone, results in errors causing motion paths to cross locally. Also, the network was found to be very sensitive to

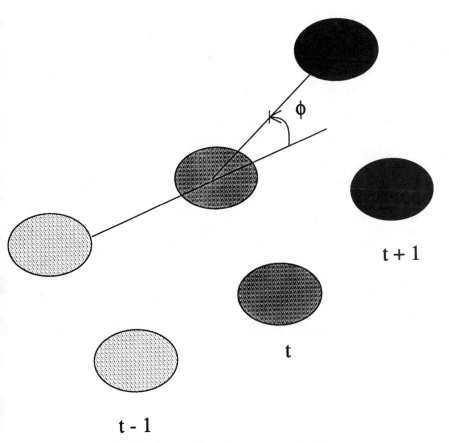

Figure 2.29.   Co-curvilinearity across motion frames.

proper setting of the weights, specifically the bias (D in Equation (6.1)). The use of the proximity constraint substantially reduced matching errors and also made the network more stable to the setting of the weights and bias. The use of the co-curvilinearity constraint helped reduce the number of matches considered, thus speeding up the computation. It also reduced the number of matching errors and the sensitivity to the weight settings, though not as much as the proximity constraint.

6.3. Graph Matching

Description hierarchies have simple representations as graphs. Thus, correspondence tasks involving description hierarchies can be formulated as graph matching problems [5]. For example, for the stereo correspondence problem defined in

Figure 2.1, the description hierarchy consists of curves and edges and can be represented by graphs with one node corresponding to a curve and all other nodes corresponding to the component edges of the curve, linked to it. The corresponding graph matching problem, is to find matches between the graphs for the left and right images. Graph matching arises more often in model matching applications.

Let **G** be a graph of n nodes represented by its interconnection matrix $G_{n \times n}$. Let the matches between graph **G** and **G'** be defined (following the notation used in [4]) by the match matrix $M_{n \times n'}$, where $M_{\alpha,i} = 1$ indicates a match between node α of graph **G** and node i of graph **G'**. We wish to match the nodes of graphs **G** and **G'** such that each node has a unique match and that the matches are consistent with the relationships (denoted as arcs in the graphs) imposed by the graphs. The graph-matching problem can be translated to a constraint satisfaction network by assigning a neuron to each match (i.e., for each potential match $M_{\alpha,i} = 1$), generate a node of the CSN. A measure of the goodness of the match between nodes α and i is fed as input to the neuron for $M_{\alpha,i}$. Negatively weighted links connect two nodes if they are alternate matches for the same features. For example, there will be a negative link between neurons for $M_{\alpha,i}$ and $M_{\alpha,j}$. Positive links are created between two match nodes $M_{\alpha,i}$ and $M_{\beta,j}$, if $G_{\alpha,\beta} = 1$ and $G'_{i,j} = 1$. Thus, the interconnection matrix $T_{M \times M}$ can be defined as:

$$T_{M_{\alpha,i}, M_{\beta,j}} = M_{\alpha,i} M_{\beta,j} \begin{cases} + cG\alpha, \beta G'_{i,j} & \text{when } \alpha \neq \beta \wedge i \neq j \\ - d & \text{otherwise} \end{cases}$$

This formulation of the graph-matching problem as a constraint satisfaction problem is similar to formulations in [4,50,51]. Mjolness, Gindi, and Anandan use the graph-matching problem to solve model matching for an artificial domain [4]. Parvin and Medioni define relationships between surfaces and contours detected in range images of an object as graphs. Graphs, obtained from range images of a particular object taken from different viewpoints, were matched to generate complete descriptions of the objects that could then be used as models [51].

7. VISION SYSTEMS

An experimental computer vision system [52,53], that employs constraint satisfaction mechanisms throughout its architecture, is under development at the IBM T.J. Watson Research Center. We first briefly summarize the system and then discuss the constraint satisfaction networks employed.

The vision system has a homogeneous architecture that supports recognition of simple partial features to complex feature assemblies and 3-D objects. At all levels of recognition, the same techniques are used, namely *parameter transforms* and constraint satisfaction networks. Parameter transforms generate hypotheses in the constraint satisfaction network, and the best hypotheses for features are selected using the CSN mechanism. Within this framework, a system which extracts surface patches and surface intersection curves from a depth map, has been implemented. These reconstructed features index into an object database to find consistent interpretations.

Figure 2.30 represents an overview of the system. The recognition task is structured as a hierarchy of layered and concurrent parameter transforms [54] for feature extraction. Features that are structurally independent, for instance, planes and linear 3-D edges, form concurrent paths of recognition. Features that depend upon other lower-level features, for instance, boxes and planar patches, are placed in hierarchical layers within a path. Parameter transforms create new hypotheses or support existing hypotheses. The best hypotheses are selected using constraint satisfaction networks.

The *generalized feature concept* states that each feature type is defined by a parameterization and a set of relationships to other features. The generalized feature concept allows a homogeneous, feature-independent control structure. This takes the form of a constraint satisfaction network, where nodes represent feature hypotheses and links represent the evidential relationships between fea-

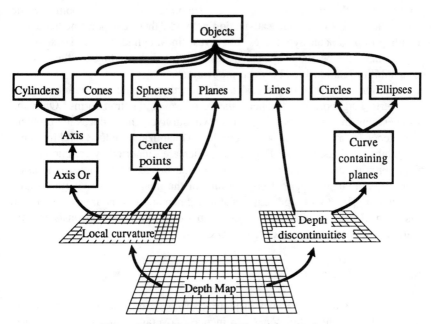

Figure 2.30.   Overview of the vision system.

tures. Parameter hypotheses for a feature are collected in a parameter space associated with that feature type. Each parameter space is a subnet of the recognition network. Parameter transforms map from some input parameter space into some other parameter space and accumulate evidence for feature hypotheses in a manner similar to the Hough transform. The constraint satisfaction network is used to select the best parameter hypotheses.

The links in the network are:

- Bottom-up connections between the data and nodes, or between lower- and higher-level nodes. These links are used to feed input to the nodes.
- Links between nodes themselves. These links can be inhibitory, in case the hypotheses are conflicting, or excitory, in case the hypotheses support one another.

Hypotheses and links are generated dynamically from the results of the parameter transforms and compatibility relations. The input I_i to node i is a measure of the corresponding hypothesis h_i based only on data measurements. Nodes supported by the same data are linked by inhibitory links. For example, in the parameter space for a plane, each hypothesis represents a plane. The input for the node for each plane hypothesis is the number of points that vote for that plane. This node is connected by negatively weighted links to other nodes representing planes with different parameters that are supported by common points in the image. In the full constraint satisfaction network, there are other nodes corresponding to parameter hypotheses for curves, lines, cylinders, etc. These nodes may or may not be linked to the nodes for planes depending on the defined compatibility relationships between the features.

Inhibition links perform several useful functions. Inhibition within a small parametric neighborhood sharpens the response of the transforms. Only the strongest unit in any neighboring cluster will survive. This reduces the problem of evidence for a hypothesis being split due to quantization into several hypotheses. Inhibition links between hypotheses which are supported by common image pixels provide an implicit segmentation of the image. Only those hypotheses which do not share support from portions of the image will survive constraint satisfaction. These will represent a spatial segmentation of the image. Inhibition links can also be used to ensure that hypotheses which are inconsistent, for example, for geometric reasons, will compete.

7.1. Feature Detection

The surface feature set consists of planes, spheres, and quadrics of revolution, specifically, cylinders and cones. To increase coverage, curves in three-space, namely lines and conic-sections, are also included. These correspond to intersections and boundaries of surface patches. Local surface features are extracted from smooth surface approximations to the depth map. That is, least-squares' second-order polynomial approximations are made within $M \times N$ areas about range point $\mathbf{q}$. From these approximations, the principal curvatures, κ_{max} and κ_{min}, and the associated principal directions in three-space, X_{max} and X_{min} are computed.

Three-dimensional points that lie on depth discontinuities are defined as local curve features. An edge detector is used to generate discontinuity maps; this gives range points $\mathbf{q}$ on, or near, zero and first-order depth discontinuities.

When a first-level hypothesis survives in its winner-take-all subnetwork, it is used as input to a parameter transform to determine higher-level feature hypotheses. These transforms generally reexamine the image points, $\{\mathbf{q_n}\}$, which support the hypothesis. For example, the radius R associated with each point in $\{\mathbf{q_n}\}$ of a sphere center hypothesis $\mathbf{p}$ is given by $R = \|\mathbf{p} - \mathbf{q}\|$.

7.2. Object Recognition

The homogeneous approach of the system is maintained for object recognition as well. The parameter transform from the feature spaces to object space uses the reconstructed features to index into a database of object models to determine possible object hypotheses.

There is no need to determine which features belong to a single object before recognition. Just as the selection via constraint satisfaction provides an implicit segmentation of the image during feature extraction, it also provides a partitioning of the features during object recognition. Hypotheses which share support from common features compete, thus assembly hypotheses which survive constraint satisfaction do not share features, and a partition on the feature set is created.

Object models in the database are represented by a feature graph. Nodes in the graph represent the primitive features of the object: surfaces and their intersection curves. Arcs represent coordinate-free geometric relationships between features, for example, the relative size of the radii of a sphere and cylinder.

Features of a model are sorted into layers, which represent the expected reconstruction resolution. The first layers contain the features that are likely to be found at a coarse resolution and, successively, later layers contain progressively finer features. This "multiple resolution" representation prunes the search for matching features as described below.

Each hypothesis in object space represents an instantiation of an object model from the database. It is identified by the set of bindings $\{B(F_i, f_j), \dots \}$ between features F_i of the object model and features f_j found in the image. Indexing consists of two steps, checking for a match with unbound model features of existing object hypotheses and checking features of models in the database. If a match is found, an object hypothesis is extended or created to include the new evidence.

In either case, there is only the need to check for matches between image features and features in active layers of an object model. For uninstantiated models in the database, only the first (coarsest resolution) layer is active. Instances of models in object hypotheses can have one or more active layers. Layers are activated whenever sufficient features of the previous layer have been bound to image features. To avoid an explosion in hypotheses with very little evidence, only models with sufficient matches in the first layer are instantiated. Matching an image feature to a feature in a model requires checking two pieces of information, intrinsic feature characteristics (e.g., feature type) and position relative to other features.

7.3. Experiments

Experiments were run on some 20-range images, obtained by a laser-range finder. Images have varied from 32×32 to 256×256. A 64×64 depth map was generated from the scene in Figure 2.31. Figure 2.32 shows the depth map

Figure 2.31. Complex real-world scene.

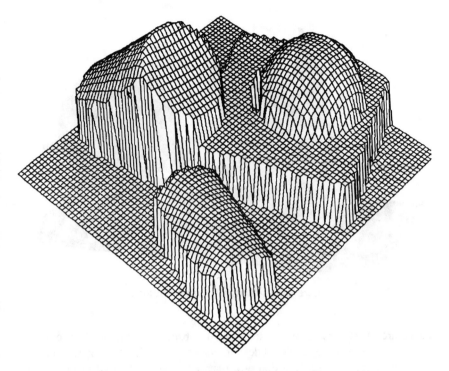

Figure 2.32.   Depth map.

obtained. Low-level processing includes finding the zero- and first-order discontinuities in the original data, and computing quadric smooth surface approximations about each point. Most surface and discontinuity features present in the image were successfully reconstructed, cf. Figure 2.33.

Constraint satisfaction causes a dramatic implosion in the number of hypotheses, as can be seen in Figure 2.34, which shows the number of hypotheses in each parameter space over time. As an example, 17 axis orientation hypotheses (partial features of axes of quadrics of revolution) were generated in the first-level quadric of revolution reconstruction process. After constraint satisfaction, two survived and generated 89 hypotheses for axes of revolution. Again, after constraint satisfaction, only the two correct axes survived to reconstruct the solids of revolution.

8. EARLY VISION

Visual processing can roughly be divided into three stages: low- (early), mid-, and high-level vision. These divisions are not mutually exclusive. The different

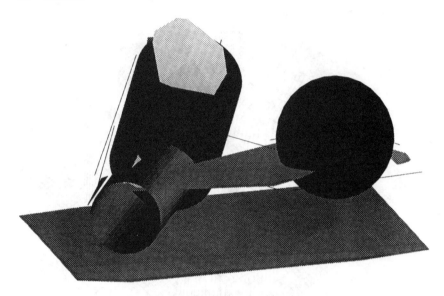

Figure 2.33. Reconstructed features.

stages are characterized by the increasingly abstract descriptors they employ. Early vision uses image-centered descriptors while high-level vision uses object-centered descriptors. Early vision processes work on pixel-based features organized in grids, usually a direct mapping from the image.

Some processes associated with early vision are edge detection, surface interpolation, shape from shading, motion (optical flow) and stereo. Early vision tasks share certain problems, the most important being the problem of smoothing

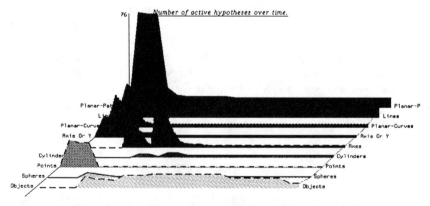

Figure 2.34. Number of active hypotheses over time.

in the presence of discontinuities. This is also reflected in the similar fashion these tasks are formulated as optimization of certain cost functions. Yuille [55] provides a survey of the cost minimization formulation and the implementation using analog networks for these tasks.

All of these processes are computationally intensive, and stand to gain much, in terms of processing images in reasonable times, by parallel implementations. The data are organized in regular patterns, usually rectangular grids, allowing similar simple geometries in the processing elements. Communication is limited to small local neighborhoods. This results in simple interconnection schemes with much fewer connections to and from each processor node, as compared to more general neural network organizations.

The standard formulations of early vision problems as a minimization of a cost function were introduced by Horn and Schunk for optical flow [56], Ikeuchi and Horn [57] for shape from shading, and Grimson [58] and Terzopolous [59] for surface reconstruction. These different formulations were unified using regularization theory [45].

8.1. Surface Interpolation

Surface interpolation, or reconstruction, involves fitting a surface across a sparse set of points. The most common application is in stereo, where stereo correspondence usually results in a sparse set of depth points, reflecting the sparse distribution of the matched features. The problem is commonly formulated as that of fitting a membrane or thin plate through the data such that the energy of the plate (or membrane) is minimized. We present the formulation given by Koch, Marroquin and Yuille [60], and Yuille [55]. The energy to be minimized is given by:

$$E(f) = \|Bf - d\|^2 + \lambda \|Sf\|^2 \qquad (8.1)$$

where the first term gives a measure of the distance of the solution f to the data d, and the second term is the regularizer needed to make the problem well posed. B is a matrix with 1 where there are data and 0 where there are none. S corresponds to the operator associated with the thin plate or membrane. This can be equated to the energy term minimized by the constraint satisfaction network, namely:

$$E(V) = \frac{1}{2} \sum_{i,j} T_{ij} V_i V_j + \sum_i V_i I_i \qquad (8.2)$$

by making $T = 2(B^T B + \lambda S^T S)$, $V = f$, $I_i = -2B^T d$ and dropping the constant term $d^T d$. Thus, one can transform the surface interpolation problems to a constraint satisfaction problem.

For the one-dimensional case:

$$E(f) = c_d \sum_i (f_i - d_i)^2 + \sum_i (f_i - f_i + 1)^2 \tag{8.3}$$

where f_i denotes points on the interpolated surface and d_i denotes data points. However, this equation does not handle discontinuities. Discontinuities are locations where the surface orientation (orientation discontinuity, for example, between the two sides of a cube) or surface depth (depth discontinuity, for example, between the surface of a cube and the background) changes sharply. In Equation (8.3) no provision has been made for discontinuities, so the interpolation will smooth over them.

Discontinuities can be elegantly handled in surface reconstruction, and in the other early vision problems, by using *line processes* [61]. A line process element is located in between two adjoining pixels (interspacial cite). It is switched on, or 1, when there is a discontinuity located between the two pixels, and is off or 0, otherwise. Line processes can be modeled as nodes in a constraint satisfaction network. Equation (8.3) can be modified to handle discontinuities by including the determination of line processes as a part of the constraint satisfaction.

$$E(f, l) = \sum_i \frac{(f_i - f_i + 1)^2}{(1 - l_i) + c_d} \sum_i (f_i - d_i)^2 + c_l \sum_i l_i \tag{8.4}$$

where l_i is the line process element and is 1 if there is a discontinuity (i.e., no smoothing is allowed across it) or 0 when there is none. As is evident from the second term of Equation (8.4), there is a cost associated with proposing a discontinuity. Therefore, a discontinuity is proposed when the cost surface gradient $(f_i - f_i + 1)$ is large, i.e., $(f_i - f_i + 1)^2$ is more than the cost c_l of introducing a discontinuity. To use constraint satisfaction networks, the value of the line processes is made continuous from 0 to 1 and is represented by V_i in the following equation:

$$E(f, V) = \sum_i (f_i - f_{i+1})^2 (1 - V_i) + c_d \sum_i (f_i - d_i)^2 + c_l \sum_i V_i$$
$$+ c_g \sum_{V=0}^{V=1} g^{-1} (V) dV \tag{8.5}$$

The general 2-D case is treated in [60], which also presents analog hardware implementation details and some experimental results.

8.2. Stereo

The stereo problem can be formulated as an energy minimization problem as [55,62]:

$$E(d) = \sum_i (L_i - R_{i+d(i)}) + \lambda \sum_i [d(i + 1) - d(i)]^2 \qquad (8.6)$$

where $d(i)$ is the disparity, and L and R are local measures on the image. The regularization (second) term insures that disparity varies smoothly (in 1-D). To allow for sharp changes in disparity, one can introduce line processes [55] as was done in Equation (8.4) for surface interpolation:

$$E(d, l) = \sum_i (L_i - R_{i+d(i)})^2 (1 - l_i) + \lambda \sum_i [d(i + 1) - d(i)]^2 (1 - l_i) + \tau \sum_i l_i$$

$$(8.7)$$

8.3. Optical Flow

Horn and Schunk formulated short-range motion (Section 6.3) as optical flow [56]. Optical flow is the apparent motion of the brightness pattern [63] and, due to the aperture problem, it may or may not correspond to the actual motion field. The optical flow problem can be formulated as minimization of [63]:

$$E(u, v) = \iint (I_x u + I_y v + I_t)^2 \, dx \, dy + \lambda [(u_x^2 + u_y^2) + (v_x^2 + v_y^2)] \, dx \, dy \quad (8.8)$$

where (u, v) is the velocity field, I is the image irradiance, and I_x, etc. are the partial derivatives. The first term states that image brightness is constant over time and the second term imposes smoothness on the velocity field. The equation can be modified to a difference equation:

$$E(u_{i,j}, v_{i,j}) = \sum_{i,j} [u_{i,j}(I_{i+1,j} - I_{i,j}) + v_{i,j}(I_{i+1,j})]^2$$

$$+ \sum_{i,j} (u_{i+1,j} - u_{i,j})^2 + (u_{i,j+1} - u_{i,j})^2 + (v_{i+1,j} - v_{i,j})^2$$

$$+ (v_{i,j+1} - v_{i,j})^2 \qquad (8.9)$$

To take into account discontinuities in the motion field, for example, at object boundaries, one can introduce horizontal and vertical line processes $h_{i,j}$ and $k_{i,j}$. Here h and k are made continuous variables ranging from 0 to 1. The energy function can then be written as [55]:

$$E(u_{i,j}, v_{i,j}) = \sum_{i,j} [u_{i,j}(I_{i+1,j} - I_{i,j}) + v_{i,j}(I_{i+1,j} - I_{i,j})]^2$$

$$+ \sum_{i,j} [((u_{i+1,j} - u_{i,j})^2 + (u_{i,j} - u_{i,j})^2)(1 - h_{i,j})$$

$$+ ((v_{i+1,j} - v_{i,j})^2 + (v_{i,j} + 1 - v_{i,j})^2)(1 - k_{i,j})] + \sum_{i,j} V(h,k) \quad (8.10)$$

The last term gives the cost of introducing a vertical or horizontal discontinuity. A similar CSN has been implemented in hardware [64].

9. SUMMARY

The constraint satisfaction problem in vision was defined. A technique to map the problem onto a network by representing the hypotheses as nodes and constraints as weighted links, was presented. The network is implemented as a neural network. An optimal solution to the constraint satisfaction problem is obtained by relaxing the network and selecting the hypotheses which correspond to the neurons with high output. This methodology allows direct use of the Hopfield network to find optimal solutions for a given constraint satisfaction problem, without first having to formulate a global energy term for the problem, by simply mapping the neural network directly to the natural structure of the problem.

There are problems which are more naturally expressed in terms of cost functions to be minimized, rather than as a set of hypotheses and constraints. Tasks in early vision are examples from this domain. For these problems, the energy term is equated to that for the constraint satisfaction network to arrive at the nodes and the interconnection weights.

The use of constraint satisfaction networks for practical applications in computer vision; namely, perceptual organization, correspondence, segmentation, and early vision, were demonstrated. It may be useful to note here that in the first two applications, each node represents a high-level feature. In contrast to neural networks that take images as input and learn internal representations [10], for constraint satisfaction networks the features to be represented, and the relationships between them, are selected by the network designer. This, however, does not require the network to be constructed manually; the nodes and their relationships get automatically formed as a by-product of the detection process or by use of simple iterative algorithms. Constraint satisfaction networks with regular geometries, for example CSN for early vision, can be easily implemented in analog hardware.

REFERENCES

[1]   S.E. Fahlman and G.E. Hinton, "Connectionist Architectures for Artificial Intelligence," *IEEE Computer,* January 1987, pp. 100–109.

[2]   R. Mohan, "Application of Neural Constraint Satisfaction Networks to Vision," *Proceedings of the International Joint Conference on Neural Networks,* San Diego, 1989.

[3]   D. Marr, *Vision,* W.H. Freeman, San Francisco, 1982.

[4]   E. Mjolness, G. Gindi, and P. Anandan, "Optimization in Model Matching and Perceptual Organization," *Neural Computation,* Vol. 1, 1989, pp. 218–229.

[5]   R. Nevatia, *Machine Perception,* Prentice-Hall, Englewood Cliffs, NJ, 1982.

[6]   M.A. Arbib, "Brain Theory and Cooperative Computation," *Human Neurobiology,* Vol. 4, 1985, pp. 201–218.

[7]   S. Kirkpatrick, C.D. Gelatt, and M.P. Vecchi, "Optimization by Simulated Annealing," *Science,* Vol. 220, 1983, pp. 671–680.

[8]   J.J. Hopfield and D.W. Tank, "'Neural' Computation of Decisions in Optimization Problems," *Biological Cybernetics,* Vol. 52, 1985, pp. 141–152.

[9]   J.J. Hopfield and D.W. Tank, "Computing with Neural Circuits: A Model," *Science,* Vol. 233, 1986, pp. 625–633.

[10] D.E. Rumelhart, J.L. McClelland, and the PDP Research Group, *Parallel Distributed Processing: Explorations in the Microstructures of Computing,* MIT Press, Cambridge, MA, 1986.

[11] S.E. Fahlman, G.E. Hinton, and T.J. Sejnowski, "Massively Parallel Architectures for AI: NETL, Thistle, and Boltzman Machines," *Proceedings of the National Conference on Artificial Intelligence,* Menlo Park, CA, 1983.

[12] J.A. Feldman and D.H. Ballard, "Connectionist Models and Their Properties," *Cognitive Science,* 1982, pp. 205–254.

[13] J.J. Hopfield and D.W. Tank, "Neural Networks and Physical Systems with Emergent Collective Computational Abilities," *Proceedings of the National Academy of Science,* Vol. 79, April 1982, pp. 2554–2558.

[14] J.J. Hopfield, "Neurons with Graded Response Have Collective Computational Properties Like Those of Two-State Neurons," *Proceedings of the National Academy of Science,* Vol. 81, 1984, pp. 3088–3092.

[15] R.A. Hummel and S.W. Zucker, "On the Foundations of Relaxation Labeling Process," *IEEE Transactions on Pattern Analysis and Machine Intelligence,* Vol. 5, No. 3, May 1983, pp. 267–287.

[16] R. Mohan and R. Nevatia, "Segmentation and Description Based on Perceptual Organization," *Proceedings of the IEEE Conference on Computer Vision and Pattern Recognition,* San Diego, CA, June 1989.

[17] M.R. Quillian, "Semantic Memory," M. Minsky (Ed.), *Semantic Information Processing,* MIT Press, Cambridge, MA, 1968, pp. 227–270.

[18] R. Mohan, "Perceptual Organization for Computer Vision," Ph.D. Thesis, IRIS Report #254, Institute for Robotics and Intelligent Systems, University of Southern California, Los Angeles, CA, 1989.

[19] R. Mohan and R. Nevatia, "Perceptual Grouping with Applications to 3-D Shape Extraction," *Proceedings of the IEEE Computer Society Workshop on Computer Vision,* Miami Beach, FL, December 1987.

[20] M. Wertheimer, "Principles of Perceptual Organization," D. Beardslee and M. Wertheimer (Eds.), *Readings in Perception,* Van Nostrand, Princeton, NJ, 1958, pp. 115–135.

[21] D.G. Lowe, *Perceptual Organization and Visual Recognition,* Kluwer Academic, Hingham, MA, 1985.

[22] R. Mohan and R. Nevatia, "Using Perceptual Organization to Extract 3-D Structure," *IEEE Transactions on Pattern Analysis and Machine Intelligence,* Vol. 11, No. 11, November 1989, pp. 1121–1139.

[23] G. Kanisza, *Organization in Vision,* Praeger, New York, 1979.

[24] S.E. Palmer, "The Psychology of Perceptual Organization: A Transformational Approach," J. Beck, B. Hope, and A. Rosenfeld, (Eds.), *Human and Machine Vision,* Academic, New York, 1983, pp. 269–339.

[25] A. Triesman, "Perceptual Grouping and Attention in Visual Search for Features and Objects," *Journal of Experimental Psychology: Human Perception and Performance,* Vol. 8, No. 2, 1982, pp. 194–214.

[26] Kubovy and Pomerantz, *Perceptual Organization,* Erlbaum, Hillsdale, NJ, 1981.

[27] A.P. Witkin and J.M. Tenenbaum, "On the Role of Structure in Vision," J. Beck, B. Hope and A. Rosenfeld (Eds.), *Human and Machine Vision,* Academic, New York, 1983, pp. 481–543.

[28] R.A. Brooks, "Goal-Directed Edge Linking and Ribbon Finding," *Proceedings of the DARPA Image Understanding Workshop,* April 1979, pp. 72–78.

[29] D.H. Ballard, G.E. Hinton, and T.J. Sejnowski, "Parallel Visual Computation," *Nature,* Vol. 306, November 1983, pp. 21–26.

[30] G.A. Carpenter, M.A. Cohen, S. Grossberg, T. Kohonen, E. Oja, G. Palm, J.J. Hopfield, and D.W. Tank, "Technical Comments: Computing with Neural Networks," *Science,* Vol. 235, March 1987.

[31] S. Amari, "Competitive and Cooperative Aspects of Dynamics of Neural Excitation and Self Organization," Amari and Arbib (Eds.), *Cooperation and Competition in Neural Networks,* Springer Verlag, New York, 1982.

[32] S. Ullman, *The Interpretation of Visual Motion,* MIT Press, Cambridge, MA, 1979.

[33] S. Ullman, "Maximizing Rigidity: The Incremental Recovery of 3-D Structure from Rigid and Non-rigid Motion," *Perception,* Vol. 13, 1984, pp. 255–274.

[34] R. Mohan, G. Medioni, and R. Nevatia, "Stereo Error Correction, Detection and Evaluation," *IEEE Transactions on Pattern Analysis and Machine Intelligence,* Vol. 11, No. 2, February 1989.

[35] G. Medioni and R. Nevatia, "Segment Based Stereo Matching," *Computer Vision, Graphics and Image Processing,* Vol. 31, 1985, pp. 2–18.

[36] K. Nakayama, "Biological Image Motion Processing: A Review," *Vision Research,* Vol. 25, No. 5, 1985.

[37] K. Aggarwal and N. Nandhkumar, "On the Computation of Motion from Sequences of Images—A Review," *Proceedings of the IEEE,* Vol. 7, No. 8, August 1988, pp. 917–934.

[38] O.J. Braddick, "A Short-Range Process in Apparent Motion," *Vision Research,* Vol. 14, 1974.

[39] G. Johansson, "Spatiotemporal Differentiation and Integration in Visual Motion Perception," *Psychological Review,* Vol. 38, 1976, pp. 379–383.

[40] E.H. Adelson and J.R. Bergen, "Spatiotemporal Energy Models for the Perception of Motion," *Journal of the Optical Society of America,* Vol. 2, No. 2, 1985.

[41] L. Chen, "Topological Structure in the Perception of Apparent Motion," *Perception,* Vol. 14, 1985, pp. 197–208.

[42] P.A. Kolers, *Aspects of Motion Perception,* Pergamon, New York, 1972.

[43] K. Mucth, I.M. Smith and A. Yonas, "The Effect of Two-Dimensional and Three-Dimensional Distance on Apparent Motion," *Perception,* Vol. 12, 1983, pp. 305–312.

[44] N.M. Grzywacz and A.L. Yuille, "Motion Correspondence and Analog Networks," *Proceedings of the American Institute of Physics Conference on Neural Networks for Computing,* Snowbird, Utah, 1986.

[45] T. Poggio, V. Torre, and C. Koch, "Computational Vision and Regularization Theory," *Nature,* Vol. 317, 1985, pp. 314–319.

[46] R.M. Bolle and D.B. Cooper, "On Optimally Combining Pieces of Information, with Application to Estimating 3-D Complex-Object Position from Range Data," *IEEE Transactions on Pattern Analysis and Machine Intelligence,* Vol. 8, No. 5, 1986, pp. 619–638.

[47] R. Mohan, "Perceptual Organization in Motion Correspondence," RC 15805, Computer Science, IBM T.J. Watson Research Center, May 1990.

[48] S.K. Sethi and R. Jain, "Finding Trajectories of Feature Points in a Monocular Image Sequence," *IEEE Transaction on Pattern Analysis and Machine Intelligence,* Vol. 9, No. 1, 1987, pp. 56–73.

[49] K.A. Stevens and A. Brookes, "Detecting Structures by Symbolic Constructions on Tokens," *Computer Vision, Graphics and Image Processing,* Vol. 37, 1987, pp. 238–260.

[50] C. von der Malsburg, "Pattern Recognition by Labeled Graph Matching," *Neural Networks,* Vol. 1, 1988, pp. 141–148.

[51] B. Parvin and G. Medioni, "A Constraint Satisfaction Network for Matching 3D Objects," *Proceedings of the International Joint Conference on Neural Networks,* San Diego, 1989.

[52] R.M. Bolle, A. Califano, R. Kjeldsen, and R.W. Taylor, "Visual Recognition Using Concurrent and Layered Parameter Networks," *Proceedings of the IEEE Conference on Computer Vision and Pattern Recognition,* San Diego, CA, June 1989.

[53] A. Califano, R.M. Bolle, R. Kjeldsen, and R.W. Taylor, "Evidence Fusion Using Constraint Satisfaction Networks," J.K. Aggarwal (Ed.), *NATO Advanced Research Workshop on Multisensor Fusion for Computer Vision, NATO ASI Series,* Springer Verlag, New York, November 1989.

[54] D.H. Ballard, "Parameter Nets: A Theory of Low Level Vision," *Proceedings of the 7th International Joint Conference on Artificial Intelligence,* August 1981.

[55] A.L. Yuille, "Energy Functions for Early Vision and Analog Networks," *Biological Cybernetics,* Vol. 61, 1989, pp. 115–123.

[56] B.K.P. Horn and B.G. Schunk, "Determining Optical Flow," *Artificial Intelligence,* Vol. 7, 1981, pp. 185–203.

[57] K. Ikeuchi and B.K.P. Horn, "Numerical Shape from Shading and Occluding Boundaries," *Artificial Intelligence,* Vol. 17, 1981, pp. 141–184.

[58] W.E.L. Grimson, *From Images to Surfaces,* MIT Press, Cambridge, MA, 1981.

[59] D. Terzopolous, "Multiresolution Computation of Visible Surface Representations," Ph.D. Thesis, MIT, Cambridge, MA, 1984.

[60] C. Koch, J. Marroquin, and A.L. Yuille, "Analog 'Neuronal' Networks in Early Vision," *Proceedings of the National Academy of Science,* Vol. 83, June 1986, pp. 4263–4267.

[61] S. Geman and D. Geman, "Stochastic Relaxation, Gibbs Distribution, and the Bayesian Restoration of Images," *IEEE Transaction on Pattern Analysis and Machine Intelligence,* Vol. 6, No. 6, November 1984, pp. 721–741.

[62] S. Barnard, "A Stochastic Approach to Stereo Vision," *Proceedings of the National Conference on Artificial Intelligence,* AAAI-86, Vol. 1, Philadelphia, PA, August 1986, pp. 676–680.

[63] B.K.P. Horn, *Robot Vision,* MIT Press, Cambridge, MA, 1986.

[64] J. Hutchinson, C. Koch, J. Luo, and C. Mead, "Computing Motion Using Analog and Binary Resistive Networks," *IEEE Computer,* Vol. 21, 1988, pp. 52–63.

3
Higher-Order Neural Networks for Position, Scale, and Rotation Invariant Pattern Recognition

Max B. Reid
Lilly Spirkovska
Information Sciences Division
NASA Ames Research Center
Moffett Field, CA

1. INTRODUCTION

In this work, the purpose of an autonomous vision system is assumed to be to allow the automatic recognition of objects. The general performance desired is for the system to classify input scenes as either belonging to a set of target objects or not, as in Figure 3.1(a), or as belonging to one of a number of distinct pattern classes, as shown in Figure 3.1(b) and (c). Here we deal with the case shown in Figure 3.1(c), where it is desired to classify an input pattern into exactly one of a set of defined classes. In particular, we consider distortion invariant pattern recognition, in which each class in Figure 3.1(c) is the set of all views of a single object which result from either translating the object within the field of view, scaling the object, or rotating the object within the plane of view. Examples of members of one distortion invariant class are shown in Figure 3.2.

Figure 3.1 is a Venn diagram wherein object classes are subsets of all possible input scenes. To be precise, the pattern space in the figure should be shown not as a two-dimensional drawing but as an M-dimensional space, where M is the number of pixels in the input scene. Every possible input scene can be represented as an M-dimensional vector, the elements of which are the values of individual pixels, which may be either binary or gray-scale. In most practical vision applications, M is a number between 10^3 and 10^6. The total number of possible inputs is therefore enormous, and the computational overhead required to determine whether the M-vector describing a given object is a member of a given subset of M-vectors rules out pattern classification by direct comparison of inputs to stored images on a pixel-by-pixel basis.

Practical pattern recognition is performed as a two-part process of feature

Pattern Space: All possible input scenes

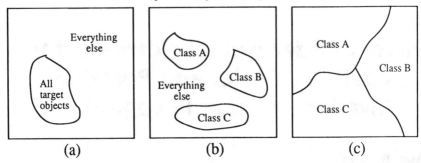

(a)   (b)   (c)

Figure 3.1.   Pattern classification. In (a) and (b), it is desired to distinguish input scenes into a single or into multiple classes, respectively. If the classes do not include the entire pattern space, an additional class for "everything else" is implicitly defined. As this additional class will have extremely diverse members, it is more practical to design classes so that every possible image will be a member of a class, as in (c).

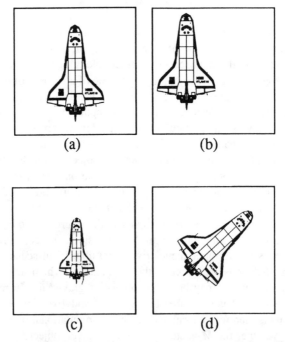

(a)   (b)

(c)   (d)

Figure 3.2.   Four members of a distortion invariant pattern class. The prototype in (a) is defined to be in the same class as each translated (b), scaled (c), or in-plane rotated view (d).

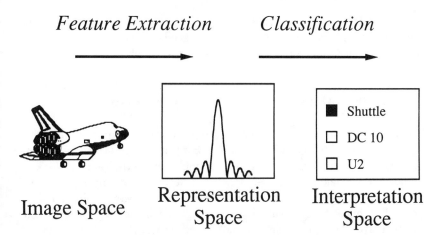

Feature Extraction   *Classification*

Image Space   Representation   Interpretation
                          Space   Space

Figure 3.3.   Pattern recognition paradigm. A scene is input in high-dimensional image space and is mapped via feature extraction into a representation space with much lower dimensionality. Classification is then performed by a subsequent mapping from representation space to interpretation space.

extraction followed by object classification, as shown in Figure 3.3 [1,2,3,4]. First, a preliminary mapping from an image to a representation space is made, resulting in a significant degree of data reduction. In representation space, the image is generally described by a set of features. The length of the feature vector, which is the dimensionality of the representation space, is much lower than M, the dimensionality of the original image. A second mapping then operates on this reduced data to produce a classification or estimation in an interpretation space. Historically, feature extraction has been performed either with mathematical mappings operating on a digitized detected image [1,2] or with optical pre-processing before the image is detected [3]. In either case, feature extraction is followed by analysis of the digitized feature set to allow classification. In order to allow full in-plane distortion invariant pattern recognition, classification requires the extraction of features which do not change when an object is translated, scaled, or rotated.

Both mappings shown in Figure 3.3 may potentially be performed using neural network models [4]. In this chapter we discuss neural networks both as classifiers in hybrid systems and as implementations of the complete pattern recognition operation. Emphasis is given to recognition invariant to distortions in scale, translational position and angular orientation. The relatively poor results achieved for this problem with neural models performing the complete mapping from image to interpretation is attributable to the unsuitability of the models used for distortion invariant feature extraction. In contrast, higher-order neural networks can be designed to implement the extraction of simple but effective features suitable for in-plane distortion invariance. Simulation results of higher-order neural networks demonstrate that simultaneous invariance to scale, translation, and in-plane rotation is obtainable with this model.

2. NEURAL NETWORKS FOR PATTERN RECOGNITION

Pattern recognition requires the nonlinear separation of pattern space into subsets representing the objects to be identified. Early research into neural networks concentrated on defining their potential for nonlinear discrimination [5,6]. It was found that a single-layer, first-order neural network can only perform linear discrimination. Figure 3.4 demonstrates the distinction between linear and nonlinear discrimination. In Figure 3.4(a) a straight line separating classes A and B can be drawn through (M-dimensional) pattern space. Figure 3.4(b) shows the case of classes which are not linearly separable because a straight line cannot be drawn between them. The most commonly cited example of this is the exclusive-or problem, shown in Figure 3.4(c). Results of research in the early 1960s showed that either multiple layer first-order networks or single-layer networks of higher order can provide nonlinear separation [6].

The capability of neural networks to perform nonlinear separation can be applied both to extract image features and to interpret images based on a feature set. Practical applications in distortion invariant pattern recognition have been found for hybrid systems utilizing neural networks for classification. Troxel, Rogers, and Kabrisky [7] successfully applied a multilayer perceptron neural network trained with a backward-error propagation (back propagation) learning

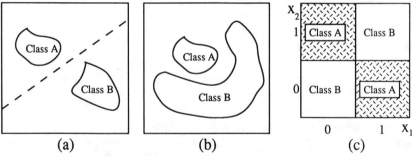

$$(a) \qquad (b) \qquad (c)$$

Figure 3.4.   Linear vs. nonlinear discrimination. The classes in (a) are separable by a straight line drawn through M-dimensional pattern space, where M is the number of distinct parameters of a pattern, such as the number of pixels in an image. In (b) some form of nonlinear discrimination is required to distinguish between classes. The most familiar example of nonlinear classes is the exclusive-or (c). M for the exclusive-or is only two, as it is defined in terms of only two inputs, x_1 and x_2.

algorithm [8,9] to classify laser radar images of targets, invariant to position, in-plane rotation, and scale. The data was first mapped into the magnitude of the log-radial/polar Fourier transform, $|F(\ln r, \theta)|$, feature space using a nonneural digital processor. Glover [10] describes a practical product inspection system based on optical Fourier transform feature extraction followed by neural classification. Rotation and scale invariance has also been described in a system using complex-log conformal mapping combined with a distributed neural associative memory [11]. In all of these approaches utilizing neural classification, distortion invariance is achieved through nonneural feature extraction techniques.

It has been argued that nonlinear neural computing is theoretically superior to methods such as matched filters or linear correlation for the complete pattern recognition operation, including feature extraction [12]. However, the performance of neural networks to date fails to fulfill this promise. For instance, several types of neural associative memories have been shown to be computationally more expensive than matched filters in a study involving the recognition of line segments [13]. Multilayer networks trained by back propagation have also been applied to recognition tasks, examples being sonar signal classification [14] and distortion invariant character recognition [15,16]. In these cases, the networks achieved $\approx$ 80–90% recognition accuracy only after being shown a training set of images several hundred [14] or thousand [15,16] times. Learning by back propagation to distinguish a "T" from a "C," invariant to translation and rotation, required over 5,000 presentations of an exhaustive training set [15]. Learning to distinguish 36 patterns in a 5 × 5 pixel array invariant to translation required over a thousand training set presentations to a network composed of two layers, each with 25 Adalines arranged in slabs [16].

The relatively poor performance of neural networks in the preceding examples, most particularly the failure to produce efficient distortion invariant recognition, is due to the fact that first-order networks are poorly suited for extracting distortion invariant features. One layer of a typical first-order network is shown in Figure 3.5. The activation level of an output node in a first-order neural network is determined by an equation of the form:

$$y_i = \Theta(\Sigma_j \, w_{ij} \, x_j), \tag{2.1}$$

where Θ is a nonlinear threshold function, the x_j's are the values of the input nodes, and the interconnection matrix elements, w_{ij}, determine the weight that each input is given in the summation.

Achieving translation, scale, and rotation invariance requires a neural network to learn relationships between the input pixels, x_j. Note that the summation within the parenthesis in Equation (2.1) is a function of individual x_j's. No advantage is taken of any known relationships between the x_j's. Multilayer, first-order networks can learn invariances, but require a great deal of training, and produce solutions that are specific to particular training sets.

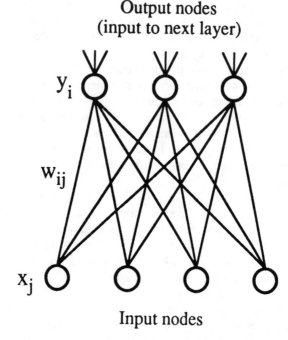

Figure 3.5.   One layer of a first-order neural network.

A further disadvantage is that the mappings learned are opaque: It is not readily evident what features are being extracted or how classification is being performed. It is generally assumed that the output of intermediate-layer hidden nodes in the network correspond to specific features, and in some applications it is possible to discern what these features are. An example is the network trained to perform sonar signal classification described by Gorman and Sejnowski [14], where the hidden nodes were shown to take the form of an audio frequency filter. In distortion invariant recognition applications, however, it is not apparent that first-order networks' hidden nodes come to represent efficient feature sets or even feature sets sufficient to allow classification by succeeding layers. What is apparent is that very extensive training is required to produce even a partial solution to the distortion invariant recognition problem.

3. HIGHER-ORDER NEURAL NETWORKS

The output of nodes in a general higher-order network is given by:

$$y_i = \Theta(\Sigma_j \, w_{ij} x_j + \Sigma_j \, \Sigma_k \, w_{ijk} \, x_j \, x_k + \Sigma_j \, \Sigma_k \, \Sigma_l \, w_{ijkl} \, x_j \, x_k \, x_l + \ldots). \qquad (3.1)$$

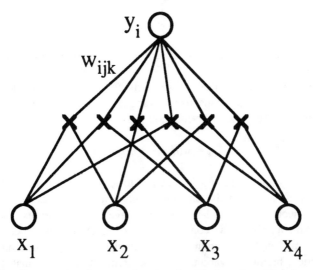

Figure 3.6.   A second-order neural network with four inputs and one output. Inputs are first multiplied together (at X) and then multiplied by a weight before being summed.

A diagram of a neural network utilizing only second-order terms is shown in Figure 3.6. Higher-order neural networks (HONNs) were evaluated in the 1960s for performing nonlinear discrimination but were rejected as impractical due to the combinatoric explosion of higher-order terms [6]. A network with M inputs and one output using only rth order terms requires M-choose-r interconnections. For higher orders and large M, this number, which is on the order of M^r, rapidly becomes excessive.

Interest in higher-order networks was rekindled by the work of Giles and Maxwell and their colleagues [17,18] who proposed that the problem of combinatoric explosion could be overcome by building invariances into the network architecture. Recent research [19,20] has shown that by using information about the relationships expected between the input x_j's, HONNs can be tailored for invariant pattern recognition by building distortion invariant feature extraction functionally into the architecture. The invariances achieved require no learning to produce and apply to any input pattern learned by the network. Further, a HONN can perform nonlinear discrimination using only a single layer so that a simple learning rule can be used, leading to rapid convergence.

As an example, translation invariance can be built into the second-order neural network with four input nodes and one output node shown in Figure 3.7. Assume that the input patterns (1 0 1 0) and (0 1 0 1) are to be identified as the same object. If $w_{i13} = w_{i24}$, then y_i is the same for both inputs. In general, translation invariance requires that the connections for equally spaced input pairs are all set equal. This is written functionally as:

$$w_{ijk} = w(i,(j-k)). \tag{3.2}$$

The weights w_{ijk} are a function of the output node, i, and the distance between input nodes j and k.

Combinations of invariances can similarly be achieved. A second-order neural network will be simultaneously invariant to scale and translation if the weights are set according to the function [18]:

$$w_{ijk} = w(i,(y_k - y_j)/(x_k - x_j)). \tag{3.3}$$

Equation (3.3) implies that w_{ijk} is set equal to $w_{ij'k'}$ if the slope of a line drawn between nodes j and k equals that formed between j' and k', as shown in Figure 3.8. Any object drawn in a 2-D plane can have lines of various slopes drawn within it. An object's relative content of lines of different slopes does not change when it is translated in position or scaled in size, as long as it is not rotated.

In practice, building invariance into the architecture means that if a weight w_{ijk} is changed during training, every other weight $w_{ij'k'}$ which is equal to w_{ijk} according to Equation (3.3) must be simultaneously updated. Simultaneously updating every affected weight need not take any more time than updating a single weight if each element w_{ijk} is implemented as a pointer to an actual numerical value. Each weight which is constrained to be equal by Equation (3.3)

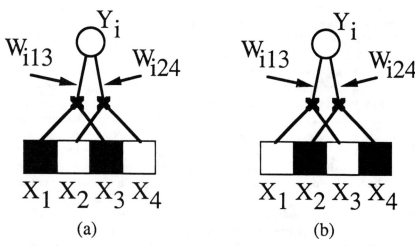

Figure 3.7. Building translation invariance into a second-order neural network. Sets of weights are constrained to be equal so that the network is unable to distinguish between distorted views. The input patterns 1010 and 0101 give the same response if $w_{i13} = w_{i24}$. In general, translation invariance requires $w_{ijk} = w_{i(j-k)}$.

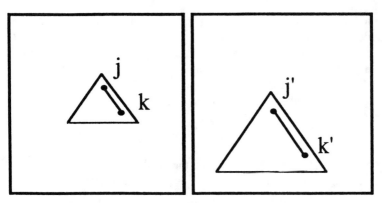

Figure 3.8. Translation and scale invariance achieved in a second-order network by setting $w_{ijk} = w_{ij'k'}$ if the slope of the line formed by nodes j and k equals that formed by nodes j' and k'.

points to the same value; when this value is changed, all the weights pointing to it are effectively updated simultaneously.

Rotational invariance can be included by using a third-order neural network, where the output is given by the function:

$$y_i = \Theta(\Sigma_j \, \Sigma_k \, \Sigma_l \, w_{ijkl} \, x_j \, x_k \, x_l). \tag{3.4}$$

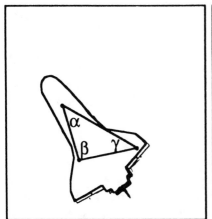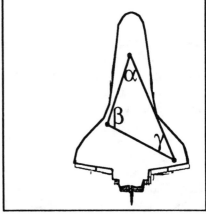

Figure 3.9. Translation, scale, and in-plane rotation invariance is achieved with a third-order network by setting all weights equal for those inputs j, k, and l which form similar triangles. Weights are defined by included angles through the formula: $w_{ijkl} = w_{i\alpha\beta\gamma} = w_{i\gamma\alpha\beta} = w_{i\beta\gamma\alpha}$ (i.e., a similar triangle is defined both by the values of the included angles and by their order).

As shown in Figure 3.9, any three points within an object define a triangle with included angles (α, β, γ). When the object is translated, scaled, and rotated in-plane, the three points in the same relative positions on the object still form the included angles (α, β, γ). In order to achieve invariance to all three distortions, all sets of three input pixels which form similar triangles are connected to the output with the same weight. The interconnection function has the form:

$$w_{ijkl} = w(i, \alpha, \beta, \gamma) = w(i, \beta, \gamma, \alpha) = w(i, \gamma, \alpha, \beta). \tag{3.5}$$

where α, β, and γ are calculated from the positions of input nodes j, k. and l. Note that the order of angles matters, but not which angle is measured first.

3.1. Simulations of Fully Connected HONNs

We have simulated both second- and third-order neural networks to achieve simultaneous invariance to: (a) translation and scale with a second-order network, and (b) translation, scale, and in-plane rotation using a third-order network. A Sun 3/60 with 20 MB memory and 30 MB swap space was used for simulations. Approximately 6.3 million (integer) interconnections could be stored with this amount of memory. The single-layer second-order network was simulated using a 16×16, or 256 node, input field fully interconnected to a single output node which was thresholded with a fixed-threshold hard limiter:

$$\Theta(\Sigma) = 1, \text{ if } \Sigma > 0,$$
$$\Theta(\Sigma) = 0, \text{ if } \Sigma \leq 0. \tag{3.6}$$

There were 256-choose-2 or 42,640 input pairs and therefore interconnections, which did not push the limit of the available memory capacity. The interconnection weights were constrained to follow Equation (3.3) in order to achieve invariance to scale and translation. The weights were initially set to zero and a learning rule was used of the form:

$$\Delta w_{ijk} = (t_i - y_i) x_j x_k, \tag{3.7}$$

where the expected training output, t, actual output, y, and inputs x, were all binary. The network was trained on just two distinct patterns—only one size and one location for each pattern. It learned to distinguish between the patterns after approximately 10 passes of the training set, and after training, the network successfully distinguished between all translated and scaled versions of the two objects with 100% accuracy. It is important to note again that training was not required to achieve this invariance, as distortion invariance was built into the architecture through Equation (3.3). The network only had to learn to distinguish between the two prototypical views of the target objects.

The system learned to distinguish between many pairs of distinct patterns, and was tested on a variety of problems, including the T-C problem. As explained in Rumelhart [15], in the T-C problem, the goal is to discriminate between the letters "T" and "C" independent of translation or in-plane rotation. Scale distortions were not considered in the problem as stated by Rumelhart, but were considered in this work. As originally suggested by Rosenblatt [5], the T-C problem requires the use of higher-order terms. Even when the "T" and "C" are considered just over all translations and 90° rotations, configurations of at least three pixels taken together must be examined to discriminate between the patterns. If only distances between pairs of pixels are considered, the patterns are equivalent.

Given the size of the input window, it was possible to scale the "T" and "C" by up to a factor of 5. Invariance over this range was demonstrated using the second-order network, with 100% recognition accuracy. Due to the limited resolution of the finite 16 × 16 input window, residual scale variance did occur which required a modification to the learning algorithm. Given the small scale of the inputs, it was possible to enumerate the number of lines of different slopes which could be drawn between pixel pairs within each pattern. From this it was seen that (T,C) pairs are distinguished by their relative content of horizontal and vertical information. For the smallest (T,C) pair, shown in Figure 3.10(a), the T has three input pair combinations arranged horizontally and three vertically, while the C has two arranged horizontally and four vertically. In the next larger scale of (T,C), shown in Figure 3.10(b), the ratio of horizontal to vertical pixel pairs is 34:34 for the T and 26:42 for the C. It is therefore easier to distinguish between the smaller (T,C) pair based on their relative horizontal/vertical content. If the system is trained on the smaller set of letters, learning is not pushed to the point where larger versions can be recognized. In contrast, if large patterns are used for training, all smaller versions are subsequently recognized.

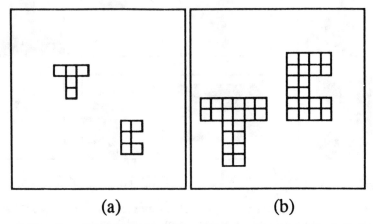

(a)   (b)

Figure 3.10.   Two different scales of T and C drawn in a 16 × 16 pixel window.

Residual scale variance was eliminated by using bipolar training values and a modified threshold function:

$$\Theta(\Sigma) = 1, \text{ if } \Sigma > K,$$
$$\Theta(\Sigma) = -1, \text{ if } \Sigma < -K,$$
$$\Theta(\Sigma) = 0, \text{ otherwise,} \tag{3.8}$$

where K is some positive constant. Learning with a sufficiently large value for K forces the network to make a greater distinction between the initial patterns, allowing easier discrimination between test patterns which are subsequently evaluated with a hard limiter thresholded at zero. Training the network on the smallest (T,C) pair using a value of $K = 1,000$ allowed correct identification of all larger test versions, without greatly increasing the training time.

For the third-order network simulation, input windows of 9×9 pixels, or 81 input nodes, were used. The 81-choose-3, or 85,320, weights were constrained to follow Equation (3.5) in order to achieve invariance to scale, translation, and in-plane rotation. The weights were initially set to zero and a learning rule was used of the form:

$$\Delta w_{ijkl} = (t_i - y_i)\, x_j\, x_k\, x_l. \tag{3.9}$$

The training set again consisted of two images, one for each object to be learned. After approximately 20 passes through the training set, the network learned to distinguish between distortions of the two objects with 100% accuracy. The T-C problem could be learned with full invariance to translation within the input

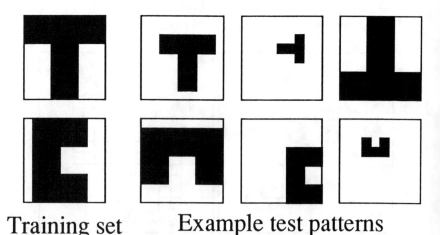

Training set   Example test patterns

Figure 3.11.   Training set and sample test patterns for distinguishing a "T" and a "C," invariant to translation, scale, and in-plane rotation.

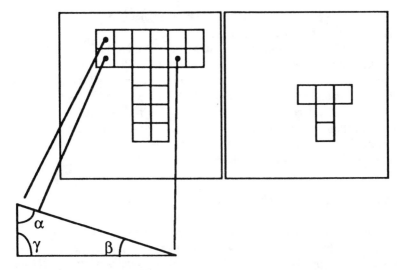

Figure 3.12.   A triangle with included angles, α, β, and γ which may be drawn between the pixels of a 6 × 6 pixel "T," but not between those of a 3 × 3 pixel "T."

field, to scale over a factor of three, and to 90° rotations, as shown in Figure 3.11. In principle, recognition is invariant for any rotation angle, given sufficient resolution to draw the image accurately at arbitrary angles.

As in the case of the second-order network, the small window size led to some residual scale variance. The triangles which can be formed between the pixels of the smallest T or C vary considerably from those which may be formed with larger versions of the letters. Figure 3.12 shows an example of a triangle with included angles α, β, and γ formed by three pixels of a 6 × 6 pixel T. These angles are not enclosed by any triangle which can be drawn on the smallest, 3 × 3 pixel, T. In this case, residual scale variance was eliminated by decreasing the resolution to which the angles α, β, and γ in Equation (3.5) and Figures 3.9 and 3.12 were calculated. Included angles were rounded off to the nearest 20°. With larger window sizes, both the image resolution and the resolution to which α, β, and γ are calculated can be increased.

In summary, simulations of fully connected networks demonstrate that a second-order neural network can be rapidly trained to distinguish between two patterns regardless of their size and translational position. One hundred percent recognition accuracy was achieved for several different training pattern pairs using a 16 × 16 pixel input field size. Additional invariance to in-plane rotation has been achieved using a 9 × 9 pixel input field. In both cases, training required only 10–20 presentations of just one example of each object to be learned. Comparing these results in terms of recognition accuracy and learning speed show HONNs to be vastly superior to multilayer, first-order networks trained by back propagation for this application.

This superiority results from the HONN architecture's ability to perform simple, transparent feature extraction. These simple features, slopes between input pixel pairs in the case of the second-order network, and included angles between input pixel triplets for the third-order network, are sufficient to allow the network to rapidly learn to classify patterns. The provision of a transparent feature extraction mechanism allows a HONN to efficiently perform the complete mapping from image to intermediate feature space to interpretation space required for distortion invariant pattern recognition.

3.2. Nonfully Connected HONNs

With invariant pattern recognition demonstrated, several additional characterization studies, including learning time vs. number of stored images and performance with noisy inputs, are called for. Preliminary studies of storage capacity using a third-order network with a 9×9 pixel input window showed that the network could learn to distinguish at least 16 separate pattern classes. However, this window is much too small to draw the type of realistic targets which are of interest in actual pattern recognition applications. Statistically, significant studies of the network's behavior with noisy inputs also require the capability of larger input windows.

The large number of connections required for a third-order neural network limits the window size which can be fully connected. Building invariances into the network greatly reduced the number of independent weights which had to be learned, but some storage was still used to associate each triplet of inputs to a set of included angles. In an $N \times N$ pixel input field, three pixels can be combined in N^2-choose-3 ways. Thus, for an 18×18 pixel input field, the number of triangles formed is 324-choose-3 or 5.6 million. Increasing the resolution to 128 $\times$ 128 pixels would increase the number of connections to 128^2-choose-3 or 7.3 $\times 10^{11}$ interconnections, a number which is too great to store on most machines for the purpose of simulation, and which is certainly far too large to allow a parallel implementation in any hardware technology that will be available in the forseeable future. Therefore, determining a method for increasing the size of the input window is the most critical step in making HONNs practical.

To reduce the interconnection requirements of third-order networks, we have evaluated various methods of connecting only a subset of input pixel triplets to the output node. Instead of simply moving to a machine with more memory, we have chosen to limit the storage used by the network to that which is available on a Sun 3/60 with 30 MB of virtual memory, which allows approximately 6.3 million (integer) interconnections. A limitation on the number of connections to not much more than 10^6 is imposed by the electronic and optical technologies which can reasonably be expected to be available within the next several years. The number of connections which can be simulated on the Sun is already large enough to severely push the capabilities of the parallel implementation technologies which will have to be employed if neural models are to fulfill their promise in terms of processing speed.

Both deterministic and probabilistic methods have been explored for choosing the set of inputs to be connected to the output layer. Four such techniques will be described: local, sampled, probabilistic, and regional connectivity. Each technique was evaluated by using the T-C problem as discussed above, was required to achieve 100% recognition accuracy, and was limited to 6.3 million interconnections.

The assumption behind *local connectivity* is that local connections are adequate for distinguishing between objects and that distant information will be represented by some combination of local information. Thus, a connection for a triplet of pixels is formed only if all three pixels are within some bounded number of pixels away from each other, as shown in Figure 3.13. Figure 3.14 shows the probability of connecting a given pixel triplet to the output node as a function of the greatest distance between any two of the three pixels. For local connectivity, the probability of connection is 1 for triplets of input pixels which are within a bounded distance away from each other and 0 for more distant pixels. In our simulations, the network was able to distinguish between a "T" and a "C" with 100% invariance to translation and in-plane rotation only if pixels that

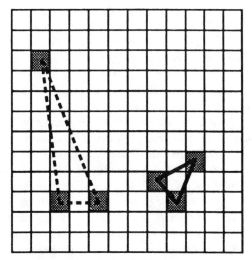

Figure 3.13.   Local connectivity. Only triplets of pixels that are close together are connected to the output (solid lines). Triangles formed using distant pixels are ignored (dashed lines).

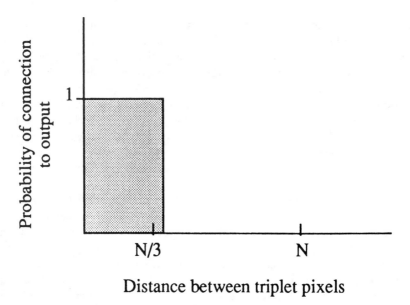

Distance between triplet pixels

Figure 3.14. Probability of connecting input pixel triplets to the output. With local connectivity, triplets are connected if all three pixels are close together (gray area). *N* is the input field width.

were at least $1/3$ of the width of the input field away from each other were included. Scale invariance was not achieved in this case, however. This method allows a field of 24×24 pixels to be represented with the available memory, increasing the number of input pixels by over 75%. The increase in image size which this technique enables is substantial, but it is not great enough to allow complicated input scenes, and the technique does not retain scale invariance.

In *sampled connectivity,* only a fraction of all possible input pixel triplets are connected to the output. Figure 3.15 shows the probability of connecting a given pixel triplet to the output node as a function of the greatest distance between any two of the three pixels. A predetermined subset of interconnections (for example, every *i*th one) was used, where the fraction used was not a function of the distance between the pixels, as shown in the figure. The expectation was that the images would be sufficiently sampled to allow discrimination. As Figure 3.16 demonstrates, however, this strategy fails to achieve 100% accuracy because distorted views of the same image may not be well represented by the same sampled connections. As an example, assuming that only the interconnections in Figure 3.16(a) are used for recognition, then in the images in Figure 3.16(b), a T is represented by triangle 1 whereas a C is represented by triangle 2. When the images are distorted as in Figure 3.16(c), triangle 1 is now associated with a C and triangle 2 with a T. Thus, accurate recognition is not achieved. In fact, 100%

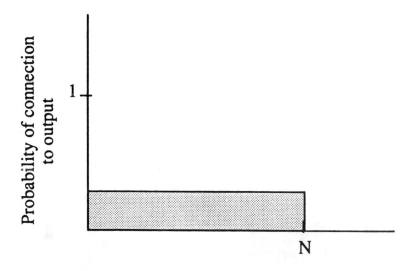

Distance between triplet pixels

Figure 3.15.   Sampled connectivity. Probability of connecting input pixel triplets to the output is constant as the fraction of triplets connected is independent of pixel separation.

accuracy can be guaranteed using this type of technique only if the fraction of interconnections used is equal to 1.

Probabilistic connectivity is a modified sampling method in which the images are sampled such that the probability of connection varies with distance. The function in Figure 3.17 shows that the probability of connecting triplets of pixels which are in very close proximity is higher than connecting pixels that are further away, but is never zero. This approach has the same drawback as sampled connectivity in that distorted views may not contain the same information as the training images, thereby not guaranteeing 100% recognition accuracy. Moreover, the same triplets must be used for each training pass as well as for testing. Thus, a record of which connections were formed during training must either be retained, requiring extra storage, or the same connections must be regenerated, requiring extra processing time.

The final approach investigated was *regional connectivity* in which triplets of pixels are connected to the output only if the distance between all the pixels falls within a set of preselected regions, as shown in Figure 3.18. Regions are chosen so as to sample the space sufficiently for accurate discrimination. Thus, some pixel triplets are connected to the output which are close to each other, some which are widely spaced, and some which are at intermediate separations. Because the connections are deterministic, it is guaranteed that the same informa-

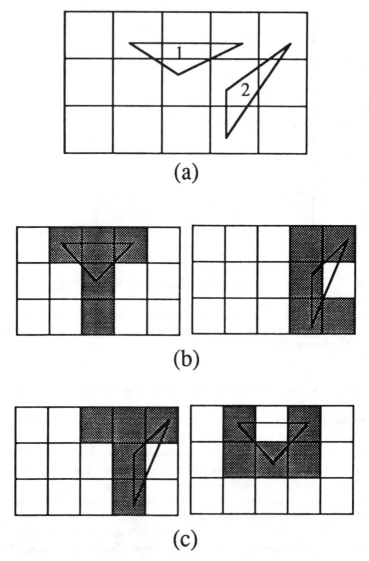

(a)

(b)

(c)

Figure 3.16. Failure of sampled connectivity. Only a predetermined, limited number of interconnections are formed (a). If the T and C shown in (b) are used for training, triangle 1 is associated with the T and triangle 2 is associated with the C. If the letters are now distorted as in (c), recognition fails because triangle 1 is now associated with a C and triangle 2 is associated with a T.

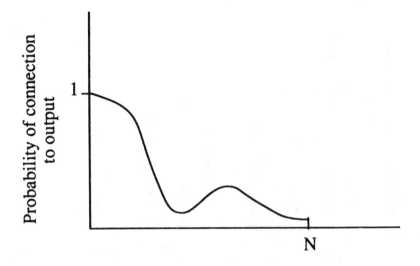

Distance between triplet pixels

Figure 3.17.   Probabilistic connectivity. Probability of connection is a function of the distance between triplets of pixels. One such function is shown here.

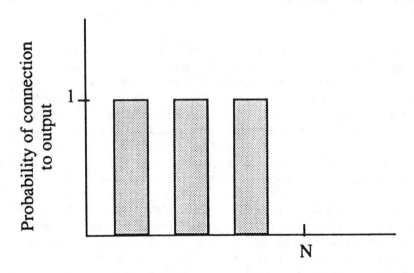

Distance between triplet pixels

Figure 3.18.   Regional connectivity. Only connections between pixels separated by distances shown in gray are used.

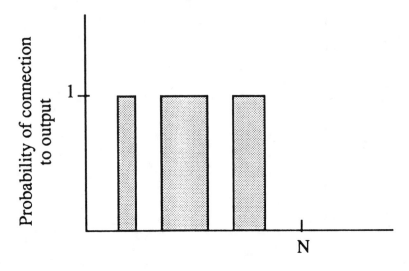

Distance between triplet pixels

Figure 3.19. Regions of connectivity distributed as shown have been found to be most effective for learning the T-C problem and for learning to distinguish between a Space Shuttle Orbiter and an F-18 aircraft. Pixels separated by intermediate distances (with respect to the width of the input field, *N*) are emphasized over pixels close together or separated by distances much greater than N/2.

tion will be sampled from a rotated or a translated test image as from the training image. Additionally, since pixel triplets of various separations are sampled, some amount of scale invariance is expected. A drawback with this method is that determining an optimal set of regions requires experimentation. Our experiments with the T-C problem and in learning to discriminate between a Space Shuttle Orbiter and an F-18 aircraft show that functions similar to the one in Figure 3.19 give the best results. That is, connections that are half the width of the input field away from each other are stressed over local or distant ones.

Using regional connectivity, we have been able to increase the input image resolution for the T-C problem to 64 × 64 pixels while still achieving in-plane rotation and translation invariant recognition with 100% accuracy. The 64 × 64 pixel network uses only 5.5 million interconnections whereas the fully interconnected network would require approximately 10^{10}. This represents a reduction of the required memory by a factor of nearly 2,000. The system has also learned to distinguish between more practical images such as a Space Shuttle Orbiter versus an F-18 aircraft (Figure 3.20) in a 64 × 64 pixel input field. The system learned to distinguish between the two aircraft in just 35 passes through the training set, which consisted of just one view of each aircraft.

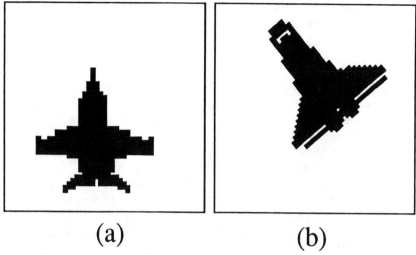

Figure 3.20. (a) A 64 × 64 pixel binary image of an F-18 aircraft. (b) A 64 × 64 pixel binary image of a Space Shuttle Orbiter.

To date, we have not fully tested the regional connectivity technique using scale distortions. However, we believe at least a limited amount of scale invariance should be attainable with this method.

4. FUTURE RESEARCH DIRECTIONS

There are several logical questions to be asked next about HONNs, including the dependence of learning time on the number of pattern classes and the performance of the model given images corrupted by noise. Answering such questions in a statistically significant way requires using images of sufficient size, with at least 32 × 32 or 64 × 64 pixels. Our studies of nonfully connected third-order networks show promise of providing for such large input images. It is hoped that continuing research will provide a robust technique for including scale invariance in nonglobally connected models, which have so far been demonstrated to provide translation and in-plane rotation invariance.

If all three in-plane distortions can be built into a nonfully connected third-order network, it could then be trained to treat out-of-plane versions of images as members of the same pattern class in order to extend the range of distortion invariance further. In the case that it is possible to achieve no or only very limited scale invariance without fully interconnecting a third-order network, it may prove more efficient to design a fully connected second-order network to be invariant to translation and in-plane rotation. The network could then be trained to treat scaled versions of images as members of the same pattern class.

Simultaneous translation and in-plane rotation invariance can be achieved with second-order weights constrained to follow the function:

$$w_{ijk} = w(i, r_j - r_k),\qquad(4.1)$$

where r_j and r_k are the distances of pixels j and k from a reference point in the image plane. Note that Equation (4.1) is simply an extension of Equation (3.2) to a two-dimensional input. As noted earlier, the distances between all pixel pairs are not sufficient features to distinguish between a "T" and a "C." However, any two patterns which can be distinguished using these features will still be distinguishable after translational and in-plane rotation distortions.

As their size grows only as N^2-choose-2, second-order networks with large N × N input fields can be formed with the same number of connections as third-order networks with much smaller input fields. Indeed, in some applications it might prove beneficial to train a second-order network to do an invariant recognition task which a third-order network could have performed without training, if the extra cost in training time is deemed worth the savings in the number of connections. This could be the case if a high-speed parallel hardware implementation is developed which has a limited number of connections. As in all image-processing research, the directions for further research into higher-order neural networks will be driven largely by the requirements of specific applications.

5. CONCLUSIONS

The results of simulations have shown that fully connected, higher-order neural networks, and specifically third-order networks, can be trained to distinguish between two patterns regardless of their position, in-plane angular orientation, or scale. The most important advantage of the HONN architecture is that distortion invariance can be built into the network before any training is performed and does not need to be learned. The HONN architecture performs simple, transparent feature extraction which is sufficient to allow the network to learn to classify noise-free patterns after training on only one view of each object to be learned and after only 10's of passes through this training set. This compares very well with the results of simulations of multilayer, first-order networks which require thousands of passes through training sets consisting of every distorted view that is to be learned.

REFERENCES

[1]   R.O. Duda and P.E. Hart, *Pattern Classification and Scene Analysis,* Wiley, New York, 1973.

[2]   C.H. Chen, *Statistical Pattern Recognition,* Hayden, Rochelle Park, NJ, 1973.

[3]   Q. Tian, Y. Fainman, Z.H. Gu, and S.H. Lee, "Comparison of Pattern Recognition Algorithms for Hybrid Processing," *Journal of the Optical Society of America A,* Vol. 5, 1988, pp. 1655–1669.

[4]   Y.H. Pao, *Adaptive Pattern Recognition and Neural Networks,* Addison-Wesley, Reading, MA, 1989.

[5]   F. Rosenblatt, *Principles of Neurodynamics,* Spartan, New York, 1962.

[6]   M.L. Minsky and S. Papert, *Perceptrons,* MIT Press, Cambridge, MA, 1969.

[7]   S.E. Troxel, S.K. Rogers, and M. Kabrisky, "The Use of Neural Networks in PSRI Target Recognition," *Proceedings of the IEEE International Conference on Neural Networks,* San Diego, California, July 24–27, Vol. 1, 1988, pp. 593–600.

[8]   P. Werbos, Beyond Regression: New Tools for Prediction and Analysis in the Behavioral Sciences, P.h.D. Thesis, Harvard University, 1974 (unpublished).

[9]   D.E. Rumelhart, G.E. Hinton, and R.J. Williams, "Learning Internal Representations by Error Propagation," *Parallel Distributed Processing,* Vol. 1, Ch. 8, MIT Press, Cambridge, MA, 1986.

[10] D.E. Glover, "An Optical Fourier/Electronic Neurocomputer Automated Inspection System," *Proceedings of the IEEE International Conference on Neural Networks,* San Diego, California, July 24–27, Vol. 1, 1988, pp. 569–576.

[11] H. Wechsler and G.L. Zimmerman, "Invariant Object Recognition Using a Distributed Associative Memory," *Neural Information Processing Systems, American Institute of Physics Conference Proceedings,* 1988, pp. 830–839.

[12] H. Szu, "Three Layers of Vector Outer Product Neural Networks for Optical Pattern Recognition," *Optical and Hybrid Computing,* SPIE Vol. 634, 1986, pp. 312–330.

[13] P.M. Grant and J.P. Sage, "A Comparison of Neural Network and Matched Filter Processing for Detecting Lines in Images," *Neural Networks for Computing, American Institute of Physics Conference Proceedings,* 1986, pp. 194–199.

[14] R.P. Gorman and T.J. Sejnowski, "Analysis of Hidden Units in a Layered Network Trained to Classify Sonar Targets," *Neural Networks,* Vol. 1, 1988, pp. 75–89.

[15] D.E. Rumelhart, G.E. Hinton, and R.J. Williams, "Learning Internal Representations by Error Propagation," *Parallel Distributed Processing,* Vol. 1, Ch. 8, MIT Press, Cambridge MA, 1986, pp. 348–352.

[16] B. Widrow and R. Winter, "Neural Nets for Adaptive Filtering and Adaptive Pattern Recognition," *IEEE Computer Magazine,* Vol. 21, March, 1988, pp. 25–39.

[17] C.L. Giles and T. Maxwell, "Learning, invariance, and generalization in high-order neural networks," *Applied Optics,* Vol. 26, 1987, pp. 4972–4978.

[18] C.L. Giles, R.D. Griffin, and T. Maxwell, "Encoding geometric invariances in higher-order neural networks," *Neural Information Processing Systems, American Institute of Physics Conference Proceedings,* 1988, pp. 301–309.

[19] M.B. Reid, L. Spirkovska, and E. Ochoa, "Rapid Training of Higher-Order Neural Networks for Invariant Pattern Recognition," *Proceedings of the Joint IEEE/INNS International Conference on Neural Networks,* Washington, D.C., June 18–22, Vol. 1, 1989, pp. 689–692.

[20] M.B. Reid, L. Spirkovska, and E. Ochoa, "Simultaneous position, scale, and rotation invariant pattern classification using third-order neural networks," *International Journal of Neural Networks,* Vol. 1, 1989, pp. 154–159.

4
Optical Implementation of Closest Vector Selection in Neural Networks*

Stanley C. Ahalt
Stuart A. Collins, Jr.
Ashok K. Krishnamurthy
Daniel F. Stewart
The Ohio State University
Department of Electrical Engineering
Dreese Laboratory

1. INTRODUCTION

Selecting a closest or "distinguished" vector from a set of vectors is a fundamental operation in many applications, including self-organizing neural networks. The Closest Vector Selection (CVS) operation determines the *exemplar* vector (drawn from a finite set of vectors) which is closest to an arbitrary input vector presented to the system. Determining the exemplar vector involves comparing the input vector to all possible exemplars; consequently the CVS operation can be computationally expensive. We describe in this chapter a number of applications for CVS, and describe an optical implementation of a CVS system. The optical system allows all comparisons to be done in parallel, and yields significantly lower CVS operation time.

CVS systems are useful in a number of applications such as self-organizing neural networks for adaptive Vector Quantization (VQ). We also describe an optical implementation of a CVS system. The novel optical CVS system will, within the space-bandwidth limits of the optical system, allow the closest vector selection operation to be completed in constant time, independent of the vector dimension or size of the exemplar vector set. This will yield significant, immediate benefits in a number of signal processing and pattern recognition applica-

* This work was supported in part by a Cray Research Award to S.C. Ahalt. Author names have been listed alphabetically.

tions. For example, if the set of exemplar vectors represents a set of image models, then CVS can be viewed as a pattern matching algorithm. Similarly, when the CVS process is combined with a suitable learning algorithm that adapts the exemplars in order to minimize distortion, the resulting system can be viewed as an adaptive Vector Quantizer. Other possible applications include Radar Target Identification (RTI) [1], associative memories, auto-associative memories, speech and image analysis [2], and vector sorting.

It is useful to use VQ as an example to illustrate the substantial computational requirements of the CVS problem. Consider the problem of encoding a 512 × 512 video image, each pixel of 8-bits resolution. If we use 6 × 6 (length 36) blocks of the image for coding, and assume a 0.5-bits/pixel resolution after VQ, the size of the codebook is 2^{18}. So for a transmission rate of one image per second, we need to perform approximately 7282 full searches through the size 262144 codebook. Assuming each closeness measure computation requires 36 multiples for this case leads to a required computation rate of over 68,000 million multiples per second! This is clearly well over the capabilities of most present day serial processors. This has led researchers to consider special purpose architectures for codebook search. For example, [3] describes a bit-serial systolic architecture for VQ. Using their linear array architecture, the image coding example would need 37 processors, each 36-bits wide. However, coding each vector will require 262144 clock cycles. At a clock rate of 10 MHz, each vector is thus coded in 26 ms. Their two-dimensional array can code one vector in each cycle, but would require 36 × 262144 processors!

Consider now an optical CVS system. Presently it should be possible to obtain liquid crystal light valves with a 600 × 600 spatial resolution and a latency of 1 ms. Furthermore, it is clear that latencies on the order of 10 μs are possible in the future. A 1 ms Liquid Crystal Light Valve (LCLV) can easily perform the 262,144 × 36 matrix by 36 element vector multiply required for the image coding example in the last paragraph. The proposed system is mainly limited by the latency of the LCLVs. To code a vector, it requires no more than five passes through LCLVs. Thus, the optical system can code a vector with no more than a 5 ms delay, searching through the entire codebook in parallel, compared with the 26 ms required for the electronic solution discussed above. With faster LCLVs (i.e., with a 1 μs latency), a complete codebook search needs only 5 μs. Further, the optical system is inherently pipelined, and a stream of vectors can be coded at one every LCLV latency.

One possible implementation of the CVS system is described later in the chapter. The optical implementation discussed uses an optical Spatial Light Modulator (SLM), such as a liquid crystal light valve, in operations that have been demonstrated in the literature, and intensity as well as spatial position coding. The operations required to realize the CVS system include analog operations such as matrix-vector multiplication as well as binary operations such as flip-flops and logic gates. These operations are combined to form a unit which will multiply a given input vector by a matrix to form a product vector. Then, the magnitude and position of the largest element of the product vector is determined. The logical extension of this work is to couple the vector selection process with a training algorithm to arrive at an adaptive signal processing system.

2. BACKGROUND

The central thesis of this chapter is that the problem of selecting the "closest" vector from a finite set of vectors is important in several areas and that the techniques of optical computing can efficiently and effectively solve this problem. In this section, we provide illustrative examples from the areas of Communications, Pattern Classification, and Neural Networks to illustrate the importance of the CVS problem. We also show how various measures of closeness can be formulated as a matrix-vector multiplication followed by a maximum element selection.

2.1. Illustrative Examples

2.1.1. Vector Quantization

Vector Quantization (VQ) is a technique for encoding a vector or block of data for transmission [4]. Basically, VQ is a pattern matching procedure; the vector or block of N numbers to be encoded is viewed as a pattern, and the encoding process determines the N-dimensional vector from a finite set of M vectors that best matches the input vector. The finite set of M vectors is called a codebook, and is usually determined off-line. Further, both the transmitter and receiver are assumed to have a copy of this codebook. The input vector is then encoded as the *index* of the closest matching vector, and it is this index that is transmitted to the receiver. The usual procedure for selecting the best matching codeword vector is to compute the distance between the input vector to be encoded and each of the codewords; the codeword with the smallest distance is the one selected. Clearly, the VQ encoding process is equivalent to the CVS problem. The Frequency Sensitive Competitive Learning (FSCL) neural network training algorithm described below is one example of a VQ codebook design technique.

In most applications, the codebook size, $M = 2^K$, is a power of 2. Thus, it takes K bits to encode the index of the "closest" codebook vector. Consequently, the number of bits needed to encode each component of the input vector is $R = K/N$. The performance of the VQ encoder improves as the codebook size $M = 2^{RN}$ gets larger; however, this also increases the computation required for encoding, and is usually the bottleneck preventing real-time implementations [3].

2.1.2. Pattern Classification

Consider a multiclass pattern classification problem with L classes. In many conventional classifiers (such as the Nearest-Neighbor algorithm), and neural network classifiers (such as the Kohonen LVQ [5]), each class is characterized by a number of exemplar patterns, with each pattern being an N-dimensional vector. Given an unknown input pattern, the classification proceeds as follows. The distance between the input vector and each of the stored exemplar patterns is computed, and the unknown pattern is classified as belonging to the same class as the closest exemplar. Clearly, this is yet another example of the CVS problem.

2.1.3. Neural Network Training—Competitive Learning Networks

The Competitive Learning (CL) [6,7] neural network can be described as follows. The network consists of a number of neural units, and a weight vector is associated with each neural unit. During the training process, a set of training vectors is presented to the network in sequence, and the weight vectors associated with the neural units are adjusted to reflect the statistics of the input data. The adjustment process involves finding the neural unit whose weight vector is closest to the input training vector (determining the "winning" neural unit), and then adjusting the weight vector of the winning neural unit towards the input vector. The CVS problem is therefore an integral part of the CL training process. Examples of CL networks are Kohonen's Self-Organizing Feature Maps [8,9], the ART neural network architectures [10,11] , and the Frequency Sensitive Competitive Learning (FSCL) network [12].

The FSCL neural network was developed to overcome the problem of under-utilization of codewords in Competitive Learning (CL). Underutilization of code-words can occur when some subset of the initial codewords are repeatedly selected as the winning codewords during training and are updated. The remaining codewords are then "underutilized" because they are infrequently updated.

Many Competitive Learning neural networks algorithms have some mechanism to solve this problem. Kohonen Self-organizing Feature Maps [7] maintain topological neighborhoods, forcing all of the codewords in a neighborhood to be updated. The Counter-Propagation network [9,13] solves the problem by temporarily withdrawing overutilized codewords from the competition. This allows other codewords to be chosen and updated.

The method used in FSCL differs from both of the methods mentioned above. In the FSCL network, the distortion measure used to determine the winner unit is modified to include a count of how frequently each unit is the winner. Thus, the chance of winning for each unit is a function of both the distortion and the number of times it has been modified.

Specifically, let $d(x, w_i(t))$ be the distortion measure that we want to minimize during the quantization process, and let $n_i(t)$ be the number of times that neural unit i has been the winner during training. Then, the modified distortion measure is defined as:

$$d'(x, w_i(t), n_i(t)) = d(x, w_i(t)) \times f(n_i(t)), \qquad (2.1)$$

where x is the input pattern in $\mathbf{R}^n$, $w_i(t)$ is the reference vector at time t, and $f()$ is the "fairness" function which determines how the count influences the modified distortion. In most circumstances, the fairness function can be set to $f(n_i(t)) = n_i(t)$.

After the training process, the weight vectors of the neural units will be roughly adapted to the statistical density function of the input vectors. Then each weight vector is assigned a class based on the majority of training vectors that are mapped to that weight vector.

2.2. Closeness Measures as Matrix-Vector Multiplication

The CVS problem involves finding the closest exemplar vector from a finite set of vectors. The notion of closeness between vectors involves the definition of a suitable distortion measure between vectors—the smaller the distortion measures between two vectors, the closer they are. In this section, we show that for many commonly used distortion measures, the closest vector selection can be formulated as a vector-matrix multiplication followed by a minimum or maximum element selection. Consequently, the proposed optical CVS system will be flexible enough for use in a variety of applications. Our development closely follows the development in [3].

In the following, let $W = \{w_i, i = 1, \ldots , M\}$ to be a set of M vectors, and let x be the input vector. Each of these vectors is assumed to be a column vector of dimension N. Also let $W = [w_1|w_2| \ldots |w_M]$ be the $N \times M$ matrix composed of the set of vectors.

2.2.1. Dot product

The first closeness measure that we discuss is the dot product between two vectors. If all vectors are normalized to unit length, then the dot product between x and w_i is:

$$x^T w_i = |x||w_i|\cos(\theta) = \cos(\theta), \qquad (2.2)$$

where θ is the angle between the two vectors. Thus, to find the w_i closest to x we need to compute:

$$x^T w_j, j = 1, \ldots , M \qquad (2.3)$$

and pick the maximum. This is equivalent to computing the vector:

$$y = x^T W, \tag{2.4}$$

and picking the maximum element of this row vector (i.e,, a matrix-vector multiplication followed by a maximum selection).

2.2.2. Euclidean distance

The squared Euclidean distance between the vectors x and w_i can be written as:

$$\|x - w_i\|^2 = \|x\|^2 - 2 \left(x^T w_i - \frac{1}{2} \|w_i\|^2 \right) \tag{2.5}$$

Since x is a fixed input vector, minimizing the Euclidean distance is equivalent to maximizing the second term in the equation above. By defining augmented $N + 1$-dimensional vectors:

$$\bar{x} = \begin{pmatrix} x \\ 1 \end{pmatrix}, \overline{w}_i = \begin{pmatrix} w_i \\ -\frac{1}{2}\|w_i\|^2 \end{pmatrix} \tag{2.6}$$

the selection of the closest vector can again be reduced to a matrix-vector multiplication followed by a maximum element selection.

3. OPTICAL COMPUTING

There are a number of optical computing techniques that support optical solutions to the CVS problem. For example, optical computing has spatial capabilities, as well as the combined capabilities of analog and digital techniques. Here, we are primarily interested in optical computing based on an optical spatial light modulator (SLM). Experience in the design of two-dimensional optical circuits [14,15] indicates that SLM device speed is expected to increase rapidly in the near future [16]. Accordingly, the two-dimensional approach will have the capability of extension to much higher throughput rates than integrated optic or acoustooptic approaches. Not only are commercial optical spatial light modulators operating in the millisecond range already available [16], but the state of the art is in the range of tens of microseconds. In addition, there is a reservoir of techniques including flip-flops, logic gates, and matrix multiplication to be used as "tools of the trade." As examples, a few of these "tools" will be described next. We conclude this section with a review of previous work concerning the optical implementation of neural networks.

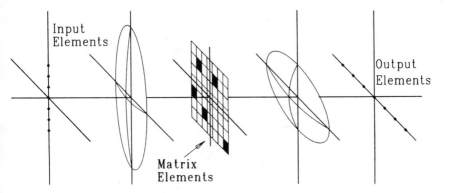

Figure 4.1. Optical matrix-vector multiplier.

3.1. Optical Matrix-Vector Multiplication

The approach to the analog matrix-vector multiplication [17] is shown schematically in Figure 4.1. In Figure 4.1, the light sources represent the input-vector elements. The intensities represent the magnitude of the elements. There is a transparency in the center with a rectangular array of spots, the transmission of which represents the numerical values of the matrix elements or weights. (In practice, the transparency is often replaced by an optical spatial light modulator.) On the right there is an output plane with a horizontal array of output positions, or detectors, if the information is not being passed on for further processing.

The elliptical, or anamorphic, lens between the input plane and transparency spreads the light out horizontally while imaging it vertically so the light from each source is imaged onto a row of matrix elements. The elliptical lens on the right images light horizontally and collects it from vertical columns so that all the light in a given vertical column goes into one output location.

The values of the vector elements and the matrix elements are assumed, for simplicity, to be either positive or zero. This restriction can be removed by using a pair of spots. The magnitudes of the vector elements are represented by the intensity of the input light sources; the values of the matrix elements or weights are represented by the transmission of the transparency at a given array location. The matrix elements are scaled in magnitude to have a maximum value of unity. The precision of this representation is limited by the precision to which light intensity can be easily set and measured, and is around one percent.

3.2. Logic Gates

Logic gates can be easily formed using polarization-logic and an optical spatial light modulator [18] such as a liquid crystal light valve which operates on the

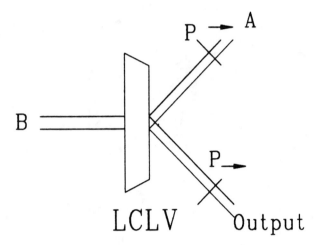

Figure 4.2.   Optical logic gate.

polarization of the read light. We give one example of an $A \cdot \overline{B}$ gate formed using polarization shown in Figure 4.2.

There we see a liquid crystal light valve with a write beam, B, incident on the input side a read beam; A, incident on the output side. The light valve is configured to leave the polarization unchanged if there is a dark input and to rotate the polarization by ninety degrees if there is a bright input. There is also a polarizer in the read beam after it strikes the light valve. It can be seen that there will be an output if and only if the light is bright at input A and dark at B (the requirement for $A \cdot \overline{B}$).

With other configurations of the polarizers [18] all sixteen logic gates can be formed.

3.3. Optical Flip-Flops

While optical flip-flops are commercially available [19], they are limited in array size. We chose to use flip-flops formed from a liquid crystal light valve with the output imaged back onto itself [20]. This is shown in Figure 4.3 where the liquid crystal light valve is located in the center of the figure.

A beam of light reflects off the output side (not seen) and is directed by way of four mirrors and two lenses onto the input side. The two lenses each have unity magnification so that each image element is imaged back onto itself. The liquid crystal light valve is configured so that a bright input produces a bright output and a dark input produces a dark output. Two states are possible. In the first, a bright output produces a bright input which then sustains itself. In the second stable state a dark output sustains a dark input. This operation holds indepen-

Input

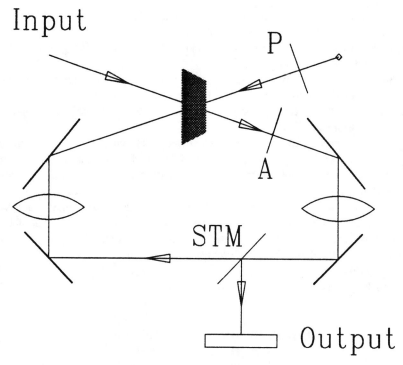

Figure 4.3.   Optical flip-flop.

dently for each image element on the light valve. The state of the flip-flop is changed by blocking the light in a bright element or illuminating the input of a dark element. The flip-flop can be used as an optical threshold. There is a given bright level required to switch the dark state to bright. This provides the threshold action.

3.4. Previous Optical Neural Network Implementations

There has been considerable activity in the optics literature dealing with neural nets [21]. Optical implementations of the Hopfield [22] model have received wide attention since the early papers of Psaltis and Farhat appeared [23,24]. In addition, there have been several modifications of the model, as described in [25,26,27]. For example, there have been discrete, rather than continuous, weights [28], problems have been put in the context of two-dimensional patterns [29], and preprocessing and postprocessing have been used to increase efficiency and effectiveness of the optical processing [30]. Others [27] have dealt with variations on the Hopfield model in a purely academic manner with no consideration of optical implementation.

Several papers [31,32] have dealt with optical neural nets involving learning capabilities. These approaches have the advantage of maintaining the higher information content associated with optical systems, and we feel this approach will be optimal in the long run.

Some papers in the optics literature have also considered neural nets in general and in association with masking fields [33], with associative memories [25], and pattern recognition and image processing [34]. However, no reference to optical implementations is given.

Only one paper [26] considers optical networks capable of closest vector selection, the problem that is being considered in this chapter. However, the scheme in [26] is an optoelectronic implementation of a winner-take-all neural network using optics to perform the matrix-vector multiply and electronic circuitry to do the winner-take-all selection. While the hybrid approach may at present be faster, it has the disadvantage of not being easily extendable to large numbers of vectors. The information content of fast linear arrays and detectors does not approach that available in optical devices. We feel that the CVS neural net is extremely useful, and that there is at least one all-optical implementation which will make it very competitive with other approaches.

4. SUGGESTED OPTICAL IMPLEMENTATION
OF THE CVS SYSTEM

Here we describe an optical implementation of the CVS algorithm. As we discussed in Section 2, CVS can be viewed as a matrix-vector multiplication followed by a maximum/minimum selection. Consider a set of N inputs nodes connected via weighted connections to a set of M nodes which sum the inputs. Mathematically, this is represented by a matrix-vector multiplication of a vector with n elements by an $M \times N$ matrix. From the resulting set of elements in the vector product, we identify the position of the brightest element. When we consider the rows of the matrix as individual vectors, we observe that this is the heart of the CVS process.

Of the two parts to the CVS algorithm, the matrix-vector multiplication and the selection of the maximum element, the matrix-vector multiplication was described earlier in Section 3. The optical scheme for selecting the maximum element will be described here in detail. The basic operations will be described schematically and sample optical layouts will be described.

The most interesting part is the optical procedure for selecting the brightest spot (closest match). We use optical intensity as a measure of magnitude, therefore, given a set of light spots, we want to select the brightest spot and document its position. This will be accomplished by means of a gray wedge, a spatial threshold detector, and optical logical image manipulations. Only the basic operations will be shown. They are all operations which have been implemented optically.

4.1. Optical CVS Operations

The first step is shown in Figure 4.4. On the left-hand side of the figure light from a string of horizontal sources serves as the input, corresponding to output of the matrix-vector multiplication. Our objective is to identify the brightest source. The light is passed through an elliptical lens to spread it out vertically and image it horizontally. The vertical streaks thus formed are applied to a gray wedge, a device whose transmission increases monotonically with distance from bottom to top. The output of the gray wedge is a set of vertical streaks whose intensity decreases with height. Next to the gray wedge is a point-by-point spatial thresholding device. Past the threshold the more intense streaks give longer lines, the longest line corresponding to the brightest input.

The position of the brightest spot is determined by a few simple optical image logical operations. Only the logic operations indicating the information flow are shown here, and not the optical configurations for implementing the operations, which will be described later.

The logical image operations are shown pictorially in Figure 4.5. First, the output of the threshold stage is shown in Figure 4.5(a). To isolate the longest line we optically smear the pattern horizontally (see Figure 4.5(b)) again using an

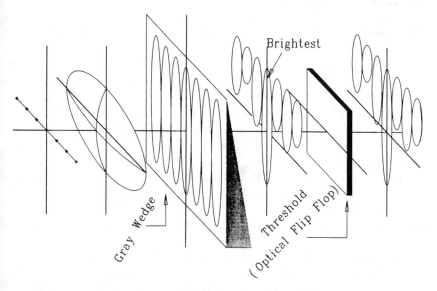

Figure 4.4.   Optical maximum selector.

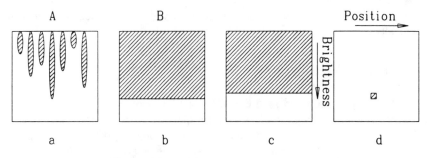

Figure 4.5.   Optical logic operations.

elliptical lens, shift the smeared pattern one image element vertically (see Figure 4.5(c)), and combine it with itself using an $A \cdot \overline{B}$ operation. Figure 4.5(d) shows the result of performing the $A \cdot \overline{B}$ operation with the original streak pattern.

A single spot then remains at the location of the tip of the longest streak. The horizontal position nicely indexes the location of the brightest spot and the vertical position gives the magnitude of the intensity. With the information contained in the spot we have the desired results. This information is available for the next step of the system—the training procedures associated with the adaptive signal or information processing tasks.

4.2. Optical CVS Implementation

The complete optical configuration for the closest vector selection procedure is presented in two parts, first the gray wedge and optical threshold followed by the optical logic. Figure 4.6 shows the start of the configuration for the gray wedge and threshold. On the left is a row of horizontal lights representing the output of the matrix-vector multiplier, the brightest of which is to be selected. The light from those spots passes through an elliptical lens where it is imaged in the horizontal plane and collimated in the vertical plane. The resulting vertical stripes are then passed through the gray wedge creating the stripes of decreasing intensity.

From the gray wedge the light then goes to an optical flip-flop configured to act as a point-by-point threshold. One can easily see the loop of the fed-back light valve. The image from the gray wedge goes to the input of the light valve and the output comes through a semitransparent mirror at the lower right in the feedback loop.

The remainder of the maximum selection procedure is shown in Figure 4.7. The input from the threshold device is shown at the top center. The light proceeds to a semitransparent mirror the reflected beam of which is imaged onto the spatial light modulator shown at the right center. This forms the A portion of the $A \cdot \overline{B}$

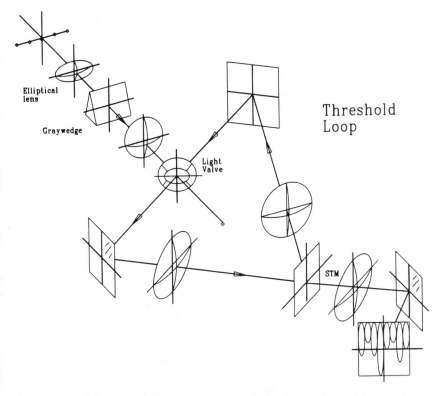

Figure 4.6.   Optical gray wedge and threshold configuration.

operation. The part of the input light which passes through the semitransparent mirror is spread horizontally by the elliptical lens shown, raised vertically one image element by the mirrors, reflected off the spatial light modulator and imaged onto the output plane at the lower right. For convenience, the semi-transparent mirror may be a polarizing beamsplitter. As shown there is only one spot left, namely that corresponding to the brightest element in the vector output of the matrix multiplier.

With the description of the $A \cdot \bar{B}$ gates; we have completed the steps showing the operation of the optical configuration of the closest vector selection apparatus. It uses a gray wedge, an optical threshold detector and an optical image $A \cdot \bar{B}$ gate array. The optical configuration for performing the desired operations has been given, thus indicating the solvability of this problem.

It might be noted that this is only one suggested approach and that this approach can undoubtedly be simplified. Ongoing efforts are directed toward reviewing this and other approaches to determine an optimum and streamlined apparatus for accomplishing closest vector selection.

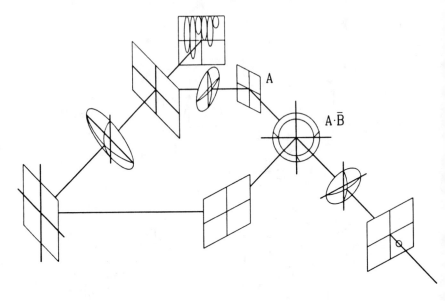

Figure 4.7.   Optical image logic configuration.

5. CONCLUSIONS

We have shown that the closest vector selection operation is important in many applications, including neural networks. We described a number of the applications to which CVS systems are easily adapted, in particular Vector Quantization and Competitive Learning (Self-Organizing) neural networks. We have described an optical solution to the CVS operation which offers a distinct advantage in that the comparisons can be carried out in parallel—yielding significantly improved response times. This novel optical CVS system will, within the space-bandwidth limits of the optical system, allow the closest vector selection process to be completed in constant time, independent of the vector dimension or size of the vector set. The results will yield immediate, significant benefits in a number of neural network, signal processing, and pattern recognition applications.

REFERENCES

[1]   S.C. Ahalt, T. Jung, and A.K. Krishnamurthy, "Radar Target Identification Using the Learning Vector Quantization Neural Network," *International Joint Conference on Neural Networks,* Washington, D.C., June 18–22, 1989.

[2]   A.K. Krishnamurthy, S.C. Ahalt, D. Melton, and P. Chen, "Neural Networks for Vector Quantization of Speech and Images," *IEEE Journal on Selected Areas in Communications,* Vol. 8, No. 8, 1990.

[3]   G. Davidson, P. Capello, and A. Gersho, "Systolic Architechtures for Vector Quantization," *IEEE Transactions on Acoustics, Speech, and Signal Processing,* Vol. 36, pp. 1651–1664, Oct. 1988.

[4]   J. Makhoul, S. Roucos, and H. Gish, "Vector Quantization in Speech Coding," *Proceedings of the IEEE,* Vol. 73, Nov. 1985, pp. 1551–1588.

[5]   T. Kohonen, "Learning Vector Quantization," *Abstracts of the First Annual INNS Meeting,* Boston, MA, Sept. 6–10, 1988, p. 303.

[6]   D.E. Rumelhart, J.L. McClelland et al., *Parallel Distributed Processing,* MIT Press, Cambridge, Massachusetts, 1986.

[7]   T. Kohonen, *Self-Organization and Associative Memory, 2nd Ed.,* Springer-Verlag, Berlin, 1988.

[8]   T. Kohonen, *Self-Organization and Associative Memory,* Springer-Verlag, Berlin, 1984.

[9]   R. Hecht-Nielsen, "Applications of Counterpropagation Networks," *Neural Networks,* Vol. 1, No. 2, 1988, pp. 131–141.

[10] M.A. Cohen and S. Grossberg, "Absolute Stability of Global Pattern Formation and Parallel Memory Storage by Competitive Neural Networks," *IEEE Transactions on Systems, Man, and Cybernetics,* Vol. SMC-13, Sept/Oct 1983, pp. 815–826.

[11] S. Grossberg, "Adaptive Pattern Classification and Universal Recording: I. Parallel Development and Coding of Neural Feature Detectors," *Biological Cybernetics,* Vol. 23, 1976, pp. 121–134.

[12] S.C. Ahalt, A.K. Krishnamurthy, P. Chen, and D.E. Melton, "Competitive Learning Algorithms for Vector Quantization," *Neural Networks,* Vol. 3, 1990, pp. 277–290.

[13] D. DeSieno, "Adding A Conscience to Competitive Learning," *Proceedings of the IEEE International Conference on Neural Networks,* Vol. I, July 1988, pp. 117–124.

[14] S.F. Habiby and S.A. Collins, Jr., "Implementation of a Fast Digital Optical Matrix-Vector Multiplier Using a Holographic Look-up Table and Residue Arithmetic," *Applied Optics,* Vol. 26, No. 21, 1987, pp. 4639–4652.

[15] M.T. Fatehi, K.C. Wasmundt, and S.A. Collins, Jr., "Optical Flip-Flops and Sequential Logic Circuits Using a Liquid Crystal Light Valve," *Applied Optics,* Vol. 23, No. 13, 1984, pp. 2163–2171.

[16] J.R. Brockelhurst, *Sales Literature.* STC Technology LTD, London Road, Harlow, Essex CM17 9NA, England, 1988.

[17] J.W. Goodman, A.R. Dias, and L. Woody, "Fully Parallel, High-Speed Incoherent Optical Method for Performing Discrete Fourier Transforms," *Optical Letters,* Vol. 2, No. 1, 1978, pp. 1–3.

[18] M.T. Fatehi, K.C. Wasmundt, and S.A. Collins, Jr., "Optical Logic Gates Using Liquid Crystal Light Valve: Implementation and Application Example," *Applied Optics,* Vol. 20, No. 13, 1981, pp. 2250–2256.

[19] *Sales Literature.* Edinburgh Instruments, Ltd., Riccarton, Currie, Edinburgh EH 14 4AP Scotland, 1988.

[20] U. Sengupta, U. Gerlach, and S.A. Collins, "Bistable Optical Spatial Device Using Direct Optical Feedback," *Optics Letters,* Vol. 3, May 1978, p. 199.

[21] G.A. Carpenter and S. Grossberg, eds., *Issue on Neural Nets and Artificial Intelligence.* Special Issue of Applied Optics, Vol. 26, Dec. 1, 1987.

[22] J.J. Hopfield, "Neural Networks and Physical Systems with Emergent Collective Computational Abilities," *Proceedings of the National Academy of Sciences,* Vol. 79, Apr. 1982, pp. 2554–2558.

[23] N.H. Farhat, D. Psaltis, A. Prata, and E. Paek, "Optical Implementation of the Hopfield Model," *Applied Optics,* Vol. 24, May 1985, pp. 1469–1475.

[24] D. Psaltis and N. Farhat, "Optical Information Processing Based on an Associate-Memory Model of Neural Nets with Thresholding and Feedback," *Optical Letters,* Vol. 10, Feb. 1985, pp. 98–100.

[25] R. Marks, "Class of Continuous Level Associative Memory Neural Nets," *Applied Optics,* Vol. 26, No. 10, 1987, pp. 2005–2010.

[26] G. Gindi, A. Gmitro, and K. Parthasarathy, "Winner-Take-All Networks and Associative Memory: Analysis and Optical Realization," *Private communication,* 1988.

[27] S.-H. Oh, T.-H. Yoon, and J. Kim, "Associative-Memory Model Based on Neural Networks: Modification of the Hopfield Model," *Optical Letters,* Vol. 13, No. 1, pp. 74–76, 1988.

[28] H. White and N. Aldridge, "Digital and Analogue Holographic Associative Memories," *Optical Engineering,* Vol. 27, No. 1, 1988, pp. 30–37.

[29] J. Jang., S. Shin, and S. Lee, "Optical Implementation of Quadatric Associative Memory with Outer-Product Storage," *Optical Letters,* Vol. 13, No. 8, 1988, pp. 693–695.

[30] T. Lu, S. Wu, X. Xu, and F. Yu., "Optical Implementation of Programmable Neural Networks." *Private communication,* 1988.

[31] A. Fisher, W. Lippincott, and J. Lee, "Optical Implementations of Associative Networks with Versatile Adaptive Learning Capabilities," *Applied Optics,* Vol. 26, No. 23, 1987, pp. 5039–5054.

[32] A.D. Fisher and J.N. Lee, "Optical Associative Processing Elements with Versatile Adaptive Learning Capabilities," *Topical Meeting on Optical Computing,* Vol. 11, 1987, pp. 137–140.

[33] M.A. Cohen and S. Grossberg, "Masking Fields: A Massively Parallel Neural Architecture for Learning, Recognizing, and Predicting Multiple Groupings of Patterened Data," *Applied Optics,* Vol. 26, May 1987, pp. 1866–1891.

[34] J. Jau, Y. Fainman, and S. Lee, "Comparison of artificial neural networks with pattern recognition and image processing," *Applied Optics,* Vol. 28, No. 2, 1989, pp. 302–305.

5
Biological Basis for Compact Artificial Neural Networks

Phyllis L. Rostykus[1]
Arun K. Somani
Department of Electrical Engineering
University of Washington
Seattle

1. INTRODUCTION

The artificial neural network field has been developed over many years, with many different models, and many different starting points. One of the indications of this diversity is in the number of different names that the networks have been given. Different researchers have called them collective models, neuromorphic systems, parallel distributed processing models, connectionist models, neural nets, neural networks, and artificial neural network systems. The field combines research in psychology, biology, neurophysiology, electrical engineering, physics, and mathematics.

The basis of the entire technology is the use of mathematical or electrical models of natural neural behavior. Various models have evolved from different disciplines, some closer and some further from what is known about neural-physiology. There is still no clear indication as to which model performs best. Some groups believe that close adherence to known neural structure will bring the capabilities of human intelligence, as "millions of years of evolution can't all be wrong". The members of this group, for the most part, are proponents of analog implementations, and detailed analysis of neural *wetware* (neurons from living organisms). They shun sequential computer simulations as painfully slow, inaccurate, and ultimately incapable of producing the advanced capabilities of the human brain. Other groups, however, cite the adage "airplanes don't flap their wings," and believe that the most efficient and powerful systems, while inspired by neural wetware, need not follow all the biochemical and bioelectrical

---

[1] The main body of this work was used in this author's MSEE thesis efforts at the University of Washington under the guidance of Dr. Arun Somani.

nuances of neural communication and processing. Most research groups in the field are somewhere between the two extremes. Most agree that the primary measurement of the validity of any model is its performance and that adherence to biologically plausible architectures is preferable.

One of the areas of interest and study is in the problems of the physical implementation of artificial neural networks (ANNs). Silicon and discrete circuit implementation is limited by the large number of interconnections necessary to emulate neural interconnect. Complete interconnection is realistically impossible, even a tiny network of 32 processors requires almost 1,000 I/O connections. For a silicon implementation, the cost of these connections is the added capacitance and related slowing of the network response. There is the limitation of only two dimensions[2] for interconnect, and the huge number of connections needed for a fully interconnected network is extremely hard to implement. Most present day silicon implementations are of the resistor and amplifier grid type. Resistors are trimmed to a specific value to provide predetermined functions. This architecture eliminates the adaptive capabilities of artificial neural networks. For a more complex, adaptive, and flexible network, there is a much larger amount of overhead for each I/O access. In either case, the cost of the implementation is related to the number of interconnections.

Another interconnect problem, especially in the summation models, is the capacity to sum across all of the connections that feed into any single processing element. For each processing element to compute its state, it must sum across the products of all its input states and weights. The number of interconnects between processing elements determines the capacity needed. The capacity of the summation is proportional to the number of interconnects, which, in the fully connected case, is proportional to the square of the number of neurons. For large networks, this again, becomes a problem.

In order to find solutions to these problems, it is possible to go back to the basis that these models were based on, the biological system of neurons. Biological systems are constrained in a manner similar to physical implementations being attempted today. Some neurophysiological background on the basis of the models is needed both to understand the motivations behind the models and to understand why a model with a partial connection scheme is more plausible than a fully connected network. Getting a feel for the computational and memory retaining capabilities of the neural system will give a feel for what is necessary in a system which strives to emulate those capabilities.[3]

---

[2] It can also be considered three-dimensional when there are multiple layers of connective material. The third dimension would be which layer the routing is on. This third dimension, however, is presently limited to one layer of polysilicon, and, at most, three layers of metal conductive layers. It gives so many less degrees of freedom than two dimensions of width and length that it does not make a significant contribution toward the solution of the problem. This is especially true for networks with thousands of processors and millions of connections.

[3] A more complete and thorough presentation of this field is in *Principles of Neural Science* [1].

The next section will cover a number of the biological findings, experiments, and theories that are used in today's mathematical or artificial models. The third section covers the various methods biology uses to deal with the connection problem and how the physical implementation of a neuron is tightly tied to the processing it is expected to do. Then, we will focus on the Local Circuit Neuron (LCN), and how they comprise the majority of neural systems. Finally, there will be a section on how those biological systems are paralleled by various artificial systems, with the main emphasis on the Compact Artificial Neural networks.

2. BIOLOGICAL BASES FOR NEURAL NETWORK MODELS

Figure 5.1 shows a very general representation for a neural processor. It has inputs, weights which modify those inputs, a Processing Element (PE) that has a certain state depending on the summation of its inputs, and the output of the processor, which is usually equivalent to the state. There is a rough similarity to the general structure of a neuron. Neurons, unlike any of the other types of cells in the body, can communicate with each other quickly, efficiently, and across relatively great distances. A neuron has four morphological regions: the *cell body* or *soma,* the *dendrites* with *postsynaptic terminals,* the *axon,* and the *presynaptic terminals.* Figure 5.2 is a schematic representation of a neuron. As can be seen, the two figures are very similar.

Each section of the cell is important to the processing done by the neuron and

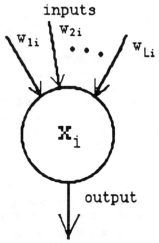

Figure 5.1.   A general processing element (PE) or neuron processor, or neural model with *L* inputs, with weights w_{1i} through w_{Li} associated with inputs 1 through *L,* and an output of the internal state.

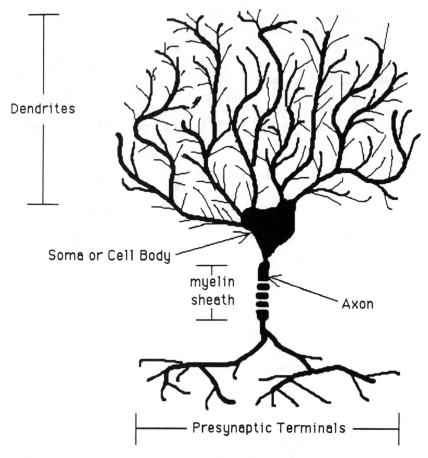

Dendrites

Soma or Cell Body

myelin
sheath

Axon

Presynaptic Terminals

Figure 5.2. A "typical" neuron with dendrites, cell body, axon, and presynaptic terminals. The axon is segmented to represent the fact that it can be meters long. This is not a proportional figure, only a conceptual figure. Dendrite ends are often in the tenths of nanometers, and the cell bodies can be in the hundreds of micrometers. Synapses are composed of a presynaptic terminal matched with a postsynaptic terminal, and therefore, not shown in this representation.

each section has a rough equivalent in the modeling world. Dendrites collect data from other neurons through postsynaptic sites, just as the inputs reach the PE through the weighting function. The cell body supplies energy for the ion pumps all along the wall of the cell. These pumps, in conjunction with selectively permeable pores in the cell membrane, maintain the resting potential of the cell at a negative voltage. In the cell body, near the junction with the axon, is the action potential triggering site, where currents from all the dendrites are integrated and measured through the cell voltage for threshold triggering. If the voltage gets higher than a certain threshold, the cell triggers an action potential, a spike of voltage that travels down the axon. This is similar to the PE processing with thresholded integration of nonlinear functions. The axon is a communication connection from the cell body to the presynaptic terminals, which are capable of triggering postsynaptic sites on other neurons' dendrites. This is like the output of the model neuron, which goes to the other PEs. Synapses (from the Greek *synapsis,* junction) are the mechanisms by which neurons communicate with each other and have various means of chemical variation and modification which affects their strengths, a clear analog to the variable weights of most models.

The basic definition of any artificial network includes: (a) a learning function for determining the weights, (b) a function involving the inputs and their weights that determines the state of the neuron or processor, and (c) a method that determines the connections between processors and neurons. A biological neuron has, as parallels: (a) the variation capabilities of the synaptic sites, (b) the current carrying function from the postsynaptic sites on the dendrites to the cell body and the current integration carried out in the cell body, and (c) the cell's physical makeup, which, as we will later see, is highly dependent on its function. What follows is a number of different artificial models with their relative advantages and disadvantages with some biological arguments as to why there were particular advantages or disadvantages to what was being done.

The earliest models were entirely linear. They had real number inputs fed into each neuron model, multiplied by real weights, and summed across all the inputs to determine the state of the neuron and the output of the system, a one-layered network without any feedback to itself. The systems were represented by a connection matrix of the connection weights. The ordering of the processors was arbitrary and most models had no strong ordering rules. The updating of states could be written as:

$$\mathbf{x}(t + 1) = \mathbf{W}\mathbf{x}(t) \tag{2.1}$$

where $\mathbf{x}(t)$ is the state of the processor at time t and $\mathbf{W}$ is the connection matrix. The weights were either predetermined by the desired function or they were formed by trial and error and the Hebbian Rule [2], if neuron A and neuron B are active at the same time, the connection between them should be increased. An input was applied and if the output was what was wanted, then the weights between responding PEs were increased, and if the output was not what was wanted, the weights were decreased.

There are a number of problems with completely linear models. The first is that repeated iterations through the same network can be modeled with some single iteration. With the above notation [3]:

$$\mathbf{x}(2) = \mathbf{T}\mathbf{x}(1)) = \mathbf{T}(\mathbf{T}\mathbf{x}(0)) = \mathbf{T}'\mathbf{x}(0) \tag{2.2}$$

Then, through an inductive proof, $x(t) = T''x(0)$ for some T''. This shows that performance will not improve through repeated iterations. A linear combination of linear functions creates another linear function. In addition, the linear nature of the network does not allow differentiation of inputs which cannot be separated by a linear function. The classic exception to linear network capabilities is the parity function. Two of the earliest networks were based on these linear models, the early Perceptron [4] and the Adaptive Linear Element (Adaline) first used by Widrow in the late 1950s and early 1960s [5]. The weaknesses of the linear models were shown in 1969 with an in-depth critique of the models in Rosenblatt's work [6].

There is no biological analog to the entirely linear network. Each input is from a synapse, which is limited by its physical size, its physical placement, and the local region's capability to support what it does to allow weights to be anything at all. The entire cell's capabilities put an upper limit on the action of all it's inputs. This means that the weights are locally limited and globally limited in their capability to affect any given cell. The voltages in the cell are not simply summed. The placement of a particular synapse severely affects how much of what it transmits that gets through to the cell body. The input from each dendrite is spread out in time, and the cell voltage is an integration over time as well as over all it's inputs. As the output travels along the axon and the presynaptic branches of the axon, it gets dispersed and affects the receiving cells in a non-linear manner. In essence, the whole neuron is entirely nonlinear.

On a higher, functional plane, the structure of the linear systems does not make sense, either. There is evidence for massive feedback within most of the neural system and that some particular input sections of the brain (most notably the visual system) have multilayering [1]. There is even a name for neurons which have their inputs and outputs contained within the functional system that they are a part of [7]. They are called Local Circuit Neurons (LCNs), and will be discussed in more detail later in this chapter. The biological neural systems, however, are so diverse, and so little is understood about how they work that there is little hard evidence on which to base a standard neurological functional subsystem.

The Hebbian rule of learning has a large number of deficiencies but is basically sound. There is no indication for how much weights should be changed, no provision for inhibition, and no mechanism for setting thresholds—all of which are very basic to how a neuron works. The basic mechanism behind the Hebbian rule, however, has validity, and it covers some important characteristics: (a) the determination for connection needs only information from the nodes it connects, (b) the correlation between activation states of the nodes and weight formation, and (c) the weights are formed over the entire activation pattern of its nodes. Most models implement some version of the Hebbian learning rule, with additions and enhancement for realistic and applicable learning methods. There also is evidence that biological cells use the same basic rule [8], but with time integration involved in both the detection of the strength of the correlation between the activation of the two cells and in determining the strength of the synaptic connection.

Models have progressed since the linear models, and most are coming close to the biological findings. Many models have added nonlinearities and found that the network performances improved. The Boltzman machines determine each weight from statistics concerning the states of the processors that were connected by the weight [3]. Grossberg's mathematical models [9] use differential equations for determination of both weights and states. Kohonen's competition network [10] has an input layer and a supervisory layer. All the neural processors in the supervisory layer inhibit all the other processors. When the network receives an input, the supervisory layer eventually shows only one active processor, the winner. Feedback through differently weighted connections and multiple layers is another method of introducing nonlinearities and is especially helpful in shaping a network to a particular function.

There are two basic types of input to output mapping, homogeneous and heterogeneous. Heterogeneous mapping is the mapping of an input to an output that is different than the input. Homogeneous mapping maps the input directly to the same output. Biological systems do both. When a homogeneous mapping network is presented with either a partial or erroneous version of an original input, it outputs the trained output. This is also a feature of Content Addressable Memories (CAMs), so many of the networks which have homogeneous mapping are also known as CAMs. The well-known Hopfield network is a CAM [11]. The Hopfield network is such a well-understood network that it is the basis of the Compact Neural Networks.

The science of neural networks is still in its infancy. The human brain contains approximately 10^{12} neurons, each with thousands of connections to other neurons. Scaling of present models up to even fractions of that size cannot be done. Learning algorithms do not scale linearly with the number of processors. Back Propagation, the algorithm which shows the most promise in terms of performance, takes $o(L^3)$ time to train the weights between L processors. Biological neurons do not seem to have a separated learning and functioning period, instead, they learn as they do. There is also the problem of implementing a system that is that large. Some researchers believe that the solution to this scaling problem is in the neuron models themselves, and that when the models approach that level of complexity they will also approach the capability of biological neurons.

3. PHYSICAL IMPLEMENTATION AS THE MEANS TO A COMPUTATIONAL END

Actual neurons come in many different shapes, with a very wide range in the number or length of any part. Some axons are more than a meter long, some do not have postsynaptic connections since they receive their inputs directly from external stimuli, some cells have thousands of dendrites, and some connect to tens of thousands of other neurons and others connect to only a few of the nearest neighbors. The connection pattern of any particular neuron usually has significance for the processing it must do, and the connections are an essential component of a neuron's capabilities. Here we will go into some of the physical complexities of some of the processes by which a neuron does its work of communication and information processing in order to see just how tightly functionality and physical implementation are intertwined.

Most communication through the connections is through fast voltage-changing action potentials, though some use a gradual change in voltage. Most of the latter communications are done between neighboring neurons and are through a special physical connection between cells called wither a *gap* or *bridged junction* synapse. Since there is a direct connection between the cells, ion currents are the main communication form, and cause gradual ramping of voltage in the postsynaptic cell. Gap junction synapses, however, are very rare and only found where there is no need for plasticity in the strength of the junction and where speed is of great importance. Since they are not plastic and are not normally in areas of the brain which need memory to complete processing, they are not normally of interest to artificial bidirectional connection between neurons.

The more common connection is the *unbridged junction* or *chemical* synapse, where there is no physical connection between cells. Instead, the presynaptic terminal releases a chemical substance called *transmitter* from vesicles. The transmitter travels the gap between the two terminals and the postsynaptic terminal uses the transmitter to initiate voltage changes in its dendrite. When a number of dendrites are affected, there is a voltage change within the entire cell body, which can trigger an action potential. It is a one-direction connection. This connection is also fairly slow, but it has the unique property of being able to remember former activity.

The basic structure of a synapse is a presynaptic terminal on the cell which is transmitting a reaction in close physical proximity to a postsynaptic terminal on the cell which is receiving the signal, with active sites on both terminals. The presynaptic terminal has vesicles, each of which contains a quantum of chemical transmitter, and the postsynaptic terminal has receptors for the transmitter. The number of transmitter types and varieties is not yet known. There are, however, two major synapse structure types which are most prevalent [12]. One (Type I) has a thicker postsynaptic membrane, a larger gap between the two terminals (about 30 nm), fairly large areas of transmitters and receivers on both terminals, and large, round vesicles on the presynaptic side. The other (Type II) has symmetric terminals, a smaller gap (about 20 nm), smaller transmitter and receiver areas, and smaller, flattened, or elliptical vesicles. Experimentally, Type I has been shown to be excitatory, and Type II is inhibitory. An excitatory synapse encourages signaling behavior in the postsynaptic neuron, whereas the inhibitory

Table 5.1.   A table of the concentrations of each of the major ions in a squid giant axon and the resulting Nernst potentials. Note how the additional organic anions within the cell balance the charges of the other ions.

Ion	Cytoplasm	Extracellular fluid	Nernst Potential
A+	400 mM	20 mM	−75 mV
Na+	50	440	+55
Cl−	52	560	−60
B+ (anions)	385	—	—

synapse has a suppressing effect. The excitatory synapses were the first to be discovered and were thought to be the most prevalent across the system. The inhibitory synapses, however, have usually been found to have more effect when they are used, and are most prevalent in areas needing regulatory control of spontaneously active cells. They determine the pattern of impulse activity.

The effect of the synapses is highly dependent on the same mechanisms which maintain the resting potential of the cell. An understanding of those mechanisms helps in understanding the effects of synaptic communication. The difference in potential across the cell membrane can be accounted for by the diffusion of certain ions. Tests on the squid giant axon show not only the concentrations of specific ions as in Table 5.1; but, also, at the normal resting potential, the cell walls were selectively permeable to only those certain ions. According to the Nernst Equation:

$$E_l = \frac{RT}{ZF} \ln \frac{[l^+]_o}{[l^+]_i} \tag{3.1}$$

where l is the ion involved, E_l is the potential when concentrations of l across a partition is at equilibrium, R is the as constant, T is the temperature in degrees Kelvin, Z is the valence of l^+, F is the Faraday constant, and $[l^+]_o$ and $[l^+]_i$ are the respective external and internal concentrations of l^+. When the equation is applied to the significant ions in a neuron, with the concentrations given in Table 5.1, they make a significant contribution to the resting potential. The ion concentrations of K^+ and Na^+ depend on ion pumps. The ion pumps an active ATP-dependent transport mechanism in the cell walls. ATP is the most common molecule used in biological systems for the transport of energy. The pumps drive K^+ into the cell and Na^+ out of the cell in a charge-balancing cycle.

Synapses affect the cell potential through the chemical control of pores in the cell membrane. The fastest and most prevalent mechanism for this effect is the increase of membrane conductances. After the binding of the transmitter to the receptors, inhibitory synapses cause a sudden increase in Cl^- and K^+ conductance. The equilibrium voltages for the two ions are both below the resting potential, -65mV and -75mV, respectively. Since the flow of ions drives the potential of the cell to be more negative, they hyperpolarize the cell and work against moving the potential of the cell towards the triggering voltage of -45mV. These synapses are inhibitory, as they inhibit the possibility of an action potential.

Excitatory synapses are not simply the reverse of the inhibitory synapses, they act quite differently. Measurement of ion currents across the membrane show that there is a simultaneous increase in both Na^+ and K^+ currents. The combination of the $+55$mV and -75mV potentials could still depolarize the membrane. They also found an increase in cation flow across the membrane, most prominently Ca^{++}. The channels involved proved to be larger and less discriminatory than the selective diffusion channels used to maintain resting potential. The effect of a single synapse is not particularly large. In measurements between input cells and muscle control neurons, each input cell only affected the membrane potential of the target cell by 200 microvolts. Both permeability increasing mechanisms go into effect quickly and last for one to five milliseconds. There are some cells which use a chemical transmitter which closes normal ion diffusion channels. The slow diffusion of K^+ out of the cell and Na^+ into the cell creates correspondingly excitatory and inhibitory responses. The diffusion reduction mechanisms are slower and can last up to 10 seconds.

The neuron body is the processor that uses its connections to integrate all the inputs that it receives from the dendrites, and the action potential is the output if the inputs are over a certain threshold. Action potentials are triggered when the cell is depolarized 15 to 20 millivolts away from the resting potential (about -45 mV to -50 mV if the resting potential is -60 mV). They are the result of an integration of all potential changes from the synaptic sites on the dendrites is both a temporal and spatial summation. The summation is nonlinear. Various factors such as position of the terminal on the dendrite, which set of branches the dendrite belongs to, and the proximity of the triggering area to the dendrites affect the triggering. When the cell fires, polarized Na^+ selective channels flip open and the ions are allowed to flow freely into the cell. The channels have large, polarized molecules that flip positions depending on the membrane potential. The positive Nernst potential of the Na^+ ions depolarizes the cell at a greater rate than when the Na^+ flow was restricted. Voltage sensitive K^+ channels copy the Na^+ channels with some small time delay, and strive to hyperpolarize the cell back towards the resting potential. The Na^+ channels are then inactivated after the cell is depolarized enough, since the membrane potential allows the channel molecules to flip closed. The K^+ flow then hyperpolarizes the cell to its Nernst potential and its channels become inactive. The resulting cell potential (see Figure 5.3) is a sharp depolarization spike of about 110mV. After the action potential, the cell cannot immediately generate another; the cell must have the time to balance its ion concentrations before it can fire again.

Influx of Ca^{++} ions during the action potential is a trigger for transmitter release [13]. One of the more interesting findings for model makers was that

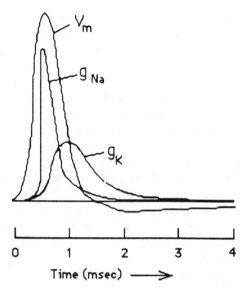

Figure 5.3. A graph of the action potential in the giant squid axon across the cell membrane, V_m, as opposed to the conductances of the Na$^+$ ion and the K$^+$ ion.

transmitter was released in quantized packets, since this implies that communication between neurons is quantized, and can, therefore, be modeled digitally with as much accuracy as in the original system. Ca^{++} concentration was found to modify the probability that any particular packet would be released. Ca^{++} concentrations affect synapse strength in three ways:

1. The concentrations of Ca^{++} control the membrane potential. Therefore, the more the cell is depolarized, the higher the influx of Ca^{++}, and the more transmitter is released. The Ca^{++} mechanism allows a cell that is more excited to have effect on the postsynaptic cell. If there is hyperpolarization, the opposite effect occurs and there is less transmitter and less effect.

2. The second source of transmitter change is through a train of action potentials. A transient saturation of the Ca^{++} buffering mechanisms occurs, and residual Ca^{++} combines with the free Ca^{++} input to enhance the following action potentials. This effect can last for several minutes to an hour.

3. Other cells may release a special transmitter that affects the Ca^{++} permeable pores, inhibiting Ca^{++} diffusion into the cell. It then inhibits the release of the transmitter. Effectively, there is a broadcast inhibition of near neurons, as the special transmitter lowers their capability to communicate. The last mechanism is rather slow, but it is also very long lasting.

All three mechanisms could be involved in the implementation of psychological medium- or short-term memory.

Synaptic increases in strength caused by usage has been experimentally shown in *Aplysia* [8]. The changes in synaptic strength are necessary for long-term memory, and they are needed in order to implement learned behavior. Geolet and Kandel used a known connection in the *Aplysia* reflex system, and tested the synaptic strength after exposing the entire synapse to 5-HT (5-Hydroxy-Tryptomine), a transmitter found in that particular synaptic connection. After a single exposure, the strength of the connection was enhanced and the enhancement lasted for several minutes. After five exposures, the synaptic strength increased twofold and lasted for a day. After long-term exposure there were three physical changes observed in the neuron: first, there was a doubling of presynaptic varicosities (about 1,300 to 2,600 in the sensory neuron); second, an increase in the incidents of active sits on these varicosities (from 40%–60%); thirdly, an increase in size of the active sites and the number of vesicles on the sites. The investigators concluded that in order to effect all these physical changes, the cell changed the expression of its DNA. These physical changes have also been postulated as one of the bases of psychological long-term memory and are modeled in most artificial neural networks with a weight on all connections into a neural processor.

While a single action potential may affect the voltage of the recipient cell, it is actually the frequency of signaling that determines the degree to which any single cell may affect another cell. The strength or weight of any synapse is dependent on its original physical structure, how many times it had been used in the immediate past (caused by the Ca^{++} residues), the long-term amount of use it has seen, and on the quantized transmitter releases. The placement of a synapse, relative to the other synapses, was also found to affect the weight of its influence on the final voltage of the cell; however, the placement of synapses is dictated more by the genetic expression of the individual neuron than by its stimulus. The summation of the voltage changes across all the synapses has been shown to be a nonlinear function. In modeling terms, the signaling and the weighting of the connection are digital, and the processing of the inputs and weights are analog and nonlinear.

Obviously, models cannot capture and effectively use all of the nuances of neural behaviors, especially since there are numerous interactions which neurophysiologists have not even identified, yet. There are, however, a number of things which can be taken from the biological implementation of a neural system. First, not all neurons are connected with all the other neurons; second, the dendrites can do a lot of informational preprocessing even before any signal reaches the cell body; and third, the entire system takes advantage of the physical means by which it does the processing. This does not mean that the only neural hardware that will work is that which is made of biological materials; what it means is that any implementation should make the best use of the technology at hand. If a silicon IC implementations are used, then the implementation should take advantage of the accurate capacitors, the multitude of transistors, the analog capabilities of matched transistors, and use the fact that longer leads will give longer delays instead of having that be one of the worst problems in implementation. It means that if the network is a simulation, then the connection scheme, the processing for weights and for the state of each PE, should be simple and quick for the processor or processors available to do the work. Another way of saying it is that biological systems specialize, and it is quite probable that artificial neural networks will have to specialize in order to be effectively and efficiently implemented.

4. LOCAL CIRCUIT NEURONS

There is a large body of work that indicates that neurons are not all connected to each other, and that, in fact, the number of neurons that are only connected among others in the same locality are in the majority. When Golgi first started exercising his method for staining neurons he was confronted with a huge variety of cells [14]. He then separated them into general classes, long-axon and short-axon cells. More recently [7], these classifications have been modified a little to take into account a number of structures which Golgi had known nothing about. The neurons which are only connected to local neurons or neurons in the same functional unit are called Local Circuit Neurons (LCN), and these include neurons which have absolutely no axon, the old Golgi type II neurons, and a vast number of other neurons which are restricted to a particular section. The neurons which connect different functional blocks are called projection neurons. The most conservative estimate put the ratio of LCNs to projection neurons at more than 3:1.

The distribution of the LCNs vary according to the functional area. Although it is very difficult to get exact numbers of all areas of the nervous system, there are a few percentages that are known. The difficulty comes from the fact that there is no reliable method for measuring the average volume of connections to all the neurons in any section of neural matter. Also, since the LCNs are very small, there are very few processes which can accurately measure them. Where the structure is very regular or very well known, there is a better capability to give an estimate of the ratio. In the candate nucleus [15] LCNs represent 95% of all the neurons. The thalamus [16] and olfactory bulb [17] is made up of a stroma of LCNs which are bound together dendrodendritically (dendrite to dendrite) and projection neurons are situated sparsely among the dendrites. The interesting aspect of this architecture is that communication is easily bidirectional, instead of the usual input to output structure of the normal axon to dendrite connection of the typical neural circuit. Blinkov and Glezar [18] found that for each Purkinje cell (a projection cell) there were 1,600 granule cells (an LCN), an overwhelming majority. More and more researchers in the area of neurophysiology are coming to believe that the number and density of LCNs is linked to the higher processing capabilities of vertebrates and man [19], and that the LCNs, because of their very smallness, are more adaptable.

5. THE COMPACT NEURAL NETWORKS

There are a number of significant differences between a biological neural network and the Hopfield network, differences which are shared by many other popular models. Hopfield's network has all the neural processors connected with all the others. Biological systems do not, as can be evidenced by the tens of thousands of connections off of single neurons with approximately 10^{12} neurons in the entire system. The Hopfield processors are extremely simple, the biological neurons are quite complex with a great deal of input preprocessing capability in the physical structure of the dendrites before signals ever reach the central processing portion of the neuron. Finally, biological systems have a connection system which takes advantage of the processing capabilities of the neuron units. Hopfield networks do not.

Compact Neural Networks (CNNs) are modified Hopfield networks [19]. They do not have each processor connected to all the others, instead they only have k connections, where k is much less than the total number of processors. There is preprocessing of input, which takes advantage of the connection architecture. The CNN connection schemes were explored in order to take advantage of the mathematically regular computing systems that they were implemented on. Some of these regular interconnected structures are shown in Figure 5.4.

For the Hopfield network, when connections are taken out at random, there is a degradation in the network's capabilities. The damaged network cannot map to as many distinct outputs and it cannot correct as many errors or complete as many missing bits of input as with full connection. The performance of partially connected networks would be close to that of a damaged network, if there were no rearrangement of the memory matrices to take advantage of the regular structure. The problem of rearrangement is an optimization problem, which can be expressed in the following manner:

Given L neurons $\{1, \ldots, L\}$
k neighbors for each neuron

Find a one to one and on-to transform from
the set $\{1, \ldots, L\}$ to $\{1', \ldots', L'\}$ such that:

$$\max \left\{ \sum_{i', j'=0}^{L} t_{i'j}, \right\} \text{ for all } i' \, j' \text{ when they are neighbors}$$

where $\mathbf{L}$ is the number of neurons, $\mathbf{T}$ is the connection matrix, and t_{ij} is the weighted connection between processor i and processor j.

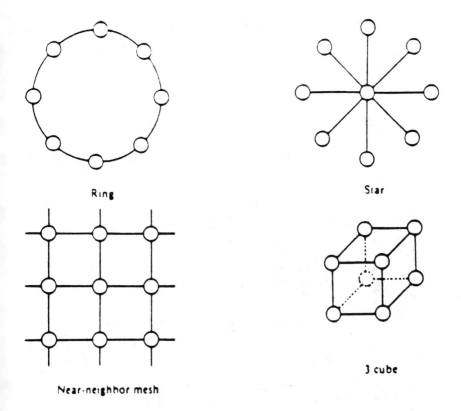

Ring

Star

Near-neighbor mesh

3 cube

Figure 5.4.   Regular inconnected structures.

A rearrangement algorithm is needed to maximize the weights that are not removed. The matrix of memory vectors may be rearranged such that the rows of the matrix which correspond to neighboring PEs have the least number of dissimilar bits[4]. The weight preservation is done best by taking the matrix of memory vectors and rearranging the rows of the matrix to make certain that the rows which correspond to neighboring PEs have the least Hamming distance. The Hopfield learning algorithm is the sum of the product of the states in the memory vector, if there are **N** memories, and all **N** memories provide the same state for the same pair of processors, the weight of the connection between those two processors is as high as it can get, as it reinforces with each like state. Most learning schemes increase the weights of connections between nodes which have the most similar (or most dissimilar[5]) states; therefore, having the rows of the

---

[4] The number of different bits between two binary numbers is also known as the *Hamming Distance*.

[5] Since negative weights and opposite states relate to each other in the same way that the positive weights and similar states do, there is just as much to be gained from pairing rows which are most

$$
\mathbf{F}^T =
\begin{pmatrix}
i & 0 & 1 & 2 & 3 & 4 & 5 & 6 & 7 & 8 & 9 & a & b & c & d & e & f \\
\\
 & + & + & + & - & + & + & + & + & + & - & - & - & - & - & - & - \\
 & + & + & + & - & - & - & - & + & - & - & + & + & + & + & - & + \\
 & - & - & + & + & + & + & - & + & - & - & + & + & - & + & - & -
\end{pmatrix}
$$

$$
\mathbf{F}_p^T =
\begin{pmatrix}
i & 0 & 1 & 2 & 3 & 4 & 5 & 6 & 7 & 8 & 9 & a & b & c & d & e & f \\
i' & 2 & 7 & 0 & 1 & 6 & 8 & 4 & 5 & 3 & a & 9 & e & c & f & b & d \\
\\
 & + & + & + & + & + & + & + & + & - & - & - & - & - & - & - & - \\
 & + & + & + & + & - & - & - & - & - & - & - & - & + & + & + & + \\
 & + & + & - & - & - & - & + & + & + & + & - & - & - & - & + & +
\end{pmatrix}
$$

$$
T_p =
\begin{pmatrix}
+3 & +3 & 0 & 0 & 0 & 0 & 0 & 0 & 0 & 0 & 0 & 0 & 0 & 0 & 0 & +1 \\
+3 & +3 & +1 & 0 & 0 & 0 & 0 & 0 & 0 & 0 & 0 & 0 & 0 & 0 & 0 & 0 \\
0 & +1 & +3 & +3 & 0 & 0 & 0 & 0 & 0 & 0 & 0 & 0 & 0 & 0 & 0 & 0 \\
0 & 0 & +3 & +3 & +1 & 0 & 0 & 0 & 0 & 0 & 0 & 0 & 0 & 0 & 0 & 0 \\
0 & 0 & 0 & +1 & +3 & +3 & 0 & 0 & 0 & 0 & 0 & 0 & 0 & 0 & 0 & 0 \\
0 & 0 & 0 & 0 & +3 & +3 & +1 & 0 & 0 & 0 & 0 & 0 & 0 & 0 & 0 & 0 \\
0 & 0 & 0 & 0 & 0 & +1 & +3 & +3 & 0 & 0 & 0 & 0 & 0 & 0 & 0 & 0 \\
0 & 0 & 0 & 0 & 0 & 0 & +3 & +3 & +1 & 0 & 0 & 0 & 0 & 0 & 0 & 0 \\
0 & 0 & 0 & 0 & 0 & 0 & 0 & +1 & +3 & +3 & 0 & 0 & 0 & 0 & 0 & 0 \\
0 & 0 & 0 & 0 & 0 & 0 & 0 & 0 & +3 & +3 & +1 & 0 & 0 & 0 & 0 & 0 \\
0 & 0 & 0 & 0 & 0 & 0 & 0 & 0 & 0 & +1 & +3 & +3 & 0 & 0 & 0 & 0 \\
0 & 0 & 0 & 0 & 0 & 0 & 0 & 0 & 0 & 0 & +3 & +3 & +1 & 0 & 0 & 0 \\
0 & 0 & 0 & 0 & 0 & 0 & 0 & 0 & 0 & 0 & 0 & +1 & +3 & +3 & 0 & 0 \\
0 & 0 & 0 & 0 & 0 & 0 & 0 & 0 & 0 & 0 & 0 & 0 & +3 & +3 & +1 & 0 \\
0 & 0 & 0 & 0 & 0 & 0 & 0 & 0 & 0 & 0 & 0 & 0 & 0 & +1 & +3 & +3 \\
+1 & 0 & 0 & 0 & 0 & 0 & 0 & 0 & 0 & 0 & 0 & 0 & 0 & 0 & +3 & +3
\end{pmatrix}
$$

Figure 5.5. A memory matrix, Rearranged Memory Matrix and T matrix for Ring-Connected Compact Neural Network.

original memory matrix rearranged to keep the closest rows together as neighbors makes the resulting weight matrix retain most of the largest values.

The ring-based CNN and the Reduced Interconnect Neural Network have been introduced in an earlier paper [19]. A rearrangement of given memory matrix is required to obtain them. The ring-based CNN, as shown in Figure 5.5, has $k = 2$ connections, or each processor is connected to its nearest neighbors on the ring. It uses either a greedy algorithm or a Grey Code approximation to determine the rearrangement of the memory and input vectors. A complete study of its performance with a larger number of neighbors has been done as well. Empirically, the single neighbor structure performed best. The Reduced Inter-

---

dissimilar. When the activation of a neuron deactivates another neuron, the weight between the two is negative. By keeping the weights of largest negative values, there is the same affect as by keeping the weights with the largest positive values. Even better performance could possibly be gotten if the weights of largest absolute value were kept; however, that is beyond the scope of this thesis.

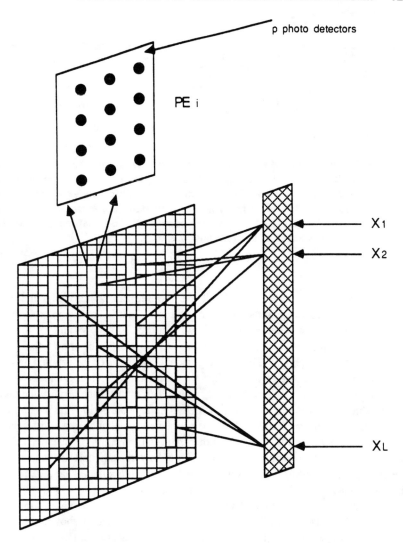

Figure 5.6.   An optical implementation of RINN.

connect Neural Network (RINN) uses the original memory matrix [20]. The RINN is given the number of weights to be preserved, and searches through the weight matrices for the largest weights. It then disconnects all the other weights by setting them to zero. A possible implementation of the RINN is shown in Figure 5.6.

The Hypercube-based CNN has $L\log_2 L$ connections between L processors. For the hypercube, Figure 5.7(a) shows a cube which has numbers corresponding to the rows of the memory matrix on its vertices. The memory matrices have

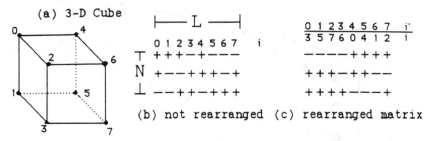

Figure 5.7.   (a) A three-dimensional cube with labeling for the corresponding processors. (b) $L = 8$, $N = 3$ memory matrix which has not been rearranged. Processor input states go from 0–7 from left to right. i is the index of the original memory matrix. (c) The rearranged matrix with Hamming distance across the connections of 8. Here, again, i is the index of the original memory matrix, compared with the index of the rearranged matrix.

been turned on their sides to make it easy to see the N individual memory vectors. The numbers along the top of each memory matrix correspond to what is referred to as the row number for each row. Figure 5.7(b) shows an $L = 8$, $N = 3$, memory matrix without rearrangement and Figure 5.7(c) shows the same matrix after rearrangement. The rearrangement of the rows of the original memory matrices can be tracked by seeing the transformed row indices (i and i') on the rearranged matrix. To get a measurement for which matrix is better, use the cube to tell which rows are connected with which; for each connection find the number of differences there are between the two connected rows, add up the differences for each connection on the cube, and the result is the Hamming distance across the cube. While the rearranged matrix may not have the smallest distance across the cube architecture, it has a distance which is much less than what the original memory matrix would have had without rearrangement.

An interconnect matrix for a three-dimensional hypercube CNN is shown in Figure 5.8(b). It is derived from the rearranged memory matrix shown in Figure 5.7(c). The hypercube matrix has more zero interconnect than the interconnect matrix in Figure 5.8(a), which was derived from the original memory matrix shown in Figure 5.7(b). The zeros are from imposing the hypercube interconnect structure onto the interconnect matrix. Knowledge about the sparser matrix of the hypercube architecture was used to lessen the amount of processing used for both simulations of the network. The choice of emphasizing positive weights with like rows is reflected in the fact that the rearranged matrix has a much higher percentage of positive weights than the original memory-basic matrix. This is highly evident when comparing the weights which correspond to those that the hypercube would have in the original matrix (the bold characters).

0	+1	-1	-1	+1	-1	-3	-1
+1	0	+1	-3	+1	-3	-1	-3
-1	+1	0	-1	-1	-1	+1	-1
-1	-3	-1	0	-1	+3	+1	+3
+1	+1	-1	-1	0	-1	-3	-1
-1	-3	-1	+3	-1	0	+1	+3
-3	-1	+1	+1	-3	+1	0	+1
-1	-3	-1	+3	-1	+3	+1	0

0	+3	+3	0	-1	0	0	0
+3	0	0	+1	0	-1	0	0
+3	0	0	+1	0	0	-3	0
0	+1	+1	0	0	0	0	+1
-1	0	0	0	0	+3	+1	0
0	-1	0	0	+3	0	0	-1
0	0	-3	0	+1	0	0	+1
0	0	0	+1	0	-1	+1	0

a) Original Memory, Full Matrix   b) Rearranged Hypercube Matrix

Figure 5.8.   Interconnection matrices for original memory matrix and rearranged hypercube matrix. a) This is the interconnection matrix for the original memory matrix shown in Figure 5.4(b), above. The bold numbers are the weights which would have been kept if this interconnection matrix was disconnected into a hypercube matrix. Note that the bold weights are about evenly distributed between positive and negative weights. b) This is the interconnection matrix for the rearranged memory matrix with all the weights left in which correspond to the hypercube connection scheme. The weights are predominantly positive.

6. CONCLUSIONS

We have presented a biological basis for deriving compact neural network. These Compact Neural Networks are based on the following three differences between most artificial neural networks and biological systems:

1. The neurons are not all connected with each other. This makes these kinds of networks more easily implemented and connected within a subsystem segment.

2. There is significant preprocessing of input, and the preprocessing is connected to and done through use of the final, physical connection scheme.

3. The connection implementation method supports the fact that the network is implemented as a simulation on a binary-based computer. The hypercube interconnect scheme is relatively simple to implement and manipulate by a binary computer, as is the ring structure.

Our studies have shown that these compact neural networks perform very well in comparison to the Hopfield networks. Furthermore, their implementation is much easier because of their regular interconnection topology. Their performance capabilities are covered in [21].

REFERENCES

[1]   E.R. Kandel and J.H. Schwartz, *Principles of Neural Science,* Elsevier Science, New York, 1981.

[2]   D.O. Hebb, *The Organization of Behavior,* Wiley, New York, 1949.

[3]   J.L. McClelland and D.E. Rumelhart, *Parallel Distributed Processing: Explorations in the Microstructure of Cognition, Vol. I,* MIT Press, Cambridge, MA, 1986.

[4]   F. Rosenblatt, *Principles of Neurodynamics,* Spartan, New York, 1962.

[5]   B. Widrow, "Adaline and Madaline—1963," *Proceedings of the IEEE First International Conference on Neural Networks,* Vol. I, SOS Printing, San Diego, 1987, pp. 143–157.

[6]   M. Minsky and S. Papert, *Perceptrons,* MIT Press, Cambridge, MA, 1969.

[7]   P. Rakic, "Local Circuit Neurons," *Neurosciences Research Program Bulletin,* Vol. 13, 1975, pp. 289–446.

[8]   P. Geolet and E.R. Kandal, "Tracking the Flow of Learned Information from Membrane Receptors to Genome," TINS, Elsevier Science, Amsterdam, October 1986, pp. 492–499.

[9]   S. Grossberg, *Studies of Mind and Brain,* Reidel, Hingham, MA, 1982.

[10] T. Kohonen, *Self Organization and Associative Memory,* Springer-Verlag, Berlin, 1983.

[11] J.J. Hopfield, "Neural networks and physical systems with emergent collective computational abilities," *Proceedings of the National Academy of Science 79,* 1979, pp. 2554–2582 (11912).

[12] A. Peters, S.L. Palay, and H. deF. Webster, *The Fine Structure of the Nervous System,* W.B. Saunders, Philadelphia, 1976.

[13] B. Katz and R. Miledi, "The Timing of Calcium Action During Neuromuscular Transmission," *Journal of Physiology,* Vol. 189, 1967, pp. 535–544.

[14] C. Golgi, "Sulla Fina Anatomia Degli Organi Centrali Del Sistema Noervoso. 4. Sulla Fina Anatomia Delle Circonvoluzioni Cerebellari (On the Detailed Anatomy of the Central Organ of the Nervous System, Section 4, On the Detailed Anatomy of Cerebral Convolution)," *Opera Omnia,* Hoepli, Milano, 1903.

[15] N.A. Bushwald, D.D. Price, L. Vernon, and C.D. Hull, "Caudate intracellular response to thalamic and cortical inputs," Rxp. Neurology, Vol. 38, 1973, pp. 311–323.

[16] M.E. Scheibal and A.B. Scheibal, "LCNs in the Ventrobasal Complex of the Dorsal Thalamus," *Neurosciences Research Program Bulletin,* Vol. 13, 1975, pp. 377–381.

[17] G.M. Shepherd, "Models of LCN function in the Olfactory Bulb," *Neurosciences Research Program Bulletin,* Vol. 13, 1975, pp. 344–353.

[18] S.M. Blinkov and I.I. Glezer, *The Human Brain in Figures and Tables: A Quantitative Handbook,* Basic Books, Plenum Press, New York, 1968.

[19] A.K. Somani and N. Penla, "Compact Neural Network," *Proceedings of the IEEE First International Conference on Neural Networks,* Volume III, SOS Printing, San Diego, 1987, pp. 191–199.

[20] A.K. Somani and N. Penla, "Reduced Interconnection Neural Network," to appear in *Neural Networks* B. Shriver (Ed.), Computer Science Press, 1991.

[21] A.K. Somani and P.L. Rostykus, "Neural Network and Their Comparison With Other Artificial Neural Networks," Vol. 1, *Progress in Neural Networks,* O. Omidvar (Ed.), 1991, pp. 57–85.

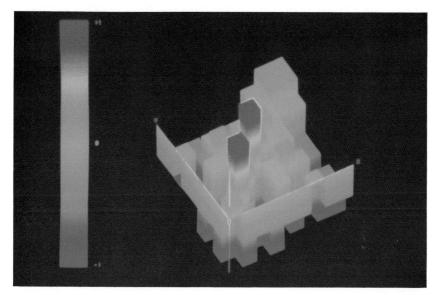

Figure 6.4. Pseudocolored, three-dimensional representation of the connection weights matrix between the zeroth hidden layer and the output layer during training at 550 iteration steps.

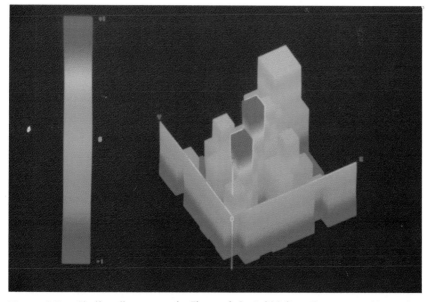

Figure 6.5. Similar diagram as in Figure 6.4 at 600 iteration steps. Note that positive and negative values in the connection matrix begin to form.

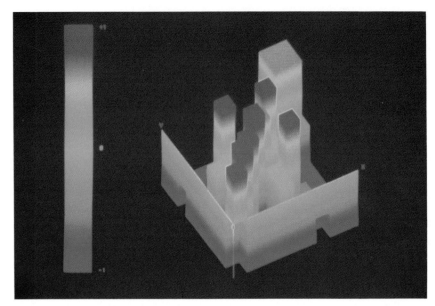

Figure 6.6. Similar diagram as in Figure 6.4 at 700 iteration steps. Note that positive correlation emerges at the diagonal, representing autocorrelated activities. The other two off-diagonal positive peaks represent positive correlation between the firing of neurons 3 and 6, and neurons 8 and 9.

6
A Hybrid Time-Shifted Neural Network for Analyzing Biological Neuronal Spike Trains*

David C. Tam
Center for Network Neuroscience
Department of Biological Sciences
University of North Texas
Denton, TX

1. INTRODUCTION

One of the differences between biological neurons in the central nervous systems in vertebrates and artificial neurons of neural networks is that the signals carried by biological neurons are pulse coded, whereas most artificial neurons use signals of continuous functions in the analog domain. That is, the input and output of a neuron in the central nervous system in most vertebrates is not represented as an analog signal, where the value is represented in the voltage amplitude, but represented as a discrete function, where the value is represented by the *time intervals* of arrival of quantal neurotransmitters on the input side and the *time intervals* of firing of the all-or-none action potentials (voltage-pulses) on the output side. In other words, the signals are represented by the occurrence of discrete quantal events. Such a discrete process is called *point process* in statistics.

In analyzing the statistics of such point processes in biological systems, these point processes can be considered as stochastic point processes since the release of neurotransmitters and the initiation of action potentials in neurons can be considered as stochastic. Since the firing of a neuron and the release of neurotransmitters can be considered as probabilistic events, the analysis of such events requires establishing statistics that describe the dynamics and interactions of the system. There are many statistical techniques designed specifically to extract the underlying interactions among the stochastic point process of action potentials in biological systems [1–8]. The analysis of such time series of action

*The support of Office of Naval Research under ONR Grant N00014-93-1-0135 is gratefully acknowledged. I thank Dr. Teresa McMullen for critical reading of the manuscript.

potentials is called *spike-train analysis*. In order to clarify the terminology used to describe biological neurons and artificial neurons, we will restrict the use of "neurons" to describe biological neurons and "units" to describe artificial neurons. Furthermore, we will use the term "neuronal networks" to describe biological neuronal networks and "neural networks" to describe artificial neural networks.

In the central nervous system as well as the peripheral nervous system, action potentials generated by a neuron usually have a stereotypical voltage profile unique to a particular type of neurons. Although the shape of the voltage profile of an action potential differs for different types of neurons, the shape is usually similar among neurons of the same type, since they have similar biophysical and biochemical properties. Although most neurons of the same type fire with action potentials of the same shape, some neurons are known to fire with two different shapes of action potentials, such as the complex spikes and simple spikes in Purkinje cells of the cerebellum. For simplicity, we will restrict our analysis of spike trains to neurons that fire with only one type of action potential.

Given the time series of pulse-coded events, without a priori knowledge of the underlying functions of the neuronal networks in the central nervous system, we would like to ask the question of how these temporal patterns would be used to deduce the functions and dynamics of interacting neurons in the network. In particular, one of the tasks of neurophysiologists is to deduce the functions of neuronal networks from electrophysiological recordings of neurons *in vivo* or *in vitro*.

With the recent development of simultaneous multineuron recording techniques, such as silicon-substrate multielectrode arrays [9–12] and optical recording from voltage-sensitive fluorescence dyes [13,14], recording from a large number of neurons is possible. One of the analytical tools for analyzing the interactions between two neurons is the cross-correlation analysis [2,6,7] in which the probability of firing one neuron can be correlated with the firing of another. The temporal patterns of interactions of firing in neurons can be deduced from the cross-correlation between the neuron pair. The task of extracting temporal coupling interactions among any pairs of neurons in a neuronal assembly using this conventional pairwise correlational analysis may require a combinatorially large number of correlograms for analysis.

In this chapter, an alternative approach is proposed to analyze the spike trains recorded from a large assembly of neurons. An artificial parallel distributed processing neural network is used to extract the correlation of firing patterns of neurons in a biological neuronal network. The parallel processing advantage of an artificial neural network is well suited in this application since the processing of the different channels of neuronal signals can be performed in parallel. The model is based on the network model developed earlier [8].

2. SIGNALS GENERATED BY BIOLOGICAL NEURONS

In most neurons, a voltage difference of 70 mV is maintained between the inside and outside ionic media of the cells at the resting state. This *resting potential* is maintained by the ionic concentration difference of the various species of charged ions separated by the membrane governed by the Nernst equation and Goldman-Hodgkin-Katz equation [15,16]. When the membrane potential is depolarized to a critical point called threshold, the voltage-dependent ionic channels in the membrane change their conductances nonlinearly, thus generating a characteristic *action potential* with a stereotypic time course. The dynamics of an action potential can be described by the Hodgkin-Huxley differential equations [17–21]. Since the time course and shape of action potentials generated by a neuron of the same type are usually similar, the action potentials can be considered as pulses with similar pulse-height and pulse-width. Thus, the signal generated by a neuron, which is transmitted along the length of the axon, can be simplified as pulses (or spikes) lasting for approximately one msec. The neural network described in this chapter is designed to detect the temporal patterns in the spike trains (i.e., the firing patterns) recorded from neurons.

As a simplification of what is described above, the output of a neuron can be approximated by a time series of events signaled by the action potentials. Since the action potentials of neurons can be recorded either extracellularly or intracellularly in experimental animals, the dynamics of interactions among neurons can be identified by analyzing the firing patterns among neurons. Identification of the serial and temporal correlation of firing among neurons may reveal the underlying mechanisms of functional connectivity among neurons.

3. DESCRIPTION OF THE ARTIFICIAL NEURAL NETWORK

Let us assume that we can record the electrical signals from n neurons from an ensemble of neurons, and obtain n spike trains. These n time series of spike train will be used as the n separate time-varying inputs to a neural network. Thus, one of our objectives is to use a neural network to identify the relationships of temporal patterns of firing among these n neurons. This objective can be further divided into the following specific aspects: (a) we want to determine if there is any correlation of firing among any given neurons in the ensemble at any given time simultaneously; (b) we want to determine what kind of correlation it is if the correlation exists (i.e., whether the correlation is positive or negative); and (c) we want to determine if there is any correlation of firing among any given neurons in the ensemble at different time intervals between firing. That is, our main objective is to identify the relationships between the time of occurrence of firing events among neurons.

Since most common artificial neural networks associate input and output patterns pairwise simultaneously without temporal order, we employ a time-shifted neural network architecture and learning algorithm to accommodate the temporal association. When the input patterns are time-shifted with respect to the output of the neural network, the association between the input and output events at different times may be established. Thus, by repeating the training cycle based on the temporal sequence of the spike trains, the pattern of input activity is correlated with the output pattern. Once the neural network is trained to produce the observed set of output spike train firing patterns in response to the input spike trains, the correlation among neurons can be revealed by the connection strengths (or connection weights) among the network units. Using this technique of analysis, the pattern of events occurring at different times may be revealed at different time intervals.

To achieve the above objectives, we designed a hybrid artificial neural network with learning rules such that the connection weights will serve as an index (or indicator) of correlation between different channels of input and output. We chose to use the Hebbian learning rule for correlation since the connection weights are modified by the simultaneity of firing of the input and output neurons [22]. With a time-shifted network architecture, the connection weights can be modified by the time-shifted intervals of the firing of the input and output neurons.

Since the connection weight between such an input–output pair is an indicator of the strength of correlation, the specific patterns of correlation between the input and output can be revealed. Therefore, we employ a time-delayed Hebbian rule to change the connection weight such that the association between the input and output is indicated by the value of the connection weight.

In addition to the Hebbian learning rule and the extended Hebbian rules we selected for the network, we also include the generalized delta rule of the back propagation, error-correction algorithm in the network [23]. We include the delta rule because it is suited for matching and reducing the discrepancies (errors) between the input and output pair during training. The algorithm we use is a time-delayed, normalized version of the generalized delta rule.

3.1. Architecture of the Hybrid Time-Shifted Correlation Network

The hybrid network has a multilayered, neural network architecture. There are n inputs to the network and m outputs from the network. There are $q + 1$ hidden layers, each containing n hidden units (see Figure 6.1). Each of the hidden layers is connected directly to all n input units in the input layer and all m output units in the output layer. The difference between the input signal received among the k different hidden layers is that the input signal is successively time-shifted by an amount of time, Δt for each hidden layer. That is, the zeroth hidden layer is

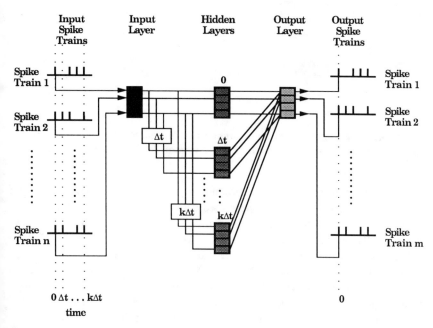

Figure 6.1. Architecture of the hybrid time-shifted multilayer artificial neural network used for temporal correlation showing the connections between the input and output spike trains.

connected to the input and output layers with no time shift to its input. The hidden units in this layer assoiciate the patterns of output with the input at the same time instant t (with no time shift). The first hidden layer is connected to the input and output with a time shift of Δt to the input signal. That is, the units in this first hidden layer associate the patterns of output at time t with the input at the previous time step, $t-\Delta t$. Similarly, the kth hidden layer is connected to the input and output with a time shift of $k\Delta t$ to the input signal. The units in this kth hidden layer associate the patterns of output at time t with the input at the kth previous time step, $t-k\Delta t$. Since each of these $q + 1$ hidden layers are situated between the input and output layers with direct connections, they can be considered as arranged in parallel with respect to each other in contrast to the series arrangement found in most other common neural network architectures.

3.2. Input and Output of the Network

If the time series of the input spike train is denoted by $x^*(t)$, then the input signals received by the ith input unit of the network can be represented by $x^*_i(t)$.

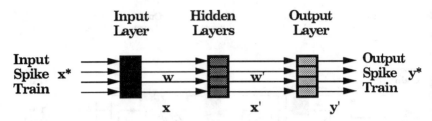

Figure 6.2. The representation of primed and unprimed notations used to distinguish the variables with respect to the hidden layer. (See text for details.)

Similarly, the time series of output produced by the jth output unit of the network can be represented by $y'_j(t)$. As described above, there are n input units and m output units in the network, and n hidden units in each hidden layer. Let us use $w_{ijk}(t)$ to denote the connection weight between the ith input and the jth hidden unit in the kth hidden layer, and $w'_{ijk}(t)$ to denote the connection weight between the ith hidden unit at the kth hidden layer and the jth output unit. Note that we use a primed notation to denote the connection on the output side of the network relative to the hidden layers and the unprimed notation to denote the connection on the input side of the network (see Figure 6.2). Since the output of a unit is also the input of the next connected unit, using this primed notation convention, the output signal produced by the ith hidden unit at the kth hidden layer of the network is

$$x_i^*(t) = \sum_{h=0}^{r} \delta(t - \tau_h) \tag{3.1}$$

with a total of $r + 1$ spikes, where spikes occur at time $t = \tau_h$. The delta function is given by:

$$\delta(t) = \begin{cases} 1, & t = 0 \\ 0, & t \neq 0 \end{cases} \tag{3.2}$$

That is, when a spike occurs within the time interval $[t, \ t + \Delta t)$, then $x_i^*(t) = 1$, otherwise $x_i^*(t) = 0$. The input signals received by each individual hidden layer are given as follows:

The units in the zeroth hidden layer receive the unmodified signal from the input units. The jth hidden unit at the zeroth hidden layer receives input from all input units at the input layer of the network without any time-shift. That is, if we denote the input to the jth unit at the zeroth hidden layer by $x_{j0}(t)$, then the total input to this jth hidden unit is given by the weighted sum of all the input from the input layer:

$$x_{j0}(t) = \sum_{i=1}^{n} w_{ij0}(t)x_i^*(t) \tag{3.3}$$

where $w_{ij0}(t)$ represents the connection weight from the ith input unit to the jth unit at the zeroth hidden layer.

The units in the first hidden layer receive input signals from the input layer time-shifted by Δt. That is, if we denote the input to the jth unit at the first hidden layer by $x_{j1}(t)$, then the total input to this jth hidden unit is given by the weighted sum of all the input from the input layer time-shifted by Δt:

$$x_{j1}(t) = \sum_{i=1}^{n} w_{ij1}(t)x_i^*(t - \Delta t) \qquad (3.4)$$

where $w_{ij1}(t)$ represents the connection weight from the ith input unit to the jth unit at the first hidden layer.

Similarly, if we denote the input to the jth unit at the kth hidden layer by $x_{jk}(t)$, then the total input to this jth hidden unit is given by the sum of all the input from the input layer time-shifted by $k\Delta t$:

$$x_{jk}(t) = \sum_{i=1}^{n} w_{ijk}(t)x_i^*(t - k\Delta t) \qquad (3.5)$$

where $w_{ijk}(t)$ represents the connection weight from the ith input unit to the jth unit at the kth hidden layer.

Finally, each jth unit in the output layer of the network receives the input signals from the ith hidden unit of all k hidden layers. That is, if we denote the total input to the jth unit at the output layer by $x'_j(t)$, and the output of the ith hidden unit at the kth hidden layer by $x'_{ik}(t)$, then the input received by the jth output unit is given by:

$$x'_j(t) = \sum_{k=0}^{q} \sum_{i=1}^{n} w'_{ijk}(t)x'_{ik}(t) \qquad (3.6)$$

where $w'_{ijk}(t)$ represents the connection weight from the ith hidden unit at the kth hidden layer to the jth output unit.

3.2.2. Outputs from of the network units

The activation rule producing the output activity, $x'_{jk}(t)$, by the jth hidden unit at the kth hidden layer is given the nonlinear mapping of the input signals:

$$x'_{jk}(t) = f\left[\frac{1}{n} \sum_{i=1}^{n} w_{ijk}(t)x_i(t - k\Delta t) \right] \qquad (3.7)$$

or:

$$x'_{jk}(t) = f\left[\frac{1}{n}x_{jk}(t)\right]$$ (3.8)

where:

$$f(x) = \frac{2}{1 + e^{-5x}} - 1$$ (3.9)

is a normalized, symmetric, sigmoidal function bounded between $+1$ and -1.

Similarly, the activation rule producing the output activity, $y'(t)$, by the jth output unit at the output layer is given:

$$y'_j(t) = f\left[\frac{1}{(q + 1)n}\sum_{k=0}^{q}\sum_{i=1}^{n}w'_{ijk}(t)x'_{ik}(t)\right]$$ (3.10)

or:

$$y'_j(t) = f\left[\frac{1}{(q + 1)n}x'_j(t)\right]$$ (3.11)

4. LEARNING RULES OF THE NETWORK

Since this network is a hybrid network model, two separate sets of rules are used in modifying the connection weights of the network. The connection weights between the output and hidden layers are modified by the time-delayed normalized Hebbian learning rule, while the connection weights between the input and hidden layers are modified by the normalized-generalized delta rule.

4.1. The Normalized Hebbian Learning Rules of the Network

The connection weight between the hidden and output layers are modified by the following equation:

$$w'_{ijk}(t + \Delta t) = w'_{ijk}(t) + \Delta w'_{ijk}(t)$$ (4.1)

where the weight change, $\Delta w'_{ijk}(t)$, is given by one of the following Hebbian rules. If the correlative firing patterns of two sets of spike trains are examined, they can be cross-correlated by supplying one set of the spike trains as the input to this neural network and the other set as the *desired* output of the network. If the input spike trains, $x*_i(t)$, are cross-correlated with the *desired* output spike trains, $y*_j(t)$, simultaneously with no time delays, then the Hebbian learning rule may be given by the following equation:

$$\Delta w'_{ijk}(t) = x^*_i(t)y^*_j(t). \tag{4.2}$$

If the input spike trains, $x^*_i(t)$, are correlated with the desired output spike trains, $y^*_j(t)$, with $k\Delta t$ time delays, then the time-delayed Hebbian learning rule may be given by the following equation:

$$\Delta w'_{ijk}(t) = x^*_i(t-k\Delta t)y^*_j(t). \tag{4.3}$$

But using such learning will produce an ever-increasing value of connection weight as long as there is simultaneous association between the input and output pair during the learning phase. In order to normalize the growth of the connection weight, we use a parametric function of the connection weight such that the connection weights will be bound by the range between $+1$ and -1:

$$\Delta w'_{ijk}(t) = \text{sgn}[x_i(t-k\Delta t), y^*_j(t)] \cdot \{|w'_{ijk}(t)| \cdot [1-w'_{ijk}(t)]\} \tag{4.4}$$

where:

$$\text{sgn}(x, y) = \begin{cases} 1, & \text{if } (x > 0) \text{ and } (y > 0) \\ 0, & \text{if } (x \le 0) \text{ and } (y \le 0) \\ -1, & \text{otherwise} \end{cases} \tag{4.5}$$

Such formulation will not only ensure bounding of the value of connection weight, but it will also provide nonlinear accelerated convergence of the weight to the desired result, which will be discussed later.

With this time-delayed Hebbian learning rule, the firing relationships between input and output spike trains can be identified. With this rule, the connection weights will increase only when both input and output are active (i.e., firing a spike). The connection weights will not increase when either the input or the output (but not both) is firing. The connection weight, $\Delta w'_{ijk}(t)$, will increase only when there is a spike in the input spike train at time $t-k\Delta t$ and there is another spike in the desired output spike train at time t. Thus, it establishes the correlation between the input and the output at a time delay of interval $k\Delta t$. To enumerate the interpretation layer by layer, the connection weights from the zeroth hidden layer to the output layer will increase only when both input and output fire a spike simultaneously (i.e., $k\Delta t = 0$). When the input spike train fires a spike preceding that of the output spike train by a time interval of Δt, then the connection weights from the first hidden layer to the output layer will increase. Similarly, when the input spike train fires a spike preceding that of the output spike train by a time interval of $k\Delta t$, then the connection weights from the kth hidden layer to the output layer will increase. To be more specific, if the ith input spike train fires a spike preceding that of the jth output spike train by a time interval of $k\Delta t$, then the connection weight, $\Delta w'_{ijk}(t)$, connecting between the ith hidden unit at the kth hidden layer and jth output unit will increase. Conversely, if after training the connection weight, $\Delta w'_{ijk}(t)$, is a maximum, it implies that there is a positive correlation between the firing of a spike in the ith input spike train preceding the firing of a spike in the jth output spike train by a time interval of $k\Delta t$.

Besides identifying the positively correlated firing between neurons, we also want to identify the pattern for which firing of the input is associated with a suppression of firing (i.e., not firing) in the output spike train. That is, if such correlated inhibition of activity occurs, there will be a negative change in the connection weights. The second condition on Eq. (4.5) provides the condition for the decrease of connection weight when either the input neuron fires but the output neuron does not, and vice versa. The connection weights will polarize to either positive values when there are positive correlations, and negative values when there are negative correlations, between the firing of the input spike train and the nonfiring of the output spike train.

Finally, when both the input and output neurons do not fire, the connection weights will not change. Therefore, if there is no correlation between the input and output neurons, the connection weights will remain unchanged.

Based on these conditions, the correlation between the temporal patterns of firing in the input spike train and the output spike train can be inferred from the value of the connection weights established after training. Positive values in the connection matrix will result from a positive correlation between the firing of input and output neurons; negative values will result from negative correlation between them; and zero values will result from no correlations.

It should be noted that the parametric functions used in the normalized Hebbian learning equations (Eq. 4.4) not only bound the value of connection weights between $+1$ and -1, but also produce a desirable effect of nonlinear rate of change of the step-size of the connection weights. Suppose the correlation between the input and output spike trains is positive, and assume that the initial value of the connection weights are near zero (but not zero), then the rate of change in the connection weights will be small initially. As the connection weight increases, the rate of change also increases. But as the weight approaches the maximal value (of one), the rate of change decreases asymptotically. This rate of change in the connection weight is automatically self-adjusting according to the distance from its desired value.

4.2. The Normalized Delta Learning Rules of the Network

While the connection weights between the time-shifted input to the hidden layers and output layers of the network is governed by one of the above time-delayed Hebbian learning rules, the connection weights between the input and the hidden layers of the network is governed by a modified-normalized delta rule. The connection weight between the ith input unit and the jth hidden unit at the kth hidden layer of the network is modified by the following equations:

$$w_{ijk}(t + \Delta t) = w_{ijk}(t) + \Delta w_{ijk}(t) \tag{4.6}$$

where:

$$\Delta w_{ijk}(t) = \left[\frac{1}{2m} \sum_{p=1}^{m} w'_{ipk}(t)e'_j(t) \right] |w_{ipk}(t)\| 1 - w_{ipk}(t)| \tag{4.7}$$

and the activity error, $e'_j(t)$, at the jth output unit is given by difference between the desired output spike train, $y*_j(t)$, and the actual output of the network, $y'_j(t)$:

$$e'_j(t) = y*_j(t) - y'_j(t). \tag{4.8}$$

5. INTERPRETATION OF THE CONNECTION WEIGHT MATRICES

Given the hybrid neural network described above, the connections established by the time-delayed Hebbian rules can be used to correlate with the strength of association between the input and output signal at any given time delay. For instance, after training, a positive correlation between the input and output at the same time will be represented by a value of $+1$ for the connection weight connecting the correlated units between the zeroth hidden layer and the output, since the connection weights are normalized. A negative correlation will be represented by a value of -1 for the connection weight connecting the negatively correlated units. If there is no correlation between the units, then the connection weight will be zero. Similarly, if the connection weight connecting the kth hidden layer and the output layer is $+1$ for the ith input unit and jth output unit, then the correlation between the firing of ith input neuron at time $t-k\Delta t$ and the firing of jth output neuron at time t is positive. If the connection weight is -1, then the correlation is negative for those neuron pairs with the time lag of $k\Delta t$ between their firing. If the correlation is zero, there is no correlation between the firing of those two neurons with a time difference of $k\Delta t$.

When the above learning rules are applied to the input and output spike trains, the pattern of input activity will be associated with the output pattern at different time shifts. Once the neural network is trained to produce the observed set of m output spike trains in response to the n input spike trains, the correlations among neurons at different lag times can be represented by the connection strengths (or connection weights) connecting the network units between the various hidden layers and the output layer. If the same set of input spike trains are used as the desired output spike trains, then the correlation will be an autocorrelation with the same set of spike trains, instead of cross-correlation between the input and output sets.

To display the correlation relationship among the input and output patterns graphically, the connection weights between the hidden and output layers can be represented in a correlation matrix format, where the rows represent the indices

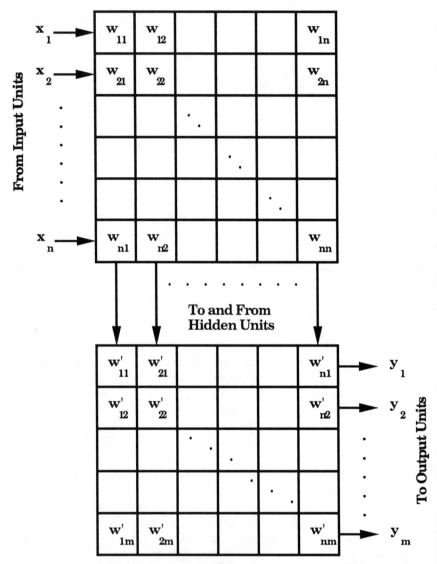

Figure 6.3. Representation of connection weights between the input and hidden layer, and between the hidden layer and output layer in correlation matrix format. The matrix of connection weights used in the analysis is the one connecting the hidden and output layer.

of the output units and the columns represent the indices of the hidden units (see second matrix in Figure 6.3). Each correlation matrix can be used to represent a separate set of connection weights between a specific (kth) hidden layer and the output layer. The correlation matrix at the kth hidden layer represents the correlation between the firing in the input spike trains and the firing in the output spike trains separated by k time-shifted steps at Δt, since the connection weight between the kth hidden layer and the output layer represents the correlation at lag time of $k\Delta t$. Therefore, the correlation patterns at any given time can easily be viewed at a glance to the corresponding correlation matrix at the hidden layer with the specified time-shift. Furthermore, the set of correlation matrices can be displayed graphically in three-dimensional form (see Figures 6.4, 6.5, 6.6).

6. RESULTS

As an example illustrating the spike train analysis performed by the neural network, we recorded the spike trains from nine neurons generated by a neuronal simulation program [24]. The biological neuronal network is constructed using a compartmental model [25] with realistic biophysical membrane properties and neurotransmitter release. The neurons are connected together with mutually excitatory and mutually inhibitory connections driven by two pacemaking neurons (see Figure 6.7). To simplify the example used for illustrating the results obtained from the correlation of the spike trains, we use the same set of spike trains as the input and the desired output of the network. In other words, the inputs and outputs are *autocorrelated* in this example. The interpretations can be generalized to show the *cross-correlational* firing relationships if different sets of input spike trains and desired output spike trains are used. In the analysis shown below, a time-shifted step, Δt, of 1 millisecond is used.

Figure 6.4 shows a three-dimensional pseudocolored representation of the values of the correlation weights between the zeroth hidden layer and the output layer. That is, it corresponds to the connection matrix for simultaneous input and output patterns (with no time-shift) obtained after 550 iteration steps of training. The pseudocolor-coding scheme is used to represent positive values as red, negative values as blue, and zero values as green. Note that the matrix is symmetrical since it is an autocorrelation between the input and output spike trains. Patterns of correlation begin to form at this training phase. Figure 6.5 shows the same connection matrix at 600 iteration steps. Correlated patterns are clearly emerging at this training cycle, particularly the positive. Finally, Figure 6.6 shows the same connection matrix after 700 iteration steps. Correlated patterns are clearly seen at this stage. Positive correlation values (red) at the diagonal suggest positive correlation of the input and output neurons, which is characteristic of autocorrelation because firing spikes are always correlated to themselves.

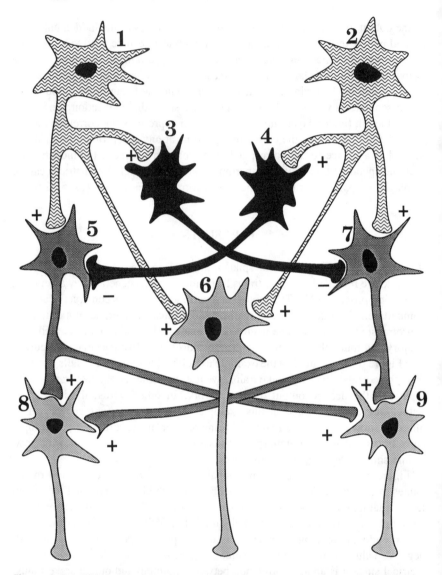

Figure 6.7. Diagrammatic representation of the nine-neurons biological neuronal network used to produce the spike trains for correlation analysis by the hybrid time-shifted artificial neural network. Neurons 1 and 2 are pacemaking neurons which drive the whole network. The positive signs indicate excitatory synaptic connections, and the negative signs indicate inhibitory synaptic connections.

The positively correlated off-diagonal points in the connection matrix show that neurons 3 and 6 are positively correlated. In other words, when neuron 3 fires, neuron 6 also fires simultaneously, whereas the rest of the neurons do not fire simultaneously. Similarly, simultaneous firing of neurons 8 and 9 is revealed from the correlation matrix of the connection matrix. Negative values (blue) for the other pairs of neurons indicate that they are negatively correlated. Zero values (green) for neurons 2 and 3 indicate that there is no correlation between the firing of neurons 2 and 3.

The correlation patterns revealed from the connection matrix of the time-shifted hybrid network clearly indicate the corresponding underlying biological network connectivity. Neurons 3 and 6 both receive inputs from the same pre-synaptic neuron 1; thus, they show positive correlation of firing between them (see Figure 6.7). Neuron 5 also receives input from neuron 1, but due to the inhibition by neuron 2, there is no associated correlation as in neurons 3 and 6. The positive correlation between neurons 8 and 9 reveals the functional connections that both neurons receive excitatory inputs from neurons 5 and 7.

7. CONCLUSION

A time-shifted, multilayer, hybrid-Hebbian neural network model is developed and shown to be capable of using the connection weights for pattern association. The patterns associated are temporal patterns of spike train recorded from neurons simultaneously. Applying the learning rules in this network, the set of correlations between pairs of spike trains can be displayed graphically as a layer of connection weights in a plane. Such a representation provides a condensed form of display showing the correlation between any pair of neurons. Any arbitrary number of neurons can be used for firing pattern recognition by sending each spike train from the neurons to the input and output channels of the neural network for processing.

After training, the firing pattern of correlation can be viewed by the positivity or negativity of the connection weights between the hidden layer and the output layer. The temporal relationship between the $k\Delta t$ time-shifted input and the output can be observed from the connection matrix between the kth hidden layer and the output layer. That is, the precise temporal firing relationship among the input and output neurons can be described by the given hidden layer. The correlational characteristics can easily be identified by inspection of the values of the correlation matrices at the hidden layer. Simulation results show that the temporal correlation characteristics among different neurons are clearly revealed by this neural network. Other types of nonneuronal time-series signals, such as speech signals, may also take advantage of the characteristics of this time-shifted neural network to reveal any temporally correlated patterns.

REFERENCES

[1]   D.H. Perkel, G.L. Gerstein, and G.P. Moore, "Neuronal Spike Trains and Stochastic Point Process, I, The Single Spike Train," *Biophysical Journal,* Vol. 7, 1967, pp. 391–418.

[2]   D.H. Perkel, G.L. Gerstein, and G.P. Moore, "Neuronal Spike Trains and Stochastic Point Process, II, Simultaneous Spike Trains," *Biophysical Journal,* Vol. 7, 1967, pp. 419–440.

[3]   G.L. Gerstein, D.H. Perkel, and J.E. Dayhoff, "Cooperative Firing Activity in Simultaneously Recorded Populations of Neurons: Detection and Measurement," *Journal of Neuroscience,* Vol. 5, 1985, pp. 881–889.

[4]   G.L. Gerstein and A. Aertsen, "Representation of Cooperative Firing Activity among Simultaneously Recorded Neurons," *Journal of Neurophysiology,* Vol. 54, 1985, pp. 1513–1528.

[5]   D.C. Tam, "Correlation of Cerebellar Purkinje Cell Activity with the Kinematics of a Voluntary Visually-Guided Closed-Loop Movement and Interactions among Purkinje Cells," Ph.D. Dissertation, University of Minnesota, Minneapolis, MN, University Microfilms International, Ann Arbor, 1987.

[6]   D.C. Tam, T.J. Ebner, and C.K. Knox, "Cross-Interval Histogram and Cross-Interspike Interval Histogram Correlation Analysis of Simultaneously Recorded Multiple Spike Train Data," *Journal of Neuroscience Methods,* Vol. 23, 1988, pp. 23–33.

[7]   D.C. Tam, C.K. Knox, and T.J. Ebner, "Cross-Interval Correlation of Firing Pattern of Simultaneously Recorded Neighboring Cerebellar Purkinje Cells," *Society for Neuroscience Abstract,* Vol. 11, 1985, p. 1035.

[8]   D.C. Tam and D.H. Perkel, "A Model for Temporal Correlation of Biological Neuronal Spike Trains," *Proceedings of the IEEE International Joint Conference on Neural Networks 1989,* Vol. 1, 1989, pp. 781–786.

[9]   G.W. Gross, "Simultaneous Single Unit Recording *in vitro* with a Photoetched, Laser Deinsulated Gold, Multimicroelectrode Surface," *IEEE Transactions on Biomedical Engineering,* Vol. 26, 1979, pp. 273–279.

[10] G.W. Gross and J.M. Kowalski, "Experimental and Theoretical Analysis of Random Nerve Cell Network Dynamics," *Neural Networks: Concepts, Applications, and Implementations,* Vol. 3, Prentice-Hall, Englewood Cliffs, NJ, 1991.

[11] G.W. Gross and J.H. Lucas, "Long-Term Monitoring of spontaneous Single Unit Activity from Neuronal Monolayer Networks Cultured on Photoetched Multielectrode Surfaces," *Journal of Electrophysiological Techniques,* Vol. 9, 1982, pp. 55–69.

[12] G.W. Gross, W. Wen, and J. Lin, "Transparent Indium-Tin Oxide Patterns for Extracellular Multisite Recording in Neuronal Cultures," *Journal of Neuroscience Methods,* Vol. 15, 1985, pp. 243–252.

[13] A. Grinvald, E. Lieke, R.D. Frostig, C.D. Gilbert, and T.N. Wiesel, "Functional Architecture of Cortex Revealed by Optical Imaging of Intrinsic Signals," *Nature,* Vol. 324, 1986, pp. 361–364.

[14] H.S. Orbach, L.B. Cohen, and A. Grinvald, "Optical Mapping of Electrical Activity in Rat Somatosensory and Visual Cortex," *Journal of Neuroscience,* Vol. 7, 1985, pp. 1886–1895.

[15] D.E. Goldman, "Potential, Impedance and Rectification in Membranes," *Journal of General Physiology*, Vol. 27, 1943, pp. 37–60.

[16] A.L. Hodgkin and B. Katz, "The Effect of Sodium Ions on the Electrical Activity of the Giant Axon of the Squid," *Journal of Physiology (London)*, Vol. 108, 1949, pp. 37–77.

[17] A.L. Hodgkin and A.F. Huxley, "Current Carried by Sodium and Potassium Ions through the Membrane of the Giant Axon of *Loligo*," *Journal of Physiology (London)*, Vol. 116, 1952, pp. 449–472.

[18] A.L. Hodgkin and A.F. Huxley, "The Components of Membrane Conductance in the Giant Axon of *Loligo*," *Journal of Physiology (London)*, Vol. 116, 1952, pp. 473–496.

[19] A.L. Hodgkin and A.F. Huxley, "The Dual Effect of Membrane Potential on Sodium Conductance in the Giant Axon of *Loligo*," *Journal of Physiology (London)*, Vol. 116, 1952, pp. 497–506.

[20] A.L. Hodgkin and A.F. Huxley, "Quantitative Description of Membrane Current and Its Application to Conduction and Excitation in Nerve," *Journal of Physiology (London)*, Vol. 117, 1952, pp. 500–544.

[21] A.L. Hodgkin, A.F. Huxley, and B. Katz, "Measurement of Current-Voltage Relations in the Membrane of the Giant Axon of *Loligo*," *Journal of Physiology (London)*, Vol. 116, 1952, pp. 424–428.

[22] D.O. Hebb, *The Organization of Behavior*, Wiley, New York, 1949.

[23] D.E. Rumelhart and J.L. McClelland, "Learning Internal Representations by Error Propagation," *Parallel Distributed Processing: Explorations in the Microstructure of Cognition. Volume I: Foundations*. MIT Press. Cambridge, MA, 1986, pp. 318–362.

[24] D.C. Tam and D.H. Perkel, "Quantitative Modeling of Synaptic Plasticity," R.D. Hawkins and G.H. Bower (eds.), *The Psychology of Learning and Motivation: Computational Models of Learning in Simple Neural Systems*, Academic, San Diego, CA, Vol. 23, 1989, pp. 1–30.

[25] W. Rall, "Core Conductor Theory and Cable Properties of Neurons," E.R. Kandel (eds.), *Handbook of Physiology, The Nervous System, Vol. 1*, Section 1, American Physiological Society, Bethesda, MD, 1977.

7

A Self-organized Neural System Extending Back Propagation to Acquire and Utilize a Knowledge Structure without a Teacher*

Bruce Y. Wu
Department of Electrical Engineering and Computer Science
EECS Building
University of Michigan
Ann Arbor

INTRODUCTION

One of the most extensively studied and applied neural network learning algorithms is one that is called "back propagation" [1–10]. This learning algorithm is applied in many problems. For instance, it has been used for the famous NETtalk project [9,10]. In that project, a multilayered neural net is trained using back propagation to "pronounce" the middle letter (i.e., output the correct phonemes) as English text is given as input. It is trained in the following fashion: during training, it is given as training input a window of seven letters wide and is moved over English text and an explicit teacher gives the correct phonemes (i.e., the correct classification) corresponding to that piece of text. This requires a teacher that is specific, omniscient, and omnipresent to tell specifically which classification/category the input belongs to and which specific part is wrong if there is an error.

Another project involves training a back propagation network to classify sonar targets. During training, the network is given the power spectral density of objects, and the corresponding objects classifications (i.e., the correct classifications) are explicitly given as the teacher [1]. In the research and applications cited above, a teacher is needed for the neural net to learn; it needs a teacher to tell specifically which classification the input belongs to and which specific part

*This research is partly supported by AT&T Foundation and AT&T Bell Lab while the author is a Bell Lab Scholar.

is wrong if there is an error, and the teacher is needed on every training instance. Therefore, the back propagation network requires a teacher which is explicit, omniscient, and omnipresent for it to learn. Learning without a teacher is important because a true learning agent (besides being taught explicitly) must be able to classify its environment without being given the correct classification for an input pattern. It should not always require explicit teaching by input-output correlations but should be able to self-organize when presented with input patterns.

There are several other shortcomings. But before we can point out in more detail the problems and issues related to it, we will first briefly review back propagation. Then we will examine a method that will help alleviate some of the problems, all within the same system. In addition, we will examine some simulation results. Finally, some concluding remarks are given.

2. BACK PROPAGATION

2.1. Brief Review

The following is a brief review of the back propagation learning algorithm and the associated network.

Neural networks consist of interconnected units with modifiable interconnection weights. The neural network under consideration is a layered feedforward network which consists of a bottom layer of input units, a top layer of output units, and one or several layers of hidden units in between (see Figure 7.1). In such a feedforward network, every unit receives its input from lower layers than its own and sends its output to higher layers than its own. When an input pattern is presented, the output pattern is calculated by passing the computed activity from the lower layer to the next higher layer and successively computing the activity of each layer higher up until the output layer is reached.

For training the network, input vectors along with its corresponding target output vectors (i.e., given by the teacher) are presented to the network. An error measure on input/output is defined to be:

$$E_v = 1/2 \times \sum_j (t_{vj} - o_{vj})^2 \qquad (2.1)$$

and an overall measure of the error is:

$$E = \Sigma E_v \qquad (2.2)$$

where t_{vj} is the jth component of the TARGET OUTPUT vector for training vector v, o_{vj} is the jth element of the ACTUAL OUTPUT vector produced by the presentation of input vector v. During training, the weights are successively modified in order to reduce the error E.

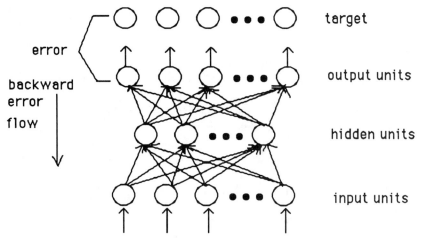

Figure 7.1.   A feedforward multilayered neural net using back propagation. (See text for detail.)

Specifically, applying back propagation involves a forward pass and a backward pass. In the forward pass, the actual output for each unit is computed from the input units by propagating activities from the bottom layer to the output layer. For each output unit, an error signal is computed by comparing the actual output with the target output. During the backward pass through the network, the error signal is passed to each unit in successively lower layers and the appropriate weight changes are made in order to decrease the error. After training and if successful, the network has an internal representation that encoded the training vector coming into the input units. The network then uses that internal representation to generate the output vector. In short, after a successful training, the network has an internal representation that generates an appropriate output vector from the corresponding input vector. (For further detail, see [7,8]).

2.2. Problems and Issues

After briefly reviewing back propagation, we now discuss the problems and issues related to it. For instance, in the research and applications such as the NETtalk project and sonar targets classification task cited in the introduction, the back propagation network requires a teacher which is explicit, omniscient, and omnipresent for it to learn; it needs a teacher to tell specifically which classification the input belongs to and which specific part is wrong if there is an error, and the teacher is needed on every training instance. Learning without a teacher is important because a true learning agent (besides being taught explicitly) must be able to classify its environment without being given the correct classification for an input pattern. It should not always require explicit teaching by input-output correlations but should be able to self-organize when presented with input patterns.

There are several other shortcomings. In the research and applications cited, besides merely performing the classification/categorization task, the same system does not make additional use and reasoning based on the knowledge it learned from the classification/categorization task. A truly intelligent agent would utilize its knowledge learned from one task to try to maximize its usage of that knowledge on other tasks when it is appropriate. Furthermore, two or more classifications/categorizations cannot be actively present at the same time so that relationships between them cannot be easily made and manipulatable. Forming relationships between classifications/categorizations might be one of the factors that is important to the formation of higher-level and larger knowledge structure, which is one of the many factors vital to the capability of neural networks to model higher-level cognitive processes and behaviors. At present, neural networks are inadequate at those tasks.

3. METHOD

Now that we have discussed some of the problems and issues related to the standard back propagation, we will examine a method extending back propagation that will help alleviate some of the problems, all within the same system. The method described below is just one way and is by no means the only way of alleviating those problems that are mentioned; there might be other ways of approaching those problems.

Since it is necessary to explain in detail, the method will be explained part by part. However, the design of one part is made in consideration of the other parts and the entire system rather than merely the part being discussed. A related point is that part of the small contribution of this chapter is perhaps not how each specific part solves a problem but how everything fit together to alleviate those problems within the same system.

3.1. Description of Method

We first describe the nature of the input and the type of neural net being used. The input could be the same input patterns that would normally be used to train a standard feedforward neural net using back propagation. But in the method described, there is no need for the teacher (i.e., the explicit target class/category is not given). Also, we take it that there may be many variants that belong to the same class/category. We use an architecture with one narrow middle layer (i.e., number of nodes in the one middle layer is fewer than the number of input nodes). More specifically, let M = the number of units in the input layer and let N = the number of units in the hidden layer. In the architecture that is being used, $N < M$. The architecture was shown in Figure 7.1. This hereafter is referred to as a subnetwork.

As described below, the resulting network is a collection of such subnetworks competing to: identify the novel input, recruit new subnetworks, form links between them, and change weights within each subnetwork as well as changing

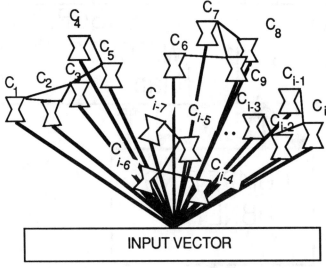

INPUT VECTOR

$\bowtie$ = SUBNETWORK

Figure 7.2. Conceptual view of the entire network. Each block is a subnetwork connected to the input vector. After being trained, each subnetwork represents a category. The lines shown between the subnetworks represent intersubnetwork weights. The intersubnetwork weights represent the relatedness between the different categories in the knowledge structure. This figure thus shows the competing subnetworks with the connection weights between the subnetworks.

weights between the subnetworks. The network is able to use its learned knowledge and its knowledge structure to reason in various ways. This is all done without an explicit and ever-present teacher. In the present system, the network modifies its own weights as well as the topology of the network as it learns.

Conceptually, the entire network can be viewed as in Figure 7.2.

The entire system can also be viewed as in Figure 7.3.

The details of each unit and the mechanisms are explained below.

3.1.1. Construction of knowledge structure

For each subnetwork, since there is no teacher, there is no target vector telling it which class/category the input should be. For each subnetwork, instead of having the target vector given by the teacher as in the standard back propagation, we use the input vector to be the target vector.[1] When a novel input is presented

---

[1]Autoassociativity has also been used elsewhere although not used in the same context as is used in this neural system. The emphasis of this chapter is not how each specific part solves a problem but how the various pieces of the resulting system fit together to alleviate those problems all within the same system. The emphasis is on integration.

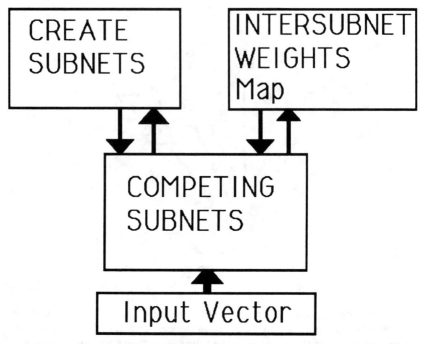

Figure 7.3. Diagram showing the competing subnetworks with intersubnetwork weights that can be formed and changed. Furthermore, additional subnetworks can be added to the set of competing subnetworks when a new category is encountered.

to the system, each subnetwork given the novel input generates it own output on the output nodes. Each subnetwork determines how closely the vector pattern generated on the output layer is related to the original input vector. This is done by computing:

$$E_v = 1/2 \times \sum_j (t_{vj} - o_{vj})^2 \tag{2.3}$$

where t_{vj} is now the input serving as the target input and o_{vj} is the vector generated by each subnetwork on presenting the input vector v. Thus, E_v is a measure of how closely the current input instance is related to the internal representation of each class/category belonging to each subnetwork.

Each subnetwork competes to classify the input into its own class/category and learns from it. The competition is based on the E_v's. Whichever subnetwork's class/category is most closely related to the current input instance and thus has the smallest error wins and classifies the input into its own class/category. More specifically, let $C_1, C_2, C_3, \ldots C_i$ be the subnetworks where i is the current total number of subnetworks in the entire network. Let E_{jv} be the error

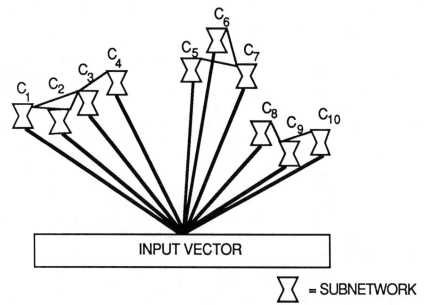

Figure 7.4. A particular network with 10 competing subnetworks C_1, C_2, C_3, ... C_{10}.

measure that belongs to the subnetwork C_j where $j = 1$ to i. If $E_{mv} = \min[E_{1v}$, E_{2v}, ... $E_{iv}]$, then C_m is the winning subnetwork. The winning subnetwork is allowed to learn and have a better internal representation of its class/category by incorporating the new instance or variant of the class/category through changing its weights within the subnetwork. The changing of weights within the subnetwork is performed using the standard back propagation (but without the teacher). That is, if the subnetwork wins and still has some error (i.e., its $E_v \neq 0$), use the back propagation algorithm to adjust the weight to reduce the error (i.e., to take the variant into account in its internal representation by changing its weights and thus have a better representation of its variants within its concept). Note that only the subnetwork that wins is allowed to learn and change its weights within its subnetwork. The weights within all other nonwinning subnetworks remain the same as they were.

For example, suppose there are competing subnetworks C_1, C_2, C_3, ... C_{10} (see Figure 7.4). If E_{5v} of C_5 is the smallest error, then C_5 is the winning subnetwork. If the subnetwork C_5 still has some error (i.e., its $E_5 v \neq 0$), use the back propagation algorithm to adjust the weight to reduce the error (i.e., to take the variant into account in its internal representation by changing its weights and thus have a better representation of its variants within its concept). The weights within all other subnetworks (C_1, C_2, C_3, C_4, C_6, C_7, C_8, C_9, C_{10}) remain the same as they were.

Moreover, if all competing classes/categories have errors so great such that it is larger than an error criterion ϵ determined by the agent and the environment, indicating that the new instance is unlikely to be an instance of any of the known class/category, a new class/category is needed to incorporate the knowledge. This is done by recruiting a subnetwork from a pool of subnetworks into the existing network[2] and let that new subnetwork learn using the back propagation algorithm without the target class/category. Specifically, for the new subnetwork, run the new input through the new subnetwork, compute the error using the input as the target vector, and adjust the weight to reduce the error so that the new instance is incorporated into the new subnetwork.

For example, from the previous example, if none of E_{1v}, E_{2v} . . . E_{10v} corresponding to the subnetworks C_1, C_2, C_3, . . . C_{10} is less than the error criterion, then another subnetwork C_{11} is added to the network. Furthermore, for the new subnetwork C_{11}, run the new input through the new subnetwork, compute the error E_{11v} using the input as the target vector, and adjust the weight to reduce the error so that the new instance is incorporated into the new subnetwork C_{11}.

So now we have a method to learn the classes/categories without the teacher. We now have a network of subnetworks and each subnetwork for a class/category has an internal representation of that class/category and also accounts for the different variants within that class/category.

In addition to the above, we can also relate the different classes/categories so that there is a structure from which one can do some additional reasoning using the knowledge obtained from the classification/categorization task. The structure might serve as a small basis for a larger knowledge structure.

The different classes/categories embodied by different subnetworks can be related to each other while the system is performing its classification task described in the previous part. Specifically, this is done by the following:

- **increment the weight between the winning subnetwork and the next closest during the competition**

and

- **decrement the weight between the winning subnetwork and a subnetwork that has the most error and that already has connection to the winning subnetwork.**

This is done so that the classes/categories that are related are connected by a larger weight and the classes/categories that are less related are connected by a smaller weight and the classes/categories that are not related at all are not connected.

The specifics of how much the intersubnetwork weight changes is as follows:

---

[2]The Nestor system also adds new units to its architecture.

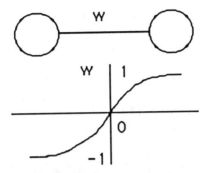

Figure 7.5. A modified sigmoid function is used for intersubnetwork WEIGHT changes. The subnetworks are pictured as circles above. W is the intersubnetwork weight. Note that the function is not the usual sigmoid function and it is not used for the activation function as in a typical neural net. (See text for detail.)

The values of the intersubnetwork weights follow the modified sigmoid function below and is also shown in Figure 7.5:

$$W = f(x) = 2/(1 + e^{-(x)})-1 \tag{3.1}$$

It is useful to derive an equation relating the old weight and the new weight after it is either incremented or decremented.

Let W_{old} = the old weight; this is the weight before weight change
X_{old} = the x value that corresponds to W_{old} in the modified sigmoid function; On the modified sigmoid function curve, this is the position on the horizontal axis that corresponds to W_{old}
X_{new} = a new position on the horizontal axis obtained by $x_{new} = x_{old} + \beta$ where β is a constant.
W_{new} = the new weight; this is the weight after weight change. This new weight corresponds to X_{new}

An equation relating the old weight W_{old} and the new weight W_{new} is obtained by the following:
From Equation (3.1),

$$W_{old} = f(x_{old}) = [2/(1 + e^{-(x_{old})})]-1 \tag{3.2}$$

solving Equation (3.2) for x_{old} corresponding to W_{old} yields the following equation:

$$x_{old} = -\ln \{]2/(W_{old} + 1)]-1\} \tag{3.3}$$

From Equation (3.1),

$$W_{new} = f(x_{new}) = [2/(1 + e^{-(x_{new})})] - 1 \qquad (3.4)$$

Since $x_{new} = x_{old} + \beta$, combining this with Equation (3.4) yields the following:

$$W_{new} = f(x_{new}) = [2/(1 + e^{-(x_{old} + \beta)})] - 1 \qquad (3.5)$$

Substituting X_{old} from Equation (3.3) into Equation (3.5) and manipulating the resulting equation algebraically yields the desired equation as follows:

$$W_{new} = \frac{2}{1 + [(1 - W_{old})/(1 + W_{old})]e^{-\beta}} - 1 \qquad (3.6)$$

To increase the intersubnetwork weight W, use a positive fraction for β in Equation (3.6); to decrease weight W, use a negative fraction for β. For example, to increase weight W, use $+0.1$ for β; to decrease weight W, use -0.1 for β. The initial weight W between any two subnetworks is 0. Given W_{old} and the appropriate β value, the new intersubnetwork weight W_{new} can be determined from Equation (3.6).

Note that the w_{old} following the curve could not have become -1 exactly, and also for a different reason stated later, the negative weights would not be allowed beyond a certain limit, so that the w_{old} would never get anywhere near -1. Thus, there would not be any divide-by-zero problem in the term $(1 - W_{old})/(1 + W_{old})$ in Equation (3.6).

Although $|\beta|$ is constant, the weight change itself is not the same every time. This is because of what impact the additional piece of evidence of relatedness has on the already existing evidence. For example, let's take what happens at both extremes. We note a nice property at both extremes. That is, the one additional piece of evidence of relatedness between classes/categories is only a small fraction if there is already a huge amount of evidence. Hence, the impact that the additional piece of evidence is not as great as it is near the middle of the curve. Hence, the weight change is not as great as it is near the middle of the curve. The property at the end is also good for preventing the explosion of weights which sometimes occurs in neural nets using the usual Hebb rule [11] if not properly formulated.

If the weight between two connected subnetworks becomes too low (say, below a limit T_c, e.g., -0.7), indicating that they are not very closely related, there is no need to keep the link between the two subnetworks.

So now we have related classes/categories that are grouped together nonrelated classes/categories apart. In addition, the classes/categories that are more related are connected by a larger weight and the classes/categories that are less related are connected by a smaller weight and the classes/categories that are not related at all are not connected. As mentioned before, in the typical neural net using back propagation, two or more classes/categories cannot be actively present at the same time so that relationships between them cannot be easily made and manipulatable. Forming relationships between classes/categories might be one of the factors that is important to the formation of higher-level and larger knowledge structure which is one of the many factors vital to the capability of neural networks to model higher-level cognitive processes and behavior; at present, neural networks are inadequate at those tasks.

In the present network, many classes/categories can be actively present at the same time and allow relationships between them to be formed easier than in the usual neural net using back propagation. Though not very sophisticated, we now have a larger structure from which one can do additional reasoning (in addition to the initial classification task). This is described later. In addition, the class/category is manipulatable and is conducive to building larger structures. Though it is not very sophisticated, perhaps it is the most one can easily obtain from input only (without other information and without a teacher). Note that higher-level structures in many systems are usually handcrafted. Though not sophisticated, the structure is one small step toward, and serves as a small basis for, larger and/or higher level structures.

3.1.2 Usage of knowledge structure

Besides being able to learn the classification without the teacher and use the subsequent knowledge to classify novel input, it can perform other reasoning using the knowledge and knowledge structure learned from the classification task. This is possible partly because there is a structure created as described previously. This is also partly because concepts can be related and two or more concepts can be actively present at the same time.

The various ways of using the knowledge structure is discussed in this section. The simulation results are described in the next section.

There are many ways that one can use the knowledge that is learned from the classification task and from the associated structure that is created. I will only mention some of them. For instance, one can find out what classes/categorizations are related to a particular class/category, c for example. This can be done by activating all the classes/categories that are directly or indirectly connected to c. Note that only the connected classes/categories with positive weights will be activated. How much the class/category c is related to the activated classes/categories is proportional to the product of the weights where the weights are positive and are along the shortest path connecting the classes/categories. Specifically, "Relatedness" $R_{cd} = k \, \Pi w_i$ where w_i's are such that $1 \geq w_i > 0$ and are along the shortest path connecting the two subnetworks c and d where k is a proportionality constant which can be taken as 1. For example, taking the simplest case, the classes/categories that are directly connected to our class/category c is merely the "relatedness weight" as we have noted in the previous section. Note that the farther away the class/category is from c, the lower the R would be. There are other ways that one can use the knowledge learned from the classification task and its associated created structure. For example, one can see if two classes/categories are related and how much. This can be done by taking one of the classes/categories and activating all its related nodes and see if there is activation coming into the other class/category. If so, they are related; if not, they are not related. In addition, one can know how much they are related. Again, how much those two classes/categories are related is proportional to the product of the weights that are along the shortest path connecting them. One can conceivably do more things with it. For example, one can regulate the activation from a class/category c by a weight parameter $p1$ and a distance parameter $p2$ such that a class is activated from a class to another class only when the weight between those two classes is above a certain weight $p1$ and that the distance from the class/category c to that class must be less than or equal to a certain distance $p2$. (Distance is the least number of weight connections from c to a particular class.)

Furthermore, the classes/categories that are activated can be thought of as belonging to a group such that the group itself can be a class/category. In other words, that group consists of those classes/categories that are activated and thus are related to each other within that same group (i.e., that group is a certain class/category that contains those activated classes/categories as its constituent members). Thus, the resulting pattern can be thought of as a distributed representation of that superclass. Depending on the parameters involved, a larger and larger pattern of activation can be thought of as moving to a larger and more general class that is represented by that particular pattern. The pattern can be thought of as a code for that more general class. Furthermore, if, for instance, there are two general classes, the amount of overlap of the two patterns would be a measure of the relatedness or similarity between those two general classes.

Thus, besides the classification task, one can make use of the knowledge learned from the classification task and from the associated structure that is created.

In addition, besides classifying the input, the subnetworks can also reconstruct the missing features if the input is partially damaged or incomplete. Since each subnetwork has its internal representation of its category and accounts for the variants in each category, given an incomplete vector pattern on its input, the subnetwork that classifies it as its own category would be able to provide the output vectors with its most probable features. Again, this categorization is based on competition between the subnetworks. As before, whichever has the least error wins. But since there are missing features, only the initially available features is compared to the corresponding features generated from the competing networks to compute the error measure E_v. That is,

$$E_v = \frac{1}{2} \times \mathrm{E}\ (t_{vj} - o_v)^2 \tag{3.7}$$

summed over j where js are the jth components corresponding to initially available features. The subnetwork with the least error is chosen providing the category as well as the microfeatures that are missing. Whereas in the standard back propagation, only the category is given but without the reconstruction of the missing features, the present network classifies it and reconstructs the missing features of the input vector for an object.

3.2. Simulation Results

This section describes some simulation results. The domain of experimentation for the neural system was category learning and construction of knowledge structure with semantic distance (i.e., how closely each concept is related to each other). Inputs were characteristics for dogs, cats, squirrels, flowers, houseplants, trees, cars, trucks, and buses. The emphasis was to learn these categories and form a knowledge structure with semantic distance and perform all the reasoning and other capabilities of the system. While many neural nets such as the ones based on standard back propagation often merely emphasize initial classification, and do not construct higher-level knowledge structure and do not perform further reasoning using that structure, the emphasis of the neural system described was more on the self-construction of a knowledge structure and the utilization of that knowledge structure. The simulation was performed to show that an artificial system can learn, construct, and utilize such a knowledge structure without a teacher; the emphasis was less on performance than on its ability to construct and utilize such a knowledge structure without a teacher.

The network architecture and learning algorithms used were the ones described in the previous sections. For each subnetwork, 12 input units were used. In addition, 12 outputs units and eight hidden units were used for each subnetwork. The classification task involved nine categories. The network was trained on a set of 700 objects form the categories and tested on another set of 400 objects. The resulting network had nine subnetworks.

The nine categories were *dog, cat, squirrel, flower, houseplant, tree, car, truck,* and *bus.* Inputs were 12 features, such as the shape of the head for animals, shape of body, size, whether the object is alive, and other characteristics, for *dog, cat, squirrel, flower, houseplant, tree, car, truck,* and *bus.* Some examples of the input vectors are in Table 7.1.

The network was trained on a set of 700 objects from the categories and tested on another set of 400 objects. The error criterion ϵ for creating a new category was 0.18. When a new subnetwork was added to the existing network, the instance that caused the addition of that new subnetwork was run repeatedly through the new subnetwork until the new subnetwork's E_v on that instance is less than one half of the error criterion E (i.e., $E_v < \epsilon/2$).

After 50 epochs, the training was stopped. During the testing phase, the number of input vectors correctly classified was recorded. No weights were modified during the testing phase. The network achieved a 92% accuracy on new objects from the test set.

In addition, the intersubnetwork weights were: cat-dog, 0.9; cat-squirrel, 0.9;

Table 7.1.   Examples of input vectors.

Position in Input Vector:	1	2	3	4	5	6	7	8	9	10	11	12
squirrel	.9	.1	.75	.9	0	0	0	0	0	0	0	0
car	0	0	0	0	0	.1	0	.1	0	0	.9	.95
house plant	0	0	.1	0	.95	0	.95	0	0	.75	0	0
bus	0	0	0	.1	0	.9	0	0	.1	0	.75	.9
dog	.9	0	0	.1	0	0	0	.8	0	.1	0	0
tree	0	.85	0	0	.9	0	.7	0	0	0	.1	0
squirrel	.95	0	.8	.85	0	0	0	0	0	0	0	0
truck	0	0	0	0	0	.65	0	0	.9	.1	0	.9
cat	.99	0	.85	.1	0	.1	0	.7	0	0	0	0
car	0	0	0	.1	0	0	0	0	.1	0	.95	.99
dog	.99	0	.1	0	0	0	0	.9	0	0	0	0
flower	0	0	0	0	.99	0	0	0	0	.95	0	0
cat	.9	0	.9	0	0	0	0	.75	0	0	0	0
house plant	0	0	0	0	.95	0	.9	0	0	.8	0	0
bus	0	0	0	0	0	.95	0	0	0	0	.8	.95
tree	0	.95	0	0	.90	0	.65	0	0	0	0	0
squirrel	.9	0	.7	.95	0	0	0	0	0	0	.1	0
flower	0	0	0	0	.95	.1	0	0	0	.9	0	0
truck	0	0	0	0	0	.75	.1	0	.85	0	0	.9
cat	.9	0	.8	0	0	0	.1	.6	0	0	0	0
bus	0	0	0	0	0	.85	.1	0	0	0	.7	.9
tree	0	.9	0	0	.99	.1	.75	0	0	0	0	0
car	0	0	0	0	0	0	0	0	0	0	.85	.9
flower	0	.1	.1	0	.9	0	0	0	0	.85	0	0
dog	.9	.1	0	0	0	0	0	.85	0	0	.1	0
truck	0	0	0	0	0	.7	0	0	.8	0	0	.99
house plant	0	0	0	0	.9	0	.8	.1	0	.85	0	0

flower-houseplant, 0.9; houseplant-tree, 0.9; car-bus, 0.9; and bus-truck, 0.9. Other intersubnetwork weights were negligible.

Related reasoning on this structure was performed. For example, the network was to find out what categories were related to a particular category. For example, when the particular category was chosen to be *dog,* it was found that the categories *cat* and *squirrel* were related to it. The *Relatedness* values were: $R_{\text{dog-cat}} = 0.9$ and $R_{\text{dog-sqirrel}} = 0.81$ where $R_{c\text{-}d}$ represents the relatedness between categories c and d. Similarly, when the particular category was chosen to be *flower,* the network returned *houseplant* and *tree* with $R_{\text{flower-houseplant}} = 0.9$ and $R_{\text{flower-tree}} = 0.81$.

To see if two arbitrary categories were related and how much they are related, the following was performed. For example, the category pair *cat* and *bus* was tested. The category *cat* was first chosen and its connections were activated and after 15 steps of activation (with each step of activation going through one intercategory weight), the concept *car* is still not activated to a significant level. In this particular experiment, *cat* and *bus* has no relationship and $R_{\text{cat-bus}}$ is 0.

The network was also able to find the most related class given a specified class. Given that the category *dog* was identified, the network returned the concept *cat* as the most related from all the concepts that is in the network. Given that the category *flower* was identified, *houseplant* was given as the most closely related in this particular experiment. Moreover, given that *car* was identified, the network returned *bus* as the most related category.

Dog, cat, and *squirrel,* were grouped together by their intersubnetwork weights as they should be since they were all animals. *Flower, houseplant,* and *tree* were grouped together since they were all vegetation. *Car, truck,* and *bus* were grouped together since they were all nonliving vehicles.

It was mentioned in the previous section that the categories that are activated can be thought of as belonging to a group such that the group itself can be a category. In other words, that group consists of those categories that are activated and thus are related to each other within that same group (i.e., that group is a certain category that contains those activated categories as its constituent members). Thus, the resulting pattern can be thought of as a distributed representation of that superclass. Furthermore, as also discussed in the previous section, one can regulate the activation from a category c, for example, by a weight parameter $p1$ and a distance parameter $p2$ such that a class is activated from one class to another class only when the weight between those two classes is above a certain weight $p1$ and that the distance from the class c to that class must be less than or equal to a certain distance $p2$. (Distance is the least number of weight connections from c to a particular class.)

In this part of the simulation, $p1 = 0.3$ and $p2 = 15$. Given *dog,* it activated *cat* and *squirrel* since they were grouped together. This group consisted of those categories (i.e., *cat, dog,* and *squirrel*). This group was the *animals.* Thus, the resulting pattern of activation can be thought of as a distributed representation of the superclass *animal.* The group for *car, bus,* and *truck* was also activated. The resulting pattern of activation can be thought of as a distributed representation of the superclass of *nonliving vehicles.* Since there was no overlap of the two patterns of these two groups, the measure of relatedness R between these two superclasses was 0.

Experiment concerning reproduction of missing features was also performed. For example, in this particular experiment, one of the input features was deleted. When the category was correctly classified, the reproduced missing input feature came on the average to about 0.2 of the typical value of the missing feature of that category.

4. CONCLUDING REMARKS

Therefore, in this chapter, we have first reviewed backpropagation and pointed out the problems and issues related to it. Then, we examined a method that helped to alleviate those problems, all within the same system. That is, the system that was described in this chapter extends backpropagation to learn classification without a teacher, forms a basis for larger knowledge structures and makes additional reasoning using knowledge learned from the classification and from its associated structure that is self-organize. In addition, we examined some simulation results. While many neural nets such as the ones based on standard back propagation often merely emphasize initial classification, and do not construct higher-level knowledge structure and do not perform further reasoning using that structure, the emphasis of the neural system described was more on the self-construction of a knowledge structure and the utilization of that knowledge structure. The simulation was performed to show that an artificial system can learn, construct, and utilize such a knowledge structure without a teacher; the emphasis was less on performance than on its ability to construct and utilize such a knowledge structure without a teacher. Although the system was explained part by part, the emphasis of this chapter was perhaps not how each specific part solves a problem, but how the various pieces of the resulting system fit together to alleviate those problems all within the same system. The emphasis was on integration.

REFERENCES

[1]   R.P. Gorman and T.J. Sejnowski, "Analysis of Hidden Units in a Layered Network Trained to Classify Sonar Targets," *Neural Networks*, Vol. 1, 1988, pp. 75–89.

[2]   Y. Le Cun, "Une Procedure D'apprentissage Pour Reseau a Seuil Assymetrique (A Learning Procedure for Assymetric Threshold Network)," *Proceedings of Cognitiva*, Paris, Vol. 85, June 1985, pp. 599–604.

[3]   Y. Le Cun, "Learning Processes in an Asymmetric Threshold Network," E. Bienenstock, F. Fogelman Souli, and G. Weisbuch (Eds.), *Disordered Systems and Biological Organization*, Springer, Berlin, 1986.

[4]   Y. Le Cun, *Modèles Connexionnistes de L'apprentissage* [Connectionist Models of Learning]. Ph.D. Thesis, University of Paris, 1987.

[5]   D.B. Parker, "Learning Logic," Invention Report, 581-64, File 1, Office of Technology Licensing, Stanford University, 1982.

[6]   D.B. Parker, "Learning Logic," TR-47, Center for Computational Research in Economics and Management Science, MIT, Cambridge, MA, 1985.

[7]   D. Rumelhart, G. Hinton, and R. Williams, "Learning Internal Representations by Back-Propagating Errors," *Nature*, Vol. 323, 1986, pp. 533–536.

[8]   D.E. Rumelhart, G.E. Hinton, and R.J. Williams, "Learning Internal Representations by Error Propagation," D. Rumelhart and J. McClelland (Eds.), *Parallel Distributed Processing: Explorations in the Microstructure of Cognition*, Vol. I: Foundations, MIT Press, Cambridge, MA, 1986.

[9]   T.J. Sejnowski, and C.R. Rosenberg, "NETtalk: a Parallel Network that Learns to Read Aloud," Technical Report No. JHU/EECS-86/01, Department of Electrical Engineering and Computer Science, John Hopkins University, Baltimore, 1986.

[10]   T.J. Sejnowski, and C.R. Rosenberg, "Parallel Networks that Learn to Pronounce English Text," *Complex Systems*, Vol. 1, 1987, pp. 145–168.

[11]   D.O. Hebb, *The Organization of Behavior*, Wiley, New York, 1949.

8

Analysis and Synthesis of Artificial Neural Networks for Modeling Complex Systems

Jun Wang
Department of Industrial Technology
Starcher Hall
University of North Dakota
Grand Forks, North Dakota

B. Malakooti
Department of Systems Engineering
Crawford Hall
Case Western Reserve University
Cleveland, Ohio

1. INTRODUCTION

The human brain possesses a bewildering capability of information processing and can resolve many complex problems which modern computers cannot. Based on our present understanding of brains, it is postulated that a model or a system, with a structure analogous to biological neural networks could exhibit similar intelligent behavior [1].

Advocated by a school of researchers called connectionists, artificial neural networks (ANNs), also known as connectionist models or parallel distributed processing (PDP) models are gaining more and more popularity in recent years. An artificial neural network is a (nonlinear) network consisting of a number of interconnected artificial neurons (processing units or computational elements). Each processing unit performs a simple transformation. The strength of interaction among these processing units is reflected by the weights on connections which determine the functional behavior of an artificial neural network. Processing in such an artificial neural network operates concurrently in a parallel distributed manner, whereas learning in the artificial neural networks commonly occurs by incrementally adjusting its parameters to refine the representation.

Artificial neural networks as complex problem solvers have been investigated extensively by the researchers from a variety of disciplines. The formal study of neurally inspired learning systems began with the seminal work of McCulloch and Pitts [2]. Stimulated by results of biological experiments and observations, McCulloch and Pitts looked upon information-processing machines as a means for modeling the brain. Consequently, their machines were built of large numbers of binary artificial neurons. One of the well-known pioneering learning systems is the Perceptron developed by Rosenblatt [3]. Essentially, a Perceptron is a single-layer adaptive feedforward network of threshold units. Another important learning machine of the early time is the Adaline [4] which is a one-layer linear network using the delta learning rule to adjust its internal parameters. The limitation of the Perceptron and Adaline are that they could converge only for problems with linearly separable patterns in feature space because, among others, they lacked an internal representation of the stimuli. After Minsky and Papert's pessimistic evaluation [5], the research of artificial neural networks diminished for a while. In recent years, there has been an exciting resurgence in the study of artificial neural networks caused by the introduction of new net topologies, new node characteristics, and new learning algorithms as well as the progresses in neuroscience, cognitive science, and biology, etc. For example, Grossberg [6] and Carpenter and Grossberg [7] developed Adaptive Resonance Theory (ART) as unsupervised learning systems for clustering. Kohonen [8] presented a neuron-like system which could reconstruct the ordering of input patterns in outputs. A stochastic learning model called the Boltzmann Machine designed by Hinton and Sejnowski [9] is a parallel implement of the simulated annealing procedure on the analogy of statistical thermodynamics. Neural models of binary and continuous activation states were proposed by Hopfield as associative memory [10,11] and by Hopfield and Tank to solve optimization problems such as the traveling salesman problem [12]. A multilayer perceptron (MLP) with an error backward propagation learning rule proposed by Rumelhart, Hinton, and Williams [13] is one of the most popular artificial neural network models. An MLP is a semilinear feedforward multilayer network. Such neural nets possess the capability of learning from examples by parameter adjustment. When trained by presenting a set of input-output pairs, the MLP adjusts the weights or strengths of their internal interconnection and their activation threshold values to accommodate the training input-output pairs and implement the underlying mapping. Rather than using threshold logic units or linear function for activation, the MLP uses differentiable sigmoid activation function to facilitate credit (blame) assignment. The information flow is fed forward in parallel from the input to the output layer, while the errors of actual output compared to desired output propagate backward, and a set of plausible weights and thresholds is obtained based on a least square error criterion in a gradient descent manner. After a number of epochs provided that the training instances are good representatives, the artificial neural network can then "discover" a mapping mechanism from the input space to the output space even if the mapping is unknown to the human user (trainer) explicitly. It has been proven that the MLP is able to approximate any continuous function [14,15]. It has also been discovered that the mapping thus learned is often very robust, and represents generalizations of examples available in the learning process.

Because of their appealing and promising characteristics in functionality and computational power, artificial neural networks have manifested significant application potential, and been proposed and applied to numerous areas. For example, as pattern classifiers, they can approximately discriminate complicated decision regions generalized from a limited number of training instances; as parallel processors, they can realize the solution procedures for a large class of combinatorics problems; as associative memories, they can store an amount of information such that the information may be retrieved with partial or distorted cues.

Although great advances have been made in the recent year, the theory and methodology of artificial neural networks are far from complete. Many interesting and challenging problems await exploration. For example, how to configure network architecture to represent a set of given training samples accurately and how to design learning algorithms to ensure fast convergence and avoid local minima is still unsolved theoretically.

This chapter is an attempt to provide formal theory and methodology for analysis and synthesis of artificial neural networks. Specifically, our primary interest is in the role of artificial neural networks for modeling complex systems. Starting with formulating the modeling processes and defining general concepts, we formalize, categorize, and characterize artificial neural networks from a systems-theoretic point of view. By introducing the general structural topologies, this chapter focuses on the analysis aspect of artificial neural networks to analyze the fundamental properties such as trainability and representability; on the synthesis aspect of artificial neural networks to derive design principles for the system modeling; on the algorithm aspect of the artificial neural networks to develop an effective and efficient learning paradigm; and on the application aspect of artificial neural networks to demonstrate the applicability of the developed theory and methodology. This chapter consists of seven sections. Section 2 formulates the complex system modeling problem in the scenario of the connectionist approach; Section 3 formalizes the concepts of artificial neural networks by introducing a set of definitions and remarks; Section 4 characterizes artificial neural networks with analysis of trainability and representability; Section 5 addresses design principles of synthesizing architectures and learning rules of artificial neural networks based on the analysis; Section 6 discusses some illustrative examples and the results of numerical simulations; finally, Section 7 is the conclusion.

2. FORMULATION OF MODELING PROBLEM

A mathematical model is an abstract representation of a system which can be formalized at set-theoretic level [16];

$$M \subset \mathbf{X} \times \mathbf{Y} \tag{2.1}$$

where M stands for the system model; $\mathbf{X} = \mathbf{X}_1 \times \mathbf{X}_2 \times \ldots \times \mathbf{X}_n$, a set of feasible input variables (stimuli); $\mathbf{Y} = \mathbf{Y}_1 \times \mathbf{Y}_2 \times \ldots \mathbf{Y}_m$, a set of possible output variables (responses). The system modeling problem can be interpreted as deriving or inferring an appropriate representation based on available knowledge and information about the system under study.

The system modeling encompasses the whole spectrum of human intelligent endeavors. At one end of the spectrum, lies the analytical approach. The analytical approach resorts to the formal methods (e.g., mathematical analysis and dimensional analysis) in deriving a system model based on existing knowledge (e.g., physical laws and chemical principles). Among the formal methods of modeling complex systems, the decomposition methods and aggregation methods appear to be the most popular. The former attempts to decompose a large system into many smaller subsystems and coordinate the solution to the original problem. In the latter method, variables of the original system are aggregated or coalesced to reduce the dimensionality of the problem [17]. At another end of the spectrum is the empirical approach. Statistical methods are a good example of the empirical approach. In statistical work, one collects data and uses techniques such as regression analysis, analysis of variance, and correlation analysis to model a system. The well-known Taylor equation for tool life estimation is a typical example of empirical models. As the complexity of a system increases, analytical approach, developed for organized simplicity, becomes impractical, whereas empirical approach, developed for disorganized complexity becomes favorable.

Similar to the empirical approach, the connectionist approach can be used for modeling complex systems. Since the ANNs can represent a variety of mappings and possess many desirable properties such as robust generalization and fault tolerance, they could be a very good representation for complex systems. It has already been demonstrated that the ANNs are able to be used to model algebraic systems [18] and dynamical systems [19].

Our emphasis of the connectionist research is on the analysis and synthesis of ANNs to capture the essence of the complex systems. Specifically, our motivation is to realize ANNs via supervised learning which resemble the stimulus-response behavior of the systems. Toward this end, let's consider an ANN as a mapping mechanism from input space $\mathbf{X}$ to output space $\mathbf{Y}$ which resembles the underlying input-output behavior of the system under study.

Artificial Neural Network N: $\mathbf{X} \times \mathbf{W} \rightarrow \mathbf{Y}$

where $\mathbf{W}$ is the set of the adaptable parameters of the ANN model.

In this scenario, the system modeling process can be decomposed into three

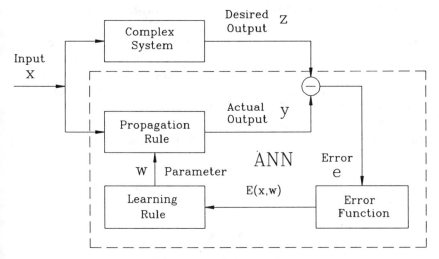

Figure 8.1.   Dynamics of the learning process.

sequential phases: preprocessing phase, training phase, and testing phase. The preprocessing phase begins with the selection of training input samples as the basis of the inductive inference assuming that the input-output data are available with adequate accuracy. The selected input samples with associated output samples constitute an information database. The data in the information database are scaled or normalized according to the maximum value of net output, and are arbitrarily or purposely divided into two sets corresponding to their usage in the two subsequent phases: training set S_{trn} and testing set S_{tst}. In the training phase, the samples in the training set and other instances generated from these representatives are presented to an ANN. The ANN is taught what the expected or probable outputs are for the training instances. Based on a prespecified performance criterion and guided by the properties of the underlying mapping, the ANN modifies its adaptable parameters according to a designed tuning scheme to learn the behavior of the underlying process represented by the training instances. Figure 8.1 illustrates the dynamics of the learning process in the training phase. In the testing phase, the tests are performed with the data in the testing set. It is important to test the performance of the inductive inference using the data different from those used in the training phase. There is the possibility of retraining the ANN if the results of tests are unsatisfactory. The purpose of this learning process is essentially to infer a general robust representation of the system based on available information; or, more precisely, to discover the mapping mechanism representing the system from a limited number of input-output training instances.

3. FORMALIZATION OF ARTIFICIAL NEURAL NETWORKS

There are a few excellent papers in the literature to formalize the concepts of artificial neural networks from different angles such as statistics [20] and cognitive science [21]. However, the concepts and properties of ANNs are not well defined from a systems-theoretic point of view. This section introduces the formal representation of ANNs and associated concepts by precise definitions and brief remarks. It is our belief that the formalization is beneficial for elucidating the concepts of the ANNs, unifying the framework and rationale of the research, and identifying new research topics.

Definition 3.1 (Artificial Neural Network): An Artificial Neural Network (ANN) is a duplet:

$$ANN \triangleq (ARCH, RULE) \tag{3.1}$$

where ARCH stands for architecture which represents the spatial structure of an ANN, and RULE denotes rules for information processing which determine the temporal feature of an ANN.

Definition 3.2 (Architecture of An ANN): The architecture of an ANN is a quintuplet:

$$ARCH \triangleq (x(t), y(t), u(t), v(t), w(t)) \tag{3.2}$$

where $x \in \mathbf{X} \subseteq \mathbb{R}^n$, an n-tuples column vector of external input variables; $y \in \mathbf{Y} \subseteq \mathbb{R}^m$, an m-tuples column vector of external output variables; $u \in \mathbf{U} \subseteq \mathbb{R}^N$, $v \in \mathbf{V} \subseteq \mathbb{R}^N$, N-tuples column vectors of aggregation input variable and activation states variable corresponding to N artificial neurons; $w \in \mathbf{W} \subseteq \mathbb{R}^M$, an M-tuples column vector of adaptable parameters which accordingly can be decomposed into three subvectors $w(t)^T = [w^{(1)}(t)^T, w^{(2)}(t)^T, w^{(3)}(t)^T]$ corresponding to weights between neurons, weights from external inputs to neurons, and thresholds, respectively; $\mathbf{X}, \mathbf{Y}, \mathbf{U}, \mathbf{V}$ and $\mathbf{W}$ are the sets of all possible external inputs, external outputs, aggregation inputs, activation states, and adaptable parameters of an ANN, respectively.

Remark 3.1: The architecture of an ANN is uniquely defined by the five elements. Specifically, $x(t)$ and $y(t)$ determine the external input and output of an ANN; $u(t)$ determines the aggregate input to every individual neuron, $v(t)$ determines the activation states of an ANN, and is usually called short-term memory (STM); $w(t)$ determines the topology of connectivity and the functional behavior of an ANN, and is usually called long-term memory (LTM), respectively.

For an ANN to process information, a set of rules have also to be specified.

Definition 3.3 (Rules of An ANN):   *RULE* of an *ANN* is a duplet:

$$RULE \triangleq (PR, LR) \tag{3.3}$$

where *PR* stands for propagation rule and *LR* for learning rule.

Definition 3.4 (Propagation Rule):   A propagation rule (PR) is a rule for information to propagate from external input to external output of an ANN, i.e., PR: $\mathbf{T} \times \mathbf{X} \times \mathbf{W} \to \mathbf{Y}$ where $\mathbf{T} = \{t | t \geq 0, t \in \mathbb{R}\}$ is a time set. Specifically,

$$PR \triangleq (E, F, G, H) \tag{3.4}$$

where E: $\mathbf{T} \times \mathbf{W} \times \mathbf{X} \times \mathbf{Y} \times \mathbf{Z} \to \mathbf{S}$, a scalar evaluation function, $\mathbf{S} \subseteq \mathbb{R}$ and $\mathbf{Z} \subseteq \mathbb{R}^m$ are a value set and a target set, respectively; $F: \mathbf{U} \to \mathbf{V}$, an N-dimensional activation function; $G: \mathbf{X} \times \mathbf{Y} \times \mathbf{V} \times \mathbf{W} \times \mathbf{S} \to \mathbf{U}$, an N-dimensional aggregation function; $H: \mathbf{X} \times \mathbf{V} \times \mathbf{W} \to \mathbf{Y}$, an m-dimensional response function, respectively. If, in addition, the aggregation function is defined in reference to the gradient of the evaluation function, then a PR with the aggregation function is referred to as a gradient-based PR.

Definition 3.5 (Learning Rule):   A learning rule (LR) is a rule to determine the parameters *w* based on the available information, i.e., *LR:* $\mathbf{T} \times \mathbf{X} \times \mathbf{Y} \times \mathbf{Z} \to \mathbf{W}$. Specifically,

$$LR \triangleq (E, L) \tag{3.5}$$

where L: $\mathbf{S} \times \mathbf{V} \times \mathbf{X} \times \mathbf{Y} \to \mathbf{W}$, an M-dimensional adaptation function. If an evaluation function is defined with respect to a whole training set, then an LR with the evaluation function is referred to as a synchronous LR; if an evaluation function is defined with respect to an individual training sample, then the LR is referred to as an asynchronous LR. If an adaptation function is defined in reference to the gradient of the evaluation function, then an LR with the adaptation function is referred to as a gradient-based LR.

Remark 3.2:   The activation function defines the node characteristics of the artificial neurons. The activation function can be deterministic or probabilistic; if deterministic, it can be continuous such as sigmoid or discrete, such as threshold logic. The aggregation function and the adaptation function are usually defined implicitly by a differential or difference equation or explicitly by a real-valued function as follows.

$$\dot{u}(t) = G'(x(t), y(t), u(t), v(t), w(t)), \ u(0) = u_0, \tag{3.6a}$$

$$\text{or } u(t + \Delta t) = G''(x(t), y(t), u(t), v(t), w(t)), \ u(0) = u_0; \tag{3.6b}$$

$$u(t) = G'''(x(t), y(t), v(t), w(t)); \tag{3.7}$$

$$\dot{w}(t) = L'(x(t), y(t), u(t), v(t), w(t)), \ w(0) = w_0, \tag{3.8a}$$

$$\text{or } w(t + \Delta t) = L''(x(t), y(t), u(t), v(t), w(t)), \ w(0) = w_0; \tag{3.8b}$$

$$w(t) = L'''(x(t), y(t), u(t), v(t)). \tag{3.9}$$

The response function, in the most of the cases, is either identity or partial identity function on $\mathbf{V}$ and null on $\mathbf{X}$ and $\mathbf{W}$, i.e., $\mathbf{Y} \subseteq \mathbf{V}$.

Remark 3.3:   The PR and LR determine the behaviors of the states (short-term memory STM) and parameters (long-term memory LTM) of an ANN, respectively.

Remark 3.4:   The LR is concerned with encoding the knowledge contained in the training instances and the prior knowledge possessed by the trainers. The LR is of primary importance to design an adaptive ANN. A good LR should be effective and efficient. Effectiveness means that a synthesized ANN can represent a certain type or class of systems; efficiency means that the computational time of the learning processes is relatively short.

The learning process can be formalized as follows. Let output(s) of an ANN be y. From a limited number of training instances, the deviations of the expected outputs z^p and actual outputs of the ANN $y(x^p, w), e(z^p, y^p)$, and evaluation function of performance, $E(e)$, for given parameters w can be computed according to predefined metric and performance evaluation function where $p = 1, 2, \ldots, P$, and P is the number of training pairs. By optimizing E with respect to w subject to constraint(s) enforced by the properties of the underlying mapping, a set of parameters w^* can be obtained. The synthesized network $y(x, w^*)$ results in a plausible fit of the data generated from the system.

Based on the above definitions, the ANNs can be categorized according to some features. For instance, according to the algebraic structure of the aggregation function, the ANNs can be categorized into semilinear ANNs, and others; according to the domain of the aggregation function, the ANNs can be categorized to feedforward ANNs and recurrent ANNs.

Definition 3.6 (Semilinear ANN):   A semilinear ANN is an ANN with a linear aggregation function, i.e., all net inputs to a neuron are aggregated by weighted summation. The aggregation function of a semilinear ANN can be expressed by a differential equation or a difference equation;

$$\dot{u}^T(t) = W^{(1)}v^T(t) + W^{(2)}x^T(t) + W^{(3)} \qquad (3.10a)$$

$$u^T(t + \Delta t) = W^{(1)}v^T(t) + W^{(2)}x^T(t) + W^{(3)} \qquad (3.10b)$$

where $W^{(1)}$, $W^{(2)}$, and $W^{(3)}$ are adaptable parameter matrices of N by N, N by n and N by 1 arranged from $w(t)$ corresponding to weights between neurons $w^{(1)}(t)$, from external inputs to neurons $w^{(2)}(t)$, and thresholds $w^{(3)}(t)$, respectively. The elements w_{ij} of $W^{(1)}$ and $W^{(2)}$ are defined as the weights on connections from neuron $i(i = 1, 2, \ldots, N)$ and from input $i(i = 1, 2, \ldots, n)$ to neuron j, respectively; the elements w_{ij} of $W^{(3)}$ are defined as thresholds for neuron $j(i = 1)$, for $j = 1, 2, \ldots, N$.

Similarly, a semimultiplicative ANN with a multiplicative aggregation function and ANNs with other higher-order aggregation functions can be defined.

Definition 3.7 (Feedforward ANN):   A feedforward ANN (F-ANN) is an ANN with unidirectional connections between neurons except between output neuron(s) in a feedforward fashion. Precisely, an F-ANN is an ANN with its aggregation function defined on only **V, W, X**, i.e., $G: \mathbf{V} \times \mathbf{W} \times \mathbf{X} \rightarrow$ **U**. Specifically, if $w_{ij}^{(1)}$ is defined as the weight parameter on connection from neuron i to neuron j, for a semilinear F-ANN the weights on and above the diagonal line of $W^{(1)}$ are always zero, only lower left $(N(N - 1) - m(m - 1))/2$ weights in W_1 can be nonzero, i.e., $w_{ij}^{(1)} = 0$ for $1 \le i \le j \le N; i \le m$.

Definition 3.8 (Recurrent ANN):   A recurrent ANN (R-ANN) is an ANN with feedback connections. Precisely, an R-ANN is an ANN with its aggregation function defined on **V, W, X**, and **Y**, i.e., $G: \mathbf{V} \times \mathbf{W} \times \mathbf{X} \times \mathbf{Y} \rightarrow$ **U**. Specifically, for a semilinear R-ANN at least one of the weights on or above the diagonal line of $W^{(1)}$ is nonzero, i.e., $\exists i, 1 \le i \le j \le N$ & $w_{ij} \ne 0$.

Remark 3.5:   The defined R-ANNs and F-ANNs are the most general forms of ANN with and without feedback, respectively, in terms of the intensity of connections. The difference between an R-ANN and an F-ANN is in their weight submatrix $W^{(1)}$. The R-ANNs and F-ANNs allow maximum degree of connectivity in terms of number of connections among existing ANNs with and without feedback, therefore, as connectionist models, the ANNs have the highest degree of plasticity. Figure 8.2 illustrates the topological structure of the F-ANN. The characteristics of specific ANN models could be properly deduced from the general properties, e.g., [22].

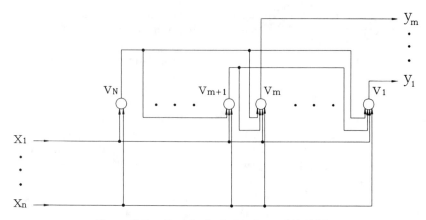

Figure 8.2.   Topological structure of F-ANN.

Remark 3.6:   This formalization unifies an array of existing ANN models. For instance, the *Perceptron* (i.e., $N = m$; *F* is threshold logic; *G* is linear), *Adaline* ($N = m$; *E* is a mean square error (MSE); *F* is linear; *G* is linear), and *multilayer Perceptron* ($N > m$; *E* is an MSE; *F* is sigmoid; *G* is linear; *L* is gradient-based) are special cases of semilinear F-ANNs. The *Hopfield nets* ($N = m = n$; $w_{ij} = w_{ji}$, $w_{ii} = 0$, $i, j = 1, 2, \ldots, N$; *E* is quadratic; *F* is threshold logic or sigmoid; *G* is linear; *H* is an identity on *V*; *L* is given explicitly), and the *Boltzmann machines* (*F* is probabilistic) are special cases of semilinear R-ANNs.

Definition 3.9 (Stability):   Given ARCH, PR, LR, and an initial state, the state of an ANN is stable if all its activation states are steady eventually. Precisely, given $v(0)$, $\forall x \in \mathbf{X}$, $\forall \epsilon > 0$, $\exists v^* \in \mathbf{V}$, $\exists T > 0$, such that for $t \geq T$:

$$\|v(t) - v^*\| \leq \epsilon, \tag{3.11}$$

where $\|\cdot\|$ is a predefined norm.

The state of an ANN is globally stable if it is stable from (almost) any initial state $x(0)$. An ANN is invariantly stable if it is stable for any parameter configuration w. An ANN is absolutely stable with respect to an evaluation function $E[v(t)]$ if its state is stable, and:

$$E[v^*] = \inf_{v \in V} E[v]. \tag{3.12}$$

Similarly, stability, global stability, and absolute stability of output of an ANN can be defined on the output $y(t)$. Since the stability of outputs of an ANN is *implied by the stability of its state, the stability of an ANN refers to the stability of its state of the ANN.*

Note that this definition of stability is equivalent to Liapunov's asymptotic stability.

Remark 3.7:   The F-ANNs are always globally stable since the F-ANNs do not allow feedback. The stability problem occurs only in the R-ANNs.

Definition 3.10 (Trainability):   Given ARCH, PR, LR, and a training set S_{trn}, an ANN is potentially trainable if a set of definite parameters w^* can be obtained; precisely, an ANN is potentially trainable if $\forall(x, z) \in S_{trn}$, $\forall \epsilon > 0$, $\exists w^* \in W$, $\exists T > 0$, such that for $t > T$,

$$\|w(t) - w^*\| \leq \epsilon. \tag{3.13}$$

An ANN is trainable if the ANN is potentially trainable, and:

$$E(w^*) \leq \delta, \tag{3.14}$$

where δ is prespecified tolerance level. *An ANN is globally trainable if it is trainable from (almost) any initial parameter $w(0)$. An ANN is invariantly trainable if it is trainable for any training set S_{trn}. An ANN is absolutely trainable with respect to an evaluation function $E[w(t)]$ if it is trainable and:*

$$E[w^*] = \inf_{\omega \in W} E[\omega]. \tag{3.15}$$

An ANN is invariantly trainable if it is trainable for any training set.

Remark 3.8:   The concept of stability is related to the PR (i.e., given x,w stability ensures definite v^* minimizing an evaluation function); the concept of trainability pertains to the LR (i.e., given x, z, trainability ensures definite w^* minimizing an evaluation function).

An ANN trained from examples is only a hypothesis of underlying mapping. It is necessary to test the synthesized ANN for the purpose of validation.

Definition 3.11 (Representability):   An ANN has the representability for an input-output system if the ANN can represent, to a satisfactory degree, the mapping mechanism of the input-output systems by testing with an arbitrary set of testing instance pairs generated from the system; precisely, given $\delta > 0$, $\forall(x^p, z^p) \in S_{tst}$,

$$\lim_{t \to \infty} \|y(x^p(t), w^*) - z^p\| \leq \delta. \tag{3.16}$$

Remark 3.9: As a special case, if $S_{trn} = X \times Z$, then the absolute trainability is equivalent to the representability.

Remark 3.10: The potential trainability ensures convergence of the *LR*, which is prerequisite for any meaningful representation. The global trainability ensures convergence of the *LR* under any initial conditon, which is necessary since in general we have little knowledge about the optima in training. The absolute trainability ensures accuracy of the representation, which is desirable for the ANNs to optimize their performances. The invariant trainability is the ideal properties for the ANNs. Nevertheless, the invariability may be too strong to be satisfied and it is not necessary for the representability. Therefore, the global and absolute trainability and the representability is the emphasis of the subsequent development.

Remark 3.11: The necessary and sufficient condition for an ANN to perform certain descriptive tasks is the representability. The representability of an ANN is implied by proper synthesis of ARCH and RULE as well as trainability.

4. CHARACTERIZATION OF ARTIFICIAL NEURAL NETWORKS

The *trainability* and the *representability* of artificial neural networks (ANNs), though mentioned in the literature, has not been explored in detail. The basic problems are what are the conditions for an ANN to be trainable, and what is the inherent relationship between the supervised learning in ANNs and statistical reasoning. This chapter is devoted to the analysis of the ANNs by revealing the characteristics of the ANNs in representing the input-output relations between the stimuli and responses. We start with a general form of the ANNs, then focus on those of our special interests.

4.1. Trainability of ANNs

Theorem 4.1: Given *ARCH, PR,* and *LR* of an ANN with a real-valued evaluation function $E[w(t)]$, if there exists M such that $E[w(t)] > M$ for any $w \in W$, and $dE_t[w(t)]/dt \leq 0$, then the ANN is potentially trainable. Furthermore, if there exists w^* such that $dE_t[w^*]/dt = 0$ iff $E[w^*] = \inf_{\omega \in W} E[\omega]$ for $w^* \in W$, and $dE_t[w(t)]/dt < 0$ for $w \neq w^*$, then the ANN is globally and absolutely trainable.

Proof: Since $E[w(t)]$ is bounded from below, $dE_t[w(t)]/dt \leq 0$, the value of the evaluation function is always monotonically nonincreasing as $w(t)$ moves along the LTM trace and eventually can reach a local minimum. Furthermore, if there exists w^* such that $E[w^*] = \inf_{\omega \in \mathbf{W}} E[\omega]$ and $dE_t[w(t)]/dt = 0$ if and only if $w = w^*$, the value of $E[w(t)]$ is always monotonically decreasing as $w(t)$ moves along the LTM trace toward w^* until w^* is reached.

Corollary 4.1:   Given an evaluation function bounded from below, the ANN with a gradient-based LR is potentially trainable.

Proof: A gradient-based LR can be described as:

$$\dot{w}(t) = \frac{dw(t)}{df} = - \eta(t) \, \nabla_w^T E[w(t)]$$

where $\eta(t) > 0$, and $\Delta_w E[w(t)]$ is a gradient vector. Since $\exists M, E[w(t)] > M$, for $w \in \mathbf{W}$, and

$$dE_t[w(t)]/dt = \nabla_w E(w(t))\dot{w}(t) = - \frac{1}{\eta(t)} [\dot{w}(t)^T \dot{w}(t)] \begin{cases} < 0, & \text{if } \dot{w}(t) \neq 0; \\ = 0, & \text{if } \dot{w}(t) = 0. \end{cases}$$

The case that $\dot{w}(t) = 0$ means the ANN is potentially trainable by definition. Since in either case, $dE_t[(w(t)]/dt \leq 0$, the ANN is potentially trainable according to Theorem 4.1.

Remark 4.1:   Corollary 4.1 is applicable to an LR defined on continuous time space (i.e., a smooth LTM trace). An LR of discrete time could result in oscillation in the neighborhood of local minima of $E[w(t)]$ because of overshoot. However, proper selection of $\eta(t)$ with very small value, or by line search along the gradient directions, can still achieve potential trainability.

Remark 4.2:   Corollary 4.1 is a sufficient condition of potential trainability for an ANN with a gradient-based LR. However, it is not for global and absolute trainability. It is quite possible for an LTM trace to get stuck at some local minima of the given evaluation function. The trainability, especially global and absolute trainability of a gradient-based LR, requires a more stringent condition.

Theorem 4.2:   Let an evaluation function be:

$$E[w] = \frac{1}{Pq} \sum_{p=1}^{P} \mu_p \sum_{i=1}^{m} |e_i^p(x^p, w)|^q \qquad (4.1)$$

where $e_i^p(x^p, w) = z_i^p - y_i(x^p, w)$ is the error on the output neuron i and $1 < q < +\infty$. An ANN with a differentiable activation function F and a synchronous gradient-based *LR* is globally and absolutely trainable at a global minimum $E[w(t)] = 0$ if and only if the rank of matrix $\Phi(x, w)$ is Pm, i.e.,

$$rank(\Phi(x, w)) = Pm \qquad (4.2)$$

where:

$$\Phi(x, w) \triangleq [J_w^T(y(x^1, w))|J_w^T(y(x^2, w))|\ldots|J_w^T(y(x^P, w))],$$

a matrix of jacobians of output $y(x^p,w)$ with respect to parameter w for every input samples x^p, $p = 1, 2, \ldots, P$; P is the number of training samples.

Proof: For a gradient-based LR, $\dot{w}(t) = 0$ if and only if $\nabla_w E[w] = 0$. Since $E[w]$ is piecewise differentiable with respect to w, $\nabla_w^T E[w(t)] = -\Phi(x, w)\bar{e}(x, w)$, where $\bar{e}(x, w) = col[\bar{e}_i^p(x^p, w)]$, $\bar{e}_i^p(x^p, w) = \mu_p/Pe_i^p(x^p, w)|e_i^p(x^p, w)|^{q-2}$, $i = 1, 2, \ldots, m; p = 1, 2, \ldots, P$, and $\Phi(x, w)$ is a matrix of M by Pm. Since $e(x, w) = 0$ iff $\bar{e}(x, w) = e(x, w)/|e(x, w)|^{2-q} = 0$ for $1 < q < \infty$, assuming that $\Phi(x, w)$ has a rank of Pm, $\dot{w}(t) = -\eta(t)\Phi(x, w)\bar{e}(x, w) = 0$ only if $e(x, w) = 0$. This proved sufficiency. For necessity, if the rank of $\Phi(x, w)$ is less than Pm then it is possible that $\dot{w}(t) = 0$ and $e(x, p) \neq 0$. Therefore, $\Phi(x, w)$ must have a rank of Pm.

Remark 4.3: The necessary and sufficient condition for global and absolute trainability is also a sufficient condition for the nonexistence of a nonglobal stationary point, and the necessary and sufficient condition for the existence of only a global minimum (minima) w^* such that $E[w^*] = 0$. If a proper initial condition can be identified, then Theorem 4.2 is a sufficient condition for absolute trainability of an ANN.

Corollary 4.2: Let all activation function(s) of output neuron(s) be strictly monotonic with respect to any finite activation (i.e., $dF_i(u_i)/du_i \neq 0$, $-\infty < u_i < +\infty$, $i = 1, 2, \ldots, m$) a linear aggregation function $u_k = \Sigma_{j=k+1}^N w_{jk}^{(1)}v_j + \Sigma_{i=1}^n w_{ik}^{(2)}x_i + w_k^{(3)}$). A semilinear F-ANN with a synchronous gradient-based LR and an evaluation function (4.1) is globally and absolutely trainable, if and only if:

$$rank(\Phi_{m+1}) = P, \qquad (4.3)$$

where $\Phi_k^T = [V_k^T|X^T]$, *and:*

$$V_k = \begin{pmatrix} v_k^1 & v_k^2 & \cdots & v_k^P \\ v_{k+1}^1 & v_{k+1}^2 & \cdots & v_{k+1}^P \\ \cdot & \cdot & \cdot & \cdot \\ \cdot & \cdot & \cdot & \cdot \\ \cdot & \cdot & \cdot & \cdot \\ v_N^1 & v_N^2 & \cdots & v_N^P \end{pmatrix},$$

an $N - k + 1$ by P matrix of hidden activation states.

$$X = \begin{pmatrix} x_1^1 & x_1^2 & \cdots & x_1^P \\ x_2^1 & x_2^2 & \cdots & x_2^P \\ \cdot & \cdot & & \cdot \\ \cdot & \cdot & \cdot & \cdot \\ \cdot & \cdot & & \cdot \\ x_n^1 & x_n^2 & \cdots & x_n^P \\ 1 & 1 & \cdots & 1 \end{pmatrix},$$

an $n + 1$ by P matrix of training samples (including the dummy input component which is always one).

Proof: Without loss of generality, let's define the first m neurons as the output neurons. For a semilinear F-ANN:

$$\Phi(x,w) = \begin{pmatrix} \bar{\Phi}_{m+1}\Delta_{11} & 0 & \cdots & 0 \\ 0 & \bar{\Phi}_{m+1}\Delta_{22} & \cdots & 0 \\ \cdot & \cdot & & \cdot \\ \cdot & \cdot & \cdot & \cdot \\ \cdot & \cdot & & \cdot \\ 0 & 0 & \cdots & \bar{\Phi}_{m+1}\Delta_{mm} \\ \bar{\Phi}_{m+2}\Delta_{1,m+1} & \bar{\Phi}_{m+2}\Delta_{2,m+1} & \cdots & \bar{\Phi}_{m+2}\Delta_{m,m+1} \\ \bar{\Phi}_{m+3}\Delta_{1,m+2} & \bar{\Phi}_{m+3}\Delta_{2,m+2} & \cdots & \bar{\Phi}_{m+3}\Delta_{m,m+2} \\ \cdot & \cdot & \cdot & \cdot \\ \cdot & \cdot & \cdot & \cdot \\ \cdot & \cdot & \cdot & \cdot \\ \bar{\Phi}_N\Delta_{1,N-1} & \bar{\Phi}_N\Delta_{2,N-1} & \cdots & \bar{\Phi}_N\Delta_{m,N-1} \end{pmatrix},$$

$$\Delta_{ij} = \begin{pmatrix} \dfrac{\partial y_i^1}{\partial u_j^1} & 0 & \cdots & 0 \\ 0 & \dfrac{\partial y_i^2}{\partial u_j^2} & \cdots & 0 \\ \cdot & \cdot & \cdot & \cdot \\ \cdot & \cdot & \cdot & \cdot \\ \cdot & \cdot & \cdot & \cdot \\ 0 & 0 & \cdots & \dfrac{\partial y_i^P}{\partial u_j^P} \end{pmatrix},$$

$i = 1, 2, \ldots, m, j = 1, 2, \ldots, N;$ diagonal matrices of P by P, (confer the detailed derivation in Appendix A.1).

Since $dF_i(u_i)/du_i \neq 0$, $-\infty < u_i < +\infty$, $\partial y_i(x^p,w)/\partial u_i \neq 0$, $rank(\Delta_{ii}) = P$ (i.e., Δ_{ii} has full rank) for $i = 1, 2, \ldots, m$. Therefore, the number of linear independent vectors in $\Phi(x, w)$ is equal to $m \cdot rank(\bar{\Phi}_{m+1})$. According to Theorem 4.2, an ANN is globally and absolutely trainable iff the rank of $\Phi(x,w)$ is Pm, the necessary and sufficient condition for global and absolute trainability (4.3) is obtained.

Remark 4.4: According to Corollary 4.2, the global and absolute trainability of a semilinear F-ANN depends on the $v(t)$, and $w(t)$. This means the global and absolute trainability can be achieved by proper selection of the STM and LTM traces.

Corollary 4.3: For an ANN with a synchronous gradient-based LR and an evaluation function (4.1) to have global and absolute trainability, the number of elements of the adaptable parameters $w(t)$, M, must not be less than the product of the number of training instances, P, and the number of output variables, m (i.e., $M \geq Pm$).

Proof: According to Theorem 4.2, an ANN with a synchronous gradient-based LR and an evaluation function (4.1) is global and absolute trainability iff $rank[\Phi(x,w)] = Pm$. Since $\Phi(x,w)$ is a matrix of M by Pm, $rank[\Phi(x,w)] = Pm$ implies $M \geq Pm$.

Remark 4.5: Since the adaptable parameters $w(t)$ represents the LTM of ANNs, and Corollary 4.3 states that the number of the components in $w(t)$, M, must not be less than the product of the number of training instances, P, and the number of output variables, m, for global and absolute trainability. For the given dimension of $w(t)$, the defined F-ANN and R-ANN require the least number of artificial neurons, and hence, have the least degree of temporal and spatial complexity.

Remark 4.6: An ANN may not be globally and absolutely trainable based on a gradient descent LR if local minima of an evaluation function with respect to w exist (i.e., if the condition (4.2) cannot be satisfied). Since the $E[w]$ is a function of x^p and y^p as well as w, a set of constraints on x^p (consequently on y^p) exists to ensure quasi-convexity in the neighborhood of w^* such that the global and absolute trainability could be achieved. From Theorem 4.2 and Corollary 4.2, we can see that the global and absolute trainability of an ANN depends on the rank of the matrices V and X, hence, can be achieved by properly selecting training instances, aggregation functions, and evaluation functions. We will elaborate on this for the F-ANNs in Section 5.

Even global and absolute trainability cannot guarantee representability. As an inductive inference, representability is implied by stability and trainability and proper synthesis of ARCH of the ANNs.

4.2. Representability of ANNs

In any modeling processes, random errors incurred from either measurement or evaluation in data acquisition and description in model specification are immutable. In training ANNs, the randomness is induced by the random parameter initialization. The errors are induced by either inadequate ANN representation or local minima. A robust model should possess a property which minimizes the total errors.

Theorem 4.3:   If $e_i^p = z_i^p - y_i(x^p, w)$ are random variables which are uncorrelated among every component, independent among every sample, and $Mod\{e_i^p\} = 0, i = 1, 2, \ldots, m; p = 1, 2, \ldots, P$ (i.e., the errors e_i^p are zero with the highest probability) then, an LR which achieves trainability is statistically equivalent to a maximum likelihood estimator (MLE).

Proof: Assuming that the errors e_i^p are uncorrelated for $i = 1, 2, \ldots, m$ and independent for $p = 1, 2, \ldots, P$, since $e^p, p = 1, 2, \ldots, P$ are independent, the likelihood function is $L\{e[w(t]\} = \Pi_{p=1}^{P} Pr(e^p[w(t)]\}$. Since $Mod\{e_i^p\} = 0$ (i.e., $maxPr(e^p) = Pr(0)$, and (4.2) is satisfied (i.e., $min\ E[e(w)] = E[0]$, maximizing $L\{e[w]\}$ is equivalent to minimizing $E[e(w)]$, the proof is obtained.

Corollary 4.4:   If e_i^p is a white noise with a symmetric probability distribution about zero, then, an LR which achieves global trainability is statistically equivalent to an MLE.

Remark 4.7:   Maximum likelihood estimates have many desirable statistical characteristics, therefore, maximum likelihood estimators can be a design objective to pursue.

Remark 4.8:   If satisfaction of the global and absolute trainability condition (4.2) cannot be guaranteed, then for certain type(s) of probability distribution of errors, obtaining an MLE is equivalent to minimizing a certain evaluation function. In other words, if only potential trainability is guaranteed, the selection of evaluation functions depends on the probability distribution of the errors to obtain an MLE. We will elaborate on this issue in Section 5.

5. REALIZATION OF ARTIFICIAL NEURAL NETWORKS

The synthesis of an ANN is an essential part of the modeling process. Synthesizing an ANN is to determine ARCH and RULE of the ANN to achieve representability. The basic problem is what are the general design principles to realize an ANN for given problems. This section discusses the guidelines for designing a semilinear feedforward ANN (F-ANN). We address the design principles in terms of ARCH and RULE. In particular, an effective and efficient LR entitled *adaptive delta rule* for the F-ANNs is proposed.

5.1. Synthesis of Architecture

In contrast to the multilayer Perceptrons (MLPs) that requires determining the number of layers and the number of neurons in each layer, the task of designing ARCH of an F-ANN requires determining only the total number of artificial neurons N.

Proposition 5.1: Let F be differentiable. A semilinear F-ANN with a synchronous gradient-based LR and an evaluation function (4.1) is globally and absolutely trainable only if:

$$N \geq P + m - rank(X). \qquad (5.1a)$$

or,

$$N_h \geq P - rank(X) \qquad (5.1b)$$

where N_h is the number of hidden neurons.

Proof: According to Corollary 4.2, a semilinear F-ANN with a synchronous gradient-based LR is globally and absolutely trainable if and only if (4.3) is satisfied. Since the rank of Φ is at most $N - m + rank(X)$, this implies $N - m + rank(X) \geq P$. The proof is complete.

Remark 5.1:   According to Proposition 5.1, the number of artificial neurons in an F-ANN should be increased as the number of output neurons and the number of training instances increases, and the number of linear independent training instances decreases. This finding seems consistent with biological neural nets.

Propositon 5.2:   Let F be differentiable. If a semilinear F-ANN of N_{gat} neurons with a synchronous gradient-based LR and an evaluation function (4.1) is globally and absolutely trainable, then a semilinear F-ANN of more than N_{gat} neurons is also globally and absolutely trainable.

Proof: According to Corollary 4.2, a semilinear F-ANN of $P + m - n - 1$ neurons with a gradient-based LR is globally and absolutely trainable iff $rank (\Phi_{m+1}) = P$. For an F-ANN, increase the number of neurons, N, only Φ_i for $i = m + 2, m + 3, \ldots, N$ may be affected. Since if $N > N_{gat}$ cannot decrease the rank of Φ_{m+1}, a semilinear F-ANN of more than N_{gat} neurons is still globally and absolutely trainable.

Remark 5.2:   Proposition 5.1 provides a "hard" lower bound for N and Proposition 5.2 suggests that there is no upper bound for N for global and absolute trainability. For a specific problem, the numbers of input and output variables, n and m, are known, and the number of training instances, P, is usually given. Therefore, the number of artificial neurons in an F-ANN can be determined accordingly (i.e., an F-ANN can be configures accordingly).

5.2. Synthesis of Rules

This subsection emphasizes the synthesis of the LR by providing principles of selecting training instances, selecting the evaluation function, and designing the training procedure.

5.2.1. Determination of training set

Before the training session, a set of training instances, $\mathbf{S_{trn}}$, must be determined. The selection of the training instances is very important for an inductive inference. The general requirements for the training instances of the training set are that they should be: (i) consistent; (ii) presentable; and (iii) informative.

The consistency means that the training instances should be consistent with the behavior underlying the system (i.e., $s_{trn}^p \triangleq (x^p, z^p)$ where (x^p, z^P) is the pair with the highest probability of association for $p = 1, 2, \ldots, P$); the presentability means that these training instances should satisfy the constraints on x such that a global minimum of the evaluation function with respect to the parameters could be obtained; the informativeness implies that the input components of training instances should distribute uniformly or as uniformly as possible on the domain of interest, and the output components should cover completely or as completely as possible, the spectrum of the output value z, and the informativeness also implies nonredundancy (i.e., without loss of information, the training set should be minimal).

Remark 5.3:   According to Corollary 4.2, an ANN is globally and absolutely trainable if and only if matrix Φ composed of X and V have rank of P. This means the global and absolute trainability can be achieved by proper selection of training instances as well as the LTM traces.

Proposition 5.3:   To minimize the size of ARCH, i.e., to minimize the total number of adaptable parameters $w(t)$, M, or the number of neurons, N, the rank of the training sample matrix X must be maximized, i.e., select the training instances such as that $\mathrm{rank}(X) = \min\{n + 1, P\}$.

Proof: According to Theorem 4.2 and Corollary 4.2, the number of adaptable parameters $w(t)$ is equal to the number of rows of $\Phi(x, w)$, and the number of linear independent rows of $\Phi(x, w)$ must be equal to Pm for global and absolute trainability. Therefore, to minimize the number of adaptable parameters, hence, minimize the number of neurons, it is necessary to maximize the number of linear independent rows of Φ given the number of training instances P. The linear independent rows in X constitutes a subset of the linear independent rows in Φ. Since X is an $n + 1$ by P matrix, $\max rank(X) = \min\{n + 1, P\}$.

Remark 5.4:   Proposition 5.3 embodies two of the above three principles: presentability and informativeness. Since linear dependent training instances require larger dimensions of adjustable parameters, hence, larger sizes of ARCH, they are redundant in terms of informativeness.

5.2.2. Determination of evaluation function

Since in general global and absolute trainability may not be guaranteed, or learning processes are artificially terminated after a specified number of epochs, the LR may not be equivalent to an MLE. However, as indicated in the previous section, if prior knowledge on the probability distribution of random errors exists, an MLE can still be obtained by proper selection of an evaluation function.

Proposition 5.4:   (1) If the errors e_i^p are random variables with zero-mean and uncorrelated (white) Gaussian probability distribution, then a maximum likelihood estimator of $w(t)$ can be obtained by minimizing:

$$E = \frac{1}{2} \sum_{p=1}^{P} \mu_p \sum_{i=1}^{m} (z_i^p - y_i^p)^2; \qquad (5.2)$$

(2) if the errors e_i^p are random variables with zero-mean and independent (white) Laplace or Triangular probability distribution, then a maximum likelihood estimator of $w(t)$ can be obtained by minimizing:

$$E = \sum_{p=1}^{P} \mu_p \sum_{i=1}^{m} |z_i^p - y_i^p|; \qquad (5.3)$$

(3) if the errors e_i^p are random variables with zero-mean and independent (white) Cauchy distribution, then a maximum likelihood estimator of $w(t)$ can be obtained by minimizing:

$$E = \prod_{p=1}^{P} \mu_p \prod_{i=1}^{m} (\lambda_i^p + (z_i^p - y_i^p)^2); \qquad (5.4)$$

(4) if the errors e_i^p are random variables with zero-mean and independent (white) student distribution, then a maximum likelihood estimator of $w(t)$ can be obtained by minimizing:

$$E = \prod_{p=1}^{P} \mu_p \prod_{i=1}^{m} \left(1 + \frac{(z_i^p - y_i^p)^2}{Pm} \right). \tag{5.5}$$

Proof: Assuming that the errors have zero-mean and independent Gaussian distribution, i.e.,

$$Pr\{e^p[w(t)]\} = (\pi)^{-m}|\Sigma_p^{-1}|\exp\{-(e^p)^T(2\Sigma_p^2)^{-1}e^p\}$$

where $e^p = z^p - y^p$, $\Sigma_p = diag(\sigma_p, \sigma_p, \ldots, \sigma_p)$.
Since $e^p, p = 1, 2, \ldots, P$ are independent, the likelihood function is:

$$L\{e[w(t)]\} = \prod_{p=1}^{P} Pr\{e^P[w(t)]\} = (\pi)^{-Pm}|\Sigma_p^{-1}|^P \exp\left\{ -\sum_{p=1}^{P} (e^P)^T e^P / 2\sigma_p^2 \right\}.$$

Maximizing $L\{e[w(t)]\}$ is equivalent to maximizing $\ln\{L\{e[w(t)]\}\}$ and equivalent to minimizing $\Sigma_{p=1}^P (z^p - y_p)^T(z^p - Y^p)/2\sigma_p^2$. Let $\mu_p = 1/\sigma_p^2, p = 1, 2, \ldots, P$, the proof of (1) is complete.

Remark 5.5:   The statistical implication of μ_p can be observed from the proof of Proposition 5.4. In general, they can be regarded as the weights of significance of the pth training instance and reflects the knowledge or confidence of the trainer on the output samples.

Remark 5.6:   If a trainer has almost full confidence on the expected output training samples, which can be regarded as that the trainer has made a large or infinite number of observations, evaluations, or measurements, then according to the Central Limit Theorem and Proposition 5.4, evaluation function (5.2) should be used in an LR to obtain an MLE. If, instead, a trainer has no knowledge on underlying probability distribution of the errors, one plausible evaluation function has to be selected, but which may not result in an MLE.

5.2.3. Determination of training procedure

Analysis and simulations have shown that the generalized delta rule (GDR) proposed by Rumelhart et al. [13] is not very efficient in terms of convergence rate. One of the causes of the inefficiency is that the GDR algorithm uses a fixed or uniformly decreasing learning rate (step length), which could result in undershoot and overshoot along the direction of gradient and oscillation near the minima. Another cause is that the GDR uses the steepest descent method, which is inherently sluggish near the minima due to the corrections vanishing as the gradient approaches zero. A great improvement of the existing learning algorithm can be made using an optimal learning rate at each iteration by applying a line- (one-dimensional) search method and using a more effective optimization technique such as conjugate direction or quasi-Newton methods to ensure better learning results. Conjugate direction methods have some advantages over the steepest descent method, and they generally would converge fast near minima.

There are many line-search strategies available [23] (e.g., direct approaches such as dichotomous search, Fibonacci search, and golden section search); curve-fitting approaches such as Newton method, quadratic and cubic fitting; and inaccurate (heuristic) approaches such as Armijo method, Goldstein method, and Wolfe method. Among these approaches, the golden-section search (GSS) method is the most effective and efficient one in this context since in general we do not know what kind of profiles will be encountered, and GSs requires only paired comparisons of output values.

A gradient-descent learning algorithm with the adaptive learning rate parameter entitled ADR (adaptive delta rule) for semilinear F-ANNs based on polak-Ribiere conjugate direction and golden section search methods, is presented as follows.

Let $W(t) = [W^{(1)}(t), W^{(2)}(t), W^{(3)}(t)]^T$ be a parameter matrix of $N + n + 1$ by N, where $W^{(1)}(t)$ is an N by N matrix corresponding to the connection weights between neurons, $W^{(2)}(t)$ is an N by n matrix corresponding to the connection weights from inputs to neurons, and $W^{(3)}(t)$ is an N-tuples row vector corresponding to the thresholds of neurons; $F_i(u_i) = (1 + e^{-u_i})^{-1}$, $i = 1, 2, \ldots, N$; $C(t)$ and $D(t)$ are matrices with the same dimensions as $W(t)$ and accordingly labeled; $E[W(t)] = \frac{1}{2}\sum_{p=1}^{P}\mu_p(z^p - y^p)^T(z^p - y^p)$ is an evaluation function of performance; $\gamma > 0$ is a mediate-sized, step length for line search; and $\epsilon, \rho > 0$ are small numbers of termination criteria.

Step 0 (Initialization): Set $W(0)$ randomly, $\tau = (\sqrt{5} - 1)/2 \approx 0.618$, $t = 0$.

Step 1 (Calculation of $c_{ij}(t) \triangleq \partial E[W(t)]/\partial w_{ij}$): (Confer the detailed derivation in Appendix A.2). *While $p = 1, 2, \ldots, P$,*

if $i = 1, 2, \ldots, N; j = 1, 2, \ldots, m$, then

$$c_{ij}(t) = -\sum_{p=1}^{P} (z_j^p - y_j^p)(1 - y_j^p)y_j^p v_i^p;$$

if $i = N + 1, N + 2, \ldots, N + n; j = 1, 2, \ldots, m$, then

$$c_{ij}(t) = - \sum_{p=1}^{P} (z_j^p - y_j^p)(1 - y_j^p)y_j^p x_{i-N}^p;$$

if $i = N + n + 1; j = 1, 2, \ldots, m$, then

$$c_{ij}(t) = - \sum_{p=1}^{P} (z_j^p - y_j^p)(1 - y_j^p)y_j^p.$$

$$\delta_j^p(t) = (z_j^p - y_j^p)(1 - y_j^p)y_j^p.$$

If $i = 1, 2, \ldots, N; j = m + 1, m + 2, \ldots, N$, then

$$c_{ij}(t) = - \sum_{p=1}^{P} \left(\sum_{h<j} \delta_n^p w_{hj}(t) \right) v_j^p (1 - v_j^p) v_i^p;$$

if $i = N + 1, N + 2, \ldots, N + n; j = m + 1, m + 2, \ldots, N$, then

$$c_{ij}(t) = - \sum_{p=1}^{P} \left(\sum_{h<j} \delta_h^p w_{hj}(t) \right) v_j^p (1 - v_j^p) x_{i-N}^p;$$

if $i = N + n + 1; j = m + 1, m + 2, \ldots, N$, then

$$c_{ij}(t) = - \sum_{p=1}^{P} \left(\sum_{h<j} \delta_h^p w_{hj}(t) \right) v_j^p (1 - v_j^p).$$

$$\delta_j^p(t) = \left(\sum_{h<j} \delta_h^p(t) w_{hj}(t) \right) v_j^p (1 - v_j^p).$$

Step 2 (Determination of conjugate direction):

If $t = 0$, then $D(t) = -C(t)$; otherwise

$$\beta_{t-1} = \frac{\sum_{i=1}^{N+n+1} \sum_{j=1}^{N} [c_{ij}(t) - c_{ij}(t-1)]c_{ij}(t)}{\sum_{i=1}^{N+n+1} \sum_{j=1}^{N} [c_{ij}(t-1)]^2},$$

$$D(t) = -C(t) + \beta_{t-1}D(t-1).$$

Step 3 (Determination of interval L for line search):

If $E[W(t)] < E[W(t) + \gamma D(t)]$, then $L = \gamma$ and go to step 4;
if $E[W(t) + \gamma D(t)] < E[W(t) + 2\gamma D(t)]$, then $L = 2\gamma$ and go to step 4;
otherwise $W(t) = W(t) + 2\gamma D(t)$ and repeat step 3.

Step 4 (performing line search):

$$W'(t) = W(t) + (1 - \tau)LD(t), \; W''(t) = W(t) + \tau LD(t),$$
if $E[W'(t)] < E[W''(t)]$, then $W''(t) = W'(t), W'(t) = W(t) + \tau(1 - \tau)LD(t)$;
otherwise $W(t) = W'(t), W'(t) = W''(t), W''(t) = W(t) + (1 - \tau)LD(t)$.

Step 5 (Adjusting the Parameters):   If $|E[W'(t)] - E[W''(t)]| \leq \rho$,

then $W(t + 1) = [W'(t) + W''(t)]/2$, and go to step 6;
otherwise $L = \tau L$ and go to step 4.

Step 6 (Checking termination criterion):

If $E[W(t + 1)] \leq \epsilon$, then $W^* = W(t + 1)$ and stop; otherwise go to step 7.

Step 7 (Restarting):   If $t > M$, then $t = 0$, $W(0) = W(t + 1)$, and go to step 1;

otherwise $t \leftarrow t + 1$, go to step 1.

In the above learning algorithm, γ serves as a step length for the search of intervals to bracket the relative minima along the directions of gradients. The optimal learning rate (step length) is determined by the algorithm autonomously based on the GSS at each epoch. It is obvious that the selection of the line search step length γ in the ADR is much less sensitive than that of the learning rate η and momentum rate α required by the GDR.

The above learning procedure was designed for the semilinear F-ANNs. It also can be extended to higher-order ANNs with the same or other activation and evaluation functions.

6. PARADIGMS OF ARTIFICIAL NEURAL NETWORKS

There are numerous areas of application or potential application of artificial neural networks. These areas include, but are certainly not limited to: pattern recognition, associative memory, combinatorial optimization, and process and robotics control. For the purpose of illustration, in this section, we consider only two examples: the parity three problem and the multiattribute preference assessment problem.

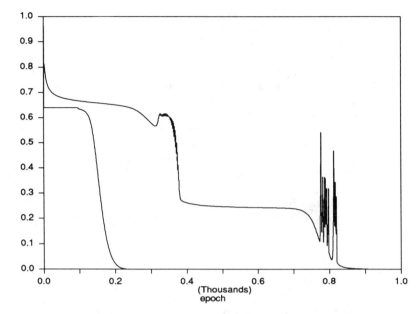

error

Figure 8.3. Convergence rates of ADR vs. GDR in the parity problem.

Example 1 (Odd-Parity Checking Problem): Let's first consider training an ANN to check three-bit odd-parity, $y = x_1 \oplus x_2 \oplus x_3$, where $x_i \in \{0,1\}$, $i = 1, 2, 3$. It is well known that the single-layer Perceptron cannot be trained to discriminate these patterns. We trained the F-ANN with ADR and MLP with GDR to represent the mapping. Both ANNs have five neurons including one output neuron. The simulation shows that the convergence rate of GDR is very sensitive to the selection of the learning rate parameter η and the momentum parameter α, whereas the convergence rate of ADR is very robust to the selection of the parameter γ. Figure 8.3 illustrates the convergence rate of the training error of both F-ANN with ADR versus MLP with GDR, where a good (if not optimal) combination of parameters η and α in GDR are chosen by comparing with convergence rates. The oscillation of GDR near the minimum of error can be easily observed from the graph. In this case, the training error monotonically decreases to zero in 250 epochs for ADR ($\gamma = 4$) while the error decreases to zero in 850 epochs for GDR ($\eta = 5$, $\alpha = 0$). Although the computation of optimal step lengths need an additional fraction of time in each epoch, the absolute computational time is still much less in ADR than in GDR.

Example 2 (Multiattribute Preference-Assessment Problem): In decision making with multiple objectives, it is often desired to assess the decision maker's (DM's) preference explicitly described by multiattribute value function; that is, to discover a mapping mechanism underlying the DM's preferential behavior. Once the DM's underlying preference structure would be assessed, a decision rule could be derived. A multiattribute value function is a mapping from attribute set to value set, $v : \mathbf{X} \rightarrow \mathbb{R}$ such that $x' > x'' \Leftrightarrow v(x') > v(x'')$, $x' < x'' \Leftrightarrow v(x') < v(x'')$, and $x' \sim x'' \Leftrightarrow v(x') = v(x'')$ where $>$, $<$, and $\sim$ stand for *is preferred to, is less preferred to,* and *is indifferent to.* The input of the model $x = (x_1, x_2, \ldots , x_n)^T$; the desired output of the model is v, the value corresponding to the outcome x provided that the DM can provide the numerical ratings. For simplicity, we also assume the DM is confident about his or her value assessments of all outcomes. Therefore, according to Proposition 5.4, a least-square evaluation function (5.3) was selected. Simulations were performed based on the proposed F-ANN with ADR to assess the preference model. Fifty efficient alternatives of three attributes were generated *randomly,* and were divided in half arbitrarily to form a training set and a testing set. Three different types of value functions, *Chebychev, additive,* and *quadratic,* were assumed to implicitly represent the underlying DM's preference in providing responses of preferential information, i.e.:

$$v_1(x_2, x_2, x_3) = \min\{x_1, x_2, x_3\}$$

$$v_2(x_1, x_2, x_3) = 0.5x_1 + 0.3x_2 + 0.2x_3$$

$$v_3(x_1, x_2, x_3) = x_1 - 0.5x_1^2 + 0.6x_2 - 0.3x_2^2 + 0.4x_3 - 0.2x_3^2$$

Since $n = 3$, $m = 1$, $P = 25$, according to Propositions 5.1 and 5.2, we choose $N = 30$. The number of epochs is 20,000. Table 8.1 summarizes the performances of synthesized ANNs in *training* and *testing* phases in assessing Chebychev, additive, and quadratic value functions, respectively. The entries of the second and third column are the mean-square error (MSE) in training and testing, respectively. The detailed results are shown in Appendix A.3. The simulations show that the configured ANN-based preference model F-ANN can rank all the alternatives in testing sets correctly and generate a set of output values very close to the desired values. The results of the simulations show that ADR converges much faster than GDR and is very robust in the selection of computational parameter(s). Besides the convergence rate and robustness, the representability of the proposed F-ANN is also better than that of layered neural networks because of the general representation. An in-depth analysis of this subject is beyond the scope of this chapter. For more detailed treatment, confer [24,25].

Table 8.1.   Summary of the simulation results.

MSE	S_{trn}	S_{tst}
Chebychev	5.40×10^{-7}	1.68×10^{-2}
Additive	6.19×10^{-7}	4.27×10^{-4}
Quadratic	1.65×10^{-6}	1.52×10^{-4}

7. CONCLUSION

In this chapter, the theory and methodology for analysis and synthesis of artificial neural networks for modeling complex systems has been presented. The modeling problem has been formulated in the context of supervised learning of artificial neural networks. The concepts and properties associated with artificial neural networks have been formalized. The conditions for trainability have been characterized and characteristics of representability have been analyzed. A set of design principles have also been derived, and a general network architecture and an effective and efficient learning algorithm have been introduced for synthesis of the artificial neural networks.

The connectionist approach opens a new horizon to complex system modeling. There are many merits in the proposed connectionist approach comparing with the existing ones. One of the merits that the proposed connectionist models possess is that their structures are independent functional forms and their parameters are error insensitive when encoding and decoding knowledge. It is shown that the synthesized artificial neural networks could represent complex systems. It is also perceived that the proposed approach could overcome some shortcomings of the existing approaches (i.e., increase the utility of information generated from processes by requiring a smaller amount or simpler form of information and minimizing representation errors); and reduce analytical work on the analyst's part by processing and organizing data autonomously based on the prespecified general rules; improve the applicability of the system representations by relaxing all restrictive assumptions on the functional forms of the models. Due to the nature of incremental learning and availability of existing computing facilities, this approach usually requires longer computational time than traditional approaches. This limitation can be improved with the progress in learning algorithm and network architecture as well as computer technology.

APPENDICES

A.1. Derivation of $\Phi(x,w)$ for Corollary 4.2

Let $\Phi(x,w) = [\Phi_1|\Phi_2| \ldots |\Phi_N]^T$, $\Phi_j = [\Phi_j^1|\Phi_j^2| \ldots |\Phi_j^m]$,

$$
\Phi_j^k = \begin{pmatrix}
\phi_{j+1,j}^{1k} & \phi_{j+1,j}^{2k} & \cdots & \phi_{j+1,j}^{Pk} \\
\phi_{j+2,j}^{1k} & \phi_{j+2,j}^{2k} & \cdots & \phi_{j+2,j}^{Pk} \\
\cdot & \cdot & \cdot & \cdot \\
\cdot & \cdot & \cdot & \cdot \\
\cdot & \cdot & \cdot & \cdot \\
\phi_{N+n+1,j}^{1k} & \phi_{N+n+1}^{2k} & \cdots & \phi_{N+n+1,j}^{Pk}
\end{pmatrix}
$$

where $\phi_{ij}^{pk} = \partial y_j^p / \partial w_{ij}$.

For $p = 1, 2, \ldots, P,$

$$\frac{\partial y_k^p}{\partial w_{ij}} = \begin{cases} \dfrac{\partial y_j^p}{\partial u_j^p} \, v_i^p, & j = k; \\ 0, & j \neq k, \end{cases}$$

where $i = 1, 2, \ldots, N; j = 1, 2, \ldots, m; k = 1, 2, \ldots, m;$

$$\frac{\partial y_k^p}{\partial w_{ij}} = \begin{cases} \dfrac{\partial y_j^p}{\partial u_j^p} \, x_{i-N}^p, & j = k; \\ 0, & j \neq k, \end{cases}$$

where $i = N + 1, N + 2, \ldots, N + n; j = 1, 2, \ldots, m; k = 1, 2, \ldots, m.$

$$\frac{\partial y_k^p}{\partial w_{ij}} = \begin{cases} \dfrac{\partial y_j^p}{\partial u_j^p}, & j = k; \\ 0, & j \neq k, \end{cases}$$

where $i = N + n + 1; j = 1, 2, \ldots, m; k = 1, 2, \ldots, m.$

$$\frac{\partial y_k^p}{\partial w_{ij}} = \frac{\partial y_k^p}{\partial u_j^p} \, v_i^p,$$

where $i = j + 1, j + 2, \ldots, N; j = m + 1, m + 2, \ldots, N; k = 1, 2, \ldots, m.$

$$\frac{\partial y_k^p}{\partial w_{ij}} = \frac{\partial y_k^p}{\partial u_j^p} \, x_{N-i}^p,$$

where $i = N + 1, N + 2, \ldots, N + n; j = m + 1, m + 2, \ldots, N; k = 1, 2, \ldots, m.$

$$\frac{\partial y_k^p}{\partial w_{ij}} = \frac{\partial y_k^p}{\partial u_j^p},$$

where $i = N + n + 1; j = m + 1, m + 2, \ldots, N; k = 1, 2, \ldots, m.$

A.2. Derivation of Gradient $E(W)$ with Respect to W for F-ANN

$$\min_{w \in W} E = \frac{1}{2} \sum_{p=1}^{P} \mu_p (z^p - y^p)^T (z^p - y^p)$$

where

$$v_j^p(t + \Delta t) = F(u_j^p) = F\left(\sum_{i>j, i>m}^{N} w_{ij} v_i^p(t) + \sum_{i=N+1}^{N+n} w_{ij} x_{N-i}^p + w_{N+n+1, j} \right),$$

$$y_k^p = v_k^p, j = 1, 2, \ldots, N; k = 1, 2, \ldots, m; p = 1, 2, \ldots, P.$$

Let's define

$$c_{ij} \triangleq \frac{\partial E}{\partial w_{ij}}, \qquad \delta_j^p \triangleq - \frac{\partial E}{\partial u_j^p},$$

where $j = 1, 2, \ldots, N; p = 1, 2, \ldots, P$.

For $j = 1, 2, \ldots, m$,

$$c_{ij} = \sum_{p=1}^{P} \delta_j^p \frac{\partial u_j^p}{w_{ij}} = \begin{cases} \sum_{p=1}^{P} \delta_j^p v_i^p \\ \sum_{p=1}^{P} \delta_j^p x_{i-N}^p \\ \sum_{p=1}^{P} \delta_j^p \end{cases}$$

$$= \begin{cases} - \sum_{p=1}^{P} (z_j^p - y_j^p)(1 - y_j^p) y_j^p v_i^p, & i = 1, 2, \ldots, N; \\ - \sum_{p=1}^{P} (z_j^p - y_j^p)(1 - y_j^p) y_j^p x_{i-N}^p, & i = N + 1, N + 2, \ldots, N + n; \\ - \sum_{p=1}^{P} (z_j^p - y_j^p)(1 - y_j^p) y_j^p, & i = N + n + 1. \end{cases}$$

For $j = m + 1, m + 2, \ldots, N$,

$$c_{ij} = \sum_{p=1}^{P} \delta_j^p \frac{\partial u_j^p}{w_{ij}} = \begin{cases} \sum_{p=1}^{P} \delta_j^p v_i^p \\ \sum_{p=1}^{P} \delta_j^p x_{i-N}^p \\ \sum_{p=1}^{P} \delta_j^p \end{cases} = \begin{cases} \sum_{p=1}^{P} \frac{\partial E}{\partial v_j^p} \frac{\partial v_j^p}{\partial u_j^p} v_i^p \\ \sum_{p=1}^{P} \frac{\partial E}{\partial v_j^p} \frac{\partial v_j^p}{\partial u_j^p} x_{i-N}^p \\ \sum_{p=1}^{P} \frac{\partial E}{\partial v_j^p} \frac{\partial v_j^p}{\partial u_j^p} \end{cases}$$

$$= \begin{cases} \sum_{p=1}^{P} \left(\sum_{h<j} \frac{\partial E}{\partial u_h^p} \frac{\partial u_h^p}{\partial v_j^p} \right) \frac{dF(u_j^p)}{du_j} v_i^p \\ \sum_{p=1}^{P} \left(\sum_{h<j} \frac{\partial E}{\partial u_h^p} \frac{\partial u_h^p}{\partial v_j^p} \right) \frac{dF(u_j^p)}{du_j} x_{i-N}^p \\ \sum_{p=1}^{P} \left(\sum_{h<j} \frac{\partial E}{\partial u_h^p} \frac{\partial u_h^p}{\partial v_j^p} \right) \frac{dF(u_p)}{du_j} \end{cases}$$

$$= \begin{cases} \sum_{p=1}^{P} (\sum_{h<j} \delta_h^p w_{hj})(1 - v_j^p) v_j^p v_i^p, & i = 1, 2, \ldots, N; \\ \sum_{p=1}^{P} (\sum_{h<j} \delta_h^p w_{hj})(1 - v_j^p) v_j^p x_{i-N}^p, & i = N + 1, N + 2, \ldots, N + n; \\ \sum_{p=1}^{P} (\sum_{h<j} \delta_h^p w_{hj})(1 - v_j^p) v_j^p, & i = N + n + 1. \end{cases}$$

A.3. Results of the Simulation for Example 2

Table 8.2: Training and Testing Errors of F-ANNs for Example 2.

Table 8.2. Training and testing errors of F-ANNs for example 2.

p	v_1: S_{trn}	v_1: S_{tst}	v_2: S_{trn}	v_2: S_{tst}	v_3: S_{trn}	v_3: S_{tst}
1	0.0002	−0.0202	0.0010	−0.0027	0.0010	−0.0028
2	−0.0002	0.0015	0.0007	0.0006	0.0026	−0.0036
3	0.0001	−0.0009	0.0006	−0.0007	0.0004	−0.0006
4	0.0000	−0.0018	−0.0009	−0.0007	−0.0031	0.0007
5	0.0000	−0.0001	−0.0019	0.0003	−0.0001	−0.0071
6	0.0006	−0.0006	−0.0005	0.0018	0.0003	0.0005
7	0.0019	−0.0020	−0.0003	0.0007	−0.0002	−0.0032
8	−0.0002	0.0062	−0.0005	0.0002	−0.0005	−0.0018
9	0.0004	−0.0199	0.0001	0.0001	−0.0016	−0.0018
10	−0.0001	−0.0334	−0.0001	−0.0004	0.0001	0.0129
11	0.0002	0.0536	−0.0007	0.0040	0.0005	−0.0149
12	0.0018	0.0036	0.0008	0.0029	0.0000	0.0031
13	0.0001	−0.0103	0.0005	−0.0006	0.0000	0.0001
14	0.0000	−0.0097	−0.0005	−0.0004	−0.0008	0.0017
15	0.0003	0.0594	0.0000	−0.0022	−0.0023	0.0316
16	−0.0001	0.0007	0.0006	−0.0001	0.0003	−0.0086
17	−0.0015	−0.1330	−0.0006	0.0022	0.0001	0.0430
18	−0.0014	0.0035	−0.0007	0.0003	0.0034	−0.0102
19	0.0001	−0.0043	0.0017	0.0024	−0.0009	0.0021
20	−0.0001	−0.0054	0.0008	0.0011	−0.0002	−0.0030
21	−0.0006	−0.0165	−0.0010	−0.0009	−0.0001	0.0026
22	−0.0008	−0.0142	−0.0002	−0.0006	0.0014	−0.0023
23	−0.0005	0.0050	−0.0006	−0.0001	−0.0001	−0.0033
24	−0.0006	−0.1195	0.0010	0.0014	0.0004	0.0155
25	0.0001	0.0317	0.0008	0.0054	−0.0001	0.0004

REFERENCES

[1] S.E. Fahlman and G.E. Hinton, "Connectionist Architectures for Artificial Intelligence," *Computer,* Vol. 20, No. 1, 1987, pp. 100–109.

[2] W.S. McCulloch and W.H. Pitts, "A Logical Calculus of the Immanent in Nervous Activity Ideas," *Bulletin of Mathematical Biophysics,* Vol. 5, 1943, pp. 115–133.

[3] R. Rosenblatt, "The Perceptron: A Probabilistic Model for Information Storage and Organization in the Brain," *Psychological Review,* Vol. 65, No. 6, 1958, pp. 386–408.

[4] B. Widrow and M.E. Hoff, "Adaptive Switching Circuits," *IRE WESCON Convention Record,* Part IV, 1960, pp. 96–104.

[5] M. Minsky and S. Papert, *Perceptrons: An Introduction to Computational Geometry,* MIT Press, Cambridge, MA, 1969.

[6] S. Grossberg, "Adaptive Pattern Classification and Universal Recoding, II: Feedback, Expectation, Olfaction, and Illusions," *Biological Cybernetics,* Vol. 23, 1976, pp. 187–202.

[7] G.A. Carpenter and S. Grossberg, "ART 2: Self-Organization of Stable Category Recognition Codes for Analog Input Patterns," *Applied Optics,* Vol. 26, No. 23, 1987, pp. 4919–4930.

[8] T. Kohonen, "Self-Organized Formation of Topologically Correct Feature Maps," *Biological Cybernetics*, Vol. 43, 1982, pp. 59–69.

[9] G.E. Hinton, T.J. Sejnowski, and D.H. Ackley, "Boltzmann Machines: Constraint Satisfaction Networks that Learn," Technical Report CMU-CS-84-119, Carnegie Mellon University, Pittsburgh, PA, 1984.

[10] J.J. Hopfield, "Neural Networks and Physical Systems with Emergent Collective Computational Ability," *Proceedings of National Academy of Sciences, USA, Biophysics*, Vol. 79, 1982, pp. 2554–2558.

[11] J.J. Hopfield, "Neurons with Graded Response Have Collective Computational Properties Like Those of Two-State Neurons," *Proceedings of National Academy of Sciences, USA, Biophysics*, Vol. 81, 1984, pp. 3088–3092.

[12] J.J. Hopfield and D.W. Tank, "'Neural' Computation of Decisions in Optimization Problems," *Biological Cybernetics*, Vol. 52, No. 3, 1985, pp. 141–152.

[13] D.E. Rumelhart, G.E. Hinton, and R.J. Williams, "Learning Internal Representations by Error Propagation in Parallel Distributed Processing," D.E. Rumelhart, J.L. McClelland, and the PDP Research Group (Eds.), *Parallel Distributed Processing-Explorations in the Microstructures of Cognition, Vol. 1: Foundations*, MIT Press, Cambridge, 1986, pp. 318–362.

[14] K. Funahashi, "On the Approximate Realization of Continuous Mappings by Neural Networks," *Neural Networks*, Vol. 2, No. 3, 1989, pp. 183–192.

[15] K. Hornik, M. Stinchcombe, and H. White, "Multilayer Feedforward Networks Are Universal Approximators," *Neural Networks*, Vol. 2, No. 5, 1989, pp. 359–366.

[16] M.D. Mesarovic and Y. Takahara, *Abstract Systems Theory*, Springer Verlag, New York, 1989.

[17] V. Vemuri, *Modeling of Complex Systems: An Introduction*, Academic Press, New York, 1977.

[18] M. Tonorio and W. Lee, "Self-Organizing Network for Optimum Supervised Learning," *IEEE Transactions on Neural Networks*, Vol. 1, No. 1, 1990, pp. 100–110.

[19] K. Narendra and K. Parthasarathy, "Identification and Control of Dynamical Systems Using Neural Networks," *IEEE Transactions on Neural Networks*, Vol. 1, No. 1, 1990, pp. 4–27.

[20] R.M. Golden, "A Unified Framework for Connectionist Systems," *Biological Cybernetics*, Vol. 59, 1988, pp. 109–120.

[21] D.E. Rumelhart and J.L. McClelland, "A General Framework for Parallel Distributed Processing," D.E. Rumelhart, J.L. McClelland, and the PDP Research Group (Eds.), *Parallel Distributed Processing-Explorations in the Microstructures of Cognition, Vol. 1: Foundations*, MIT Press, Cambridge, MA, 1986, pp. 45–76.

[22] J. Wang and E.P. Teixeira, "On the Design Principles of the Functional Link Nets," *Proceedings of the IEEE International Conference on Systems Engineering*, Pittsburgh, PA, 1990, pp. 613–616.

[23] D.G. Luenberger, *Linear and Nonlinear Programming*, Addison-Wesley, Reading, MA, 1984.

[24] J. Wang and B. Malakooti, "Artificial Neural Networks for Multiple Criteria Decision Making," *Proceedings of INNS/IEEE International Joint Conference on Neural Networks*, Vol. II, Washington, DC, June 1989, pp. 387–393.

[25] J. Wang, "Artificial Neural Networks versus Natural Neural Networks: A Connectionist Approach to Preference Assessment," Ninth International Conference on Multiple Criteria Decision Making, Fairfax, VA, August 1990.

9
Gradient-Type Neural Systems for Computation and Decision Making

Jacek Zurada
Electrical Engineering Department
University of Louisville, Kentucky

1. INTRODUCTION

Models of neural networks are receiving widespread attention as potential new architectures for computation and decision making. Such models consist of highly interconnected structures of simple computing elements. Since computation is performed collectively, such networks have the potential to solve complex problems quickly.

The neural network approach offers a replacement for digital computation in which the finite state machine is performing a sequence of steps in a discrete space [1,2,3]. A neural network discussed in this chapter represents a dynamical system evolving in a continuous, or discrete, space under the following conditions: (a) it usually has many degrees of freedom, (b) it is nonlinear, and (c) it is dissipative and converges to an asymptotically stable solution being a minimum of an energy function.

It has been found that the example hardware discussed in [4], and consisting of a batch-trained analog processors solves specific optimization problems, or reaches the minima in specific useful cases like analog/digital conversion, signal component identification, and linear programming. In the general case, however, batch training of the neural network may not be easy since the analytical form of the computational energy function is usually not available. Learning rules and algorithms may be used as an alternative in such cases.

The knowledge about existing neural networks architectures and learning procedures is advancing rapidly. When it is fully realized, it would enhance the computational power of neural networks considerably. In addition, novel implementations in planar silicon technology and new optical technologies are under intensive investigation [5,6,7,8,9].

This chapter discusses the single-layer feedback neural networks which converge to a stable equilibrium point. They are based on Hopfield's postulate seminally published in [1,2,3]. Such networks display interesting properties from the standpoint of system theory. But their real usefulness results from the decision-making capability of the neuromorphic hardware.

Specifically, the gradient-type networks converge to one of the stable minima in the state space in the general direction of the negative gradient of a certain objective (penalty) function called an energy function. The fundamentals and examples of such networks will be discussed next. The discussion is based mainly on the concept of the energy function, and it stresses transients in actual single-layer feedback networks.

2. SYSTEM ANALYSIS AND ITS MATHEMATICAL FOUNDATIONS

2.1. Postulated Neural System and its Description

Neural networks of gradient type are examples of nonlinear, dynamic, and asymptotically stable systems. In discussion of their properties, it will be useful to define a scalar energy function $E(\mathbf{V}(t))$ in the n-dimensional output space V^n.

The nonlinear portion of the postulate network is comprised of neurons as illustrated in Figure 9.1. It shows a symbol of neuron: (a), a set of typical activation functions (b), and an example CMOS implementation of a neuron (c). The neuron is built of two inverters in cascade yielding a high value of gain λ, and it is supplied symmetrically by V_{DD} and $V_{SS} = -V_{DD}$. These supply voltages would correspond to ± 1 values of activation functions upon the normalization of the neurons' voltage transfer characteristics with respect to their supply voltage.

The model of a gradient-type neural system using electrical components is shown in Figure 9.2(a) [1,2,3]. It consists of n neurons each mapping the input voltage u_i of the ith neuron into the output voltage V_i through the activation function f($\cdot$) being the common static voltage transfer characteristic (VTC) of the neuron. Conductance T_{ij} connects the output of jth neuron to the input of ith neuron. The inverted neuron outputs $\bar{V}_i$ are available to avoid negative conductance values T_{ij} connecting in inhibitory mode the output of the jth neuron to the input of ith neuron. Note that the postulated network is symmetric, i.e., $T_{ij} = T_{ji}$. Also, since it has been assumed that $T_{ii} = 0$, neurons are not connected to their own inputs.

The input of the ith neuron is shown in Figure 9.2(b). The KCL equation for the input node can be obtained as:

$$I_i + \sum_{j=1}^{n} T_{ij} V_j - u_i G_i = C_i \left(\frac{du_i}{dt} \right), \tag{2.1}$$

a)

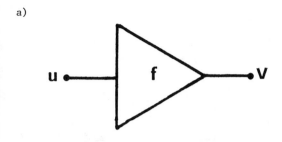

b)

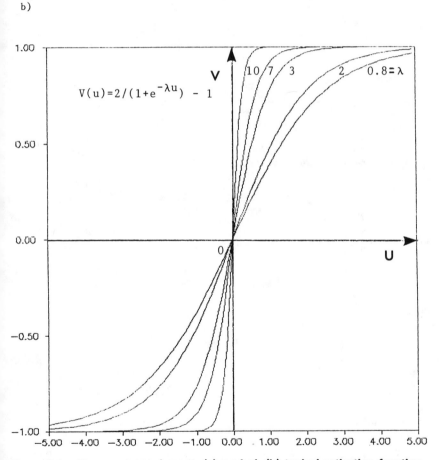

$$V(u)=2/(1+e^{-\lambda u}) - 1$$

Figure 9.1.   Neuron as an element: (a) symbol, (b) typical activation function, and (c) sample CMOS implementation.

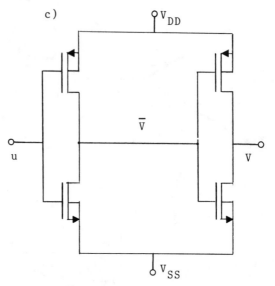

Figure 9.1. (*continued*).

where the total conductance connected to the node i is denoted as G_i:

$$G_i \triangleq \sum_{j=1}^{n} T_{ij} + g_i.$$

Now introducing matrices C, G, T defined as:

$$C \triangleq \text{diag } [C_1, C_2, \ldots C_n], G \triangleq \text{diag } [G_1, G_2, \ldots G_n],$$

and:

$$T \triangleq \begin{bmatrix} T_{11} & T_{12} & \cdot\cdot & T_{1n} \\ T_{21} & T_{22} & \cdot\cdot & T_{2n} \\ \cdots & \cdots & \cdots & \cdots \\ T_{n1} & T_{n2} & \cdot\cdot & T_{nn} \end{bmatrix},$$

and introducing n-dimensional column vectors $\mathbf{u}(t)$, $\mathbf{V}(t)$, and the bias currents vector $\mathbf{I}$, the final matrix equations of the entire model net consisting of the state (2.2a) and output equation (2.2b) become

$$C \frac{du(t)}{dt} = T V(t) - G u(t) + I \qquad (2.2a)$$

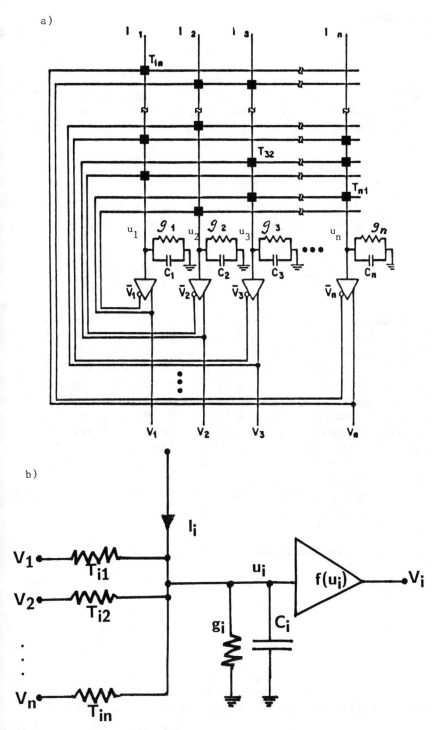

Figure 9.2. The model neural network using electrical components: (a) diagram, and (b) input node to the *i*th neuron.

$$V(t) = f(u(t)) \tag{2.2b}$$

Let us consider the stability of a system described by the ordinary differential equations (2.2). The stability of the equations can be determined using a generalized computational energy function $E(V(t))$. The function $E(V(t))$ is a scalar function. The time derivative of $E(V(t))$ can easily be obtained using the chain rule as:

$$\frac{dE(V(t))}{dt} = \nabla E^t(V)\dot{V} \tag{2.3}$$

where the superscript t denotes transposition, and $\nabla E(V)$ denotes the gradient vector:

$$\nabla E(V) \triangleq \left[\frac{\partial E(V)}{\partial V_1}, \frac{\partial E(V)}{\partial V_2}, \ldots, \frac{\partial E(V)}{\partial V_n} \right]^t$$

The discussion below in Sections 2.1–2.3 is based on the system's gradient function. Although no new results are presented here as compared with [1,2,3], the gradient-based method provides a uniform, compact approach for discussion of the network's properties. It may be noted that the computational energy function is spanned in the output space V^n where the designed neural system specifications are usually known. The corresponding energy function in the state space u^n of an asymptotically stable system would be the system's Liapunov function. If its time derivative is found to be negative, then the energy function in the output space also has a negative derivative since Equation (2.2b) describes monotonic mapping of u^n into V^n space. The formal substantiation of this property will be presented in the next section.

The solution of Equation (2.2) based on the scalar energy function and the properties of its gradient vector will now be considered.

2.2. Mathematical Foundations of Gradient-Type Networks

The postulated energy function for the system in Figure 9.2 has the following form:

$$E(V) = -\frac{1}{2} V^t TV - I^t V + \sum_{i=1}^{n} G_i \int_0^{V_i} f_i^{-1}(z)dz \tag{2.4}$$

Calculating the speed of energy changes as in Equation (2.3) for symmetric **T**, and including the result from the computation of the gradient $\nabla E(\mathbf{V})$ yields:

$$\frac{dE}{dt} = (- TV - I + Gu)^t \frac{dV}{dt} \tag{2.5}$$

Using the gradient vector expression in parenthesis of Equation (2.5), the state Equation (2.2a) can be rewritten as follows:

$$- \nabla E(V) = C \frac{du}{dt} \tag{2.6}$$

It can easily be seen from Equation (2.6) that the negative gradient of the energy function $E(V)$ is directly proportional to the speed of the state vector $\mathbf{u}$, capacitance C_i being the proportionality coefficients of its ith component. The appropriate changes of u_i are in the general direction of the negative gradient component $\partial E/\partial V_i$. This is illustrated in Figure 9.3 showing the equipotential, or equal

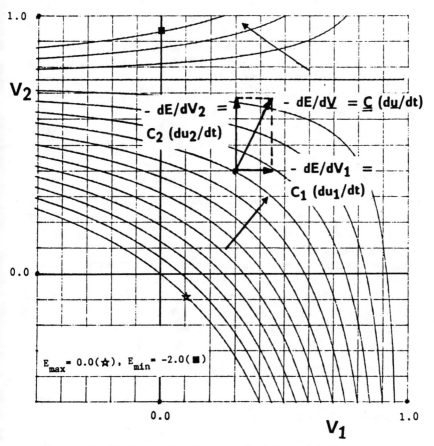

Figure 9.3.   Illustration to energy gradient descent in V^2 space.

energy lines in V^2 space of an example network. The network is able to perform addition of analog values [9,10,11]. The class of networks and its properties will be discussed in more detail in a subsequent section.

It is now interesting to see how the energy E of this system varies with time. Combining Equations (2.3) and (2.4) yields:

$$\frac{dE}{dt} = - \left(C \frac{du}{dt} \right)^t \frac{dV}{dt} \tag{2.7}$$

Using the inverse function $f^{-1}(V_i)$ of the VTC, the directions of changes of the vector $V(t)$ can now be computed as follows:

$$\frac{du_i}{dt} = f^{-1'}(V_i) \frac{dV_i}{dt} \tag{2.8}$$

Since $f^{-1'}(V_i) > 0$, then it can be noticed that du_i/dt and dV_i/dt are of identical signs. But as stated previously, the values of du_i/dt are of the same sign as the negative gradient components $\partial E/\partial V_i$. It follows thus that the changes of E in time are in the general direction towards lower values of the energy function in V^n space. The changes do not follow the direction of the gradient itself since $C_i f^{-1'}(V_i)$ provides here such scaling that:

$$\frac{dV_i}{dt} = \frac{\dfrac{dE}{dV_i}}{C_i f^{-1'}(V_i)} \tag{2.9}$$

This unique property of the system discussed here lends the name to it of a gradient-type system. It offers the replacement of the convergence *to the minimum of E in time,* as it occurs in real hardware, with the convergence *to the minimum of E(V)* in the V^n space. Such solution for minimum $E(V)$ results from solving the nonlinear, but purely algebraic equations, describing the nondynamic system (i.e., system as in Figure 9.2 but with *capacitors removed*).

As the system comes to rest at the minimum of $E(V)$ after it has moved toward a minimum in V^n space, it can be seen from Equation (2.9) that it has also reached equilibrium in u^n which is a state space of this system.

2.3. Existence of Minima of Energy Function

As discussed in previous paragraphs, finding the equilibrium point corresponds to the solution V^* of the following algebraic equation:

$$\nabla E(V) = 0 \tag{2.10a}$$

or briefly:

$$-TV - I + Gu = 0 \qquad (2.10b)$$

with the additional relationship Equation (9.2b) mapping state into output space $u^n \rightarrow V^n$.

Equation (2.10) solved for V^* without consideration of constraints to V^n (0,1) hypercube leads to:

$$V^* = -T^{-1}I \qquad (2.11)$$

where the additional assumption is made of high λ gain neurons, thus eliminating the last term in Equation (9.10b). It can also be noted that the Hessian matrix of the unconstrained system is:

$$\nabla^2 E(V) = -T. \qquad (2.12)$$

By having chosen $T_{ii} = 0$ for this neural network model, the Hessian matrix—T has intentionally been made *not* positive definite. Thus, the function E(**V**) possesses no unconstrained minima. In the case of limitation of space V^n to (0,1) hypercube, the constrained minima of $E(V)$ must be located at the hypercube's boundary—being edges or faces of the cube [12]. If a solution V^* of the constrained system within the cube (0,1) exists, it must then be a saddle point.

The energy function (2.4) evaluated on faces and on edges simplifies to the following expressions, respectively:

$$E = -\frac{1}{2}(T_{ij} V_i V_j + T_{ji} V_j V_i) - I_i V_i - I_j V_j \qquad (2.13a)$$

$$E = -I_i V_i \qquad (2.13b)$$

Since the Hessian matrix of $E(V_i, V_j)$ as in Equation (2.13a) has again zero diagonal, no minima can exist on the faces of the cube. Since Equation (2.13b) is a monotonic function of V_i, the minima may not occur on the edges either, except for possibly 0,1 vertices.

The discussion has shown that the gradient-type network converges, in time, to one of the minima of E(**V**) located in the corners of the hypercube (0,1). That convergence implemented and reached in actual gradient-type network hardware ensures that one of the desired solutions is generated. However, the solution reached by the system may not be completely satisfactory due to the existence of a preferred solution.

2.4. Relaxation Modeling for Neural Optimization Networks

As stated before, the solution of nonlinear differential equations (2.2) can be replaced with solving algebraic equations (2.10b) with additional conditions (2.2b). It can be noticed that the equation in (2.10b) has the form:

$$\sum_{j=1}^{n} T_{ij} V_j + I_i = G_i u_i, \qquad i = 1, \ldots n \qquad (2.14a)$$

In order to apply the above considerations for electronic hardware transients, or simulated numerical relaxation thereof, it should be realized that transients in actual hardware strongly depend on the energy storage capability of the actual net. Capacitances of very large values would make the system almost nonrelaxing, or relaxing very slowly, as opposed to the lack of capacitances which would cause the system to be without memory.

The stationary point solution of Equation (2.14a) based on contraction mapping theorem may now be derived by observing the sequential behavior of transients. First, an initial value V^0 chosen, the input u is next submitted, then the response V computed and fed back to the input of the neural net to replace the initial state. This sequence of events can be modeled through the following numerical recursion:

$$V_i^{k+1} = f\left[\frac{1}{G_i} \left(\sum_{j=1}^{n} T_{ij} V_j^k + I_i \right) \right], \quad i = 1, \ldots n \qquad (2.14b)$$

where the superscript $k = 0, 1, \ldots$, denotes the index of recursion. Introducing, for brevity:

$$t_{ij} \triangleq \frac{T_{ij}}{G_i}, \text{ and } i_i \triangleq \frac{I_i}{G_i}$$

allows rewriting the formula (2.14b) as:

$$V_i^{k+1} = f\left(\sum_{j=1}^{n} t_{ij} V_j^k + i_i \right), \quad i = 1, \ldots n \qquad (2.15a)$$

or, briefly:

$$V^{k+1} = f(t \, V^k + i) \qquad (2.15b)$$

This is the computational relaxation model for recursive calculations of V_i^{k+1} values. The model is valid for actual networks including network's parasitic

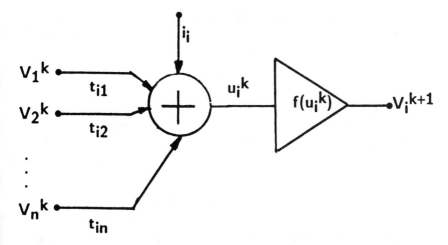

Figure 9.4. Model for recursive calculation of V^{k+1} using the gradient-type property of $E(V)$.

components, and it is depicted in Figure 9.4. Note that the coefficients t_{ij} of the model are dimensionless. The presented model is somewhat more complete than models found elsewhere in the literature, as it includes the input conductances G_i, biasing currents I_i, and finite neuron gains.

The computation algorithm (2.15) presented and based on the relaxation formula of the network is a static "neural" algorithm. The sufficient condition for its convergence is discussed in [13]. A number of dynamic (time-domain) neural algorithms can be used for evaluation of the actual convergence versus time. It has been verified in [14] that the Backward-Euler Gauss-Seidel relaxation method involves more complex techniques for an efficient matching into a parallel architecture of the net, but it is computationally more efficient than both Gauss-Jacobi and Forward-Euler methods.

In summary, the $V(t)$ converges in time to the minimum of $E(V)$ dependent upon the initial condition $V(0) = f(u(0))$. The system settles there with disregard to its dynamics near the minimum, although capacitors determine the actual rate of convergence to the minimum of E(V). The properties of trajectories depicting actual transients of the class of neural networks have been discussed and a simple recursive solution scheme has been outlined. This computational model called the *relaxation model*, although purely static, captures, if convergent, one of the final solutions of the time domain, or of the transient movement of the network.

3. EXAMPLES OF NEURAL OPTIMIZATION NETWORKS

3.1. Summing Circuit with Digital Output

Assume that the circuit from Figure 9.1 is to compute the sum of N analog voltages x_k with corresponding weighting coefficients a_k. Digital representation of the output sum is required, thus $V_i = 0, 1$, for $i = 0, 1, \ldots, n - 1$. Let us momentarily assume that the accurate analog sum of the signals is x, thus:

$$x = \sum_{k=0}^{N-1} a_k x_k \tag{3.16}$$

The computational energy which needs to be minimized for this circuit behaving momentarily as an n-bit A/D converter can be expressed as a squared error:

$$E_i = \frac{1}{2} \left(x - \sum_{i=0}^{n-1} V_i 2^i \right)^2 \tag{3.17a}$$

Expansion of the sum indicates that Equation (3.17a) will contain square terms $(V_i 2^i)^2$, thus making T_{ii} terms equal to 2^{2i}, instead of equal to zero as required. Thus, a supplemental term E_c as in (3.17b) should be added which, in addition to eliminating diagonal entries of T, will have minima at V_i equal to 0 or 1.

$$E_c = -\frac{1}{2} \sum_{i=0}^{n-1} 2^{2i} V_i (V_i - 1) \tag{3.17b}$$

Summing E_i, E_c and using Equation (2.4) for high-gain neurons leads to the relationship between the specific energy function value on the left side of Equation (3.18), and its general form as in Equation (2.4).

$$\frac{1}{2} \left(x - \sum_{i=0}^{n-1} V_i 2^i \right)^2 - \frac{1}{2} \sum_{i=0}^{n-1} 2^{2i} V_i (V_i - 1) = -\frac{1}{2} VTV - I^t V \tag{3.18}$$

Comparing coefficients on both sides of Equation (3.18) yields the conductance matrix and bias current vector as reported in [4]:

$$T_{ij} = -2^{i+j} \tag{3.19a}$$

$$I_i = -2^{2i-1} + 2^i x \tag{3.19b}$$

In the example case of a four-bit A/D converter, the results are:

$$T = - \begin{bmatrix} 0 & 2 & 4 & 8 \\ 2 & 0 & 8 & 16 \\ 4 & 8 & 0 & 32 \\ 8 & 16 & 32 & 0 \end{bmatrix} \qquad I = - \begin{bmatrix} \frac{1}{2} & - & x \\ 2 & - & 2x \\ 8 & - & 4x \\ 32 & - & 8x \end{bmatrix} \tag{3.19c}$$

In order to obtain the full diagram of the summing circuit, the value of x as in Equation (3.16) should be plugged into the left-hand side of formula (3.18), yielding the energy function as:

$$E = \frac{1}{2} \left(\sum_{k=0}^{N-1} a_k x_k - \sum_{i=0}^{n-1} V_i 2^i \right)^2 - \frac{1}{2} \sum_{i=0}^{n-1} 2^{2i} V_i (V_i - 1) \qquad (3.20a)$$

Rearranging the above expression results in the energy function for the summing circuit equal to:

$$E = -\frac{1}{2} \sum_{\substack{i=0 \\ i \neq j}}^{n-1} \sum_{j=0}^{n-1} - 2^{i+j} V_i V_j - \sum_{i=0}^{n-1} \left(- 2^{2i-1} + 2^i \sum_{k=0}^{N-1} a_k x_k \right) V_i$$
$$+ \frac{1}{2} \left(\sum_{k=0}^{N-1} a_k x_k \right)^2 \qquad (3.20b)$$

Comparing Equation (3.20b) with the right-hand side of Equation (3.18) allows the identification of the conductance matrix entries T_{ij} and neurons' input currents I_i of network T as:

$$T_{ij} = - 2^{i+j} \qquad (3.21a)$$

$$I_i = - 2^{2i-1} + 2^i \sum_{k=0}^{N-1} a_k x_k \qquad (3.21b)$$

Figure 9.5 shows the resulting network T with appropriate conductance values labeled. Conductances connect voltage sources x_j with inputs of neurons to produce current according to formula (3.21b). Note that the original negative signs of conductance values and of the current contribution as in Equations (3.19c) and (3.21b) have been absorbed by the feedback signal derived from inverted neuron outputs, and by the negative reference voltage $-1V$ applied to network T, respectively.

The approach presented in the preceding paragraphs can be extended to the case of binary addition. For binary-coded values of signals x, y, the corresponding energy function similar to the one obtained in Equation (3.20a) becomes:

$$E = \frac{1}{2} \left(\sum_{k=0}^{n-1} 2^k x_k + \sum_{k=0}^{n-1} 2^k y_k - \sum_{i=0}^{n} V_i 2^i \right)^2 - \frac{1}{2} \sum_{i=0}^{n} 2^{2i} V_i (V_i - 1) \qquad (3.22)$$

a)

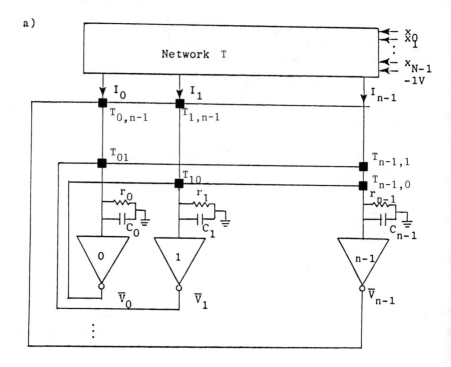

b)

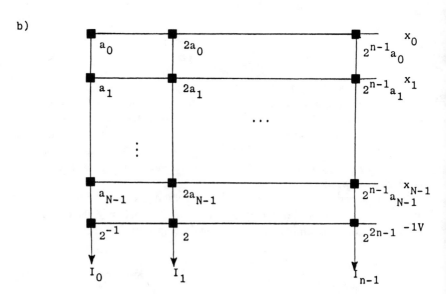

Figure 9.5. Neural network adder: (a) block diagram, and (b) network *T*.

Rearrangements of Equation (3.22) lead to the expression for values T_{ij} identical with Equation (3.21a). The conductances of network T are now the only difference, and they are specified by the following expression:

$$I_i = -2^{2i-1} + 2^i \left(\sum_{k=0}^{n-1} 2^k x_k + \sum_{k=0}^{n-1} 2^k y_k \right), \quad i = 0, 1, \ldots, n \qquad (3.23)$$

The binary adder's network T generating bias current vector $\mathbf{I}$ consists of $(2N + 1)(n + 1)$ conductances. The "neural" part of the adder remains unchanged and identical to previous cases of an A/D converter and analog signal adder.

3.2. Transient Analysis of Network

The convergence of transients for this network has been evaluated for different initial conditions for the NMOS neuron circuit [11,15]. For the simple two-dimensional case, and under the assumption of ideal network ($\lambda \rightarrow \infty$), energy functions have been computed, and convergence versus time evaluated, for $x = 0,1,2,3$. The resulting equipotential lines and related trajectories have been shown in Figure 9.6(a,b,c,d). The distance between each of the two neighboring lines is equal to $^1/_{16}$ of the total energy difference within the cube. As it may be seen, none of the energy functions has local minima distinctly within the cube; they are located in the vertices. Transitions in time take place towards one of the minima and generally not in the gradient direction.

In cases of $x = 1.3, 1.8$, the corresponding energy functions have minima at 01, 10, respectively, and a separating saddle point within the cube. The convergence of transients is to the desirable minimum in both cases if zero initial conditions are chosen. For other choices of initial conditions, the transients may end in the shallower of the two minima, thus yielding an incorrect response at the output of this neural type A/D converter. The case is depicted in Figure 9.6(e, f).

It has been expected that for small slopes of the energy surface the convergence will be slow. This has actually been observed in Figure 9.6(b,c) for curves leaving initial points most distant from the right solutions being 01, 10, respectively, and showing slowly varying transients near $V_1 = 0.25$ (Figure 9.6b), $V_1 = 0.75$ (Figure 9.6c), respectively. Slight discontinuities on all curves of Figure 9.6 are also noticeable. They are due to the shape of the voltage transfer characteristics near $u = 0$ for actual NMOS neurons simulated.

The results of transients simulation at the circuit level using the SPICE2G1.6 program for a four-bit summing network with zero initial conditions have been correct for 145 of 155 values. Input x has varied in the region [0, 15.5] with the step of 0.1 applied to a four-bit summing network. In all 10 cases of erroneous convergence, however, the settled binary output was adjacent to the correct

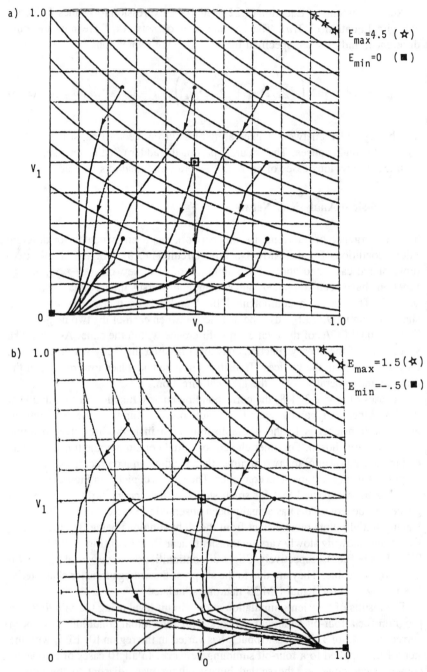

Figure 9.6. **Energy contours and transients for two-bit adder for different inputs (• denotes initial points, □ denotes zero initial conditions point): (a) 0, (b) 1, (c) 2, (d) 3, (e) 1.3, (f) 1.8.**

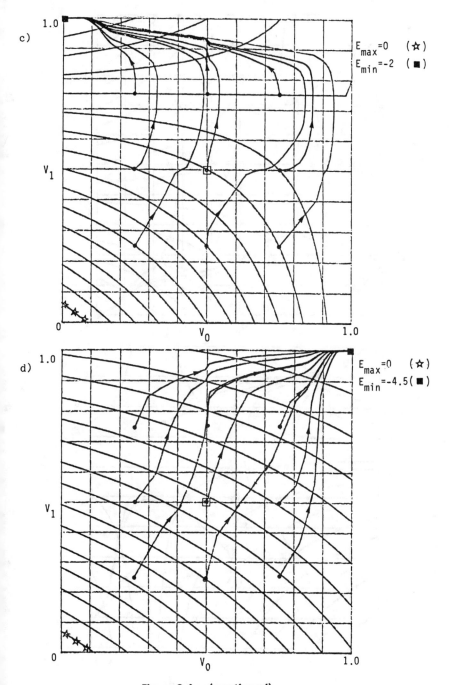

Figure 9.6. (*continued*).

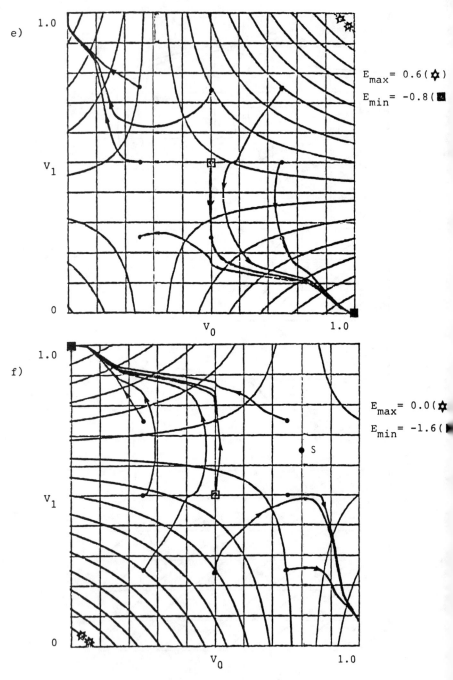

e)

$E_{max} = 0.6(\,✿\,)$

$E_{min} = -0.8(\,■\,$

f)

$E_{max} = 0.0(\,✿$

$E_{min} = -1.6(\,■$

Figure 9.6. (*continued*).

Table 9.1. Simulation results for input × from the range [0, 15.5], four-bit adder.

Input Integer Part	Input Decimal Part									
	0	.1	.2	.3	.4	.5	.6	.7	.8	.9
0	0	0	0	0	0	0.5	1	1	1	1
1	1	1	1	1	1	1	1	2	2	2
2	2	2	2	2	2	2.5	3	3	3	3
3	3	3	3	3	3	3	3	3	3	4
4	4	4	4	4	4	4.5	5	5	5	5
5	5	5	5	5	5	6	6	6	6	6
6	6	6	6	6	6	6.5	7	7	7	7
7	7	7	7	7	7	8	8	8	8	8
8	8	8	8	8	8	8.5	9	9	9	9
9	9	9	9	9	9	9	9	10	10	10
10	10	10	10	10	10	10.5	11	11	11	11
11	11	11	12	12	12	12	12	12	12	12
12	12	12	12	12	12	12.5	13	13	13	13
13	13	13	13	14	14	14	14	14	14	14
14	14	14	14	14	14	14.5	15	15	15	15
15	15	15	15	15	15					

answer, thus still making the resulting error small. Results of the transient analysis and subsequent thresholding of V are shown in Table 9.1.

Interesting results have been observed for the case when the integer answer for the sum problem does not exist because it is exactly equidistant from the adjacent integers. The V_0 bit has remained undetermined and it settled very close to 0.5 for eight of fifteen such cases. Evaluation of energy values (2.4a) or (2.6) has indeed shown flat minima spread between adjacent integers.

Sample transients illustrating such cases are shown in Figure 9.7. It may be seen from Figure 9.7(a) (case $x = 0.5$) that the energy function is monotonic, it has no saddle point within the cube and the output of the net converges to 0.5. Otherwise, if $x = 1.5$, the convergence is erroneous as shown in Figure 9.7(b), because the saddle point at $V_0 = V_1 = 0.5$ divides symmetrically the two monotonic subsurfaces of E.

Inspection of corresponding energy surface functions has also shown that for erroneous results listed in Table 9.1 in a four-dimensional case, the network outputs have converged to shallow local minima. The convergence to correct minima has usually been more reliable when started from a higher initial energy level, and in the vicinity of the minimum.

The network has also unmistakably rejected all obviously incorrect suggestions. Additions with negative results have all been rounded to the lowest sum 00. . 0. Additions with overflow sums have been rounded by the net to the highest sum 11 . . 1.

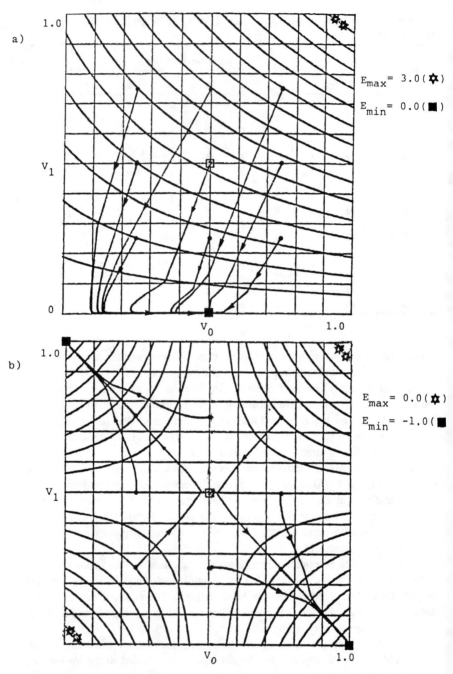

Figure 9.7. Energy contours and transients for two-bit adder for different inputs (• denotes initial points, □ denotes zero initial conditions point): (a) 0.5, (b) 1.5.

3.3. Energy Maps of Actual Example Network

The energy maps used for depicting transients in Section 2.2 have been generated for very high neuron gain values. The third term in the expression (2.4) has been vanishingly small in such a case. Using results obtained in (3.19c) for T and I leads to the following simplified energy function of an ideal two-bit summing network:

$$E = 2V_0 V_1 + \frac{V_0}{2} - x(V_0 + 2V_1) \qquad (3.24a)$$

In actual single-layer feedback neural networks, both finite λ values and conductances g_i are of significance, however. It can be seen that the accurate energy function for an actual network involves the third term in Equation (2.4) and it becomes:

$$E = 2V_0 V_1 + \frac{V_0}{2} - x(V_0 + 2V_1) + \sum_{i=0}^{1} G_i \int_{1/2}^{V_i} f_i^{-1}(z)\, dz \qquad (3.24b)$$

The actual energy contours of the example network have been shown in Figure 9.8 for three different conductance values g_i, $i = 0,1$, $x = 1.8$, $\lambda = 10$. The figure depicts the energy functions (3.24b) as compared with the ideal network's energy function (3.24a) shown in Figure 9.6(f). The case $x = 1.8$ has been selected because the energy function contains two minima and one saddle point, and the energy surface documents interesting properties of the network itself. The energy gradient for an ideal network ($\lambda \rightarrow \infty$) can be computed using (9.24a) as:

$$\nabla E(V) = \begin{bmatrix} 2V_1 + \dfrac{1}{2} - x \\ 2V_0 + 2 - 2x \end{bmatrix} \qquad (3.25)$$

Based on the discussion of Section 1.3, the solution of the equation below for $x = 1.8$:

$$\nabla E(V) = 0$$

results in a saddle point $S(0.8, 0.65)$ as referenced in Figure 9.6(f).

The saddle point of the actual network with $g_i = 1\Omega^{-1}$ shows only slight displacement from S as illustrated in Figure 9.8(a). The third term of the energy function (3.24b) becomes more contributing for $g_i = 1\Omega^{-1}$, and the energy contours in Figure 9.8(b) do not indicate the presence of the saddle point any

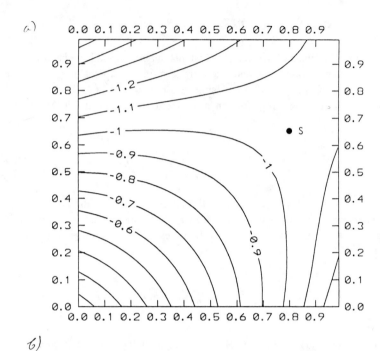

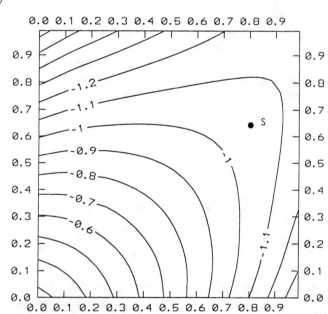

Figure 9.8. Energy contours for actual two-bit adder network with $\lambda = 10$, $x = 1.8$: (a) $g_i = 1\Omega^{-1}$, (b) $g_i = 0.1\Omega^{-1}$, (c) $g_i = 10\Omega^{-1}$.

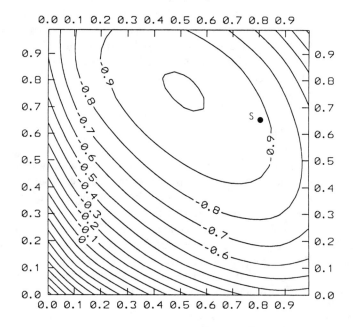

(S denotes the saddle point of an 'ideal', or
very high gain network shown in Figure 6f)

Figure 9.8. (cont.).

longer. It should be noted from Figure 9.8(b) that although the saddle point has been vanishing for cases of the dominant third term in energy expression, the minima of the constrained system still persist close to corners (1,0), (0,1). In the reference/ideal case from Figure 9.6(f) they are exactly in cube's corners.

Finally, using large values of $g_i = 10\Omega^{-1}$ causes drastic reshaping of the network's energy function. It can be seen from Figure 9.8(c) that the once useful network entirely lost its conversion error minimization properties. The network does not converge any longer to a digital representation of x. The energy surface displays neither saddle nor any of the two minima. The energy has become a convex function with a single minimum around (0.52, 0.75).

4. ASSOCIATIVE MEMORY

4.1. Basic Properties

One of the characteristics of a gradient-type net is that, if suitably trained, it can function as an associative memory. A number of different pattern vectors called prototypes can be stored in such a memory. If one of the stored vectors is presented to the memory for retrieval, the memory will remain in that state. If a distorted or incomplete prototype vector is presented, the memory is expected to evolve from that initial state to the nearest stable state being this prototype. Both auto- and heteroassociations can be stored in associative memory, and thus recovered in the presence of prototype vectors with noise, including the recovery of incomplete prototype vectors.

4.2. Training Algorithm

A memory learns in batch mode by modifying its conductance (weight) matrix T. Vectors can be stored, or memory trained, through the superposition of partial matrices T describing each pattern vector. The circuit diagram of an associative memory is shown in Figure 9.2. One necessary modification needed for the gradient-type net shown to represent an associative memory is that the neurons have to have bipolar output, or spanned between $(-1, 1)$, at least during the weight coefficients training phase. This corresponds to the transformation of the activation function $V(u)$ if it is defined as in Equation (4.26a) or transformation of the vector V, according to the relation (4.26b):

$$V(u) = \frac{1}{1 + e^{-\lambda u}} \tag{4.26a}$$

$$V \rightarrow 2\,V - 1 \tag{4.26b}$$

where 1 denotes the identity matrix. In subsequent discussion it will be assumed that transformation (4.26b) of the output vector V has been performed if needed, and that the bipolar response neurons with $f(u)$ as shown in Figure 9.1(b) are used to store bipolar pattern vectors. The associative memory design and analysis typically assumes that if the bias current vector I is zero, then the energy as in Equation (2.4), and as on the right-hand side of Equation (3.18) reduces to the simple quadratic form [1]:

$$E = -\frac{1}{2}\,V^t T\,V = -\frac{1}{2} \sum_{i=1}^{n} \sum_{j=1}^{n} T_{ij}\,V_i\,V_j. \tag{4.27}$$

Let us further assume that m prototype vectors $V^1, V^2, \ldots, V^m$ are to be stored. It will be postulated now that the conductance matrix T be chosen as:

$$T = \sum_{s=1}^{m} V^s\,V^{st} \tag{4.28}$$

This postulate leads to the following expression for energy (4.27):

$$E = -\frac{1}{2} V^t \sum_{s=1}^{m} V^s V^{st} V \tag{4.29a}$$

The above expression can be rewritten as:

$$E = -\frac{1}{2} \sum_{s=1}^{m} (V^t V^s)(V^{st} V) \tag{4.29b}$$

Each expression in parenthesis of (4.29b) is a scalar product of two vectors containing $+1$, -1 entries and its possibly largest value is clearly n. This takes place when vectors V and V^s are identical. Thus, it can be concluded that the lowest value of energy $E(V)$ as in Equation (4.29b) is at $V = V^s$, $s = 1, 2, \ldots,$ m, and this minimum is equal to [1]:

$$E_{\min} = -\frac{1}{2} n^2 \tag{4.29c}$$

As stated in Section 1.3, the final conductance matrix T requires additionally zero diagonal entries. Thus, the following final choice for T based on postulate (4.28) can be made:

$$T = \sum_{s=1}^{m} V^s V^{st} - m I \tag{4.30}$$

The formula (4.30) will satisfy the conditions for the minima of energy function being at $V = V^2$, $s = 1, 2, \ldots, m$ as formulated earlier in this chapter. The minima will be equal to:

$$E_{\min} = -\frac{1}{2} (n^2 - mn)$$

The learning algorithm expressed in Equation (4.30) is known as Hebbian-type learning. It is an algorithm easy to implement, however, its capacity and retrieval performance can be modified to yield a better memory [16,17] derived from this type of memory.

Figure 9.9 shows an example of a four-bit associative memory with $(3)_{10}$, $(6)_{10}$ stored as:

$$V^1 = \begin{bmatrix} -1 \\ -1 \\ 1 \\ 1 \end{bmatrix}, \quad V^2 = \begin{bmatrix} -1 \\ 1 \\ 1 \\ -1 \end{bmatrix} \tag{4.31a}$$

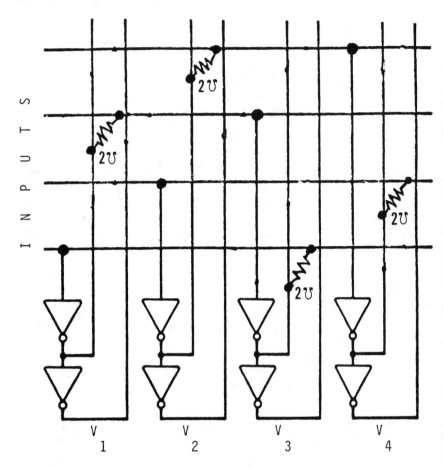

Figure 9.9.   Implementation of the example memory storing 3 and 6.

The weights T_{ij} have been computed using Equation (4.30) and are of the following values:

$$T = \begin{bmatrix} 0 & 0 & -2 & 0 \\ 0 & 0 & 0 & -2 \\ -2 & 0 & 0 & 0 \\ 0 & -2 & 0 & 0 \end{bmatrix} \Omega^{-1} \qquad (4.31)$$

The energy levels computed from Equation (4.29b) yield for this particular example memory value of 4 at 0, 5, 10, 15, value of 0 at 1, 2, 4, 7, 8, 11, 13, 14 and value of -4 at 3, 6, 9, 12. It should be noted that the numbers k stored and their 2's complements have the same values of minima. Since the Hamming distance from a slightly distorted prototype to a complement of the prototype is large, the retrieval of the complement is not immediate.

The capacity of the Hopfield associative memory has been studied in [18]. If m prototypes are chosen at random, the maximum asymptotic value of m in order that most of the prototypes are exactly recoverable is $n/2 \ln n$. For the exact recovery of every one of the m prototypes, the m value lowers to 50% of the heuristic answer above, as n approaches infinity. In the case of 100 nodes, the ordinary model can store about five patterns. For an increased order of correlations, both the capacity and the number of connections of associative memory increase dramatically.

Although the weights for Hopfield's associative memory are typically computed using formula (4.30) yielding a conductance matrix having zero diagonal elements with zero current vectors, the biasing currents may also be helpful in establishing certain stored prototypes. Conventional electronic multivibrators will be considered below as examples of associative memory converging to the closest stable prototype vectors stored.

4.3. Flip-Flops as Associative Memories

Commonly known bistable multivibrators can be viewed as circuits with two stored stable states being the following vectors:

$$V^1 = \begin{bmatrix} -1 \\ 1 \end{bmatrix} \quad \text{and} \quad V^2 = \begin{bmatrix} 1 \\ -1 \end{bmatrix} \tag{4.32}$$

Formula (4.30) can now be used for computation of the conductance matrix $\mathbf{T}$ as:

$$T = \begin{bmatrix} 0 & -2 \\ -2 & 0 \end{bmatrix} \Omega^{-1} \tag{4.33}$$

The corresponding computational energy function obtained from (4.27) is:

$$E = -\frac{1}{2} [V_1 \ V_2] \begin{bmatrix} 0 & -2 \\ -2 & 0 \end{bmatrix} \begin{bmatrix} V_1 \\ V_2 \end{bmatrix} \tag{4.34a}$$

or, simply:

$$E = 2V_1 V_2. \tag{4.34b}$$

The energy function computed according to the formula (4.34b) is shown in Figure 9.10(a), and the corresponding bistable multivibrator circuit diagram is shown in Figure 9.10(b). The energy function from Figure 9.10(a) consists of the

a)

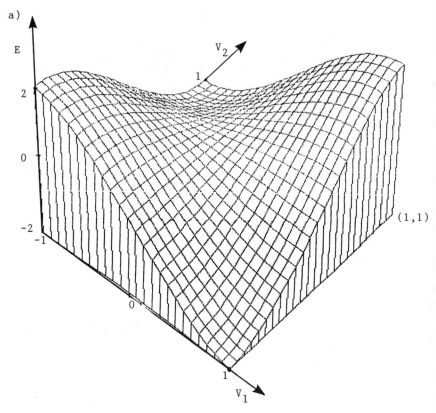

Figure 9.10. Bistable flip-flop as an associative memory: (a) energy surface, (b) circuit diagram, and (c) realizable version of (b).

two monotonically decreasing surfaces. One surface decreases toward the prototype V^1 below the line $V_1 = V_2$, and the other toward the prototype V^2 above the line $V_1 = V_2$. The plot depicts clearly that this bistable neural net has perfect recall capability to the closer prototype. It should be noted that conductances of negative values $-2\Omega^{-1}$ would change signs when inverting neurons are used as shown in Figure 9.10(c).

A monostable circuit similar to the one presented in Figure 9.10 can also be designed based on the associative memory concept. Assume that the prototype stored will be vector V^1 as in Equation (4.32). It is obvious that the computation of the conductance matrix **T,** and of the energy function E as in (4.33), (4.34), respectively, leads to the result:

$$T = \begin{bmatrix} 1 & -1 \\ -1 & 0 \end{bmatrix} \Omega^{-1} \qquad (4.35a)$$

b)

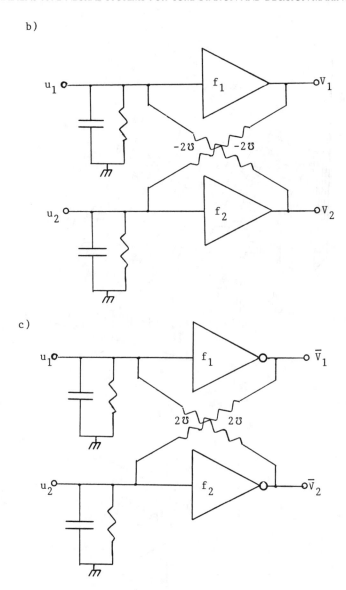

Figure 9.10.   (cont.).

$$E = V_1 V_2 \tag{4.35b}$$

The correct recall capability would now be limited to the area below the line $V_1 = V_2$ as it can be seen from Figure 9.10(a), and the circuit actually, in addition to V^1, also retains one complementary spurious prototype V^2 as defined in

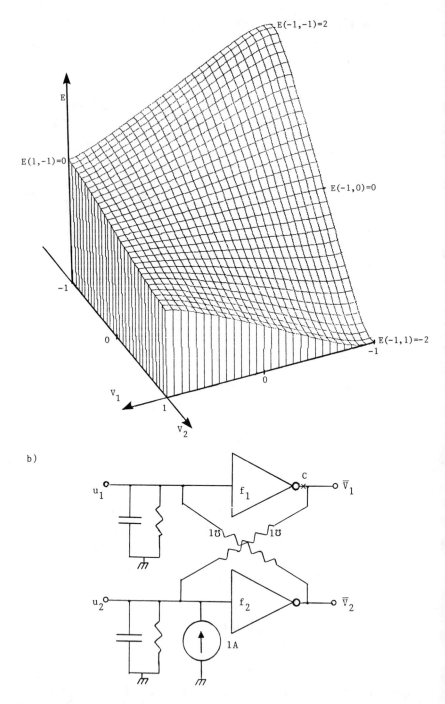

Figure 9.11. Monostable circuit as an associative memory: (a) energy surface, and (b) circuit diagram.

Equation (4.32). Thus, it seems indispensable to reshape the energy surface so that there exists only one single association, namely V^1, within the entire hypercube $(-1,1)$. The arbitrary choice of current vector as:

$$I = \begin{bmatrix} 0 \\ 1 \end{bmatrix}$$

and computation of the energy from Equation (2.4) leads to the modified energy value as:

$$E = V_1 V_2 - [0\ 1] \begin{bmatrix} V_1 \\ V_2 \end{bmatrix}, \qquad (4.36a)$$

or, simply:

$$E = (V_1 - 1)V_2 \qquad (4.36b)$$

It can now be seen from Figure 9.11(a) showing the energy function (4.36) that the only association produced by the network can be V^1. Figure 9.11(b) depicts the circuit diagram of this single-prototype vector associative memory with two neurons. Negative conductances have again been eliminated by virtue of inverting neurons used. It should be noted that this circuit does not exactly correspond to the monostable multivibrator since it has no quasi-stable state V^2. The circuit responds instantaneously to any association with convergence to V^1 as soon as the association is enforced at its input, and it does not stop in V^2. The modification of the circuit from Figure 9.11(b) by inserting a single capacitance in the point marked C would result in such a stop-over in the quasi-stable state and it could be observed at the output V_2.

4.4. Concluding Remarks

It has been shown that analog neural networks can be used to perform specific optimization, or decision, tasks. The Hopfield model network discussed here can be trained in batch mode either through fitting of the objective function being the computational energy function to be minimized to its standard form, or by using the Hebbian learning algorithm. Hebbian learning is especially valid for associative memory design. The examples shown have been based on a discussion of surfaces of relevant energy functions and illustrated by the actual simulations of transients in neural circuits to be evaluated. Both ideal and actual neural network energy surfaces have been demonstrated to provide insight into the network behavior.

The main aspect of the report has been the emphasis of an existing link between the transient behavior of a class of neural networks, its energy functions, and its static algorithmic solutions. It has been shown that the exploration of the neural network model can lead to the novel circuit configurations able to perform useful tasks such as addition or conversion. Also, certain conventional nonlinear circuits such as flip-flops have been revisited and considered as special cases of associative memories.

REFERENCES

[1] J.J. Hopfield and D.W. Tank, " 'Neural' Computation of Decisions and in Optimization Problems," *Biological Cybernetics,* Vol. 52, 1985, pp. 141–154.

[2] J.J. Hopfield, "Neurons with Graded Response Have Collective Computational Properties Like Those of Two State Neurons," *Proceedings of the National Academy of Sciences,* Vol. 81, 1984, pp. 3088–3092.

[3] J.J. Hopfield and D.W. Tank, "Computing with Neural Circuits: A Model," *Science,* Vol. 233, 1986, pp. 625–633.

[4] D.W. Tank and J.J. Hopfield, "Simiple 'Neural' Optimization Networks: An A/D Converter, Signal Decision Circuit and a Linear Programming Circuit," *IEEE Transactions on Circuits and Systems,* Vol. CAS-33, No. 5, May 1986, pp. 533–541.

[5] M.A. Silviotti, M.R. Emerling, and C.A. Mead, "VLSI Architectures for Implementation of Neural Networks," *Proceedings of the Conference on Neural Networks in Computing,* American Institute of Physics, 1986, pp. 408–411.

[6] W. Hubbard, D. Schwartz, J. Denker, H. Graf, R. Jackel, B. Straughn, and D. Tennant, "Electronic Neural Networks," *Proceedings of the Conference on Neural Networks in Computing,* American Institute of Physics, 1986, pp. 227–234.

[7] R.E. Howard, L.D. Jackel, and H.P. Graf, "Electronic Neural Networks," *AT&T Technical Journal,* May 1988, pp. 58–64.

[8] H.P. Graf, L.D. Jackel, and W.E. Hubbard, "VLSI Implementation of a Neural Network Model," *IEEE Computer (Special Issue on Artificial Neural Systems),* March 1988, pp. 41–49.

[9] J. Alspector, R.B. Allen, V. Hu, and S. Satyanarayana, "Stochastic Learning Networks and Their Electronic Implementation," *Proceedings of the IEEE Conference on Neural Information Processing Systems—Natural and Synthetic,* Denver, CO, November 8–12, 1987, pp. 9–21.

[10] J.M. Zurada and M.J. Kang, "Summing Networks Using Neural Optimization Concept," *Electronics Letters,* Vol. 24, No. 10, May 12, 1988, pp. 616–617.

[11] J.M. Zurada and M.J. Kang, "Computational Circuits Using Neural Optimization," *Proceedings of the 1988 International Conference on Neural Networks,* San Diego, CA, July 24–27, 1988.

[12] S. Park, "Signal Space Interpretation of Hopfield Neural Network for Optimization," *Proceedings of the 1989 IEEE International Symposium on Circuits and Systems,* Portland, OR, May 9–12, 1989, pp. 2181–2184.

[13] J.M. Zurada and W. Shen, "Sufficient Condition for Convergence of Relaxation Algorithm in Actual Single-Layer Neural Networks," *IEEE Transactions on Neural Networks,* Vol. 1, No. 4, Dec. 1990, pp. 300–303.

[14]   E. DiZitti, G.M. Bisio, D.D. Caviglia, M. Chirico, and G. Parodi, "Analysis of Neural Algorithms for Parallel Architectures," *Proceedings of the 1989 IEEE International Symposium on Circuits and Systems,* Portland, OR, May 9–12, 1989, pp. 2187–2190.

[15]   J.M. Zurada and M.J. Kang, "Computational Circuits Using neural Optimization Concept," *International Journal of Electronics,* Vol. 67, No. 3, 1989, pp. 311–320.

[16]   M.S. Hassoun, "Discrete Dynamic Neural Memories: Training and Performance," *Proceedings of the 1989 IEEE International Symposium on Circuits and Systems,* Portland, OR, May 9–12, 1989, pp. 470–473.

[17]   M.H. Hassoun and A.M. Youssef, "High Performance Recording Algorithm for Hopfield Model Associative Memories," *Optical Engineering,* Vol. 28, No. 1, January 1989, pp. 47–54.

[18]   R.J. McElice, E.C. Posner, E.R. Rodemich, and S.V. Venkatesh, "The Capacity of the Hopfield Associative Memory," *IEEE Transactions on Information Theory,* Vol. IT-33, No. 4, July 1987, pp. 461–482.

10
Computation on Graphs: From Neural Networks to Cellular Automata

Max Garzon*
Stan Franklin**
Department of Mathematical Sciences and Institute for Intelligent Systems
Memphis State University
Memphis, TN

1. INTRODUCTION

Classical computational theories originated in attempts to understand calculations as performed by humans. All the resultant models (Turing machines, Church's λ—calculus, Chomsky grammars, Markov algorithms, etc.) are based on the seemingly sequential nature of conscious human calculation. They are inherently sequential. As a consequence, their common physical realizations, von Neumann computers, are now running headlong into fundamental limitations such as the speed of light.

In the past four decades, our notion of computation has changed radically as a result of a paradigm shift in cognitive science. That *cognition is essentially computation* is now the working hypothesis of many contemporary cognitive scientists. In this new sense, it is becoming clear that the classical models of computation barely scratch the surface of a satisfactory theory.

The massively parallel nature of the human nervous system immediately suggests parallel models for a theory of computation that would encompass cognition. Parallel, coarse-grained[1] models of computation have been explored. One such is illustrated by the PRAM-parallel random-access machine, a shared-memory model. But coarse-grain models appear ill-suited for studying cognition. In more applicable models the activity of the various processes must be tightly orchestrated. Hence, the processors must be highly interconnected. This leads to

---
* Partially supported by NSF Grant DCR–8602319.
** Partially supported by ONR Grant N0014–88–K–0110.
[1] For example, consisting of relatively few, but relatively powerful, processors.

models of *computation on digraphs,* with nodes supporting processors, and links carrying communication. A number of such models have been proposed including cellular automata, automata networks and, of course, neural networks.

Cellular automata have been used successfully to create digital models of a physical universe [1,2] and their phenomena (chemical reactions [3], diffusion processes [4], hydrodynamics [5], mechanics [1,6], etc.). Their homogeneity appeals to physical intuition. Also common tools of physics, such as energy functions or statistical mechanics, can be used to analyze their long term behavior. Cellular automata are, in many respects, far more suitable for physical modeling than traditional models of computation.

On the other hand, neural networks have been successfully applied to create computational models of a cognitive universe [7] and their phenomena (associative memory [8], learning [9] and adaptation [10], pattern recognition [11], speech [12], artificial life [13], etc). Their similarity to vertebrate nervous systems appeals to cognitive intuition. Again neural networks are, in many respects, far more suitable for cognitive modeling than traditional models. Moreover, combinatorial problems that are hard in the classical sense can be given quick, good-enough solutions using neural networks [15,16].

The more general concept of an automata network provides a natural generalization of both cellular automata and neural networks [17]. They are natural models of computer networks, but as yet, little is known about their applications and potential for discrete modeling.

Thus, the time seems ripe to ask whether these models are as fundamentally different in nature as their applications seem to suggest. Since they are all models of computation on graphs, one might hope to provide a unified theory to encompass them all. Such a theory would allow us to precisely formulate several important questions. First, what sort of tasks are amenable to processing by these models? Second, how does their computational power compare to one another and to classical models? Third, are there general-purpose, rather than application-specific, devices for computing on graphs?

This chapter surveys recent progress toward providing such a unified theory and toward answering these questions. In this theory, automata networks define a transformation of their global states. This transformation naturally iterates into a dynamical system. This dynamical systems approach to neural computing allows precise formulations of significant problems about the computational power of neural networks. In particular, *cellular automata, neural networks and automata networks turn out to be equivalent in computational power for a large class of digraphs. If implemented on infinite graphs, they are strictly more powerful than a Turing machine. However, within this class there remain unsolvable problems such as the Stability Problem. The existence of a universal neural network, of interest in its own right, plays an important role in establishing these results. It also raises the possibility of implementing a general-purpose neurocomputer.*

The next two sections provide key definitions which allow a precise formulation of problems solvable by computation on graphs. Section 4 deals with characterizing those transformations which are computable on graphs. They play the role in this theory that partial recursive functions play in classical computibility. Section 5 is concerned with the problem of comparing the computational power of three major models. Section 6 is concerned with the existence of unsolvable problems.

2. ALGORITHMIC AND DYNETIC PROBLEMS

Classical computability theory is concerned with solving algorithmic problems (i.e., problems that could, in principle, be solved using a computer). For example, one cannot hope to determine whether or not an arbitrary real number is rational by using a computer. An arbitrary real number cannot even be *given* to a Turing machine since, regardless of the choice of representation, some reals will require infinitely many digits. An *algorithmic problem* consists of a possibly infinite list of questions expressible as *finite* strings over some *fixed*, finite alphabet (for instance, decimal digits). For example, one may ask whether or not a rational number is an integer, since every rational number is expressible as a finite string of symbols over the decimal alphabet. In this case, an *instance* of the algorithmic problem is a rational number given as a finite string. The "INTEGER PROBLEM FOR THE RATIONALS" consisting of the infinite list of finite strings involving all possible such instances, is commonly stated in the following format:

INPUT: a binary string ω over $\{0, 1, \overline{1}\}$

OUTPUT: $\begin{cases} \textbf{yes,} \text{ if } \omega \text{ represents an integer;} \\ \textbf{no,} \text{ otherwise.} \end{cases}$

Thus, classical computibility theory implicitly assumes that all kinds of information be encodable as finite *strings* of symbols.

An ever-increasing body of evidence, however, points to human use of pictorial representations rather than strings, even in the use of ordinary language. Although finite images are certainly encodable as strings, processing the semantic content of translated images turns simple tasks into expensive string processes. Sequential processing of images via a single processor only compounds the problem. What is needed is a representation of pictorial information that preserves local relations among image elements (pixels) while still requiring only finitely many symbols. The same kind of representation is also naturally applicable to other computational problems.

Digraphs seem to be an ideal tool for this task. Nodes can be used to represent pixels and links to represent local relations among them. But, in order for the digraph to be physically realizable, each node must have only finitely many

incoming and outgoing arcs (i.e., the digraph must be *locally finite*). In order to
have full computational ability [18,19], we will simply assume a *countably
infinite* number of nodes. Thus, we are led to the notion of a cellular space. A
cellular space $\langle D,\{Q_i\}_i \rangle$ consists of a countable (finite or infinite), locally finite,
directed graph D (which may be a symmetric digraph, i.e., just a graph, in the
case of a cellular automaton) with vertex set V and a family of finite sets Q_i (each
containing the *quiescent* state 0), the possible activation levels (or states) of each
cell i. Associated with every cellular space is a *configuration space* $\Pi_i Q_i$ (or
simply C) consisting of all *configurations* (or *total states*, or *state vectors*).

   Cellular spaces allow us to generalize the concept of an algorithmic problem
for pictorial information processing. The current paradigm in neural-network
problem solving takes roughly the following form. Some nodes of a network are
singled out as *input* nodes. Some others are assigned as *output* nodes. Initially,
suitable states (activation levels) are clamped to the input nodes, and the network
is then *repeatedly updated*. After a certain period of time, the network stabilizes
and the output is then "collected" from the output nodes. From an abstract point
of view, one just has a set of initial configurations and a mapping (functional or
relational) that associates other configurations with them. Thus, we can formulate the most general type of problem that could, in principle, be solved using
graphical representations.

Definition 2.1:   Let C be the configuration space and $I,J \subseteq C$ arbitrary but fixed
subsets of C. A (functional) *dynetic problem P* is a function

$$P: I \to J.$$

The members of I are called instances or inputs of the problem P and the
members of J are called solutions or outputs of the problem P. The symbol
P can also stand for a relation $P \subseteq I \times J$ (more than one output is allowed
for a given input).

   Dynetic problems are those one might expect to solve via computation on
digraphs. The next step is to define precisely what is meant by a solution. We
will take a dynamical systems approach. Any model of computation on digraphs
can be viewed in a natural way as a dynamical system. At a given time, the
processor at each node assumes a certain state or activation. The nodes of the
digraph, each labeled with its corresponding state, specify the global state or
configuration of the system at the given time. The system starts in an initial
configuration and, at each tick of the clock[2], computes its next configuration and
updates itself. The system updating itself defines a function $T: C \to C$ called the
global dynamics of the system. The global dynamics of the system is a self-map
of configuration space.

---

   [2] We assume all our models are discrete.

Systems of this type will be generically refered to as *automata networks*. Automata networks, and in particular, neural networks and cellular automata, will be carefully defined in Section 4.

Definition 2.2: A *solution* of a dynetic problem is the global dynamics of some automata network $T: C \rightarrow C$ that, upon iteration, stabilizes on each instance of the problem at the correct output, i.e., it satisfies the following condition:

for each $x \in I$, there exists a positive integer t (which may depend on x) such that:

$$T^{t+1}(x) = T^t(x) = P(x).$$

If P has a solution it is said to be *neurally solvable*. In case P is a relation, $P(x)$ can be any element in J so that $(x, T(x)) \in P$. A dynetic decision problem $P: I \rightarrow J$ is one with only two possible answers (YES/NO configurations) in its range J. For example, the Stability Problem for neural networks consists of a set I of encodings $\langle N,x \rangle$ of a network and its input, where:

$$P(\langle N,x \rangle) := (N \text{ stabilizes on input } x).$$

A dynetic decision problem is *weakly solvable* if there exists a neural network N that stabilizes on an input $x \in C$ if and only if $P(x) = $ YES.

A dynetic problem is solvable on a network of a certain type if the global dynamics that solves it is induced by a network of that type.

One may illustrate the distinction between the notions of algorithmic problems[3] and dynetic problems with the Halting Problem for Turing machines, a fundamental Turing unsolvable problem. We show below that this problem is solvable by infinite neural networks. That discussion will require the reducibility of one dynetic problem to another, a concept of interest in itself.

Definition 2.3: A dynetic problem $P: I \rightarrow J$ is *reducible* to a dynetic problem $Q: I' \rightarrow J'$ (denoted $P \leqslant Q$) if there exist solvable dynetic problems $H: I \rightarrow I'$ and $H': J' \rightarrow J$ such that $P = T'' \circ Q \circ T'$, where T', T'' are the solutions of H, H', respectively. $\square$

3. GRAPHICAL MODELS OF COMPUTATION

As graphical models of computation we consider neural networks, and generalized cellular automata over homogeneous digraphs (Cayley graphs of arbitrary

---

[3] See [20] for a detailed definition.

finitely generated groups—see definition below), as particular cases of a very general type of *automata network*. Although other types of networks (asynchronous, continuous, and/or probabilistic) lead to important models, we have restricted our attention to automata networks that are discrete, synchronous, and deterministic.

It is *necessary* to have precise formal definitions of parallel models of computation in order to be able to make meaningful and precise statements about their relative computational power. While the definition of cellular automata on Euclidean digraphs (lattices) is standard, there are many varieties of neural networks, and virtually no commonly accepted definition of automata network. Below, we propose fairly general definitions of discrete neural networks and automata networks.

Although it may be attractive to postulate an infinite number of cell states or activation levels, the issue of physical realizability and our real inability to *physically* control and *manipulate* an infinite number of activation levels suggests that it would be better to first develop a general theory of automata networks with finitely many cell states. Hence, we assume that each cell i is capable of storing some information represented by a state from a *finite* set Q_i with a special *quiescent* activation level (or state) denoted 0. This state set may be peculiar for a given cell (as in neural or automata networks) or uniform for all cells (as in cellular automata). It may also have a restricted structure (a finite ring in neural networks) or be arbitrary (cellular automata or automata networks). We also assume that the underlying communications digraph of each network is locally finite (each cell directly communicates only with finitely many others).

3.1. Automata Networks

After much informal discussion of automata networks, the time has arrived for their precise definition.

Definition 3.1: An *automata network* is a pair $A = \langle D, \{M_i\} \rangle$ consisting of a cellular space $(D, \{Q_i\})$ and an associated family of finite-state machines M_i (only finitely many of which are distinct) with input alphabet $\Sigma_i := Q_{i_1} \times \ldots \times Q_{i_{d_i}}$, and local transition functions:

$$\delta_i : Q_i \times \Sigma_i \to Q_i$$
$$(x_i, x_{i_1}, \ldots, x_{i_{d_i}}) \mapsto \delta_i(x_i, x_{i_1}, \ldots, x_{i_{d_i}}),$$

where $i_1, \ldots, i_{d_i}$ are the cells with a link into cell i in D. $\square$

An automata network operates locally as follows. A copy of a finite-state machine M_i (called the *computing* or *processing* element) occupies each vertex i

of D, which is then called a *cell*—or also a *site* or *node*. *Synchronously,* each copy M_i looks up its input in the states $x_{i_1}, \ldots, x_{i_{d_i}}$ of its neighbor cells and its own state x_i, and then changes its state according to a prespecified local dynamics δ_i. The automata network thus performs its calculation by repeating this atomic move any number of times, possibly very many.

The global operation of an automata network is best viewed as a discrete dynamical system. Given a configuration at a certain instant of time t, an automata network transforms the current configuration of the cellular space into a new configuration by its local action. This induces a global dynamics $T: C \to C$ defined by:

$$T(x)_i = \delta_i(x_i, x_{i_1}, \ldots, x_{i_{d_i}}), \qquad (3.1)$$

where $i_1, \ldots, i_{d_i}$ are the cells adjacent to i, and x_j is the state of j. Moreover, since the underlying digraph is locally finite, the restriction of T to C_0 (configurations with only finitely many nonquiescent cells) maps into C_0. The tth iteration of T will be denoted T^t.

This general definition captures the classical models of parallel computation as well as most synchronous discrete models including neural networks and cellular automata.

3.2. Cellular Automata

The cellular space for a cellular automaton is defined on a homogeneous graph determined by a group G with finitely many generators X. A *Cayley graph* $\Gamma(G,X)$ is the graph whose vertices are the elements of G and whose edges, colored with generators j (and their inverses j^{-1}) from X, connect vertices i and $i.j$ (or $i.j^{-1}$, respectively), the product "." being taken as elements in G. Thus, a Cayley graph is a symmetric digraph (i.e., a graph).

Familiar examples are hypercubes of dimension d on 2^d vertices (the Cayley graph of the elementary abelian two-group of rank d with the standard generating set), finite or infinite euclidean lattices (the Cayley graph of the free abelian group of rank d with the standard set of free generators), and uniform trees (the Cayley graph of the free group of finite rank with the standard set of free generators). Other examples, as well as detailed definitins of the group theoretical terms used above, can be found in the classical book by Coxeter and Moser [21].

Definition 3.2: A *cellular automaton* is a triple $M = \langle \Gamma, N, M \rangle$ consisting of a cellular space (Γ, Q) with common state set Q over a Cayley graph Γ, a finite set N (the neighborhood of M) of vertices of Γ, a copy of a single finite-state machine M at each node i with input alphabet $Q^d := Q \times \ldots \times Q$ (d times) and local transition function:

$$\delta: Q \times Q^d \to Q$$
$$(x_i, x_1, \ldots, x_d) \mapsto \delta(x_i, x_1, \ldots, x_d) \tag{3.2}$$

where $d = |N|$ is the number of cells in the neighborhood N.[4] $\square$

The global dynamics of a cellular automaton is defined by Equation (3.1) with $d_i := d$ and $\delta_i := \delta$ for all sites i.

3.3. Neural Networks

Neural networks differ from cellular automata primarily in two aspects: (a) the underlying network is no longer homogeneous but an arbitrary locally finite digraph; and (b) the transition functions first compute weighted sums of inputs from neighboring cells (which makes the cell unable to detect from whence specific inputs come). Thus, we assume that the state set is a finite ring R with unity, although some of the results of this chapter carry over to weights and activations from arbitrary rings, including the real numbers. (A theory of computability over infinite rings has been initiated, by Blum, Schub, and Smale [23] among others.)

Each arc from vertex j to vertex i is labeled with a weight w_{ij}. Cells sum their weighted inputs and apply an *activation function* $f_i: R \to R$. Each f_i satisfies $f_i(0) = 0$ (in order to avoid spontaneous generation of activation). For some results presented below we must also assume that $f_i(1)$ is a unit (to avoid trivial networks). The weighted sum of the inputs to each cell from its neighbors is given by a function called net_i, which plays a role reminiscent of that of δ_i. Thinking of a neural network as a discrete dynamical system, at any time $t + 1$ (t a nonnegative integer), the net-input at i is given by:

$$net_i(t + 1) = \sum_j w_{ij} \, a_j(t), \tag{3.3}$$

where:

$$a_j(t) = f_j(net_j(t)) \tag{3.4}$$

is the activation of the cell j at time t, and the sum is taken over all cells j supporting links into i.

Definition 3.3: A (discrete) *neural network* is a triple $N = \langle D, R, \{f_i\} \rangle$ consisting of a cellular space (D, R) whose state space R is a finite ring with unity, a countable (finite or infinite), locally finite, arc-weighted, digraph D, and a

---

[4] which may be different from the generating set X.

family of activation functions f_i, one for each vertex i in D. The local dynamics of N is defined by Equations (3.3) and (3.4) above. □

There are two possible interpretations of the notion of configuration of a neural network. One might look at the vector of all net-inputs to individual cells during a particular time step, or one might choose the vector of all activations of individual cells during that time step, as is done in the definition above. At a fixed time t, the network has at each cell i its net input $net_i(t)$ and its activation $a_i(t)$. The vector of net-inputs x has in its ith component the net-input $x_i = net_i(t)$ of the ith cell of D, a value from the ring R, and is thus a member of R^V. (Recall that R^V is the set of all functions from V to R, or the cartesian product of R with itself the cardinality of V times.) Similarly, the vector of activations $(a_i(t))$ is also a member of R^V. In the following, we shall use C to refer to activation space and call it the configuration (activation) space of the network, and use R^V to refer to the net-input space.

Each of these possibilities gives rise to its own global dynamics. At each tick of the time clock, the current net-input vector changes, as does the activation vector. These changes reflect the two distinct global dynamics of the network.

More formally, the family of functions f_i mapping R into R gives rise to a product function $F: R^V \to C$ so that the following diagram commutes under composition of functions:

$$
\begin{array}{ccc}
& F & \\
R^V & \to & C \\
\pi_i \downarrow & & \downarrow \pi_i \\
R & \to & R \\
& f_i &
\end{array}
$$

where π_i is the projection from R^V onto R. This means that for each cell i and each net-input vector $x \in R^V$, $F(x)_i = f_i(x_i)$.

We are now able to define the *net-input global dynamics* $T_{net}: R^V \to R^V$ of the network. For any net-input vector $x \in R^V$ put:

$$T_{net}(x)_i = net_i(F(x)) \tag{3.5}$$

This gives rise to the following commutative diagram:

$$
\begin{array}{ccc}
& T_{net} & \\
R^V & \to & R^V \\
F \downarrow & & \downarrow \pi_i \\
C & \to & R \\
& net_i &
\end{array}
$$

This global dynamics T_{net} describes the evolution of the entire network via the net-input vectors.

In a manner similar to the definition of F above, for each cell i, the net-input function net_i maps R into R. This family of functions gives rise to a product function $net: C \rightarrow R^V$ so that the following diagram commutes under composition of functions:

$$
\begin{array}{ccc}
 & net & \\
C & \rightarrow & R^V \\
id \downarrow & & \downarrow \pi_i \\
C & \rightarrow & R \\
 & net_i &
\end{array}
$$

where π_i is the projection from R^V onto R and id is the identity map. This means that for each cell i and each activation vector $x \in C$, $net_i(x) = \pi_i(net(x))$.

In an analogous fashion we now define the *activation global dynamics* $T_{act}: C \rightarrow C$ of the network. For any activation vector $x \in C$ put:

$$T_{act}(x)_i = f_i(net_i(x)) \tag{3.6}$$

This gives rise to the following commutative diagram:

$$
\begin{array}{ccc}
 & T_{act} & \\
C & \rightarrow & C \\
net_i \downarrow & & \downarrow \pi_i \\
R & \rightarrow & R \\
 & f_i &
\end{array}
$$

The *global dynamics* $T: C \rightarrow C$ of the neural network N is defined as follows. For any configuration $x \in C$, put:

$$T(x)_i = f_i(net_i(x)) \tag{3.7}$$

Thus, both global dynamics of neural networks are also self-maps of their respective configuration spaces.

3.4. Finite Bandwidth

Some of the results presented below, particularly the comparisons of computational power of neural networks and cellular automata, require an additional hypothesis. We restrict our attention to the large class of digraphs of finite bandwidth. This class encompasses the communications digraphs of virtually all discrete neural networks of practical interest.

Definition 3.4:   A *labeling* of a digraph D is a one-one mapping $\ell\colon V(D) \to \mathbf{N}$ that assigns a positive integer to each vertex of D. The *bandwidth* of a labeling ℓ is the maximum of the differences $|\ell(i) - \ell(j)|$ for every pair of adjacent vertices i,j or ∞ if there is no maximum. The *bandwidth* of a (di)graph is the minimum bandwidth of any of its labelings. **AN (CA,NN)** represent the classes of global dynamics induced by automata networks (cellular automata, neural networks, respectively), while $\mathbf{AN_0}$ ($\mathbf{CA_0}$,$\mathbf{NN_0}$, respectively) are their subclasses consisting of global dynamics defined on digraphs of finite bandwidth. $\square$

Note that finite bandwidth in a digraph implies bounded-degree. That is, there is a uniform bound on the number of links entering or leaving any node.

4. GLOBAL DYNAMICS

The configuration space of several models of parallel computation is essentially the Cantor middle-third set of real numbers. Recall that the Cantor set is the set of points left in the unit interval $[0,1]$ of the real line after first deleting its middle third $[1/3,2/3]$, and then continuing to delete the middle thirds of all remaining intervals *ad infinitum*. It is sometimes refered to as the Cantor dust. Its elements are characterized by ternary expansions not containing the digit 1. The Cantor set is characterized topologically as a perfect, totally disconnected, compact metric space [14, p. 97].

The configuration space of any cellular space is a countable cartesian product of its sets of states. Give each of these finite sets of values the discrete topology. The configuration space then becomes a countable product of finite discrete spaces with the usual product topology. It then has the very topological properties that characterize the Cantor set. Thus, every configuration space is homeomorphic to the Cantor set. Transformations of configuration space thus become self-maps of the Cantor set.

Not all self-maps of the Cantor set happen to arise as the global dynamics of some network. Those that do will be called *graphically computable* or simply *computable*[5] in the remainder of this chapter. More particularly, if the self-map arises as the global dynamics of a neural network (cellular automaton) it is called *neurally computable. Determining just which self-maps are computable by neural networks is of fundamental importance in neural computing.*

For cellular automata, this question is answered satisfactorily by Richardson's Theorem [21]. (A one-dimensional version of this result follows from earlier work by Hedlund [24].)

---

[5] not to be confused with the notion of Turing or effectively computable.

Theorem 4.1: A self-map $T: C \rightarrow C$ is computable by a Euclidean cellular automaton if and only if:

1. $T(O) = O$;
2. T commutes with shifts;
3. T is continuous;

Analogous theorems characterizing the computability of self-mappings of the Cantor set as global dynamics of neural networks have recently been established [25,26]. Local dynamics give rise to global dynamics on two interpretations of configuration space, namely the net-input space and the activation space of the network. Here we give both net-input and activation characterizations of neurally computable global dynamics.

The computability of a self-map of C as net-input global dynamics is characterized by the following theorem, which was proved in [25] for R a field. The same proof applies to the slightly more general case stated next.

Theorem 4.2: A self-map $T: C \rightarrow C$ is computable as the net-input global dynamics of a neural network with activation functions $\{f_i: R \rightarrow R\}$ (where R is a finite ring with unity and each $f_i(1)$ is a unit) if and only if:

1. $T(O) = O$;
2. T is continuous;
3. $T(e^k)$ has finite support for each pixel configuration e^k; and
4. T and $\{f_i\}$ are related, for all x_j in R, by

$$T\left(\sum_j x_j e^j \right)_i = \sum_j \frac{f_j(x_j)}{f_j(1)} T(e^j)_i$$

Here e^k denotes the pixel configuration with activation 1 at the kth cell and quiescent elsewhere.

Theorem 4.2 has natural applications. In the important case of a *finite* neural network, Conditions 2 and 3 are automatically satisfied. It also implies that, under natural conditions, the uniform limit [25] of net-input global dynamics is also a global dynamics. A direct proof of this result may be somewhat involved.

Theorem 4.3: A self-map $T: C \rightarrow C$ is computable by a neural network with given activation functions $(f_i: R \rightarrow R)$ if it is the uniform limit of a sequence of neural network global dynamics $T_n: C \rightarrow C$ with the same activation functions and uniformly bounded support of pixel images $T_n(e^k)$.

If the underlying digraph of a neural network happens to be a cellular space, it is reasonable to ask under what conditions the global dynamics might be that of a cellular automaton. The following result is a partial converse to Theorem 5.2 below.

Theorem 4.4:   Let $T: C \to C$ be a self-map arising from a neural network whose activation functions are $\{f_i: R \to R\}$ and let F be the product of the f_i. If:

1. the underlying digraph of the network is a Euclidean cellular space;
2. the activation functions of the network are identical and onto;
3. T commutes with shifts of pixels.

then there is a mapping $\tau: C \to C$ that is realized by a cellular automaton on D so that the following diagram commutes:

$$
\begin{array}{ccc}
 & T & \\
C & \to & C \\
F \downarrow & & \downarrow F \\
C & \to & C \\
 & \tau &
\end{array}.
$$

While the net-input space of a neural network and its associated global dynamics are technically easier to handle, the activation space of the network and its associated dynamics are more natural objects of study. One normally thinks of the current configuration of a neural network as its vector of activation values at the given time. The following theorem characterizes the computability of self-maps of the Cantor set as activation global dynamics of a neural network. Again R is a finite ring with unity.

Theorem 4.5:   A self-map $T: C \to C$ is computable over a finite ring R with unity as an activation global dynamics of a neural network if and only if:

1. $T(O) = 0$;
2. T is continuous;
3. $T(e^k)$ has finite support for each pixel configuration e^k; and
4. $T = F \circ L$, where L is a linear self-map of C and F is strictly local.

Here, F is strictly local if $F(x)_i = F(x_i e^i)_i$ for all x and i.

Note that Condition 4 holds with linear activation map F if and only if T is linear.

In both Theorems 4.2 and 4.5, Condition 1 disallows spontaneous generation within the network. Condition 2 allows the recovery of the underlying network structure. Condition 3 reflects the local finiteness of the network. Condition 4 mirrors the type of local dynamics of the network. Thus, as one would expect, the first two conditions are two of those from Richardson's theorem, while the other two result from the less regular type of architecture of the network, and from the characteristic form of its local dynamics. (It follows from conditions 1 and 2 that the sum in the right-hand side of Condition 4 in Theorem 4.2 is finite.)

Theorem 4.5 makes it easy to find common self-maps of the Cantor set that are not neurally computable. The mapping defined by $T(x) = 1 - x$ reflects the Cantor set about $x = \frac{1}{2}$. It fails to satisfy Condition 1. Since the mapping defined by $T(x) = 3x$ mod 1 is not continuous at $x = \frac{1}{3}$, if fails to satisfy Condition 2. Finally the self-map that converts from ternary to binary representation of points of the Cantor set fails to satisfy Condition 3 since $\frac{1}{3}$ is a ternary pixel $1000 \cdots$ with a finite binary representation $010101 \cdots$.

A characterization of global dynamics of automata networks is given next. Here, we let $C = \Pi_{i \in V}Q_i$ be an encoding of the Cantor set. Each Q_i is a finite set of states contained in a common finite set Q, and V is a countably infinite index set.

Theorem 4.6: A self-map $T: C \rightarrow C$ is computable as the global dynamics of an automata network if and only if:

1. $T(O) = O;$
2. T is continuous;
3. each $j \in V$ T-influences only finitely many $i \in V$.

Here j T-influences i (for $i,j \in V$) if for some $x \in C$ there is some $y \in C$ so that $y_k = x_k$ for all k different from j and $T(y)_i \neq T(x)_i$.

In this section, we have presented several solutions to the problem of which self-maps of the Cantor set are computable on digraphs, that is, via neural networks, cellular automata or automata networks. Next, we will explore their computational power.

5. COMPUTATIONAL POWER

McCulloch and Pitts, in their original chapter on neural networks [27], asserted that neural networks were computationally universal, suggesting that a neural implementation of the finite control of a Turing machine be somehow attached to a read-write head and tape. This assertion, though widely believed and oft quoted, leaves open the issue of exactly how a network can simulate a Turing machine. A concrete and detailed neural network implementation of a Turing machine was provided in [18]. The *Turing* undecidability of the Stability Problem for a relatively simple class of neural networks (synchronous, binary, linear-threshold) is a consequence of this effective implementation (see Section 6 below). The primary consequence is, of course, that any algorithmic problem that is Turing solvable can be encoded as a dynetic problem that is neurally solvable. Neural networks are at least as powerful as Turing machines.

The converse has been widely presumed to be true [19], since computability had become synonymous with Turing computability. The next theorem, shows that, *if* we are willing to allow potentially infinite digraphs, *infinite* neural networks are strictly more powerful computing devices than Turing machines.

Recall that the Halting Problem asks for a general algorithm to determine whether or not any given Turing machine will eventually halt when given some specified, but arbitrary, input. Turing showed that no such algorithm exists. Nonetheless, the Halting Problem, when encoded as a dynetic problem, can be solved by an infinite neural network.

Theorem 5.1:   The membership problem for any countable set of finite strings is neurally solvable. In particular, the Halting Problem for Turing machines is solvable as a dynetic problem by an infinite neural network of bandwidth 2.

Despite its appearance, Theorem 5.1 is *not* a counterexample to the Church-Turing thesis since the Thesis concerns only algorithmic problems solvable by *finitary* means, whereas the network involved in the proof of the theorem above requires the use of an essentially infinite object, namely the underlying digraph. The point here is that a simple infinite *finitary* object solves the problem.

Since this result may be surprising, we will include a proof for neural solvability of the Halting Problem. A similar argument can be used to show that the membership problem for any countable set is neurally solvable.

The Halting Problem is formulated as a dynetic decision problem as follows. An instance $\langle M,x \rangle$ consisting of a Turing machine M and its input x is encoded as a configuration:

$$1 \cdots 11311 \cdots 113000 \cdots \qquad (5.8)$$

(to be explained below). The proof requires the construction of a network N and two configurations x_{yes} and x_{no} such that N stabilizes on every input at either x_{yes} or x_{no}, depending on whether M halts on x or not.

Each instance of the Halting Problem can be regarded as a positive integer (see, [28], Section 8.3). The cells of the network N are in one-to-one correspondence with the instances of the Halting Problem and are arranged in increasing order of instance. The underlying digraph consists of two disjoint one-way infinite paths of cells, called the *halting* and *nonhalting* cells, respectively, depending on whether the corresponding instance halts or not. Each halting cell is connected to the next *halting* cell while each nonhalting cell, except the first, is connected to the previous *nonhalting* cell. Thus, the digraph consists of two distinct connected components. The ring of activations will be Z_6, the integers modulo 6. *All weights will be 1.*

Table 10.1. Activation Functions for a Solution of the Halting Problem.

x	0	1	2	3	4	5
$f_{halting}(x)$	0	0	1	0	3	0
$f_{nonhalting}(x)$	0	0	2	3	0	0

Since, for the purpose of computing its bandwidth, the (non)halting cells can be labeled with (odd) even numbers in consecutive order, this digraph has bandwidth 2.

Table 10.1 describes the activation functions of halting and nonhalting cells, respectively. The leftmost nonhalting cell is exceptional in that it is *persistent* (it has a self-link to feed back its own activation), while all the others are not.

With these activation functions, the network operates as follows. A given instance $\langle M, x \rangle$ is encoded and clamped as a configuration (5.8) consisting of a row of 1s up to the cell representing $\langle M, x \rangle$, except at the position of the first halting cell and the given instance itself, whose initial values are both 3. The remaining cells are always quiescent. The activation functions and the connections of the halting cells are set up in such a way that the 3 in the left-most halting cell will begin traveling right erasing intermediate 1s, until it reaches the rightmost 3 or a 0, at which point it becomes a 0, so that the halting path always stabilizes at the quiescent configuration. Likewise, the nonhalting cells (except the first) all become quiescent after the first time-step, except when the rightmost cell is a 3 representing the original instance of the Halting Problem. In this case, the 3 turns into a 2 which moves left along the nonhalting path until it reaches the leftmost persistent cell (without loss of generality, assume that the leftmost cell is nonhalting), at which point the nonhalting path stabilizes at a quiescent configuration with a 2 at the leftmost cell. In the second case, on a halting instance, the nonhalting path (hence, the entire network) stabilizes likewise, but with a 1 instead of a 2 at the leftmost cell. Hence, one can put $x_{yes} := 1000 \cdots$ and $x_{no} := 2000 \cdots$. Thus, the digraph "knows" in advance which instances are or are not halting. All its dynamics will do is single out in which of the two paths the original input was clamped. $\square$

Another fundamental problem is to what extent two network models (be they neural networks, cellular automata, or automata networks) perform *essentially* the same computation. Clearly few cellular automata, as given, *are* neural networks or vice versa, although both are particular cases of automata networks. The characterization of any automata network by a self-map of the Cantor set C makes possible the comparison of computation by different types of networks by comparing the self-maps that they compute.

Since Turing machines can be simulated by one-dimensional cellular automata, the class of Turing computable (partial recursive) functions **TM** is included in **CA**. This inclusion is proper for the class **CA** considered here since the prototypical, recursively unsolvable algorithmic problem, the Halting Problem is solvable by a simple neural network (see Theorem 5.1 above). In a different vein, it is not too hard to prove that a one-dimensional cellular automaton can take as input a real number (as an *infinite* binary expansion) and stabilize if and only if it is an integer. This means that *the integer problem for real numbers* is weakly solvable (see Definition 2.2). A Turing machine cannot solve this problem since the integer 1 could be given as 0.9999 . . . and hence, the machine cannot even finish reading its input. This problem can also be solved by a neural network, as shown next. The following theorem summarizes this discussion.

Theorem 5.2:   Every self-map $T: C \to C$ computable on a cellular automaton can be implemented by some neural network, i.e., **TM $\subset$ CA $\subseteq$ NN $\subseteq$ AN**.

As an example of the power of this theorem, suppose a self-map T of the Cantor set simply shifts the digits in the ternary representation of x one place to the left and then drops the left-most one. (Here, elements of the Cantor set are represented by ternary expansions without 1s.) This left-shift map is easily computable by a one-dimensional cellular automaton and hence, by the theorem, must also be neurally computable. Thus, it must also satisfy all the conditions of Theorem 4.5, the last of which is not obvious.

Theorem 5.2 raises the possibility that these classes of abstract dynamics **CA $\subseteq$ NN $\subseteq$ AN** are one and the same (i.e., that every automata network dynamics can be realized on a cellular automaton and/or a neural network). In approaching this question, one recalls Grossberg's call for higher abstraction if one is to capture the "deeper architectural level on which a formal model lives" [10].

Nevertheless, the usual diagonalization argument used to prove the Turing unsolvability of the Halting problem can still be used to show that not all dynetic problems are solvable. Theorem 6.1 below provides a specific and important unsolvable dynetic problem.

The following is a converse of Theorem 5.2 for finite neural networks.

Theorem 5.3:   Every solution of a dynetic problem on a finite neural network of n cells can be implemented on a cellular automaton with $O(n^3)$ cells.

We show below that the converse is true, even for infinite networks of finite bandwidth.

The implementation in the proof of Theorem 5.3 is uniform in the sense that two dynetic problems on the same network are implemented by cellular automata defined on the same cellular space. This raises the question of whether the uniformity of this implementation can be extended to local dynamics (i.e., whether universal neural networks exist).

The extent of this question requires some discussion. One might argue that *infinite* neural networks acting on finite initial configurations are essentially equivalent to Turing machines. If so, the existence of a universal neural network would be tantamount to the existence of a universal Turing machine, a well-known result in the classical theory of computability. Although it is true that neural networks (even those of finite-bandwidth acting on finite initial configurations) are at least as powerful as Turing machines [18], the converse is not true by Theorem 5.1. Turing machines can only be given the *finite* amount of information contained in its transition table and its finite initial input. The *possibility of storing an infinite amount of information*[6] in the pattern of interconnections among the nodes of an infinite neural network is a fundamental advantage indeed. Therefore, the existence of a universal neural network is *not* a consequence of the existence of a universal Turing machine.

In analogy with the Turing notion of a (sequentially) universal machine, however, it is natural both from a theoretical and a practical point of view to ask whether there exist dynetic problems *P: I → J* which are universal in the class of all dynetic problems. The solution of such a universal problem would amount to a network that is capable of simulating, modulo a reduction, the action of every neural network *N* on any input *x*, if given some encoding of both *N* and *x*. In the proof of the following theorem [29] we provide the blueprint of a specific neural network that accomplishes precisely that for all networks of finite bandwidth, both finite and infinite.

Theorem 5.4:   [26] There exists a universal neural network (over an extended finite ring) for neural networks of finite bandwidth over any finite ring with unity.

This universal network U'' has a row of cells numbered $1, 2, 3, \cdots$ and auxiliary cells some of whose states represent weights on the links of its input *N*. The network *N* is encoded simply by arbitrarily numbering its nodes $1, 2, \cdots$ and clamping their initial activations as well as *N*'s weights onto the corresponding cells of U''. Thus, U'' is a *programmable* neural network whose programs are configurations (real numbers in the Cantor set).

The existence of a universal neural network allows us to complete our comparison of the relative computational power of neural networks, cellular automata, and automata networks.

Theorem 5.5:   Any dynetic problem solvable on a neural network of finite bandwidth is also solvable on a three-dimensional Euclidean cellular automaton.

---

[6] This "infinity" is again to be distinguished from that "finitary" infinity exhibited by a periodic decimal expansion.

Theorem 5.6: All three models, neural networks, cellular automata, and automata networks, are computational equivalent when restricted to digraphs of finite bandwidth, i.e.:

$$CA_0 = NN_0 = AN_0.$$

The proofs of these results, as well as of those in the next section, can be found in the full version of [30].

6. THE STABILITY PROBLEM

As mentioned in Section 5, the Stability Problem of a certain relatively simple class of neural networks is Turing undecidable [18]. In view of the neural solvability of the Halting Problem, a more germaine question is *whether it is neurally unsolvable* as well. This problem is formally analogous to the classical Halting Problem for Turing machines.

Every pair consisting of a finite bandwidth network N and its input x has been encoded as a configuration $\langle N,x \rangle$ of the universal network U in Section 5. This encoding has the following properties:

1. the universal network U can simulate N on x when given $\langle N,x \rangle$ as an initial configuration.
2. it preserves finiteness of N (i.e., it has finite support if N only has finitely many cells).
3. N stabilizes on input x if and only if U stabilizes on input $\langle N,x \rangle$.

Now consider the dynetic problem of membership in the set of configurations:

$$L_s(R) := \{\langle N,x \rangle : N \text{ has finite bandwidth \& does } not \text{ stabilize on } x\}.$$

The complement of this set is called *the Stability Problem* for neural networks of finite bandwidth. Recall that a neural network weakly solves this problem if it stabilizes on $\langle N,x \rangle$ if and only if $\langle N,x \rangle \in L_s(R)$.

Theorem 6.1: The dynetic problem of instability[7] for neural networks of finite bandwidth is not weakly solvable (i.e., no neural network of finite bandwidth over a given finite ring takes as input some encoding of an arbitrary network over the same ring and stabilizes if and only if its input does not).

---

[7] which was inadvertantly stated as *stability* in [30]

Weak unsolvability is a stronger notion of unsolvability than the one implied by Definition 2.1. Since neural solvability of a problem clearly implies weak solvability of the problem and its complement, it follows that:

Corollary 6.1: The dynetic problem of stability for neural networks of finite bandwidth is neurally unsolvable (i.e., no neural network over a given finite ring takes as input some encoding of an arbitrary network over the same ring and decides whether it eventually stabilizes).

Proof of Theorem 6.1: If the stability problem were weakly solvable by a network of finite bandwidth N_0 over R, it would also be weakly solvable (after suitable recoding) by the universal network U by Theorem 5.5 (see the end of its proof). But, on input $\langle N_0, x_0 \rangle$, U either:

1. stabilizes, i.e., $\langle N_0, x_0 \rangle \in L_s(R)$, hence N_0 does not stabilize on x_0, and neither will U stabilize, a contradiction.
2. on the other hand, if U does not stabilize on x_0, then $\langle N_0, x_0 \rangle \in L_s(R)$. Hence, N_0 does stabilize on x_0, and so also U should stabilize on $\langle N_0, x_0 \rangle$, a contradiction.

This is once more the well-known diagonalization argument: such a network N_0 does not exist. $\square$

The notions of problems solvable and weakly solvable by (infinite) neural networks can be thought of as natural analogs of the classical notions of recursive and recursively enumerable sets. But unlike the situation for recursively enumerable sets, problems which are not weakly solvable can be made so by a *finite* extension of the ring of activation values (here playing the role of the tape alphabet of a Turing machine).

Theorem 6.2: The dynetic problem of stability for neural networks of finite bandwidth over a ring R is weakly solvable by a neural network over some extended finite ring R'.

Theorem 6.1 suggests that this solution cannot be of finite-bandwidth.

Corollary 6.2: The dynetic problem of stability for neural networks of finite bandwidth is weakly solvable by a three-dimensional euclidean cellular automaton.

Pursuing the analogy with recursive and recursively enumerable sets one might conjecture that a dynetic decision problem is solvable if it and its complement are weakly solvable.

Finally, Theorem 6.2 follows since, by construction, the network U stabilizes if and only if its input network stabilizes on its initial configuration.

7. SOME ISSUES AND OPEN PROBLEMS

The fundamental theme of this chapter is computation on graphs. This requires some justification.

One might argue that only finite networks can be physically implemented. Since *finite* neural networks are implementable by finite-state or Turing machines, it would follow that a formal theory of neural network computation would be subsumed under classical computability theory. However, finite neural networks bear the same relation to infinite neural networks that finite-state machines do to Turing machines. Turing machines are strictly more powerful than finite-state machines. In the same way, infinite neural networks are strictly more powerful than finite neural networks, and in fact, than Turing machines (see Theorem 5.1 above). More importantly, although every physical machine is in principle a finite state machine, the concept of Turing machines is necessary for a deeper understanding of the full computational power of sequential computers. In the same way, an understanding of the computing power of neural networks on infinite graphs may provide a better understanding of parallel computing.

The issue of *scalability* of *finite* networks also leads naturally to consideration of infinite networks. The scaling problem deals with how *uniformly* a neural network solves a problem as a function of the input size (i.e., how easy it is to adapt the solution to a similar problem on larger inputs). Scalability requires the use of finite networks of arbitrarily large size. Moreover, in order to have full computational ability (i.e., that of Turing machines [18,19,29]) neural networks must allow for an arbitrarily large number of cells. As with Turing machines in the sequential case, one simply assumes a *countably* infinite universe. That way solutions for the infinite model would also provide *uniform* solutions for finite networks of all sizes.

There is yet another pragmatic concern that justifies a detailed study of the computational capabilities of infinite neural networks. Classical computation has been incapable of dealing satisfactorily with numerical computation. The basic shortcoming lies in its finitistic character, which prevents it from handling *arbitrary* infinite representations of real numbers. Infinite neural networks, on the other hand, afford a real possibility of modeling infinite precision arithmetic (see [33] for a specific implementation of 'carry-free' arithmetic operations) thereby reconciling the computational and theoretical aspects of numerical analysis. Thus, convergence issues in numerical analysis would be equivalent to asymptotic solutions in a very precise sense. For instance, the examples following Theorem 4.5 suggest the following problem. Consider self-maps f of the full real interval $[0,1]$. Represent points in $[0,1]$ by binary expansions, and regard them as ternary representations of elements of the Cantor set. Thus, f can be considered as a self-map of the Cantor set. Under this encoding, *what exactly are the neurally computable functions on the unit interval?*

Viewing the dynamics of any of these three types of networks as a self-map of the Cantor set makes possible the comparison of the computational power of parallel models of computation. We have shown that three of these computational models are equivalent over digraphs of finite bandwidth. The question of their relative power over arbitrary digraphs remains.

A related problem that seems to be of fundamental importance in both computer science and cognitive science is the *encoding problem*. Intuitively, the images of a pattern of activation under various bijective (or just injective) neurally computable maps are just encodings of the given pattern. A first step in characterizing just what tasks are computable by neural networks would be to determine equivalent reformulations (encodings) of the given task. In the view taken here, this problem precisely asks for a *characterization* of the *bijective neurally computable self-maps of the* Cantor set.

A more general problem concerns a *characterization of injective global dynamics and their relation to the class of surjective dynamics*. It is well-known that for a cellular automaton, injectivity of its global dynamics automatically implies surjectivity [22].

The characterizations in Section 4 of the neurally computable self-maps of the Cantor set are strongly dependent on the encoding of C. It would be of interest to *find an encoding-independent characterization of self-maps of the Cantor set.*

The less theoretical question of *physical* implementation of models of computation on graphs has been ignored in this chapter. That this should be a proper concern in theoretical considerations is not currently accepted. However, this is in fact a very important issue, as argued in [34].

Finally, Theorem 5.1 shows that all the algorithmic problems which constitute the subject matter of classical computability are actually solvable by computing on graphs. One might be tempted to conclude that the classical paradigms are of no value to a theory of pictorial computation. In fact, however, the results in this chapter only illustrate how robust and valid classical paradigms will remain in any theory of computation.

REFERENCES

[1] T. Toffoli and N. Margolus, *Cellular Automata Machines*, MIT Press, Cambridge, MA, 1987.

[2] G. Vichniac, "Simulating Physics with Cellular Automata," *Physica* 10D, 1984, p. 96. (Reprinted in *Cellular Automata, Proceedings of the Los Alamos Conference*, North-Holland, Amsterdam).

[3] Y. Oono and C. Yeung, "A Cell Dynamical System of Chemical Turbulence," *Journal of Statistical Physics*, Vol. 48, No. 3/4, 1987, pp. 593–644.

[4] A. Winifree, E. Winifree, and H. Seifert, "Organizing Centers in a Cellularly Excitable Medium," *Physica D*, Vol. 17, 1985, p. 109.

[5] N. Margolus, T. Toffoli, and G. Vichniac, "Cellular Automata Supercomputers for Fluid Dynamics Modeling," *Physical Review Letters*, Vol. 56, 1986, pp. 1694–1696.

[6]   P. Rujan, "Cellular Automata and Statistical Mechanical Models," *Journal of Statistical Physics,* Vol. 49, No. 1/2, 1987, pp. 139–232.

[7]   J. L. McClelland and D.E. Rumelhart (Eds.), *Parallel Distributed Processing,* MIT Press, Cambridge, MA, Vol. 2, 1986.

[8]   B. Kosko, "Constructing an Associative Memory," *BYTE,* September 1987, pp. 137–144.

[9]   D.E. Rumelhart, G. Hinton, and R.J. Williams, "Learning Internal Representations by Error Propagation," D.E. Rumelhart and J.L. McClelland (Eds.), *Parallel Distributed Processing,* MIT Press, Cambridge, MA, Vol. 1, 1986, pp. 318–362.

[10]   S. Grossberg, "Competitive Learning: From Interactive Activation to Adaptive Resonance," D. Waltz & J.A. Feldman (Eds.) *Connectionist Models and Their Applications,* Ablex, Norwood, NJ, 1988.

[11]   T. Kohonen, "An Introduction to Neural Computing," *Neural Networks,* Vol. 1, 1988, pp. 3–16.

[12]   T.J. Sejnowski and C.R. Rosenberg, "Parallel Networks that Learn to Pronounce English Text," *Complex Systems,* Vol. 1, 1987, pp. 145–168.

[13]   M. Langton, *Artificial Life,* MIT Press, Cambridge, MA, 1989.

[14]   J.G. Hocking and G.S. Young, *Topology,* Addison-Wesley, Reading, MA, 1969, pp. 97–100.

[15]   J.J. Hopfield, "Neural Networks and Physical Systems with Emergent Collective Computational Abilities," *Proceedings of the National Acadamy of Science,* Vol. 79, 1982, pp. 2554–2558.

[16]   J.J. Hopfield and D.W. Tank, "Computing with Neural Circuits: A Model," *Science,* Vol. 233, No. 4764, 1986, pp. 625–633.

[17]   F. Fogelman-Soulie, Y. Robert, and M. Tchuente, *Automata Networks in Computer Science,* Princeton University Press, Princeton, NJ, 1987.

[18]   S.P. Franklin and M. Garzon, "Neural Computability," Omid Omidvar (Ed.) *Progress in Neural Networks, Vol. 1,* Ablex, Norwood, NJ, 1991, pp. 127–146.

[19]   R. Hartley and H. Szu, "A Comparison of the Computational Power of Neural Network Models," *Proceedings of the IEEE First International Conference on Neural Networks III,* 1987, pp. 17–22.

[20]   M.R. Garey and D. Johnson, *Computers and Intractabillity: A Guide to the Theory of NP-Completeness,* H. Freeman, San Francisco, 1978.

[21]   H.S.M. Coxeter and W.O. Moser, *Generators and Relations for Discrete Groups,* Springer-Verlag, New York, 1972.

[22]   D. Richardson, "Tessellation with Local Transformations," *Journal of Computer and Systems Science,* Vol. 6, 1972, pp. 373–388.

[23]   L. Blum, M. Shub, and S. Smale, "On a Theory of Computation and Complexity Over the Real Numbers; NP-completeness, Recursive Functions and Universal Machines," *Bulletin American Mathematical Society,* 1989, pp. 1–46.

[24]   G.A. Hedlund, "Endomorphism and Automorphism of the Shift Dynamical System," *Mathematical Systems Theory,* Vol. 3, 1969, pp. 320–375.

[25]   S.P. Franklin and M. Garzon, "Global Dynamics in Neural Networks," *Complex Systems,* Vol. 3, No. 1, 1988, pp. 29–36.

[26]   M. Garzon and S.P. Franklin, "Global Dynamics in Neural Networks II," *Complex Systems,* Vol. 4, No. 5, 1990, pp. 509–518.

[27]   W.S. McCulloch and W. Pitts, "A Logical Calculus of the Ideas Immanent in

Nervous Activity," *Bulletin of Mathematical Biophysics,* Vol. 5, 1943, pp. 115–133.

[28]   J.E. Hopcroft and J.D. Ullman, *Introduction to Automata Theory, Languages and Computation,* Addison-Wesley, Reading, MA, 1979.

[29]   M. Garzon and S.P. Franklin, B. Boyd and D. Dickerson, "Design and Testing of a general purpose neuro-computer" *Journal of Parallel and Distributed Computing,* 14(1992), 203–220.

[30]   M. Garzon and S. Franklin, "Neural Computability II (Extended Abstract)," *Proceedings of the 3rd International Joint Conference on Neural Networks,* Washington, D.C., Vol. I, 1989, 631–637.

[31]   D.E. Rumelhart, G. Hinton, and J.L. McClelland, "A General Framework for Parallel Distributed Processing," D.E. Rumelhart and J.L. McClelland (Eds.), *Parallel Distributed Processing,* MIT Press, Cambridge, MA, Vol. 1, 1986, pp. 45–76.

[32]   J. von Neumann, *Theory of Self-Reproducing Automata,* University of Illinois Press, Chicago, IL, 1966.

[33]   K. Hwang, "Optical Multiplication and Division Using Modified Signed-Digit Symbolic Substitution," *Journal of Optical Engineering* [Special Issue], April 1989.

[34]   C. Fields, "Consequences of Nonclassical Measurement for the Algorithmic Description of Continuous Dynamical Systems," *Journal of Experimental and Theoretical Artificial Intelligence,* Vol. 1, 1989, pp. 171–178.

[35]   S. Wolfram, *Theory and Applications of Cellular Automata,* World Scientific, Singapore, 1986.

11
Non-Gaussian Feature Analyses Using a Neural Network*

Wei Gong
Hung-Chun Yau
Michael T. Manry
Department of Electrical Engineering
University of Texas at Arlington

1. INTRODUCTION

In this chapter, a neural net classifier is applied to non-Gaussian features calculated from numeric hand-printed (NHP) characters. Rule-based and nearest neighbor classifiers are applied to the same data for comparison. Others have shown that neural nets can be optimal. In this chapter, a neural net is used to verify that the performances of the conventional classifiers are near optimal. A feature selection approach is proposed and demonstrated which utilizes the neural net. A method for fast learning is demonstrated on the neural net. A reject category is developed, so that bad characters are not classified. Therefore, the neural net is allowed to express uncertainty.

1.1. Background

In many pattern analysis problems, a set of features is developed, and many example feature vectors from each class are available for training and testing. In most cases of interest, the feature vectors do not have the same joint probability density for each class and do not have Gaussian or even unimodal joint densities [1]. Rule-based classifiers and assymptotically optimal pattern classifiers, such as those of the nearest neighbor type [2–5], can sometimes be developed in spite of these difficulties. However, these classifiers are much more difficult to design

---
* We gratefully acknowledge the assistance of Hei-Lun Han, who developed the loop-related features, and Mu-Song Chen, who helped us refine the measure of feature usefulness.

This research was supported by a grant from Recognition Equipment Incorporated of Irving, Texas.

than those of the Gaussian type. Several problems remain to be solved for these classifiers. How can a classifier's closeness to optimality be measured? How can bad input data be detected and rejected? How can feature selection be performed?

1.2. Objectives

The research described in this chapter has two main objectives. The first objective is to develop neural net techniques for analyzing non-Gaussian feature data and the associated conventional classifiers. The second objective is to add capabilities to the neural network which will enhance its usefulness. The neural network used in this chapter is the back propagation network [6].

The raw data used in the research consists of images of numeric handprinted (NHP) characters. Non-Gaussian features calculated from (NHP) characters are described in Section 2. Rule-based and nearest neighbor classifiers for this data are described. Section 3 introduces the neural net notation and classifier. In Section 4, the repetitive training algorithm for neural networks is introduced. A method for allowing neural networks to reject useless input data is also presented. Neural feature selection is developed and compared to conventional feature selection in Section 5. The performances of the classifiers are discussed in detail. Conclusions are given in Section 6.

2. FEATURES AND CONVENTIONAL CLASSIFIERS

The NHP characters analyzed in this chapter are stored in 32×24 pixel arrays, denoted as $f(i, j)$, with 1 bit per pixel. Here, i is the row number and j is the column number. A pixel with an intensity of 1 is black and a pixel with intensity 0 is white. When the character array's pixels are processed into a vector of features, the 0's and 1's are treated as integers. All characters are scaled equally in the horizontal and vertical directions. Thus, the top and bottom or left and right edges of the character touch the edges of the array.

In this section a set of non-Gaussian features, calculated from the character images, is described. Two conventional classifiers for this data are presented.

2.1. Feature Descriptions

It is desirable for each character class to correspond to a unique feature vector. This does not happen in reality because the character images and the features are imperfect. Five types of topological features are used in our feature set [7,8]. These feature types are convexity features, width features, energy distribution features, loop-related features, and slope features. It has not been necessary to make the features rotation- or scale-invariant, since all characters are oriented normally and are scaled.

Four binary-valued features have been developed which describe the convexity of NHP characters. The upper-right, upper-left, lower-right, and lower-left convexities are 1 if the character is convex in that region and 0 otherwise. In our software, the above four features are denoted by x_1, x_2, x_3 and x_6, respectively. As an example, the upper-right convexity is calculated as follows. Find the right-most dark pixel in the top half of the character. Scan downward, following the right edge of the character, until row 16 is reached. If the right-most pixel's column number shifts left by less than 2 pixels between rows, or by 2 or 3 pixels only once, the top-right area is convex. The other convexities are found similarly.

Three binary-valued width features have been developed. The bottom width, x_4, is set to 0 if the maximum width in the bottom one fourth of the character is seven columns or more. It is set to 1 otherwise. The whole width x_7 is set to 1 if the maximum width over all rows is less than or equal to 7. Otherwise, it is set to 0. The top width x_5 is set to 0 if the maximum width in the top one-fourth of the character is seven columns or more. It is set to 1 otherwise.

There are five feature describing the characters' loops and their locations. The number of loops is denoted by x_8. It is calculated as follows. First calculate the number of dark regions in each row and also in each column. Scanning from the top row downward, potential loops are located in regions of adjacent rows which have two regions of dark pixels. Mark the top row and bottom row of each such region. Scanning the columns from left to right, each potential loop is a true loop if at least one column has dark regions at its top and bottom. Although this loop detector is not perfect, it has the advantage of detecting loops in some open-loop fours. The location (average row number) of the top loop is denoted by x_9 and the location of the second loop is denoted by x_{10}. The "stick out" length x_{11}, which is the width of the horizontal bar below the top loop, is found as follows. If a loop exists in the top half of a character, the rightmost column of the character is followed from the top of the loop to its bottom. x_{11} is the rightmost column number minus the average column number. The amount of energy in the upper portion of the top loop is x_{12}. This is the number of black pixels above the topmost row having two regions.

The energy distribution features describe the distribution of black pixels in the character. Let the top energy be defined as the number of black pixels in the top 16 rows of the image and let the left energy be the number of black pixels in the first 12 columns of the image. The bottom and right energies are similarly defined. The reduced top and bottom energies are calculated using the top 10 and bottom ten rows of the image. Feature x_{13} is the ratio of the left to right energies. Feature x_{14} is the ratio of the top to bottom energies. x_{16} is similar to x_{14}, except that the reduced energies are used. The slope feature x_{15} is the sum of the squared errors for a straight line fit to the rightmost pixels in the image.

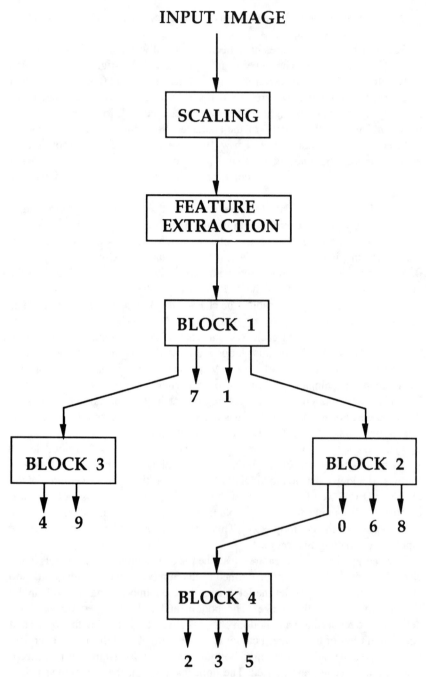

Figure 11.1. Rule-based classifier.

2.2. Rule-Based Classifier

Our rule-based classifier [7,8] was designed based on intuition using the mean feature values for each class. From Figure 11.1, the classifier recognizes all characters 0 through 9 by using 14 features, which are x_1 through x_{14}. The functions of the blocks in Figure 11.1 are briefly summarized as follows.

Block 1 uses features x_4, x_5, x_6, and x_8. Its functions are to:

1. Divide characters 0–9 into two groups. Characters belong to the group (0, 2, 3, 5, 6 and 8) if ($x_4 = 0$) or ($x_8 = 2$) or ($x_1 = x_2 = 1$ and $x_3 = x_6 = x_8 = 0$) or ($x_2 = x_3 = 1$ and $x_1 = x_6 = x_8 = 0$). Otherwise, the characters belong to the group (1,4,7, and 9).
2. Distinguish 1 from 4,7, and 9 using the fact that a 1 has $x_5 = 1$.
3. Distinguish 7 from 4 and 9, using the fact that $x_8 = 0$ for the 7.

Block 2 uses features x_2, x_6, x_7, x_8, and x_9. Its functions are to:

1. Distinguish 8 from 0, 2, 3, 5, and 6, using the fact that $x_8 = 2$ for the 8.
2. Distinguish 0 from 2, 3, 5, and 6, using the fact that a 0 has $x_8 = 1$ and x_9 close to 16.
3. Distinguish 6 from 2, 3, and 5, using the fact that a 6 has $x_8 = 1$ and x_9 significantly greater than 16.
4. Go to block 4 to recognize characters 2, 3, and 5.

Block 3 uses features x_8, x_{11} and x_{12} to classify characters 4 and 9. Given that $x_8 = 1$, the 4 has larger values for x_{11} and the 9 has larger values for x_{12}.

Block 4 uses features x_1, x_2, and x_3 to recognize characters 2, 3, and 5. If the character has two left concavities, one on the top of the character and one on the bottom of the character, it is a 3. If it has a left concavity on the top of the character but not at the bottom, it is 2. If it has no left concavity on the top, it is a 5.

2.3. Nearest-Neighbor Classifier

The second conventional classifier to be used with the feature data is the nearest neighbor classifier [2–5]. Its advantages are that: (a) it doesn't require a knowledge of the joint probability density of the feature vectors, and (b) it asymptotically approximates the minimum error Bayesian classifier as the number of reference vectors gets large [1,9]. The most important disadvantage is that the computational requirements become overly burdensome as the product of the numbers of classes and reference vectors increases.

In designing a nearest neighbor classifier, the first step is the clustering of the

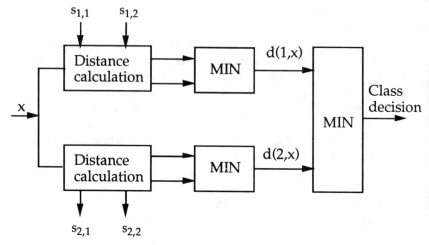

Figure 11.2. Nearest neighbor classifier for 2 classes and 2 reference vectors per class.

training vectors. Given the training vectors for a given class, we divide the vectors into subsets or clusters. Each cluster consists of vectors which are similar to each other. The sequential leader clustering algorithm is used because of its simplicity and good performance [4]. In this algorithm, one pass is made through the training vectors. The first vector is assigned to cluster number 1. For every subsequent vector, if it is beyond a user chosen distance from each of the existing cluster mean vectors, it becomes the first vector in a new cluster. Every time a new vector is added to a cluster, the mean vector of that cluster is updated. The result is that each of the cluster mean vectors is a reference vector for its class. In this chapter, the reference set consists of 100 vectors, 10 cluster mean vectors for each class.

The second design step is the choice of a distance measure. Let $s_{i,k}$ denote the kth reference feature vector corresponding to class i. Let $D(s_{i,k}, x)$ represent the Mahalanobis distance between vectors $s_{i,k}$ and x, under the assumption of statistically independent features. Although the features are not statistically independent, this distance measure is easy to calculate and is better than the Euclidean distance. Let $d(i, x)$ denote the minimum of $D(s_{i,k}, x)$ over all reference vectors in the ith class. Assume that the distance for the jth class, $d(j, x)$, is less than or equal to $d(i, x)$ for all i not equal to j. Then the nearest neighbor classifier assigns the vector x to the jth class. In Figure 11.2, a nearest neighbor classifier is shown for the case of two classes and two reference vectors per class.

3. NEURAL NETWORK CLASSIFIER

In this section notation is given for a feedforward back propagation neural net [6]. The net's parameters, developed for use in unconstrained character recognition, are listed. A preliminary comparison is made between the performances of the two conventional classifiers and the neural net.

3.1. Neural Network Notation

The neural network paradigm used here is a feedforward back propagation network with one or more hidden layers [6]. The basic notation for the network is defined as follows.

Let Ln denote the number of layers in the network, including the input and output layers. Let Nu_i denote the number of units in layer i for $i = 1$ to Ln. Nu_1 or Nf is the number of input units. The hidden layers are therefore numbered 2 through $Ln - 1$ and the number of hidden units is:

$$Nh = \sum_{i=2}^{Ln-1} Nu_i$$

Lf_i denotes the first layer number with connections to layer i. Lo_i denotes the last layer which the layer i feeds. Lo_i can be any integer between $i + 1$ and Ln. If the input layer and every hidden layer feeds to every subsequent layer and the output layer, then $Lo_i = Ln$ for $i = 1$ to $Ln - 1$. Lf_2 equals 1 and Lf_1 is not used. x_k denotes the input to the kth input unit for a given input pattern. $Tout_{i,j}$ denotes the desired output for output unit j for the ith pattern. $Npat$ denotes the number of training patterns for the network. $O_{m,n}$ denotes the output for unit n of layer m. $W_{Ld,Ls,Nd,Ns}$ denotes the weight for the connection from unit Ns of layer Ls to unit Nd of layer Ld, where $Ld = 2$ to Ln, $Ls = Lf_{Ld}$ to $Ld - 1$, $Nd = 1$ to Nu_{Ld}, $Ns = 1$ to Nu_{Ls}. $A_{m,Nd}$ denotes the threshold for the mth unit of layer Nd. In Figure 11.3, a back propagation neural network is shown for the case of $Ln = 4$, $Nu_1 = 5$, $Nu_2 = 6$, $Nu_3 = 5$, $Nu_4 = 4$, $Lf_3 = 2$, and $Lf_4 = 3$. The dummy input units are drawn smaller than the processing units. Nc denotes the number of classes.

For a regular back propagation network [6], the net is:

$$Net_{m,Nd} = A_{m,Nd} + \sum_{Ls=Lf_m}^{m-1} \sum_{Ns=1}^{Nu_{Ls}} W_{m,Ls,Nd,Ns} O_{Ls,Ns} \qquad (3.1)$$

and the standard output activation is:

$$O_{m,n} = f(Net_{m,n}) = \frac{1}{1 + \exp(-Net_{m,n})}$$

In back propagation learning [6], the goal is to minimize the error function:

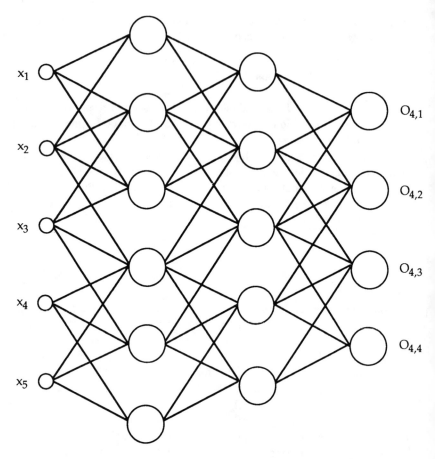

Figure 11.3.   Back propagation neural network classifier.

$$E = \sum_{i=1}^{Npat} \sum_{j=1}^{Nu_{Ln}} [Tout_{i,j} - O_{Ln,j}]^2 \qquad (3.2)$$

with respect to the weights $W_{Ld,Ls,n,m}$ and the thresholds $A_{m,Nd}$. As this is done, the hope is that the classification error percentage for the network is reduced.

3.2. Neural Net for Character Recognition

Through experimentation, we have chosen a four-layer net ($Ln = 4$). The input layer has 14 or 16 units, corresponding to features 1–14 or 1–16 ($Nu_1 = 14$ or 16). The output layer has four units, as four bits are necessary to specify the ten classes corresponding to NHP characters 0 to 9 ($Nu_4 = 4$). The two hidden layers have 12 and 10 units, respectively ($Nu_2 = 12$ and $Nu_3 = 10$). Each layer connects to the input layer ($Lf_2 = Lf_3 = Lf_4 = 1$). When the net is being trained, each successive pattern comes from successive classes. In another words, the input patterns are from classes 0, 1, 2, . . , 9, 0, 1, 2, and so on.

The training data set consists of 1,000 feature vectors, 100 from each class. The testing data set is the same size, but has no feature vectors in common with the training data set. The images used were provided by Recognition Equipment Incorporated (REI) of Irving, TX, and came from IRS forms. In this chapter, one "iteration" of the back propagation algorithm corresponds to presentations of all 1,000 training images to the net.

3.3. Classifier Evaluation

Several researchers have shown the near optimality of neural net classifiers [10,11,12,13]. Theforefore, a reasonable method for evaluating a nonneural pattern classifier is to compare its performance to that of a neural net. The

Table 11.1.   Classification results for testing data.

Case	Classifier	Features	Error %	Reject %	D1	D2	Constant Feature
					\multicolumn{2}{c}{Threshold}	
1	Rule-Based	14	11.8	0.0			none
2	Nearest Neigh.	14	11.2	0.0			none
3	Neural	14	11.1	0.5	0.5	0.5	none
4	Neural	14	10.4	3.4	0.4	0.6	none
5	Neural	14	8.5	6.2	0.3	0.7	none
6	Neural	14	7.8	8.9	0.2	0.8	none
7	Neural	14	6.1	14.3	0.1	0.9	none
8	Neural	16	9.3	1.4	0.5	0.5	none
9	Neural	16	7.5	4.4	0.4	0.6	none
10	Neural	16	5.9	7.7	0.3	0.7	none
11	Neural	16	4.1	12.0	0.2	0.8	none
12	Neural	16	9.9	1.5	0.5	0.5	x(5)
13	Neural	16	8.8	3.3	0.4	0.6	x(5)
14	Neural	16	7.7	5.8	0.3	0.7	x(5)
15	Neural	16	6.3	8.7	0.2	0.8	x(5)
16	Neural	16	5.0	12.3	0.1	0.9	x(5)
17	Neural	16	10.3	2.8	0.5	0.5	x(13)
18	Neural	16	8.8	5.6	0.4	0.6	x(13)
19	Neural	16	7.5	8.0	0.3	0.7	x(13)
20	Neural	16	6.2	11.2	0.2	0.8	x(13)
21	Neural	16	4.8	17.0	0.1	0.9	x(13)

classifiers are compared in cases 1, 2, 3, and 8 of Table 11.1. The testing data (second set of feature vectors) was used. Comparing the results, it is clear that the neural net performs the same as the rule-based and nearest-neighbor classifiers when the first 14 features are used. At this point, we can be satisfied that the rule-based and nearest-neighbor classifiers are not very suboptimal. All three classifiers have error rates in the 11% range. However, the introduction of the new features, x_{15} and x_{16}, improves the neural net's performance as seen in case 8. This shows that the feature set is not complete.

4. UNCERTAINTY AND REPETITIVE TRAINING

In the previous section, the performance of a neural network classifier has been used to evaluate another classifier's closeness to optimality. In this section: (a) uncertainty is introduced into the neural net, (b) the net is used for simple feature selection, and (c) a new training regime is described for the net.

4.1. Uncertainty

In expert systems, numerical or nonnumerical pieces of evidence are processed, heuristically, into decisions. Many techniques have been developed for specifying the reliability, or conversely the uncertainty, of these input pieces of evidence. After processing, the decisions made by such systems also have various amounts of uncertainty associated with them. Methods for dealing with uncertainty [14] include fuzzy logic, the Demster-Shafer method, and Bayesian networks.

In many pattern recognition problems, including character recognition and target recognition, it is necessary to produce some measure of the uncertainty about the decisions being made. It is unacceptable to force the classifier to make a classification when the input feature vector is bad and the identity of its class is uncertain. In such a case, a human operator can examine the data and make a decision. This is very clear for the case of the IRS data which we analyze in this chapter. Clearly, the concept of uncertainty is of critical importance, in spite of the fact that it is ill-defined.

A neural net can be allowed to express uncertainty about the input feature vector, by allowing it to reject bad vectors. First, if the rounded output vector, which has four elements, has an output corresponding to a decimal number between 10 and 15, it is rejected. Second, if any output elements, before rounding, fall between the user-specified thresholds D1 and D2, the input feature vector is rejected. Examining cases 3–7 and 8–11 in Table 11.1, it is clear that the thresholds D1 and D2 can be adjusted, producing a trade-off between the error and reject percentages.

4.2. Repetitive Training

One problem with back propagation neural networks is their slow rate of learning, including their tendency to get stuck in local minima [6]. A second problem is that minimizing the probability of error for a neural net is equivalent to minimizing the maximum output unit error over all of the training patterns, which is clearly not equivalent to back propagation learning.

The slow learning problem is sometimes attacked through the use of a momentum term, when the weights are updated [6]. A second approach is the gradient reuse algorithm of [15]. The probability or error issue can be addressed as well. Minimizing the probability of error for the classifier is equivalent to minimizing the p-error function [16]:

$$Ep = \sum_{i=j}^{Npat} \sum_{j=1}^{Nu_{Ln}} [Tout_{i,j} - O_{Ln,j}]^{2p} \tag{3.3}$$

if p is increased enough. A modified back propagation algorithm can easily be developed for minimizing Ep. However, the resulting error surface will probably have more local minima for large p values than for the $p = 1$ case [16].

Suppose that a neural net is being trained in a region where learning is very slow. Both problems discussed above can be attacked by changing the slope of the surface E through changing the contents of the training data set. Consider the following algorithm. Assume that if the ith input pattern is misclassified, we resubmit it to the net until: (a) it is correctly classified or (b) it has been submitted Lt times, where Lt is a positive integer chosen by the user. Let $Nt(i)$ denote the number of times the ith input is put into the net. Clearly $1 < Nt(i) < Lt$. If the weight changes are scaled to be small, the error function being minimized is approximately:

$$Ett = \sum_{i=1}^{Npat} \sum_{j=1}^{Nu_{Ln}} Nt(i) \cdot [Tout_{i,j} - O_{Ln,j}]^2 \tag{3.4}$$

The minimizations of Ep and Ett are similar in that large errors are penalized far more than in conventional back propagation. However, the Ett error surface is constantly being changed. Thus this second approach, which we call repetitive training, may avoid the local minima of the Ep error surface. It is related to the gradient reuse algorithm of [15], with a batch size of 1. However, the goals in the present approach and its justification are somewhat different. Also, the gradient is recalculated before each use and is only used a maximum of Lt times or until the input pattern stops being misclassified. This is quite different from the termination criterion of [15].

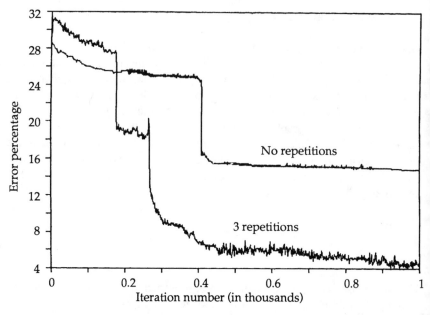

Figure 11.4. Error percentage vs. iteration number for training data.

In measuring the mean square error and the classification error percentage for repetitive training, only the error from the first submission of each pattern is used. The iteration number for ordinary back propagation corresponds to the presentation of 1,000 patterns, once each. The measurement of iteration number is slightly different for repetitive training. Here, the iteration increment equals the number of total presentations divided by the number of unique patterns (1,000). Thus, one iteration of repetitive training and one iteration of back propagation involve the same amount of computation, and the performances for the two training procedures can be fairly compared. Commonly, the net is trained with $Lt = 1$ in the first 100 iterations. Consider the plots of error percentage vs. iteration number in Figure 11.4 for $Lt = 3$. From the figure it is clear that repetitive training can increase learning speed. It is also apparent from the figure that repetitive training can result in a reduced error classification percentage.

If one repetitively trains a back propagation network with a single pattern, the network will be forced to recognize that pattern and to forget those previously learned. Because of this effect, the network's learning speed tends to be degraded as Lt values are increased beyond 3 or 4.

5. FEATURE SELECTION

In NHP character recognition problems, as in other recognition problems, there are often a large number of features that have been developed intuitively. A subset of the original feature set is sought which minimizes the probability of misclassification. However, existing feature selection approaches are suboptimal [17,18,19,20]. Because of the near-optimality of neural net classifiers, a reasonable approach to feature selection is to determine which input units contribute most heavily to the output patterns. These features or units are selected. The noncontributing features or units can be deleted. In other words, a function will be developed for measuring the usefulness of input and hidden units. In this section, conventional and neural network approaches to feature selection are briefly described and demonstrated.

5.1. Conventional Feature Selection

There are two important components to many conventional subsetting methods for conventional feature selection. These are: (a) the subset usefulness function which estimates the usefulness of a given feature subset, and (b) the algorithm for subset determination. The subset usefulness function developed by P.M. Narendra and K. Fukunaga in [18] has been extended to the case of Nc classes as:

$$D(x) = \left\{ \sum_{i=1}^{Nc} [M(i) - M] \right\}^T \cdot \left[\sum_{i=1}^{Nc} \frac{C(i)}{Nc} \right]^{-1} \cdot \left\{ \sum_{i=1}^{Nc} [M(i) - M] \right\}$$

where $M(i)$ and $C(i)$ are, respectively, the mean feature vector and mean covariance matrix for the ith class, and the M is the mean vector over all classes. Although this function is easy to use, it does not have a direct relationship to the probability of error for the Bayes classifier.

The subset determination algorithm used here is the branch and bound algorithm, which has been described by several authors [18,19,20]. Given a desired subset size, this algorithm finds that subset which maximizes the subset usefulness function. If the function gave a value consistent with the classifier's probability of error, the branch-and-bound technique would yield the best feature subset.

5.2. Neural Feature Selection

Many investigators have found that neural nets can closely approximate Bayesian classifiers [10,11,12,13]. Therefore, a reasonable approach to feature selection is to determine which input units contribute most heavily to the output patterns. These features or units are selected. The noncontributing features or units can be deleted. One past approach is that of the network-pruning procedure of Sietsma and Dow [21], they eliminate units which: (a) have constant outputs over the set of all training patterns, or (b) which have outputs which completely correlate with another unit's output. This pruning approach is an important advance, but it has problems. First, a large network must be completely trained; second, the autocorrelation matrix for each layer's outputs must be calculated using the entire training set.

One measure for the usefulness [22] of input feature $x(n)$ is:

$$Xm(n) = G(n) \max_{} \max_{i=1}^{Nu_{Ln}} \left\{ \frac{\partial O_{Ln,i}}{\partial x_n} \right\}$$

$$G(n) = \max\{x_n\} - \min\{x_n\}$$

where the outer max operation is taken over all possible input patterns and where n equals 1 to Nf. $Xm(n)$ tends to be large for more useful features and small for less useful features. The partial derivative is expressed using the chain rule as:

$$\frac{\partial O_{Ln,j}}{\partial x_n} = f'(\text{Net}_{Ln,j})[W_{Ln,1,j,n}$$

$$+ \sum_i \sum_k W_{Ln,k,j,i} f'(\text{Net}_{k,i})[W_{k,1,i,n} + \dots$$

This can be bounded using the fact that $\max\{f'(\text{net})\} = 1/4$, thus eliminating the necessity for calculating the partial derivative for each input pattern.

A second approach [7,8] for measuring the importance of feature x_n is to calculate the sum of the magnitudes of all weights leaving input unit n. The effects of the average feature magnitude are then removed. The resulting feature importance function $Xm(n)$ is calculated as:

$$Xm(n) = G(n) \sum_{Ld=2}^{Lo_1} \sum_{m=1}^{Nu_{Ld}} |W_{Ld,1,m,n}|$$

for $n = 1$ to Nu_1. $Xm(n)$ tends to be large for more useful features and small for less useful features. We have found this second approach to be simpler but equally as effective as the first approach. The function Xm is used for feature selection as follows.

1. Train the network for a large number of input units or features.
2. Measure $Xm(n)$ for each feature after more than 1,000 iterations. Order the values of $Xm(n)$ in a list from the largest to the smallest.
3. To obtain a set of N good features, pick the features corresponding to the top N features in the list.

Table 11.2.   Measure of feature usefulness.

n	Xm(n)
1	0.0124
2	0.0065
3	0.0095
4	0.0048
5	0.0077
6	0.0095
7	0.0089
8	0.0099
9	0.2090
10	0.1487
11	0.0451
12	0.1257
13	0.3748
14	0.0274

5.3. Experiments

After the training of the neural network, the $Xm(n)$ values listed in Table 11.2 were calculated. Features x_5 and x_{13} are apparently the least important and most important features, respectively. In order to test the relative usefulness of these two features, the corresponding input unit was held constant at an activation value of .5 for these two features separately. The network was then retrained for 500 additional iterations. As seen in Figure 11.5 and cases 12–21 in Table 11.1, the neural net performance is more damaged by removing feature x_{13} than by removing feature x_5.

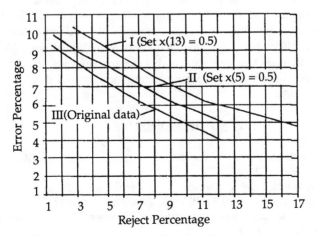

Figure 11.5.   Example of feature importance.

As an experiment, two ten-feature subsets were selected. The branch-and-bound algorithm chose features 1, 4, 5, 6, 7, 8, 10, 12, 13, and 14. The neural feature selector chose features 1, 3, 6, 8, 9, 10, 11, 12, 13, and 14. Two nearest-neighbor classifiers were then designed from scratch for the two subsets. For the 10 features selected via the neural network, there was a 7% error for the training data and a 13.9% error for the testing data. For the 10 features chosen via the conventional branch-and-bound algorithm, there was a 12% error for the training data and a 17% error for the testing data. It is obvious that the neural network method is better than conventional selection algorithms.

6. CONCLUSIONS

In this chapter, several techniques have been discussed for improving a back propagation network and for using it to analyze data. Even when the neural net is not practical to implement, it can be used to bound the performance of conventional classifiers. It has been shown that a neural net can easily be made to handle uncertainty, through the introduction of a reject capability. The reject and error percentages can be adjusted as desired.

A method for changing the network's error surface, through repetitively applying misclassified input patterns, has been developed. It can be used to help the net escape from local minima during training. It has been verified that one can read a trained neural net for the purpose of feature selection. The feature subset chosen by the neural network proved to be better than the feature subset chosen via the branch-and-bound technique.

The research presented in this chapter is being continued. Although the neural network feature selection technique has proved superior to conventional methods on the data set in this chapter and on others, it is still unfinished. A better subset determination method should be developed.One important remaining problem is that the optimal topology of a back propagation neural network, for a given problem, is difficult to determine. Most people find good topologies through experimentation, as has been done in this chapter. However, many researchers, including the authors, are developing better procedures for this.

REFERENCES

[1] K. Fukunaga, *Introduction to Statistical Pattern Recognition*, Academic Press, New York, 1972.

[2] M.D. Srinath and P.K. Rajasekaran, *An Introduction to Statistical Signal Processing with Applications*, John Wiley & Sons, New York, 1979.

[3] J.T. Tou and R.C. Gonzalez, *Pattern Recognition Principles*, Addison-Wesley, Reading, MA, 1974.

[4] J.A. Hartigan, *Clustering Algorithms*, John Wiley & Sons, New York, 1975.

[5] T.M. Cover and P.E. Hart, "Nearest Neighbor Classification," *IEEE Transactions on Information Theory,* Vol. IT-13, No. 1, pp. 21–27.

[6] D.E. Rumelhart and J.L. McClelland, *Parallel Distributed Processing,* Vol. I, MIT Press, Cambridge, MA, 1986.

[7] W. Gong, "Unconstrained Character Recognition Using Neural Network," Master's Thesis, Department of Electrical Engineering, University of Texas at Arlington, May 1989.

[8] W. Gong and M.T. Manry, "Analysis of Non-Gaussian Data Using a Neural Network," *Proceedings of the International Joint Conference on Neural Networks,* Washington D.C., Vol. II, June 1989, p. 576.

[9] R.O. Duda and P.E. Hart, *Pattern Classification and Scene Analysis,* John Wiley and Sons, New York, 1973.

[10] D.J. Burr, "Experiments on Neural Net Recognition of Spoken and Written Text," *IEEE Transactions on Acoustics, Speech, and Signal Processing,* July 1988, pp. 1162–1168.

[11] R.P. Lippmann, "An Introduction to Computing With Neural Nets," *IEEE ASSP Magazine,* April 1987, pp. 4–22.

[12] J.S. Draper, D.S. Frankel, H. Hancock, and A.S. Mize, "A Microcomputer Neural Net Benchmarked Against Standard Classification Techniques," *Proceedings of the IEEE First International Conference on Neural Networks,* Vol. 4, San Diego, CA, June 1987, pp. 651–658.

[13] T. Kohonen, G. Barna, and R. Chrisley, "Statistical Pattern Recognition with Neural Networks: Benchmarking Studies," *Proceedings of the IEEE International Conference on Neural Networks,* Vol. 1, San Diego, CA, July 1988, pp. 61–68.

[14] J. Pearl, *Probabilistic Reasoning in Intelligent Systems: Networks of Plausible Inference,* Morgan Kaufmann, San Mateo, CA, 1988.

[15] D.R. Hush and J.M. Salas, "Improving the Learning Rate of Back-Propagation With the Gradient Reuse Algorithm," *Proceedings of the IEEE International Conference on Neural Networks,* Vol. I, San Diego, CA, July 1988, pp. 441–447.

[16] E.W. Cheney, *Introduction to Approximation Theory,* McGraw-Hill, New York, 1966.

[17] A.N. Mucciardi and E.E. Gose, "A Comparison of Seven Techniques for Choosing Subsets of Pattern Recognition Properties," *IEEE Transactions on Computers,* Vol. C-20, 1971, pp. 1023–1031.

[18] P.M. Narendra and K. Fukunaga, "A Branch and Bound Algorithm for Feature Subset Selection," *IEEE Transactions on Computers,* Vol. C-26, 1977, p. 920.

[19] J. Kittler, "Feature Set Search Algorithm," C.H. Chen (Ed.), *Pattern Recognition and Signal Processing,* Sijthoff and Nordhoff, The Netherlands, 1978, pp. 41–61.

[20] W.L.G. Koontz, P. Narenda, and K. Fukunaga, "A Branch and Bound Clustering Algorithm," *IEEE Transactions on Computers,* Vol. C-24, September 1975, pp. 908–914.

[21] J. Sietsma and R.J.F. Dow, "Neural Net Pruning—Why and How," *Proceedings of the IEEE International Conference on Neural Networks,* San Diego, CA, Vol. I, July 1988, pp. 325–333.

[22] C.B. Ware, "An Analysis of a Nonlinear Neural Network," Masters Thesis, Department of Electrical Engineering, University of Texas at Arlington, December 1988.

12
Primacy and Recency Effects in Back Propagation Learning*

Shelly D.D. Goggin
Kristina M. Johnson
Karl Gustafson
Center for Optoelectronic Computing Systems
University of Colorado

1. INTRODUCTION

The analysis presented here provides insight into the sequential response of the back propagation learning algorithm (also known as the generalized delta rule and learning logic) [1,2,3], with momentum and weight decay parameters. Analogies to similar effects in human and optical memory systems are also presented. In the back propagation algorithm, the use of the momentum parameter causes the first patterns to have a larger effect on the current values of the weights than the most recently learned patterns. Depending upon how the patterns interfere during the learning process, this effect may result in better recall of patterns presented earlier in a sequence. We refer to this effect as primacy. The primacy effect occurs in human list memorization under some circumstances. A similar effect occurs when recording multiple-exposure holograms in photographic recording materials. Holograms recorded first are recalled brightest [4,5]. The use of the weight-decay parameter in the back propagation algorithm enables a phenomenon of recency to occur. Recent patterns have a greater influence on the value of the weights than earlier patterns. The recency effect also occurs in human list learning. A similar effect occurs in multiple-holographic storage in photorefractive materials, where the last hologram to be recorded is brightest when recalled [6,7,8]. In this chapter, we present the mathematical analyses of

* This work was performed under NSF Engineering Research Center for Optoelectronic Computing Systems Grant CDR8622236. Shelly Goggin gratefully acknowledges fellowship support from GTE. The back propagation simulator used for the simulations was written by Mike Fellows at the University of Colorado. The simulation results were checked using the general neural network simulator, "SunNet," version 5.2, written by Yoshiro Miyata.

primacy and recency effects in the back propagation learning algorithm. Applications of these effects for back propagation learning in previously trained neural networks are also presented.

2. PRIMACY AND RECENCY IN MEMORY SYSTEMS

A memory system is defined here as any system, biological, physical, or numerical, in which items can be stored and later recalled with some degree of accuracy. The memory systems of concern here are: a) human memory systems, b) holographic memory systems, and c) artificial neural network memory systems. Human memory systems receive information through the senses and recall these items through the storage capability of the conscious mind. The memory media is understood through psychological experiments. In holographic memories, information is encoded as images and stored through the interaction of light and matter [9,10,11]. The memory media for an artificial neural network is typically storage in a digital or analog computer. The data to be stored are presented as vectors and the neural network algorithm has provisions for learning and for recall. While the data that can be stored in neural networks and holography are very simple, the memory mechanisms for neural networks and holographic memories are better understood than the mechanism for human memory. Because of this understanding, we draw analogies to the causes of primacy and recency effects between the former and the latter, while acknowledging the limitations of these analogies.

The primacy and recency effects are fundamental to any memory system in which the information to be learned is presented sequentially. The primacy effect occurs when the memory system is biased towards the earlier presentations in the sequence, and the recency effect occurs when the memory system is biased towards later presentations in the sequence. These biases can be due to internal repetitions of the previously stored information or internal decay of the stored memory. These internal processes arise from temporal properties of the memory media, or contention for memory resources. In psychological processes and neural networks, the effects of the order of learning are mainly due to the temporal properties of the memory media. In optical holographic memory, these effects are mainly due to contention for memory resources. Externally, the effects are very similar, although a mixture of primacy and recency effects is difficult to achieve in an optical system with finite memory resources.

The next two sections discuss primacy and recency effects in psychology and holography. The remainder of the paper analyzes primacy and recency in the back propagation learning algorithm. Comparisons are made to the psychological and holographic effects.

2.1. Primacy and Recency in Psychology

The psychological terms primacy and recency refer to the phenomena that when a list of items is memorized, the first and last items in the list tend to be recalled best. These effects have been extensively researched. Earlier works [12] used the experimental methods of paired associates, anticipation, and free recall to study the effects of serial position upon memorization. Under the paired associates method, the subject is presented with pairs of items to remember (such as colors and numbers), then the subject is asked to recall the corresponding item when one of the items is presented. Under the anticipation and free recall methods, a list of items is presented with a prescribed interval between presentations. In the anticipation method, the subject must recall the list in its original order, and when an item is incorrectly recalled, the correct item is provided. In the free recall method, the list can be recalled in any order, without prompting or correction. Later experiments used the Brown-Peterson method [13]. Here, each item presentation has five time intervals. First a ready signal is presented, followed by the item to be remembered. After the item is presented, a distractor task is performed, then the recall signal is used to prompt the recall of the item. Finally, an intertrial interval occurs before the sequence is repeated for the next item. The different experimental methods for list memorization each allow different levels of control over the subject's ability to use rehearsal, short-term memory, and long-term memory.

The primacy (or primary) effect has been disputed in the psychological community, since not all experiments produce the effect. The primacy effect can be eliminated when the subjects are told to concentrate only on the item currently being learned, or when the time between presentation of items in the learning phase is short [14]. The primacy effect can be enhanced by incorporating sequential structure into the list of items to be learned [15].

The cause of the primacy effect is not yet well understood. One suggested explanation is that rehearsal of earlier items may create the primacy effect in experiments with large intervals between presentations [12]. Increased attention to earlier items may also cause those items to be transferred from primary memory (PM) to secondary memory (SM) [16]. Currently, proactive inhibition (PI) is the most popular explanation for the primacy effect [17,18]. Information presented earlier in a sequence inhibits the learning of information presented later in the sequence. The neurobiological mechanisms for PI has not yet been determined.

The recency effect is much more prominent in the psychological data than the primacy effect. Even in experiments in which the primacy effect is suppressed, the recency effect remains. Several explanations exist for the recency effect in human memory, which are similar to the explanations for the primacy effect. The recency effect may be due to the existence of short-term memory, which cannot

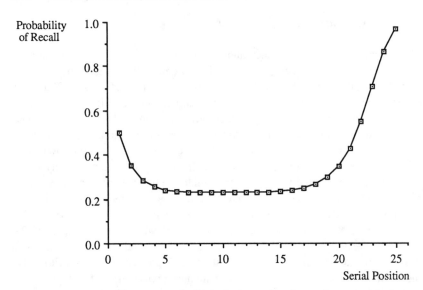

Figure 12.1. Curve fit to psychological data showing primacy and recency (copyright American Psychological Association, 1962) [37].

store all the items in the list [16]. The longer an item is in short-term memory, the less likely it will be recalled correctly. A similar theory is temporal distinctiveness [19], in which the probability of recall is proportional to the size of the search set, and earlier memories are associated with larger search sets. This theory tends to imply the existence of associated temporal information. Retroactive inhibition (RI) is a third possible explanation [20]. With retroactive inhibition, each item inhibits the items that were learned earlier. Since no items are learned after the last item, the last item has the least retroactive inhibition, and therefore, is recalled with the highest probability.

Although the recency effect can appear without the primacy effect, the primacy effect does often not appear without the recency effect. Figure 12.1 is an example of the curve fit to the data for a psychological experiment. Note that the recency effect is larger than the primacy effect. Similar curves have been obtained for laboratory animals [21]. Murdock's Theory of Distributed Associative Memory (TODAM) [22] is a linear psychological model which has been used to fit the psychological data using parameters that are similar to the neural network learning parameters discussed in Section 3.

2.2. Primacy and Recency in Holographic Memory

A hologram is a three-dimensional representation of an object, as compared to a photograph, which is capable of imaging in only two dimensions. To produce a

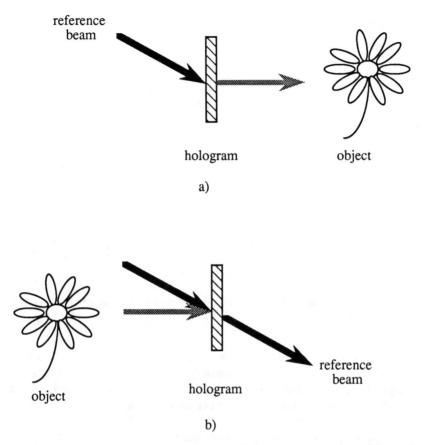

reference
beam

hologram   object

a)

object   hologram

reference
beam

b)

Figure 12.2.   Associative memory through hologram reconstruction. a) The reference beam can reconstruct the object, or b) the object can reconstruct the reference beam.

hologram, an interference pattern light either reflected by or transmitted through an object, and a reference wavefront is recorded in a suitable medium [23]. To reconstruct an image of the original object the recorded interference pattern, or hologram, is illuminated by the reference beam (see Figure 12.2). Several researchers in the late 1960s and early 1970s [9,10,11] noted that holograms could be used to implement associative memory. In fact, the hologram itself is the association between light originating from a particular object, and the reference illumination, which may be another object. By analogy to artificial neural networks, lines in the interference pattern can be thought of as the synaptic connections between sources of light emanating from the object and reference beams, which represent the neurons, or activation values.

Storing more than one hologram in the same recording medium can result in

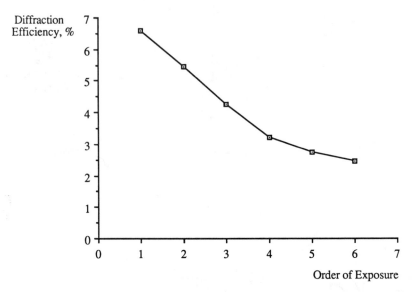

Figure 12.3. Primacy effect in diffraction efficiency vs. order of exposure in film [5].

primacy and recency effects. The primacy effect occurs when holograms recorded earlier in a sequence of recordings, reconstruct brighter images than holograms recorded later in the sequence. Recency occurs when holograms recorded later in the sequence reconstruct brighter images than objects exposed earlier in the sequence.

The primacy effect is most prominent when multiple-exposure holograms are stored in silver halide recording materials [4] (see Figure 12.3). This is due to the nature of the holographic recording process in silver halide materials. When light illuminates the silver halide crystalline grains in the film, electron-hole pairs are generated. The electrons combine with silver ion interstitial defects to form single silver atoms. The lifetimes of these single silver atoms is on the order of two seconds [24]. If during the lifetime of these single silver atoms, another single atom is created, the two combine to form a stable diatomic molecule. The lifetime of this sublatent image cluster is years. Subsequent photo-generation of electrons increases the size of these silver clusters, until eventually, they reach the threshold for development (four or more silver atoms). The lifetimes of these clusters is also years, and hence, in terms of competing for a finite set of resources (silver atoms), it makes intuitive sense that objects recorded earlier in a sequence would have more unexposed grains to make developable, and hence, diffract more light into their reconstructed images. A complete explanation involves the role of the single silver atoms, and can be found in reference [5].

The recency effect is present in nonpermanent holographic recording materials such as photorefractive $LiNbO_3$ [25]. When light illuminates a photorefractive material, there is a photo-induced perturbation of the material index of refraction due to the generation and migration of charged carriers. An interference pattern between a reference wave and an object wave produces a spatially varying index of refraction in the material. This index change diffracts light incident upon the medium by the linear electro-optic effect. Since the interference pattern is generally not a permanent recording of the association between object and reference wavefronts, objects recorded later in the superposition can rearrange, and hence erase, spatially varying perturbations of earlier recorded holograms (see Figure 12.4).

Although both holographic primacy and recency effects can be compensated for by appropriate energy of exposure schedules [5,26], there are applications of these phenomena. For example, in order to learn new information, or modify previous concepts, the capability of forgetting is essential. Selective forgetting requires erasing portions of previously recorded information (recency), while still maintaining intact other prerecorded data (primacy). By choosing an appropriate exposure schedule, this may be possible to achieve in holographic associative memories.

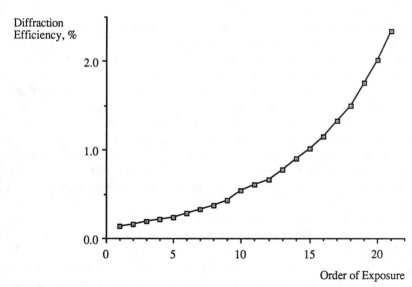

Figure 12.4.   Recency effect in diffraction efficiency vs. order of exposure in $LiNbO_s$ [8].

3. PRIMACY AND RECENCY IN NEURAL NETWORKS

Artificial neural networks models are inspired by the information processing capability of the brain. These models vary between those that model the chemical processes of the brain [27] to those which are simply parallel versions of iterative methods [28]. Here, we are concerned with those models that iteratively learn patterns.

Neural networks are composed of independently operating units, or neurons. Each unit in the neural network model has connections to other units in the model, which represent synaptic weights. The input to a unit is the sum of the output of the connected units multiplied by the weights represented by the connections. These weights determine the patterns that the units recognize. The weights are iteratively updated as the training patterns are presented. In this manner, the neural network finds a good solution to the problem of learning patterns, but not necessarily the best solution.

3.1. Neural Networks Which Exhibit Primacy and Recency

Three types of neural networks have been shown to have primacy and recency effects: adaptive resonance theory neural networks [29], brain-state-in-a-box neural networks [30], and back propagation neural networks. Primacy and recency in the first two neural networks has been analyzed elsewhere. A brief review is presented here.

Adaptive resonance theory was developed to use neural networks to reproduce psychological phenomena. The neural network has a layer of input units, a layer of output units and a gain control unit (see Figure 12.5). A pattern is placed on the input units, which activate the output units. The output units participate in a winner-take-all process until one output unit is chosen. If the chosen output unit meets the vigilance condition, then its weights are adapted and a new pattern is presented. If the chosen output unit does not meet the vigilance condition, then that unit is reset by the gain control unit, and removed from the winner-take-all competition. A new output unit is then chosen. This process continues until an output unit is chosen that meets the vigilance condition. In this manner, the neural network learns to respond to different input patterns with different output units.

Primacy and recency are used in adaptive resonance theory to describe the effect of the sequence of pattern presentations on recall in neural network theory [30,31]. As with some of the psychological studies, primacy is considered to be the effect of long-term memory interactions and recency is considered to be the effect of short-term memory interactions. In adaptive resonance theory, the long-term memory interactions are the iterative adaptation of the weights. The momentum term in the weight update formula causes the primacy effect, as will be

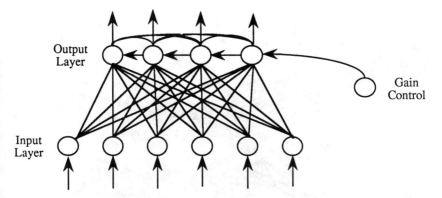

Figure 12.5.   Architecture for an adaptive resonance theory neural network.

seen in the analysis of the back propagation neural network. The short-term memory interactions are the result of the reset of the network to successively recall the stored patterns. The reset operation causes the most recently presented patterns to be recalled best, which produces a recency effect.

Brain-state-in-a-box has a neural network architecture in which all of the units are connected to each other (see Figure 12.6). This architecture is similar to the output layer of the adaptive resonance theory neural network, but the weights are adaptable in the brain-state-in-a-box neural network. The weights are learned with a decay factor, which will be shown in the analysis of the back propagation neural network to result in a recency effect. This "positive recency" effect is attributed to limited short-term storage capacity (e.g., as may be the case in the human memory).

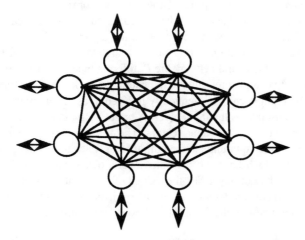

Figure 12.6.   Architecture for a brain-state-in-a-box neural network.

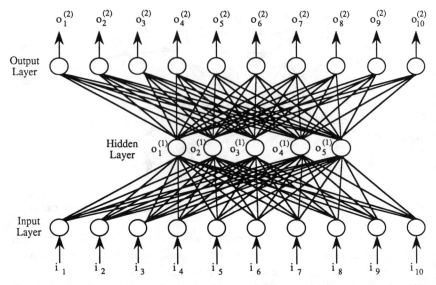

Figure 12.7. Architecture for a back propagation neural network for the 10-5-10 encoder-decoder problem.

3.2. Back Propagation Neural Networks

Back propagation neural networks are multilayer, feed-forward neural networks that use a generalized delta rule to iteratively determine weights for hetero-associative processing [1,2,3]. Back propagation is based on the least-means squared (LMS) algorithm and does not require that the target values for the intermediate layers be known a priori. Other schemes for finding the weights in a multilayer neural network have been developed based on the conjugate gradient algorithm [31] and the successive over-relaxation algorithm [28].

A typical back propagation neural network architecture is shown in Figure 12.7. The inputs to the neural network are P different input vectors $i(p)$ of length N. Only pth input vector is presented to the neural network at a given time. The N elements of the input vector are frequently referred to as the N input units. This set of units is referred to as the input layer. A target vector $d(p)$ of length M is to be associated with each of the input vectors. The M elements of the target vector are referred to as the output units in the output layer. Each hidden layer k is made up of $H^{(k)}$ units, which have the previous layer's output values as inputs. For example, the first hidden layer has the values of the input units as inputs. The output value $o_j^{(k)}(t)$ of a hidden unit j in layer k is determined by a thresholded value of the weighted outputs from the previous layer, at time t,

$$o_j^{(k)}(t) = f\left[\sum_{i=1}^{H^{(k-1)}} w_{ij}^{(k)}(t) o_i^{(k-1)}(t) \right] \qquad (3.1)$$

where $w_{ij}^{(k)}(t)$ is the weight between unit i in layer $k - 1$ and unit j in layer k, at the tth iteration. The threshold function, f, is usually a sigmoid function of the form:

$$f(x) = \frac{1}{1 + e^{-x}}.$$ (3.2)

For the first hidden layer,

$$o_i^{(0)}(t) = i_i(p),$$ (3.3)

where p depends on whether the algorithm uses pattern mode, in which $p = t$ mod P, or batch mode, in which t is not always an integer and $p = P(t - \lceil t \rceil)$. The weights are updated according to the error with respect to the target vector. For a neural network with L layers, not including the input layer, the error for the mth output unit in the final output layer is:

$$e_m(t) = d_m(p) - o_m^{(L)}(t).$$ (3.4)

The error is back propagated through the layers to determine the weight changes. Following McClelland and Rumelhart [32], define the error signal for the output layer as:

$$\delta_m^{(L)}(t) = o_m^{(L)}(t)[1 - o_m^{(L)}(t)]e_m(t).$$ (3.5)

The error signal for unit j in hidden layer k is:

$$\delta_j^{(k)}(t) = o_m^{(k)}(t)[1 - o_m^{(k)}(t)] \sum_{i=1}^{H^{(k+1)}} w_{ji}^{(k+1)} \delta_i^{(k+1)}(t).$$ (3.6)

The formula for the weight update of a weight w_{ij} at time t is:

$$w_{ij}^{(k)}(t) = \gamma w_{ij}^{(k)}(t - 1) + \Delta w_{ij}^{(k)}(t),$$ (3.7)

where γ is the weight-decay parameter and $\Delta w_{ij}(t)$ is the weight change at time t. The two most common algorithms for determining $\Delta w_{ij}(t)$ are pattern learning and batch learning. In pattern learning, the weights are incremented after each pattern presentation by:

$$\Delta w_{ij}^{(k)}(t) = \alpha \Delta w_{ij}^{(k)}(t - 1) + \eta \delta_i^{(k)}(t) o_j^{(k)}(t),$$ (3.8)

where α is a constant known as the momentum parameter, η is a constant known as the learning parameter. In batch learning, the weights are incremented after a complete presentation of the pattern set by:

$$\Delta w_{ij}^{(k)}(t) = \alpha \Delta w_{ij}^{(k)}(t-1) + \eta \sum_{p=1}^{P} \delta_i^{(k)}\left(t - 1 + \frac{p}{P}\right) o_j^{(k)}\left(t - 1 + \frac{p}{P}\right). \quad (3.9)$$

Let us define $\epsilon_{ij}(t)$ as the effect of the state of the network on the weight update at time t:

$$\epsilon_{ij}^{(k)}(t) = \begin{cases} \eta \delta_i^{(k)}(t) o_j^{(k)}(t), & \text{if pattern learning is used.} \\ \eta \sum_{p=1}^{P} \delta_i^{(k)}\left(t - 1 + \frac{p}{P}\right) o_j^{(k)}\left(t - 1 + \frac{p}{P}\right), & \text{if batch learning is used.} \end{cases} \quad (3.10)$$

The analyses that follow are for a generic weight within a neural network model, therefore, the references to the layer will be dropped. The general formulas for the weight change can therefore be written as:

$$w_{ij}(t) = \gamma w_{ij}(t-1) + \Delta w_{ij}(t), \quad (3.11)$$

with:

$$\Delta w_{ij}(t) = \alpha \Delta w_{ij}(t-1) + \epsilon_{ij}(t). \quad (3.12)$$

This is the form which will be used throughout the remainder of the chapter.

4. PRIMACY EFFECT IN BACK PROPAGATION

The primacy effect in back propagation can be created by using large values of the momentum parameter. As will be shown in the following analysis, the momentum parameter causes the previous errors to be reintroduced into the calculations, which creates a preference for learning earlier inputs. This effect is analogous to rehearsal in human memory and saturation in grains in film. Simulations confirm the existence of the primacy effect, but the temporal effects due to the errors are dominant effects in many simulations.

4.1. Analysis of the Primacy Effect of Momentum

The analysis of the primacy effect begins by setting γ equal to one in Equation (3.11). The weight update equation is then:

$$w_{ij}(t) = w_{ij}(t-1) + \alpha \Delta w_{ij}(t-1) + \epsilon_{ij}(t). \quad (4.1)$$

The effect of the sequence of pattern presentations on the weights due to α is apparent when the back propagation algorithm is rewritten as a time series with index n. The index n goes from the initial time 0, to the current time t. Removing the recursion in Equation (4.1) yields the following time series for the weight change at time t,

$$\Delta w_{ij}(t) = \sum_{n=1}^{t} \alpha^{t-n} \epsilon_{ij}(n). \tag{4.2}$$

Substituting Equation (4.2) for Equation (4.1) and removing the recursion yields:

$$w_{ij}(t) = \sum_{m=1}^{t} \sum_{n=0}^{m-1} \alpha^{n} \epsilon_{ij}(m - n) + w_{ij}(0), \tag{4.3}$$

where $w_{ij}(0)$ is the initial state of the weight. This equation can then be rewritten as a time series for the value of the weight at time t,

$$w_{ij}(t) = \sum_{m=0}^{t-1} \alpha^{m} \epsilon_{ij}(1) + \ldots + \sum_{m=0}^{t-n} \alpha^{m} \epsilon_{ij}(n) + \ldots + \epsilon_{ij}(t) + w_{ij}(0). \tag{4.4}$$

The function of α which modifies each term in the time series will be referred to as the momentum function at time n,

$$m_t(n) = \sum_{m=0}^{t-n} \alpha^{m}. \tag{4.5}$$

The momentum function determines the relative amount that the pattern presented at time n contributes to the current value of the weight. For simplicity, we assume that the dependence of $\epsilon_{ij}(n)$ on the network state at earlier times is secondary to its dependence on the network state at time n. This assumption allows the contribution of each term in the time series to be analyzed through the momentum function, ignoring the effects of $\epsilon_{ij}(n)$. This assumption is reasonable when new patterns are added to a previously trained network such that the error stays fairly constant with time. When the assumption is not valid, as is frequently the case, the effect of $\epsilon_{ij}(n)$ on the current value of the weight cannot be separated from the effect of momentum, and the primacy effect will not be observed.

The primacy effect is caused by a decrease in the momentum function as n goes from 0 to t. The mathematical confirmation of the primacy effect is different for different values for α.

If $\alpha > 1$, then Equation (4.4) simplifies to:

$$w_{ij}(t) = \sum_{n=1}^{t} \alpha^{t-n} \frac{1 - \alpha^{-(t-n+1)}}{1 - \alpha^{-1}} \epsilon_{ij}(n) + w_{ij}(0), \tag{4.6}$$

which has a momentum function of:

$$m_t(n) = \alpha^{t-n} \frac{1 - \alpha^{-(t-n+1)}}{1 - \alpha^{-1}} \tag{4.7}$$

The derivative of the momentum function with respect to n is:

$$\frac{d}{dn} \alpha^{t-n} \frac{1 - \alpha^{-(t-n+1)}}{1 - \alpha^{-1}} = -(\ln \alpha) \frac{\alpha^{t-n}}{1 - \alpha^{-1}} < 0. \tag{4.8}$$

Therefore, when $\alpha > 1$, the momentum function decreases with n. Note that $\alpha > 1$ is not a very good choice of parameters since α^t becomes very large after only a few time steps.

If $\alpha = 1$, Equation (4.4) simplifies to:

$$w_{ij}(t) = \sum_{n=1}^{t} (t - n)\epsilon_{ij}(n) + w_{ij}(0). \tag{4.9}$$

Therefore, the momentum function for $\alpha = 1$ is:

$$m_t(n) = t - n. \tag{4.10}$$

The derivative of the momentum function with respect to n is:

$$\frac{d}{dn} (t - n) = -1 < 0. \tag{4.11}$$

Therefore, when $\alpha = 1$ the momentum function decreases with n.

If $\alpha < 1$, then Equation (4.4) simplifies to:

$$w_{ij}(t) = \sum_{n=1}^{t} \left(\frac{1 - \alpha^{t+1-n}}{1 - \alpha} \right) \epsilon_{ij}(n) + w_{ij}(0). \tag{4.12}$$

The momentum function for $\alpha < 1$ is:

$$m_t(n) = \frac{1 - \alpha^{t+1-n}}{1 - \alpha}, \tag{4.13}$$

which has the following derivative with respect to n:

$$\frac{d}{dn} \left(\frac{1 - \alpha^{t+1-n}}{1 - \alpha} \right) = \frac{\alpha^{t+1-n} \ln \alpha}{1 - \alpha} < 0. \tag{4.14}$$

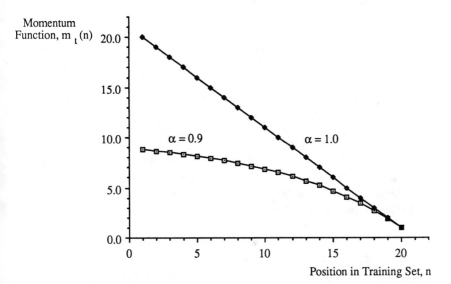

Figure 12.8.   The relative influence of the weights by the pattern presented at time *n* due to the momentum function (*t* = 20).

Therefore, when $\alpha < 1$, the function of α decreases as n approaches the current presentation t.

In summary, for any positive value of α, the momentum function is always decreasing. This decrease results in earlier patterns having a greater influence on the current value of the weights than recent patterns. As the value of α increases, the difference in the relative influence of the first and last patterns on the current value of the weights also increases (see Figure 12.8). The primacy effect occurs for any sequence of patterns, even if the sequence consists of iterating through a training set, as in batch learning.

4.2. Computer Simulation of Primacy Effect

To show the primacy effect, a simple 10–5–10 encoder-decoder neural network was simulated with pattern learning for twenty different training sets. The back propagation neural network has 10 input units, 5 hidden units, and 10 output units. The input vector is the same as the desired output vector. The hidden units are trained to perform the encoder-decoder function. Each of the training sets contained one pattern which was duplicated 19 times and one test pattern. In the ith training set, the test pattern was placed in the ith position, where $i = 1, \ldots,$ 20. The duplicated pattern was:

$$[0, 0, 0, 0, 0, 1, 1, 1, 1, 1,],$$

whereas, the test pattern was:

[1, 1, 1, 1, 1, 0, 0, 0, 0, 0,].

The assumption that the temporal effects of $\epsilon_{ij}(n)$ can be ignored is not usually very accurate for back propagation simulations, so the simulation presented here was constructed so that many of the temporal effects of $\epsilon_{ij}(n)$ have been eliminated. Orthogonal patterns were chosen, since these patterns tend to interfere the least with each other during learning. A large training set was used, so that the primacy effect was pronounced. Nineteen of the patterns in the training set are the same, so that $\epsilon_{ij}(n)$ is nearly constant. By placing the test pattern in different positions in the training set, the effect of the temporal variation in the error was separated from the effect of position. Since the effect of position is cumulative over the iterations through the training set, we used data taken after 50 iterations. To further emphasize the effect, the error for the weight update at each position was normalized to the error at the first position.

The relative error for the test pattern after 50 passes through the training set is shown in Figure 12.9. When the test pattern was presented earlier in the training set, the error was less than when the test pattern was presented later in the training set. This implies that earlier patterns have greater influence on the weights than later patterns.

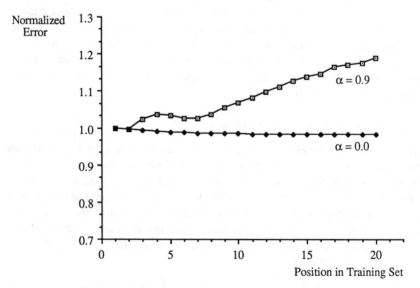

Figure 12.9. Simulation of primacy effect of relative position within a training set. Errors are normalized to the error at the first position.

5. RECENCY EFFECT IN BACK PROPAGATION

The weight decay parameter γ in the back propagation algorithm can be used to generate a recency effect in the back propagation algorithm. In applications in which the characteristics of the patterns change over time, more recent patterns can be considered more heavily in determining the value of the weights than earlier patterns, when the weight-decay parameter is used. This effect is analogous to decay in short-term memory in human memory, and to the rearrangement of charges in photorefractive materials. As with the primacy effect, the temporal effect of the error tends to cause the recency effect to be weak in back propagation simulations.

5.1. Analysis of Recency Effect of Weight Decay

The analysis of the recency effect begins with Equation (3.12) with $\alpha = 0$,

$$w_{ij}(t) = \gamma w_{ij}(t - 1) + \epsilon_{ij}(t), \qquad (5.1)$$

where $0 < \gamma \leq 1$ for most applications, and $\epsilon_{ij}(t)$ is defined by Equation (3.10). The recursion can be removed to yield the time-series form. The time-series form of Equation (5.1) is:

$$w_{ij}(t) = \sum_{n=1}^{t} \gamma^{t-n} \epsilon_{ij}(n) + \gamma^t w_{ij}(0). \qquad (5.2)$$

From this equation, the weight-decay function for $\gamma \neq 1$ is:

$$M_t(n) = \gamma^{t-n}. \qquad (5.3)$$

The derivative of the weight-decay function is given by:

$$\frac{d}{dn} \gamma^{t-n} = -\gamma^{t-n} \ln\gamma, \qquad (5.4)$$

which shows that the weight-decay function increases as n increases when $\gamma < 1$, and the weight-decay function decreases when $\gamma > 1$. Therefore, both recency and primacy effects can be obtained with γ. However, $\gamma > 1$ is usually impractical since the weight-decay functon will increase too rapidly for large t. The usual case is for γ to be less than one, which produces the recency effect (see Figure 12.10).

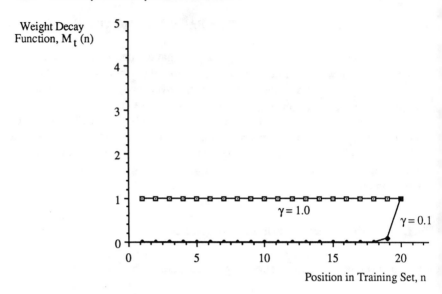

Figure 12.10. **The relative influence of the weights by the pattern presented at time *n* due to the weight-decay function ($t = 20$).**

If $\gamma = 1$, then the weight-decay function is:

$$M_t(n) = 1, \tag{5.5}$$

which has neither a primacy effect nor a recency effect.

The exponential recency effect is also apparent in other iterative methods. Back propagation learning is very similar to second-order autoregressive schemes used in time-series analyses [33]. A typical second-order autoregression has the form:

$$x(k) = a_1 x(k-1) + a_2 x(k-2) + b_1 u(k-1) + b_2 u(k-2). \tag{5.6}$$

The *forgetting factor,* a_1 has been shown to have an exponential profile [36]. The analogous back propogation weight update formula has:

$$a_1 = \gamma, \, a_2 = 0,$$
$$b_1 = 1, \, b_2 = \alpha, \tag{5.7}$$

where γ is the weight-decay parameter and α is the momentum parameter.

For stability in the random process, the restriction is placed that the roots of the following polynomial in s lie within the unit circle,

$$s^2 + a_1 s + a_2 = 0. \tag{5.8}$$

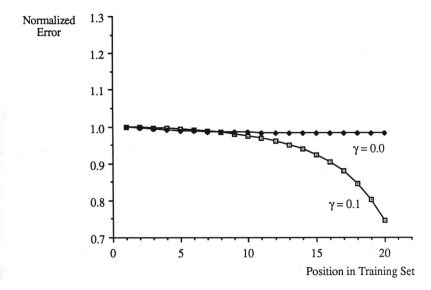

Figure 12.11. Simulation of recency effect of relative position within a training set. Errors are normalized to the error at the first position.

The stability requirement translates into the restriction that $\gamma < 1$ in the back propagation algorithm. This restriction agrees with the preceding analysis for the back propagation algorithm.

5.2. Computer Simulations of Recency Effect

Similar to the primary effect for α, the recency effect for γ is significant only if the value of $\epsilon_{ij}(n)$ is primarily dependent on time n. The recency effect was simulated using the same 10-5-10 encoder–decoder network used to simulate the primacy effect. Figure 12.11 shows simulation results for which the test pattern was learned best in the last position. As in human memory, the recency effect appears here to be stronger than the primacy effect. This increase is to be expected, since $\epsilon_{ij}(n)$ also tends to favor later patterns.

6. COMBINED PRIMACY AND RECENCY EFFECTS

The primacy and recency effects in back propagation can be combined to provide an effect that is not very similar to the combined primacy and recency effects in human memory. The momentum and weight-decay parameter can also be used to compensate for each other so that the algorithm has the convergence advantages of the momentum and weight-decay parameters without the serial presentation effects. Compensation to eliminate the primacy or recency effect is often performed in holography [4,5,6,7,8,25,26]. However, if compensation is a concern in an application of back propagation, batch learning on a static set of inputs also eliminates the serial presentation effects.

6.1. Combined Effect in Back Propagation

When both momentum and weight decay are used then the primacy and recency effects may not be observed. The combination of the two parameters can be used to emphasize areas of the list which are not necessarily the beginning or the end.

The weight update formula in the case when both momentum and weight decay are used is:

$$w_{ij}(t) = \gamma w_{ij}(t-1) + \Delta w_{ij}(t), \tag{6.1}$$

where:

$$\Delta w_{ij}(t) = \alpha \Delta w_{ij}(t-1) + \epsilon_{ij}(t). \tag{6.2}$$

Removing the recursion for $w_{ij}(t-1)$ in Equation (6.1) yields:

$$w_{ij}(t) = \gamma^t w_{ij}(0) + \sum_{m=1}^{t} \gamma^{t-m} \Delta w_{ij}(m). \tag{6.3}$$

Substituting Equation (4.2) for $\Delta w_{ij}(m)$ yields:

$$w_{ij}(t) = \gamma^t w_{ij}(0) + \sum_{m=1}^{t} \gamma^{t-m} \sum_{n=0}^{m-1} \alpha^n \epsilon_{ij}(m-n), \tag{6.4}$$

which can be rearranged so that the combined momentum and weight-decay function is evident,

$$w_{ij}(t) = \gamma^t w_{ij}(0) + \gamma^{t-1} \sum_{m=0}^{t-1} \left(\frac{\alpha}{\gamma} \right)^m \epsilon_{ij}(1) + \ldots$$

$$+ \gamma^{t-n} \sum_{m=0}^{t-n} \left(\frac{\alpha}{\gamma} \right)^m \epsilon_{ij}(n) + \ldots + \epsilon_{ij}(t). \tag{6.5}$$

The combined function for α and γ is:

$$C_t(n) = \gamma^{t-n} \sum_{m=0}^{t-n} \left(\frac{\alpha}{\gamma} \right)^m. \tag{6.6}$$

For $\alpha < \gamma$, the combined function simplifies to:

$$C_t(n) = \gamma^{t-n} \frac{1 - \left(\dfrac{\alpha}{\gamma}\right)^{t-n+1}}{1 - \dfrac{\alpha}{\gamma}}. \qquad (6.7)$$

For $\alpha > \gamma$,

$$C_t(n) = \alpha^{t-n} \frac{1 - \left(\dfrac{\gamma}{\alpha}\right)^{(t-n+1)}}{1 - \dfrac{\gamma}{\alpha}}. \qquad (6.8)$$

For $\alpha = \gamma$,

$$C_t(n) = \begin{cases} \gamma^{t-n}\,[t - n] \text{ for } n < t. \\ 1 \text{ for } n = t \end{cases} \qquad (6.9)$$

Graphs of these functions are in Figure 12.12. For the case when $\alpha = \gamma$, the inflection point occurs at:

$$n = t + \frac{1}{\ln\gamma}. \qquad (6.10)$$

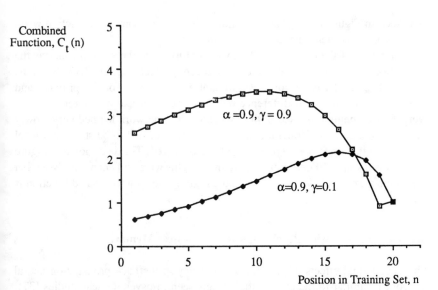

Combined Function, $C_t(n)$

Position in Training Set, n

Figure 12.12.   The relative influence of the weights by the pattern presented at time _n_ due to the combined function ($t = 20$).

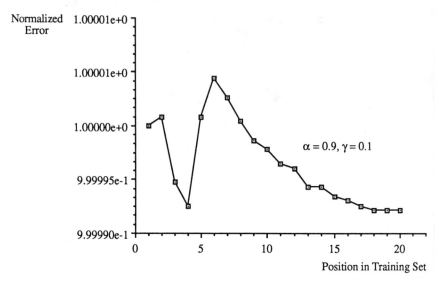

Figure 12.13. Simulation of combined primacy and recency effect of relative position within a training set. Errors are normalized to the error at the first position.

For example, for $\gamma = \alpha = .9$, the inflection occurs at

$$n = t - 9.5, \tag{6.11}$$

as is seen in Figure 12.12. The inflection points for the combined function when $\alpha \neq \gamma$ cannot be determined in closed form.

Simulation of the combined effect was performed in the same manner as the simulations for the primacy effect and the recency effect. Figure 12.13 shows the results. The results were not as significant as the results for the primacy and recency simulations. This difference may have been caused by different areas of weight space being traversed in the two cases. The network learned very slowly in this simulation. At 50 iterations, the algorithm seemed to be stuck in a local minima, so that no temporal results could be observed. The data shown in Figure 12.13 was taken at 20 iterations, where the weights were still changing. Note that the simulation does have low errors in the region where the combined function is high.

6.2. Comparison with Psychological and Optical Memories

The exponential effects of primacy and recency in the back propagation neural network is similar to the exponential effects seen in psychological studies [37]. An empirical equation for the probability of recall from Murdock is:

$$p = 1.00 + 0.27(0.463)^{(x-1)} - 0.772(0.042)^{0.555(L-x)}, \qquad (6.12)$$

where x is the position in the list that was learned and L is the length of the list (see Figure 12.1). This is approximately:

$$p \approx -1.447 + 0.27(0.463)^{(x-1)} + 2.447(0.555)^{(L-x)}. \qquad (6.13)$$

The general exponential form agrees well with the form of Equations (6.7) and (6.8). Lewdowsky and Murdock's TODAM [22] results in a similar exponential form. One would not expect the equations to correspond exactly, since the mechanisms involved are very different.

The exponential form for the recency and primacy effects also agrees well with the exponential forms for the data in the holographic experiments [26]. The space charge field of a hologram in a photorefractive crystal is approximately:

$$E_{sc} = E_o[1 - e^{-t/\tau_r}], \qquad (6.14)$$

which agrees with the exponential form of the weight-decay function.

7. APPLICATIONS OF PRIMACY AND RECENCY IN BACK PROPAGATION

Other than the interesting comparisons with optical and human memory, the primacy and recency effects may be too subtle to be applicable for general back propagation applications. The ravines and local minima tend to dominate convergence. The momentum and weight-decay parameters certainly can be used to improve convergence for many applications, but the improved convergence may be due to providing a means to escape local minimum and more quickly traverse ravines in the error function. In addition, the primacy and recency effects are not generally considered to be desirable in memory applications. In human memory and holography, schemes are frequently devised to compensate for these effects. However, some situations do exist in which primacy and/or recency are desirable. Two situations in which the primacy and recency effects may be useful for back propagation neural networks is for adding patterns to a neural network that was trained with a different set of patterns, and allowing the training set of patterns to evolve over time.

7.1. Adding Patterns to Trained Neural Network

One of the problems with back propagation [38,39,40] is that training new patterns tend to interfere with the ability of the neural network to recall previously learned patterns. Therefore, the training set must be repeated many times before all patterns are learned. In addition, after a back propagation neural network has been trained on one set of patterns, the network must be retrained with the old patterns as well as the new patterns, when new patterns are added. If some loss of performance on the old patterns can be tolerated, or if the old patterns are no longer available, then the back propagation algorithm could be used for just the new patterns with a high level of primacy. The primacy effect can be obtained with a high value for the momentum parameter α and a low value for the learning rate parameter η. This approach would incorporate into the weight changes the errors from the original patterns, which is stored in the momentum term. Solutions for the weights that are close to the original weights would be encouraged. If a large number of iterations are performed with the new patterns, the weights can be changed enough so that the original patterns are no longer correctly classified. Also, the weight changes for the old patterns may be too small or difficult to obtain.

7.2. Learning Over Time

When the patterns to be learned are changing over time, a recency effect may be desired to decrease the influence of earlier patterns that may no longer be relevant. The recency effect will be enhanced with a small value of the weight decay parameter γ and a large value of the learning rate parameter η. This approach removes the influence of previous weights on the current weights, which allows the later patterns to have more influence on the current weights than the earlier patterns. The recency effect can even enhance batch learning, if the sets of patterns evolve over time.

The weight-decay parameter creates a decaying exponential term. The decaying exponential approach to incorporating the past into present calculations has also been used for neural networks in which the inputs are temporally varying, even after the weights have been learned. One example of this type of neural network is Parker, Gluck, and Reifsnider's pulse-coded neural network [41]. Given a decay parameter μ, the output of a unit in this neural network model is:

$$o_j^{(k)}(t) = f\left[\mu\, o_j^{(k)}(t-1) + \sum_{i=1}^{H^{(k-1)}} w_{ij}^{(k)}(t) o_i^{(k-1)}(t)\right], \qquad (7.1)$$

where f in this case is a hard-limiting function,

$$f(x) = \begin{cases} \text{a pulse, if } x > \theta \\ \text{no pulse, if } x \geq \theta \end{cases} \qquad (7.2)$$

and θ is the threshold value. Another example is the recurrent back propagation neural networks [42,43], which use sigmoidal thresholding and the following form for the output value of a unit,

$$o_j^{(k)}(t) = \mu\, o_j^{(k)}(t - 1) + f\left[\sum_{i=1}^{H^{(k-1)}} w_{ij}^{(k)}(t) o_i^{(k-1)}(t) \right]. \tag{7.3}$$

A similar form is used for the input units in a motion-detector neural network, where the second term is replaced with one weighted input [44]. The decay parameter performs the same function for the output states as the weight-decay parameter performs for the weight states.

A charging time parameter τ for the output state has been used in fully interconnected temporal neural networks in a manner that is analogous to the use of the momentum parameter [45]. The formula for the output of a unit is:

$$o_j^{(k)}(t) = \mu\, o_j^{(k)}(t - 1) + f\left[\sum_{i=1}^{H^{(k-1)}} w_{ij}^{(k)}(t) o_i^{(k-1)}(t) \right]. \tag{7.3}$$

In this model, τ represents the charging time of the unit due to its resistance and capacitance. Therefore, the effect of the momentum can also be considered to be a capacitive effect in electrical engineering terminology.

8. CONCLUSIONS

For any particular neural network application, this analysis provides an approach to determining how the values of the momentum and weight-decay parameters can be chosen to influence the performance of a back propagation algorithm. Important aspects of a given application will be the smoothness of the error space, the amount of noise in the patterns, and the effect of time on the information in the patterns.

The momentum parameter α is used when a primacy effect is desired. Increasing the effect of earlier patterns on the values of the weights is appropriate when the patterns contain a large amount of noise, and the error space is assumed to be fairly smooth. The current value of the weight will then be less susceptible to noise since the algorithm responds to an average of the presented patterns. Averaging the response to the patterns cancels noise with mean zero. As α approaches one, the relative response of the back propagation algorithm to recent patterns decreases.

The weight-decay parameter γ is appropriate for applications where the information in the patterns is assumed to be changing with time. The weight decay parameter can also be used with batch learning to discount the effects of earlier responses to the error space.

The inclusion of both momentum and weight decay parameters may be desirable in certain implementations. For example, both parameters could be used when the beginning and ending segments of a training sequence are believed to be less important than the middle segment. The most interesting aspects of the momentum function and the weight decay function are the analogies with similar effects in psychological and holographic memory.

REFERENCES

[1] D.E. Rumelhart, J.L. McClelland, and the PDP Research Group, *Parallel Distributed Processing: Explorations in the Microstructure of Cognition, Volume I: Foundations,* MIT Press/Bradford Books, Cambridge, MA, 1987.

[2] D.B. Parker, "Learning Logic," Stanford University Invention Report S81–64, 1982.

[3] P.J. Werbos, Beyond Regression: New Tools for Prediction and Analysis in the Behavioral Sciences, Ph.D. Thesis, Harvard University, Cambridge, MA, 1974.

[4] N. Nishida and M. Sakaguchi, "Improvement of Nonuniformity of the Reconstructed Beam Intensity from a Multiple-Exposure Hologram," *Applied Optics,* Vol. 10, No. 2, February 1971, pp. 439–440.

[5] K.M. Johnson, L. Hesselink, and J.W. Goodman, "Holographic Reciprocity Law Failure," *Applied Optics,* Vol. 23, No. 2, January 15, 1984, pp. 218–227.

[6] D.L. Staebler, J.W. Burke, W. Phillips, and J.J. Amodei, "Multiple Storage and Erasure of Fixed Holograms in Fe-doped $LiNbO_3$," *Applied Physics Letters,* Vol. 26, No. 4, February 15, 1975, pp. 182–184.

[7] D. Psaltis, D. Brady, and K. Wagner, "Adaptive Optical Networks Using Photorefractive Crystals," *Applied Optics,* Vol. 27, 1 May 1988, pp. 1752–1759.

[8] A.C. Strasser, E.S. Maniloff, K.M. Johnson, and S.D.D. Goggin, "Procedure for Recording Multiple-Exposure Holograms with Equal Diffraction Efficiency in Photorefractive Media," *Optics Letters,* Vol. 14, No. 1, January 1989, pp. 6–8.

[9] P.J. van Heerden, "A New Optical Method of Storing and Retrieving Information," *Applied Optics,* Vol. 2, April 1963, pp. 387–392.

[10] D. Gabor, "Associative Holographic Memories," *IBM Journal of Research and Development,* Vol. 13, March 1969, pp. 156–159.

[11] M. Sakaguichi, N. Nishida, and T. Nemoto, "A New Associative Memory System Utilizing Holography," *IEEE Transactions on Computing,* Vol. C–19, December 1970, pp. 1174–1181.

[12] E.S. Robinson and M.A. Brown, "Effect of Serial Position Upon Memorization," *The American Journal of Psychology,* Vol. 26, No. 4, Winter 1926, pp. 538–552.

[13] D.S. Gorfein, "Explaining Context Effects on Short-Term Memory," D.S. Gorfein and R.R. Hoffman (Eds.), *Memory and Learning: The Ebbinghaus Centennial Conference,* Erlbaum, London, 1987, pp. 153–172.

[14] G. Raffel, "Two Determinants of the Primacy Effect," *The American Journal of Psychology,* Vol. 48, No. 4, Winter 1936, pp. 654–657.

[15] J. Deese and R.A. Kaufman, "Serial Effects in Recall of Unorganized and Sequentially Organized Verbal Material," *Journal of Experimental Psychology,* Vol. 54, No. 3, March 1957, pp. 180–187.

[16] N.C. Waugh and D.A. Norman, "Primary Memory," D.A. Norman (Ed.), *Memory and Attention: An Introduction to Human Information Processing,* Wiley, New York, 1969, pp. 89–97.

[17] T.C. Lorsbach, "Buildup of Proactive Inhibition as a Function of Temporal Spacing and Adult Age," *American Journal of Psychology,* Vol. 103, No. 1, Spring 1990, pp. 21–36.

[18] U. Talasli, "Proactive Inhibition After Self-Paced Study: An Analysis of Encoding in the Brown-Peterson Paradigm," The Journal of General Psychology, Vol. 116, No. 3, July 1989, pp. 256–265.

[19] A.R. Glenberg, "Temporal Context and Recency," D.S. Gorfein and R.R. Hoffman (Eds.), *Memory and Learning: The Ebbinghaus Centennial Conference,* Erlbaum, London, 1987, pp. 173–189.

[20] C.C. Chandler, "Specific Retroactive Interference in Modified Recognition Tests: Evidence for an Unknown Cause of Interference," *Journal of Experimental Psychology: Learning, Memory and Cognition,* Vol. 15, No. 2, March 1989, pp. 256–265.

[21] P. Reed, T. Chih-Ta, J.P. Aggleton, and J.N.P. Rawlins, "Primacy, Recency and the von Restorff Effect in Rats' Nonspatial Recognition Memory," *Journal of Experimental Psychology: Animal Behavior Processes,* Vol. 17, No. 1, January 1991, pp. 36–44.

[22] S. Lewandowsky and B.B. Murdock, "Memory for Serial Order," *Psychological Review,* Vol. 96, No. 1, January 1989, pp. 25–57.

[23] D. Gabor, "A New Microscope Principle," *Nature,* Vol. 161, 15 May 1948, p. 777.

[24] E. Katz, "On the Photographic Reciprocity Law Failure and Related Effects. I. The Low Intensity Failure," *Journal of Chemical Physics,* Vol. 17, No. 11, November 1949, pp. 1132–1141.

[25] W.J. Burke and P. Sheng, "Crosstalk Noise from Multiple Thick-Phase Holograms," *Journal of the Applied Physics,* Vol. 48, No. 2, February 1977, pp. 681–685.

[26] E.S. Maniloff and K.M. Johnson, "Dynamic Holographic Interconnects Using Static Holograms," *Optical Engineering,* Vol. 29, No. 3, March 1990, pp. 225–229.

[27] R.J. MacGregor, *Neural and Brain Modeling,* Academic Press, San Diego, CA, 1987.

[28] K.E. Gustafson, S.D.D. Goggin, and K.M. Johnson, "Iterative Methods for Connectionist Architectures," *Mathematical Modelling and Scientific Computing,* Vol. 1, 1993, pp. 67–87.

[29] S. Grossberg, "Adaptive Pattern Classification and Universal Recoding: I. Parallel Development and Coding of Neural Feature Detectors," *Biological Cybernetics,* Vol. 23, March 1976, pp. 121–134.

[30] J.A. Anderson, J.W. Silverstein, S.A. Ritz, and R.S. Jones, "Distinctive Features,

Categorical Perception, and Probability Learning: Some Applications of a Neural Model," *Psychological Review,* Vol. 84, October 1977, pp. 413–451.

[31]   S. Grossberg, "Behavioral Contrast in Short-Term Memory: Serial Binary Memory Models or Parallel Continuous Memory Models?," *Journal of Mathematical Psychology,* Vol. 17, June 1978, pp. 119–219.

[32]   Z. Schreter and R. Pfeifer, "Short-Term Memory/Long-Term Memory Interactions in Connectionist Simulations of Psychological Experiments on List Learning," L. Personnaz and G. Dreyfus (Eds.), *Neural Networks, Proceedings of Euro'88,* I.D.S.E.T., Paris, 1989, pp. 36–42.

[33]   J. Leonard and M.A. Kramer, "Improvement of the Back-propagation Algorithm for Training Neural Networks," *Computers and Chemical Engineering,* Vol. 14, No. 3, March 1990, pp. 337–341.

[34]   J.L. McClelland and D.E. Rumelhart, *Explorations in Parallel Distributed Processing: A Handbook of Models, Programs and Exercises,* MIT Press/Bradford Books, Cambridge, MA, 1988.

[35]   D.G. Luenberger, *Optimization by Vector Space Methods,* Wiley, New York, 1969.

[36]   L. Ljung and T. Soderstrom, *Theory and Practice of Recursive Identification,* MIT Press, Cambridge, MA, 1985.

[37]   B.B. Murdock, Jr., "The Serial Position Effect of Free Recall," *Journal of Experimental Psychology,* Vol. 64, No. 5, May 1962, pp. 482–488.

[38]   R.S. Sutton, "Two Problems with Back-propagation and Other Steepest-Descent Learning Procedures for Networks," *Proceedings of the 8th Annual Conference of the Cognitive Science Society,* 1986, pp. 823–831.

[39]   M. Mc Closkey and N.J. Cohen, "Catastrophic Interference in Connectionist Networks: The Sequential Learning Problem," K.W. Spence and J.T. Spence (Eds.), *The Psychology of Learning and Motivation,* Volume 24, Academic Press, New York, 1989, pp. 109–165.

[40]   R. Ratcliff, "Connectionist Models of Recognition Memory: Constraints Imposed by Learning and Forgetting Functions," *Psychological Review,* Vol. 97, No. 2, April 1990, pp. 285–308.

[41]   M. Gluck, D.B. Parker, and E.S. Reifsnider, "Learning with Temporal Derivatives in Pulse-Coded Neuronal Systems," D.S. Touretzky (Ed.), *Advances in Neural Information Processing Systems 1,* Morgan Kaufmann, San Mateo, CA, 1989, pp. 195–203.

[42]   M.I. Jordan, Serial Order: A Parallel Distributed Processing Approach, Institute of Cognitive Science Technical Report No. 8604, University of California, San Diego, 1986.

[43]   M.B. Ottaway, P.Y. Simard, and D.H. Ballard, "Fixed Point Analysis for Recurrent Networks," D.S. Tourtezky (Ed.), *Advances in Neural Information Processing Systems 1,* Morgan Kaufmann, San Mateo, CA, 19889, pp. 149–159.

[44]   W.S. Stornetta, T. Hogg, and B.A. Huberman, "A Dynamical Approach to Temporal Pattern Processing," D.Z. Anderson (Ed.), *Neural Information Processing Systems,* American Institute of Physics, New York, 1988, pp. 750–759.

[45]   D. Kleinfeld, "Sequential State Generation by Model Neural Networks," *Proceedings of the National Academy of Science,* Vol. 83, December 1986, pp. 9469–9473.

13
Neural-Logic Networks

S.C. Chan
L.S. Hsu
K.F. Loe
H.H. Teh
National University of Singapore

1. THREE-VALUED LOGIC

Artificial intelligence research aims ultimately to model human intelligence. Until recently, it was believed that symbolic logic programming is both an essential and sufficient tool to achieve such an objective.

Today, however, researchers in AI begin to realize that the design of ingeneous computer programs is insufficient to capture the nature of intelligence, for the functions of the human brain are far too complex to be modeled by purely symbolic sequential machines. This growing conviction is reflected by the recent resurgence in neural network computing as an alternative approach to modeling intelligence.

The re-emergence of research interest in this area is mainly due to the works of Hopfield [1], Carpenter and Grossberg [2], Hinton, Sejnowski, and Ackley [3], Kohonen [4], Fukushima [5], Amari [6,7], and Rumelhart and McClelland [8] etc. They independently proposed and studied various network models each of which is an improvement on the classical neural network model: *The perceptron,* proposed by Rosenblatt [9] in 1958, and later studied by Minsky and Papert [10] in 1969. The multilayer perceptron, with back propagation learning algorithm introduced by Rumelhart and others [8], is certainly an important breakthrough in the study of pattern processing.

Unfortunately, the multilayer perceptron approach does not seem to be the right tool to study logical inferences. Although it is possible to model logical OR, AND, and XOR using multilayer perceptrons, there is no way to model logical NOT, which is one of the most basic logical operations. We introduce a neural network that uses ordered pairs of real numbers for weight and for activation [11,12]. This allows the network to perform inference.

Table 13.1. NOT operator for two-value logic.

P	Not P
1	0
0	1

Table 13.2. AND and OR operators for two-value logic.

P	Q	P AND Q	P OR Q
1	1	1	1
1	0	0	1
0	1	0	1
0	0	0	0

Table 13.3. NOT operator for three-value logic.

P	Not P
(1, 0)	(0, 1)
(0, 1)	(1, 0)
(0, 0)	(0, 0)

Table 13.4. AND and OR operators for three-value logic.

P	Q	P AND Q	P OR Q
(1, 0)	(1, 0)	(1, 0)	(1, 0)
(1, 0)	(0, 1)	(0, 1)	(1, 0)
(1, 0)	(0, 0)	(0, 0)	(1, 0)
(0, 1)	(1, 0)	(0, 1)	(1, 0)
(0, 1)	(0, 1)	(0, 1)	(0, 1)
(0, 1)	(0, 0)	(0, 0)	(0, 0)
(0, 0)	(1, 0)	(0, 0)	(1, 0)
(0, 0)	(0, 1)	(0, 1)	(0, 0)
(0, 0)	(0, 0)	(0, 0)	(0, 0)

1.1. Three-Valued Logic

Classical boolean logic is developed based on two truth values TRUE and FALSE, usually represented by "1" and "0," respectively. All logical operations are defined in terms of three basic operations: AND, OR, and NOT, which are defined by truth tables: Table 13.1 and Table 13.2.

In three-valued boolean logic, the three basic truth values are TRUE, FALSE, and UNKNOWN, which are represented by $(1, 0)$, $(0, 1)$ and $(0, 0)$, respectively.

By doing so, we are able to define the three basic logical operations AND, OR, and NOT, by three-valued neural networks.

The truth table of the three basic logic operations are given in Table 13.3 and Table 13.4.

We note that three-valued logic is much more complicated than two-valued logic. Not all the binary logical operations in three-valued logic can be defined in terms of the operations AND, OR, and NOT. In fact, there are a total of $3^8 = 6,561$ distinct meaningful binary logical operations for three-valued logic. This is because when both P and Q are UNKNOWN, any operation must produce UNKNOWN as the result. Hence, there are only 3^8 and not 3^9 distinct meaningful binary operations.

In the following sections, we shall show how three-value logic can be implemented by using a NEural LOgic NETwork to be abbreviated called NELONET.

1.2. Neural-Logic Networks (NELONET)

To define a NELONET we need to:

1. Define a set of nodes, usually represented by small circles drawn on a plane. These nodes will be called the "process units" of the network.
2. Define a set of directed arcs linking some pairs of nodes. These arcs are represented by line segments or curves with arrow heads. Their lengths are not important. A node may be linked to itself to form a loop. Two different nodes may be linked in two different directions represented by two distinct arcs.
3. Every arc is attached with an ordered pair (x, y), where x and y can take any real numbers, positive, negative or zeros. These ordered pairs are called the "weights" of the arcs.
4. A subset of nodes is chosen to be the *input nodes*.
5. Another subset of nodes is chosen. These nodes will be called the output nodes or the output units. An output node may also serve as an input node.
6. All other nodes which are neither the input or output nodes will be called the hidden nodes or the hidden units.

An example of a NELONET with two hidden layers is shown in Figure 13.1.

input layer   hidden layer   hidden layer   output layer

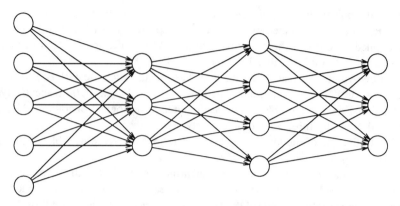

Figure 13.1.   A NELONET.

1.3. Three-Valued Logical Operation in NELONET

We now consider a special case in which each node can only be assigned an ordered pair which is (1, 0), (0, 1), or (0, 0) to represent TRUE, FALSE, and UNKNOWN. The network formed with such nodes is called *three-valued logic NELONET.*

The network is activated by assigning values (1, 0), (0, 1), or (0, 0) to the input nodes. We then follow the rule of propagation which is defined as follows:

Let R be a given node of our network. Let $P_1, P_2, \ldots \ldots , P_N$ be all possible nodes which have links to the node R. Values associated with the node P_i is denoted by (a_i, b_i), and the weight for the line connecting P_i to R is denoted by (α_i, β_i). The network is shown in Figure 13.2.

The rule of propagation defines a net input to node R:

$$\text{net} = \sum_{i=1}^{N} (a_i\alpha_i - b_i\beta_i)$$

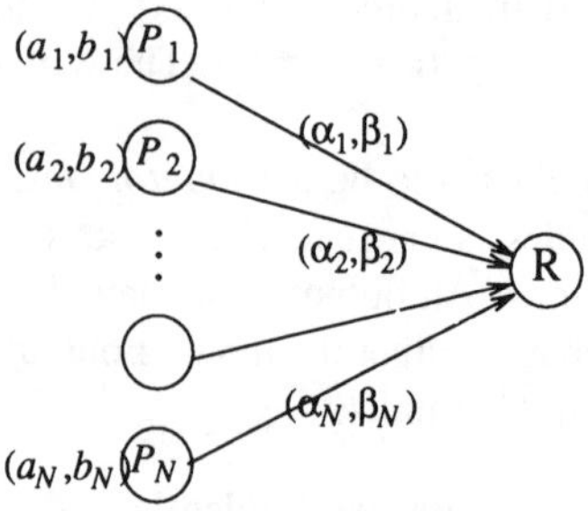

$(a_1,b_1)\,\widehat{P_1}$

$(a_2,b_2)\,\widehat{P_2}$ (α_1,β_1)

$\vdots$ (α_2,β_2) $\widehat{R}$

(α_N,β_N)

$(a_N,b_N)\,\widehat{P_N}$

Figure 13.2.   Weights and activations.

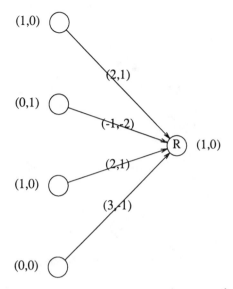

Figure 13.3.   Example for rule of propagation.

The activation rule says that if the absolute value of the net input is greater than or equal to the threshold value, the activation is either (1,0) or (0,1). If it is less than the threshold value, the activation is (0,0). Taking the threshold value to be 1, the rule defines the activation of R to be:

- (1,0) if $net \geq 1$
- (0,1) if $net \leq -1$
- (0,0) Otherwise.

The following example which is shown in Figure 13.3 is used to illustrate the rule of propagation and the rule of activation.

The following computation is used to find the net input to node R:

$$
\begin{array}{rcl}
(1, 0) \times (2, 1) & = & (2, 0) \\
(0, 1) \times (-1, 2) & = & (0, 2) \\
(1, 0) \times (2, 1) & = & (2, 0) \\
(0, 0) \times (3, -1) & = & \underline{(0, 0)} \\
& & (4, 2)
\end{array}
$$

After threshold, the activation of node R is (1,0).

The same propagation process is repeated, until no further change of value is needed. The neural network has then reached a "stable" state. At this point the values of the output nodes are the output values of the given input values.

input nodes   hidden nodes   output node

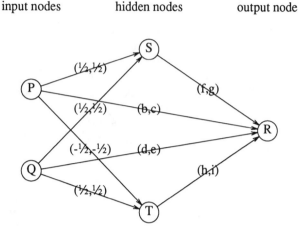

Figure 13.4.   Weights for general binary operator.

1.4. General Binary Operations in NELONETs

There are a total of 2^8 binary operations for neural logic. Each of these operations can be defined by giving values to parameters in Figure 13.4.

Suppose $(1,0)$ and $(0,1)$ are ordered pair values given to the input nodes P and Q, the activation values (after threshold computation on the activation) for the nodes S and T can be calculated as follows in Figure 13.5.

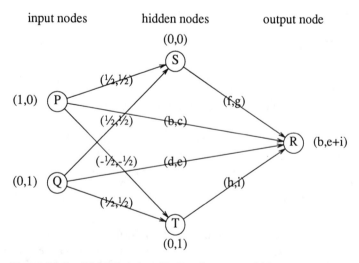

Figure 13.5.   Weight determination for general binary operator.

- At node S:

$$(1,0)*(\tfrac{1}{2}, \tfrac{1}{2}) + (0, 1)*(\tfrac{1}{2}, \tfrac{1}{2})$$
$$= (\tfrac{1}{2}, \tfrac{1}{2}) \rightarrow (0, 0)$$

- At node T:

$$(1, 0)*(-\tfrac{1}{2}, -\tfrac{1}{2}) + (0, 1)*(\tfrac{1}{2}, \tfrac{1}{2})$$
$$= (-\tfrac{1}{2}, \tfrac{1}{2}) \rightarrow (0, 1)$$

- The output from node R is therefore:

$$(0, 0)*(f, g) + (1, 0)*(b, c) + (0, 1)*(d, e) + (0, 1)*(h, i)$$
$$= (b, e + i)$$

The same can be done for the other input pairs. The results are summarized in the following table.

For rows 1 to 8, let:

- $\alpha_i = 1$ if the ith row is true
- $\alpha_i = -1$ if the ith row is false
- $\alpha_i = 0$ if the ith row is unknown

Then we obtain the set of equations:

$$b + d + f = \alpha_1 \qquad b - e - i = \alpha_2$$
$$b = \alpha_3 \qquad d + h - c = \alpha_4$$
$$-(c + e + g) = \alpha_5 \qquad -c = \alpha_6$$
$$d = \alpha_7 \qquad -e = \alpha_8$$

Table 13.5.   Activation of node R for general binary operator.

P	Q	S	T	R
(1, 0)	(1, 0)	(1, 0)	(0, 0)	(b + d + f, 0)
(1, 0)	(0, 1)	(0, 0)	(0, 1)	(b, e + i)
(1, 0)	(0, 0)	(0, 0)	(0, 0)	(b, 0)
(0, 1)	(1, 0)	(0, 0)	(1, 0)	(d + h, c)
(0, 1)	(0, 1)	(0, 1)	(0, 0)	(0, c + e + g)
(0, 1)	(0, 0)	(0, 0)	(0, 0)	(0, c)
(0, 0)	(1, 0)	(0, 0)	(0, 0)	(d, 0)
(0, 0)	(0, 1)	(0, 0)	(0, 0)	(0, e)
(0, 0)	(0, 0)	(0, 0)	(0, 0)	(0, 0)

Table 13.6.   Connecting weights for AND operator.

P	Q	"AND"	α
(1, 0)	(1, 0)	(1, 0)	1
(1, 0)	(0, 1)	(0, 1)	−1
(1, 0)	(0, 0)	(0, 0)	0
(0, 1)	(1, 0)	(0, 1)	−1
(0, 1)	(0, 1)	(0, 1)	−1
(0, 1)	(0, 0)	(0, 1)	−1
(0, 0)	(1, 0)	(0, 0)	0
(0, 0)	(0, 1)	(0, 1)	−1
(0, 0)	(0, 0)	(0, 0)	0

The result is:

$$b = \alpha_3 \qquad\qquad c = -\alpha_6$$
$$d = \alpha_7 \qquad\qquad e = -\alpha_8$$
$$f = \alpha_1 - \alpha_3 - \alpha_7 \qquad g = \alpha_5 + \alpha_6 + \alpha_8$$
$$h = \alpha_4 - \alpha_6 - \alpha_7 \qquad i = \alpha_3 + \alpha_8 - \alpha_2$$

As an example, we consider the weights for Kleene's AND operation. Therefore:

$$c = 1 \quad e = 1 \quad f = 1 \quad g = -1$$

and the rest are zero.

Although in the proof of our theorem we need two hidden units to take care of the most general situation, for special operations, such as AND and OR, no hidden units are needed. For XOR we need one hidden unit, as is depicted in Figure 13.8.

1.5. Principle of Duality

Hsu, Teh, Chan, and Loe [13] discovered one very interesting feature of defining logical operations using NELONETs. Most operations have a unique dual-operation. This is obtained by revising the ordered pairs on each of the links. For example, the dual operation of AND is OR. The dual operation of NOT is equal to itself. Hence, NOT is a self-dual operation. The operation XOR should have a dual operation XAND.

The following self-dual binary operations will play an important role in the study of three-valued logic. These operators can be represented by the following network diagrams.

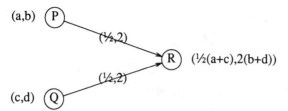

Figure 13.6.   The AND operaton.

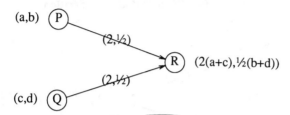

Figure 13.7.   The OR operation.

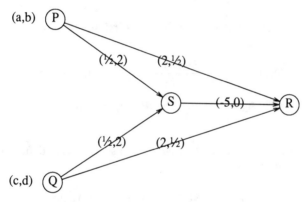

Figure 13.8.   The XOR operation.

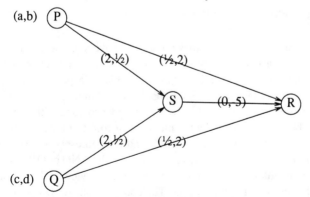

Figure 13.9.   The XAND operation.

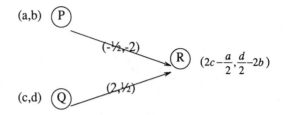

Figure 13.10.   The IMPLICATION operation.

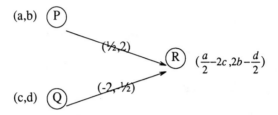

Figure 13.11.   The COMPLEMENT operation.

Figure 13.12.   The NOT operation.

Of course, the three-valued NELONET can also be used to define compound statements such as the following:

$$S = (P\ AND\ (NOT\ Q))\ OR\ (Q\ and\ (NOT\ P))$$

1.6. Human-Logic and NELONET

The process of human reasoning does not always have to conform to the rules of formal logic, but instead it is often guided by certain subjective opinions or biases. Classical Logic is too rigid to model this biased aspect of "human" logic effectively. However, the three-valued NELONET is more flexible and capable to represent biases and human subjectivities in order to cope with varying situations. It thus becomes an excellent framework or tool to model human reasonings. The conventional definitions of AND and OR represent too extreme cases of human judgment. In the semantics point of view, the AND or OR operations in our model may be interpreted as having a "pessimistic" view and an "optimistic" view, respectively, of a given situation. The conventional AND operation yields FALSE just as long as one of the inputs is FALSE, even if all the other inputs are

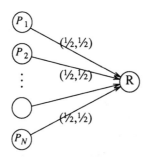

Figure 13.13.   Majority win.

TRUE. Hence, for the semantic interpretation of "pessimistic" as the chance of having a negative outcome is more likely than that of a positive outcome. Conventional OR operation, on the other hand, will yield TRUE as long as one of the inputs is TRUE, regardless of the truth values of the other inputs. Thus, it represents a more optimistic view, as the probability of a positive outcome is higher than that of a negative outcome. However, there are many intervals of human judgment in between these two extremities which cannot be expressed by conventional logic operations, but can be modeled effectively using three-valued NELONET.

Suppose we wish to model a situation in which the outcome is dependent on the votes of several people. It is agreed that if the majority vote in "Yes" (i.e., true), then the outcome will be positive (i.e., true also); otherwise, negative. However, certain persons' votes carried more weights than all the others, and may overrule the majority to 'veto' the positive decision. We cannot use conventional logic to represent this situation, for it does not conform to any of the existing logical operations. The three-valued NELONET shown in Figure 13.3, however, is an effective model of the situation and draws inference to the outcome when the "votes" are cast.

We now introduce the *generalized OR* and *generalized AND* operations to model the intervals of human judgment between the two extremities of conventional logic. Consider the following three-valued NELONET:

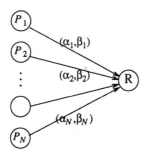

Figure 13.14.   Generalized AND and OR operators.

Suppose for each i = 1, 2, . . . , N,

$$\alpha_i > \beta_i > 0$$

then we call the function a *generalized OR*.

Suppose for each i = 1, 2, . . . , N,

$$0 < \alpha_i < \beta_i$$

then we call the function a *generalized AND*.

Each of the *generalized* operations may have a different bias which can be represented by adjusting the weights appropriately. Here we see the advantage of using ordered pair weights, for it allows the model to be more flexible than a single-value model which emphasizes both positive and negative input equally.

The flexibility of the three-valued NELONET allows us to define many other variations of conventional logical operations which are closer models of human inference or decision patterns. For example, we may wish to introduce operators such as *unless, neither nor,* or *not both,* which are often used in human reasoning processes. The following are some such examples:

1. When P_1 gives his view, his view is the outcome. If P_1 withholds his view, i.e., $P_1 = (0, 0)$, then P_2's view will be the outcome. Only when both P_1 and P_2 withhold their views, then iP$_3$'s view is the outcome.

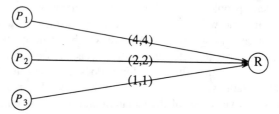

Figure 13.15.   Example 1 of Modeling Human's Decision.

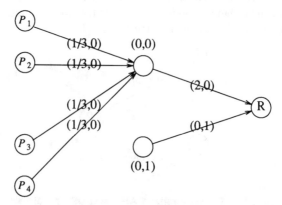

Figure 13.16.   Example 2 of Modeling Human's Decision.

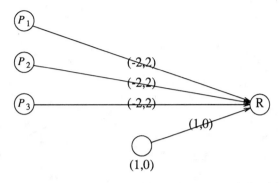

Figure 13.17.   Example 3 of Modeling Human's Decision.

2.   The outcome is true if at least three of the inputs are true or else it is false.
3.   The outcome is true only if none of P_1, P_2, P_3 expresses his view, or else it is false.

1.7. Logical Inferences

Suppose we are given a number of contingent statements about a situation, and are asked to predict the outcome assuming we possess some background knowledge. We would then go through a process of reasoning that would lead us to a conclusion, as long as sufficient information was given. Using the three-valued NELONET, we can build a representation of such a process of inference. Consider the following statements:

1.   John will go to the party if Jane is going.
2.   Jane will go unless Cindy is going.
3.   Cindy will go as long as neither Dave nor Tom is going.
4.   Tom will go unless he has to work.
5.   Dave will go if he can get a ride and it is not raining.
6.   Tom can give Dave a ride if he is not working.
7.   If it is raining, then Tom does not have to work.

We would like to determine whether John will be at the party, and we know that it is not raining. The corresponding three-valued NELONET as shown in Figure 13.18 is a model of the logical inference procedure that a human would go through to reach a conclusion.

Each node in Figure 13.18 represents a proposition, and there is only one input node, which is assigned the value (1, 0). The input node represents the statement: It is not raining. All other nodes are output nodes. They are all assigned the value (0, 0). A new value for each node is then calculated according to the process of propagation described in Section 2. The process is repeated until all new values are equal to the old values. At this stage, if the value of the output

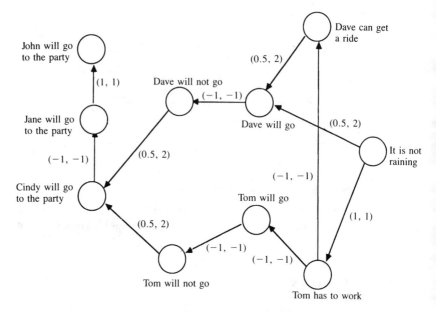

Figure 13.18. A NELONET for modeling John's decision.

node is still (0, 0), then it means that not enough information is available to reach a conclusion; otherwise, the network will yield an answer of TRUE = (1, 0) or FALSE = (0, 1). In this case, the network predicts correctly that John will not be at the party. The weights are assigned according to how the logical operations have been defined for the system. Note that nonstandard operations such as *unless* and *neither . . . nor* are represented in the model.

Representing a three-valued NELONET by a diagram will help us to see the interlinks of the nodes more easily. However, diagrams are useful only when the networks are not too large and not too complicated.

When implementing a three-valued NELONET using a traditional computer, the network is usually represented by a two-dimensional array, where each entry is an ordered pair representing the weight of the link. Even when there is no links from node i to node j say, we still represent the (i, j) entry by the ordered pair (0, 0).

On the other hand, the values of the nodes are represented by a sequence, where each term is an ordered pair of values either (1, 0), (0, 1), or (0, 0).

1.8. Pattern Processing

The NELONET Model is developed not only to study logical inferences but also pattern processing, because these are the two most important features of human intelligence.

m input units   *n* hidden units   *t* output units

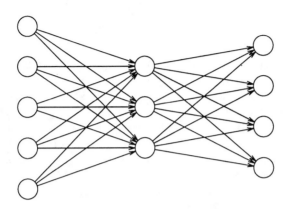

Figure 13.19.   A pattern processing NELONET.

To see how three-valued NELONET may be used to study pattern processing, consider Figure 13.19 representing a three-valued NELONET with *m* input nodes, *n* hidden nodes and *t* output nodes.

Let $S = \{(1, 0), (0, 1), (0, 0)\}$ and S^m denote the set of all sequences of the form:

$$\alpha = (X_1, X_2, \ldots \ldots , X_m),$$

where each X_i is a member of S. We call such a sequence α a feature-vector of dimension *m*. Three examples with $m = 5$ are:

$$\alpha_1 = ((1, 0), (0, 1), (0, 0), (1, 0))$$

$$\alpha_2 = ((0, 1), (0, 1), (1, 0), (0, 0))$$

$$\alpha_3 = ((1, 0), (1, 0), (1, 0), (0, 1))$$

Similarly let S^t denote the set of all sequences of the form:

$$\beta = (X_2, X_2, \ldots \ldots , X_t),$$

where each X_i is a member of S. We call such a sequence β a response-vector of dimension *t*. Three examples with $t = 4$ are:

$$\beta_1 = ((1, 0), (0, 1), (1, 0), (0, 1))$$

$$\beta_2 = ((0, 1), (0, 1), (1, 0), (1, 0))$$

$$\beta_3 = ((0, 1), (0, 1), (1, 0), (0, 0))$$

The problem is to construct a three-valued NELONET N with m inputs and t outputs such that for each i = 1, 2, . . . , n, α_i is mapped into β_i.

The following fundamental theorem tells us under what conditions such a NELONET exists.

Existence Theorem: Let m, n, t be any three given positive integers. Let $S = \{(1,0), (0,1), (0,0)\}$. Let $\alpha_1, \alpha_2, \alpha_3, \ldots \ldots, \alpha_k$ be k (distinct) members of S^m such that each α_i (i = 1, 2, . . . , k) contains at least one term equal to either (1,0) or (0,1).

Let $\beta_1, \beta_2, \beta_3, \ldots \ldots, \beta_t$ be k (not necessarily distinct) members of S^t. Then there exists at least one three-valued NELONET N which maps $(\alpha_1, \alpha_2, \alpha_3, \ldots \ldots, \alpha_m)$ to $(\beta_1, \beta_2, \beta_3, \ldots \ldots, \beta_t)$. In fact, an infinite amount of such networks exist.

Proof

1. Construct a directed graph with three layers, the first layer has m nodes, the second layer has n nodes and the last layer has t nodes. Define the nodes in the first layer as input nodes, the nodes in the second layer as hidden nodes and the nodes in the last layer as output nodes.

   From every node in the first layer, draw a directed arc to every node in the second layer, and from every node in the second layer draw a directed arc to every node in the last layer.

2. Take one node say the *ith* node of the first layer and take any node say the *jth* node of the second layer. Attach the edge joining the *ith* node to the *jth* node by the ordered pair (x, y), where x and y are real numbers obtained as follows:

   Let (a,b) be the *ith* term of the vector α_j.
   1. If (a, b) = (1, 0), we define $(x, y) = (1/c, 0)$
   2. If (a, b) = (0, 1), we define $(x, y) = (0, -1/c)$
   3. If (a, b) = (0, 0), we define $(x, y) = (-1/(d + 1), 1/(d + 1))$
   In the above, c is the number of terms in α_j which is either (1, 0) or (0, 1), and d is the number of terms in α_j equal to (0, 0). Hence $d + c = m$.

   This operation will be performed on every pair of nodes between layer 1 and layer 2.

3. Take one node, say the ith node of column 2 and another node, say the jth node of column 3. Attach the edge joining these two nodes by the ordered pair (x', y'), where x', y' are real numbers obtained as follows:
   Let (a', b') be the *jth* term of the vector β_i.
   1. If $(a', b') = (1, 0)$, we define $(x', y') = (1,0)$.
   2. If $(a', b') = (0, 1)$, we define $(x', y') = (-1, 0)$.

3.   If $(a', b') = (0, 0)$, we define $(x', y') = (0, 0)$.
    Do this to every pair of nodes between layer 2 and layer 3.
4.   Assign the value $(0, 0)$ to each of the hidden nodes.

This defines a three-valued NELONET.

It can be verified that this three-valued NELONET maps the sequence $(\alpha_1, \alpha_2, \alpha_3)$ to the sequence $(\beta_1, \beta_2, \beta_3)$.

1.9. Discussions

In the above proof, we need n hidden nodes; as many as the number of patterns in the given pair of sequences $(\alpha_1, \alpha_2, \alpha_3, \ldots \ldots, \alpha_n)$ and $(\beta_1, \beta_2, \beta_3, \ldots \ldots, \beta_n)$. In many special situations, a three-valued NELONET with much less hidden nodes can be constructed to map the given pair of sequences of patterns.

Instead of assigning precise weights to each of the links, we may first assign random weights to all the links and then apply some learning algorithm to adjust the weights gradually until the network maps the given pair of sequences with patterns. However, the amount of computations needed will grow exponentially with the number of patterns involved.

The three-valued NELONET constructed using precise weights is so exact that it will not tolerate any error. That is to say, if it is a member of S^m which is different from any member in $(\alpha_1, \alpha_2, \alpha_3, \ldots \ldots, \alpha_n)$, the network will map to the All-UNKNOWN output, i.e., $((0, 0), (0, 0), \ldots, (0, 0))$. On the other hand, NELONET that is constructed through some learning algorithm usually can tolerate a certain degree of error. That is to say, if α is a member of S^m, even α is different from each of $(\alpha_1, \alpha_2, \alpha_3, \ldots \ldots, \alpha_n)$, the network may map to some member say β_i of $(\beta_1, \beta_2, \beta_3, \ldots \ldots, \beta_n)$. This will happen if α is "quite similar" to α_i.

The ability to recognize patterns with some degree of error is very useful in the study of pattern recognition.

In order to obtain a NELONET which can recognize patterns with a certain degree of error while at the same time it does not involve too much computation time, we recommend the following method:

1.   First construct the three-valued NELONET N using the precise method described in the above theorem.
2.   Add a small random number to each of the weights in N. (N will no longer map the given pair of sequences of patterns.)
3.   Apply some learning algorithm (whatever learning algorithm is available) to N until it maps the given pair of sequences of patterns.

A bit-map pattern recognition system based on the above described technique has been implemented. The system is coded in C and in running on a model 60, PS/2 microcomputer. A set of 400 Chinese characters represented by 16×16 bit-map images are used to test the matching accuracy under a various amount of random noise environments. The following figures are some sample test results: bit-map pattern matching system based on three-value neural-logic network.

Error tolerance: 10% of random noise
Matching accuracy: 100%

Error tolerance: 15% random noise
Matching accuracy: 100%

Error tolerance: 20% random noise
Matching accuracy: 100%

The matching accuracy drops below 100% when the random noise is increased to 25%.

NELONET are natural generalizations of Hopfield Networks, Multilayer Perceptions and Inferences Networks. Hence, they can be used to study both pattern processing and logical inferences. Since pattern processing and logical inferences are the two most important components of human intelligence, NERONET should prove to be useful in modeling human intelligence, especially, NELONET can be used to model human-logic, which is fuzzy and biased better than many existing logical models.

One important aspect of NELONET is that both pattern processing and logical reasoning activities of the model are defined totally in terms of numerical computations. In fact, they are based on the very basic arithmetic operations such as addition, multiplication, and comparison (threshold operation). Hence, they can be easily implemented on conventional computers coded in conventional programming languages such as C, PASCAL, FORTRAN, BASIC, APL, etc. The simplicity of the model also implies that special-purposed NELONET can be easily implemented on VLSI chips.

Another important aspect of NELONET, like all other neural network models, is that the value-propagation process, which is the main computation activities, is extremely parallel. Hence, they are best implemented on massively parallel computers. One immediate application of the NELONET Model is the study of *connectionist expert system methodology.*

2. PROBABILISTIC INFERENCE

The objective of this section is to extend the idea of the NELONET to incorporate with the theory of probability. For human-logic reasoning, the absolute "trueness" or "falseness" is usually too strong to make decision, to give opinion, or to pass judgment in many real-life incidents.

Human-logic reasoning usually involves a certain degree of bias, fuzziness, or uncertainty. To take into account the probability factor in TRUE and FALSE, a Probabilistic NELONET Model is proposed [14]. Instead of representing the value of an input or output node by one of the three values: $(1, 0)$, $(0, 1)$, and $(0, 0)$, the node is represented by an ordered pair (a, b), where a and b represent the "TRUE" and "FALSE" probability, with:

$$0 \leq a \leq 1$$

$$0 \leq b \leq 1$$

$$0 \leq a + b \leq 1$$

Thus, the probability of UNKNOWN will be $1 - (a + b)$.

2.1. Algorithm for Probabilistic NELONET

Consider a set of random numbers X_1, X_2, X_3, X_4, X_5 as input nodes in the NELONET in Figure 13.20(a), the probabilistic features can be illustrated by Figure 13.20(b) to show the probabilities of TRUE, FALSE, and UNKNOWN, in each node.

To illustrate the algorithm of the probabilistic NELONET we use the results of the OR and AND operations in Table 13.4. There are nine different combinations with nine solutions. For the "OR" operation, the probabilities of getting the TRUE, FALSE, and UNKNOWN, solutions are: 5/9, 1/9, and 3/9, respectively.

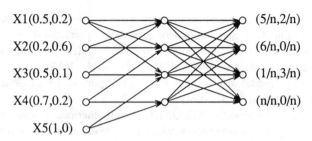

Figure 13.20.   (a) Probabilistic NELONET.

Likewise, for the "AND" operation, the probabilities for TRUE, FALSE, and UNKNOWN, are: 1/9, 5/9, and 3/9, respectively.

To consider the propagation of probability through an inference network, we shall first consider basic unary and binary logic operations. More complex operations can be constructed from that; the truth of P is given in Table 13.7.

The truthfulness of P is obtained by adding all the entries in the third column that correspond to $(1, 0)$ for P. This gives 'a' in the present case. The probability that P is false is obtained by summing up all the entries that correspond to $(0, 1)$ for NOT P. This gives b. The probabilities that correspond to $(0, 0)$ is $(1 - a - b)$, this can be used to check that the total probability is 1.

We therefore conclude that: If the probability of node P is (a, b), the probability of NOT P is (b, a).

We now consider the binary logic operations. For this purpose, we consider

```
X1:|_____(1.0)_____|__(0.1)|_____(0.0)__|
   0_____0.5____0.7_____1

X2:|__(1.0)__|_____(0.1)_____|__(0.0)____|
   0_____0.2_____0.8_____1

X3:|_____(1.0)_____|(0.1)|_____(0.0)_____|
   0_____0.5_0.6_____1

X4:|_____(1.0)_____|(0.1)|(0.0)_|
   0_____0.7__0.9____1

X5:|_____(1.0)_____|
   0_____1
```

Figure 13.20.   (b) Random number distribution for probabilistic NELONET.

Table 13.7.   NOT operations with probability.

P	NOT P	truthfulness of P
(1, 0)	(0, 1)	a
(0, 1)	(1, 0)	b
(0, 0)	(0, 0)	$(1 - a - b)$
(a, b) |_____$(-1, -1)$_____|		$(-a, -b)$ or (b, a)

two nodes P and Q, which are characterized by the probabilistic ordered pairs (a, b) and (c, d), respectively, where:

$$0 \leq a, b, c, d \leq 1$$

$$0 \leq a + b \leq 1$$

$$0 \leq c + d \leq 1$$

For the OR operations, see the following truth table, Table 13.8.

The last column in the above table gives the probability that the truthfulness of P and Q are as shown in the first two columns. To obtain the truthfulness of the binary operation, we add up all the entries in the last column that correspond to (1, 0) in the third column. This gives $a + c - ac$. To obtain the probability of falsefulness, we add up all the entries in the last column that correspond to (0, 1) in the third column. There is only one entry that corresponds to (0, 1) in the third column, and this gives bd. Therefore, the ordered pair for (P OR Q) is ($a + c - ac$, bd). As before, the rows with (0,0) do not provide new information and can only be used for checking.

The result is shown in the diagram in Figure 13.21.

Table 13.8.   OR operation with probability.

P	Q	OR	probability that (P OR Q) is true
(1, 0)	(1, 0)	(1, 0)	ac
(1, 0)	(0, 1)	(1, 0)	ad
(1, 0)	(0, 0)	(1, 0)	$a(1 - c - d)$
(0, 1)	(1, 0)	(1, 0)	bc
(0, 1)	(0, 1)	(0, 1)	bd
(0, 1)	(0, 0)	(0, 0)	$b(1 - c - d)$
(0, 0)	(1, 0)	(1, 0)	$(1 - a - b)c$
(0, 0)	(0, 1)	(0, 0)	$(1 - a - b)d$
(0, 0)	(0, 0)	(0, 0)	$(1 - a - b)(1 - c - d)$

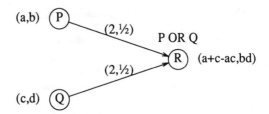

Figure 13.21.   Probabilistic NELONET for OR.

Table 13.9.   AND operation with probability.

P	Q	AND	probability that (P and Q) is true
(1, 0)	(1, 0)	(1, 0)	ac
(1, 0)	(0, 1)	(0, 1)	ad
(1, 0)	(0, 0)	(0, 0)	a(1 − c − d)
(0, 1)	(1, 0)	(0, 1)	bc
(0, 1)	(0, 1)	(0, 1)	bd
(0, 1)	(0, 0)	(0, 1)	b(1 − c − d)
(0, 0)	(1, 0)	(0, 0)	(1 − a − b)c
(0, 0)	(0, 1)	(0, 1)	(1 − a − b)d
(0, 0)	(0, 0)	(0, 0)	(1 − a − b)(1 − c − d)

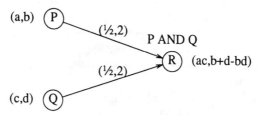

Figure 13.22.   Probabilistic NELONET for AND.

Table 13.10.   Binary operations with probability.

P	Q	P→Q	P⌐Q
(1, 0)	(1, 0)	(1, 0)	(0, 1)
(1, 0)	(0, 1)	(0, 1)	(1, 0)
(1, 0)	(0, 0)	(0, 0)	(0, 0)
(0, 1)	(1, 0)	(1, 0)	(0, 1)
(0, 1)	(0, 1)	(1, 0)	(0, 1)
(0, 1)	(0, 0)	(1, 0)	(0, 1)
(0, 0)	(1, 0)	(1, 0)	(0, 1)
(0, 0)	(0, 1)	(0, 0)	(0, 0)
(0, 0)	(0, 0)	(0, 0)	(0, 0)

Table 13.11.   Summary of binary operations.

OPERATION	probability
P OR Q	$(a + c - ac, bd)$
P AND Q	$(ac, b + d - bd)$
$P \rightarrow Q$	$(b + c - bc, ad)$
$P \sim Q$	$(ad, b + c - bc)$

Similarly, for the AND operation, we have:

From the above we find that the ordered pair for $(P \text{ AND } Q)$ is given by $(ac, b + d - bd)$.

The result is shown in the diagram in Figure 13.22.

Two other binary operations are defined Table 13.10.

Results for normal binary logic operations are collected in Table 13.11.

The probabilistic NELONET is very useful in pattern recognition and in expert system development. In the former application, it is ideal in dealing with patterns with noise. Instead of saying that a given pattern matches with a standard pattern, it says how many percent probable that it matches with the given pattern. This gives the user an indication of the reliability of the conclusion. In the latter application, probabilities can be assigned to rules and premises, and the probability of the conclusion being true will be predicted.

3. FUZZY INFERENCE

The three-valued logic described above can be generalized to deal with uncertainties in inferencing. There are three sources of these uncertainties: the facts that we based our inference on may contain uncertainties, the rules that we used may not be exact, and even the logical connectives AND, OR, and NOT, may not have the crisp meaning defined in logic.

One way of handling the first two types of uncertainties in an expert system is to introduce Fuzzy logic [15]. The idea of Fuzzy logic originated from the concept of Fuzzy set and inherited certain limitations. The most serious one is that not all the strengths of the conditions are taken into consideration in determining the strength needed for the corresponding action. Consider the following rule:

If
    the premise "A" is true   (a)
and
    the premise "B" is true   (b)
and
    the premise "C" is true   (c)
Then
    the conclusion "D" is true (d)

where the upper case letters represent conditions and action and the corresponding lower case letters represent the strengths of the conditions and the strength of the action. Fuzzy logic would take (d) to be the minimum of (a), (b), and (c). If we replace the AND in the above rule by OR, the maximum of (a), (b), and (c) would be used as the value for (d). There are many situations where this is not a good model of the real world.

Suppose we are building an expert system for the buying of properties. The expert may say that:

> If
>> the location is good   (a)
>
> and
>> the price is reasonable   (b)
>
> and
>> the property tax is not too high (c)
>
> Then
>> buy the house   (d)

Surely the case where the values of (a, b, c) are (0.8, 0.8, 0.5) and the case where the values are (0.5, 0.5, 0.5) merit different consideration. In most decision-making processes, it is more realistic to take a weighted average of the strengths of the conditions rather than just the maximum or the minimum.

The following sections describe a method of combining the strengths of the conditions [13,16,17] and point out how it can be naturally implemented in a NELONET.

3.1. Network Structure

The NELONET used to implement the decision-making expert system consists of n input nodes I, m output nodes O, and p hidden nodes H. A simple case in which $n = 4$, $m = 2$ and $p = 5$ is shown in the diagram in Figure 13.23.

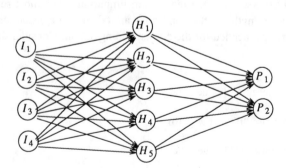

Figure 13.23.   NELONET for a simple expert system.

Each of the I nodes corresponds to a primitive condition in the system. The strength of a node is denoted by an ordered pair of real, nonnegative numbers (a, b). These numbers are normalized in such a way that $a + b \leq 1$. The numbers are assigned by the user and they have the following meaning:

1. The quantity a denotes the amount of evidence that is for the condition represented by the node,
2. The quantity b denotes the amount of evidence against the condition, and,
3. The expression $1 - a - b$ expresses the lack of evidence regarding the condition.

For example, if we ask the opinion of 100 experts, 70 of them think that the condition is true, 20 of them consider it untrue, 10 of them do not know the answer, then $(a, b) = (0.7, 0.2)$.

Each hidden node H represents a logical operation. It has a strength that is denoted by an ordered paired of real, nonnegative numbers (c, d). These numbers are computed from methods to be described in the next section, and they satisfy the normalizing condition $c + d \leq 1$. There is also a threshold value θ attached to each hidden node. When θ is less than 1, the system performs a threshold operation after the strength is calculated. If its value is 1, no threshold operation is needed, and the calculated strength is stored at the node right away.

Each output node O represents a possible recommended action. The strength of each node is given by an ordered pair of real, non-negative numbers (e, f). The values are computed from the weights of the internode connections as well as the strengths of the input and hidden nodes. The rule of computation makes sure that the normalization condition $e + f \leq 1$ is satisfied. The values of e and f represents the eagerness with which the system recommend the action to be or not to be taken. A large $1 - e - f$ shows that the system does not know whether to recommend for or against the action.

The three types of nodes described above are connected by a set of arrows to form a directed graph. A weight is assigned to each connecting arrow. Each weight is an ordered pair of real numbers (α, β). Unlike the strengths, the weights are not normalized, and negative value is allowed. The actual values depend on the number of conditions used in the rule and the type of logical operations involved.

3.2. Propagation of Strengths

To show the propagation of strengths, we shall focus our attention on one of the nodes R. Let there be n incoming arrows connecting it to n other nodes P_i whose strengths are (a_i, b_i). This portion of the network is shown in Figure 13.24.

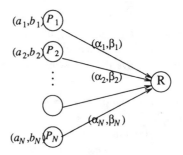

Figure 13.24.   Strengths in a fuzzy NELONET.

The strength of the node R is calculated by the following steps:

1. Compute the total uncertainty of the incoming nodes:

$$uncert = \sum_{1 \le i \le n} 1 - a_i - b_i$$

2. Compute the products $a_i \alpha_i$ and $b_i \beta_i$ for all i.
3. Let *pos* be the sum all the positive terms and *neg* be the absolute value of the sum of all the negative terms.
4. The strength of the node R is given by (a_r, b_r), where $a_r = pos/(pos + neg + uncert)$ and $b_r = neg/(pos + neg + uncert)$. Note that $a_r + b_r \le 1$ just as it should be.
5. Perform threshold calculation. If $a_r - b_r \ge \theta_r$ then we set $a_r = 1$ and $b_r = 0$. For nodes that do not reach the threshold, the values of a_r and b_r are not changed.

3.3. Determination of Weights

The computation described in the last paragraph made use of strengths of incoming nodes as well as weights of the connecting lines. The weights depend on two factors: the number of incoming nodes, and the type of logical operation. We shall describe the determination of weights for a few logical operations.

The criteria used is very simple. From the definition of the logical operation, we know whether R is true or false for a given set of inputs. We choose a set of weights so that R agrees with this result. For this purpose, we note that R is true if $a_r - b_r \ge 1$. It is false if $a_r - b_r \le -1$.

3.3.1. The AND operation

Let:

$$R = P_1 \text{ "AND" } P_2 \text{ "AND" } \ldots \ldots \text{ "AND" } P_n$$

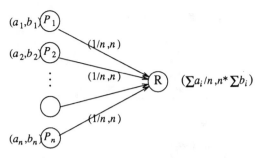

Figure 13.25.   Fuzzy NELONET AND.

then we set:

$$\alpha_i = 1/n$$

and:

$$\beta_i = n$$

The relevant part of the network is shown in Figure 13.25.

Table 13.12, from Kleene's strong three-valued logic [18] gives a definition of the binary AND operation.

It can be easily verified that the above assignment of weights does produce the desired result when we note that:

1. For the input nodes, the strengths are (1, 0) for true, (0, 1) for false, and (0, 0) for unknown.
2. Let (a, b) be the strength of node R. R is true if $a - b \geq 1$. R is false if $a - b \leq -1$. R is unknown otherwise.

Inductive argument shows that the assignment is valid for the case with n incoming nodes.

To model different worlds, other types of three-valued NELONET may be defined. This results in a different table of definition and consequently a different set of weights for the lines connecting nodes to an AND node. We have developed a program which produces the weights by reading in a table of definition.

Table 13.12.   Kleene's strong three-valued logic for AND operation.

AND	true	false	unknown
true	true	false	unknown
false	false	false	false
unknown	unknown	false	unknown

Table 13.13.   Kleene's three-valued OR operation.

OR	true	false	unknown
true	true	true	true
false	true	false	unknown
unknown	true	unknown	unknown

3.3.2. The OR operation

Similarly, it can be verified that for the OR operation, whose definition is given in Table 13.13.

The weight assignment is:

$$\alpha_i = n$$

and:

$$\beta_i = 1/n$$

and the corresponding portion of the network is in Figure 13.26.

3.3.3. The negation operation

The negation operation is a unary operation. The table of definition is very simple (see Table 13.14).

There is only one connecting line:
and the weight is:

$$\alpha_i = -1$$

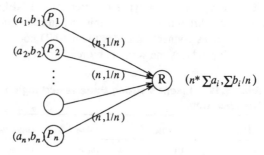

Figure 13.26.   Fuzzy NELONET for OR.

Table 13.14.   Fuzzy NOT operation.

P	NOT P
true	false
false	true
unknown	unknown

and

$$\beta_i = -1$$

The NELONET suggested above is useful in developing expert systems that helps in decision making. It allows for fuzziness in the facts as well as rules in a natural way. It is more realistic than the classical fuzzy logic because for both AND and OR operations, all evidences are weighed and taken into account.

The expert system can operate in two modes. In the normal mode, rules are given by experts and weights are assigned values given in the last section. In the learning mode, weights are allowed to vary while the system is fed with examples.

4. NELONET AND AI APPLICATIONS

On the one hand, NELONET is the generalization of the perceptron, so that the learning rule for the perceptron can easily be adapted for a NELONET. In addition, the matching of input patterns to output patterns can be constructed based on existence theorem in Section 1.8 using a three-layer NELONET. On the other hand, the order-pair construction of NELONET logic function permits it to realize various kinds of nonclassical logic systems. Various kinds of three-valued logic systems can be realized by selecting the appropriate connection weights, as given earlier.

The most attractive feature of neural networks, such as perceptron and many PDP models, is their capability in discriminating patterns which have been learned from examples. However, the lack of inferencing mechanism in most of the neural network models is the drawback for applying neural network in artificial intelligence. NELONET possesses both the pattern-matching mechanism and inferencing mechanism, as explained earlier. In the following section, we shall provide a prospective view on how such mechanisms can be applied to certain areas of artificial intelligence study.

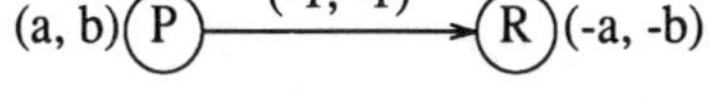

$$(a, b)\;\boxed{P}\xrightarrow{\;(-1, -1)\;}\boxed{R}\;(-a, -b)$$

Figure 13.27.   Fuzzy NELONET for NOT.

4.1. Expert System

The connectionist expert system was first developed using perceptron network. Connectionist expert system acquired knowledge through learning by examples in such a way that input nodes are used to represent a set of attributes of the knowledge domain so that every example would have a unique pattern of true values for the set of input attributes. Expected output for these examples are used for cramping the output during the learning stage. After the learning stage, the system can be used to provide answers to queries by users. The underlying principle of the design of connectionist expert systems is based on pattern matching rather than logical inferencing. This is because the user's answers to questions generated by the system are equivalent to create an input pattern for retrieving an output pattern as an appropriate solution to the queries.

Connectionist export system can also be implemented using three-layer NELONET instead of a perceptron network. A long learning process to acquire knowledge in large-knowledge domain is the shortcoming of connectionist expert system using back propogation and the delta learning rule. Using NELONET knowledge can also be acquired directly by a construction algorithm without going through the iterative learning process using a delta learning rule. However, knowledge acquisition by a constructing algorithm based on the existence theorem given in Section 1.8 is suitable for matching exact input to exact output and this may limit the adaptability of the system to respond to queries slightly deviated from the standard pattern the system has constructed. In order for the network to tolerate some degree of deviation, delta learning rule can be enforced after the exact knowledge has been acquired through the construction algorithm. Knowledge acquisition first by construction algorithm and followed by learning rule is usually more efficient.

In most of the expert system applications, some of the attributes for input and output required information taken from a range of values instead of a simple answer of true, false, or unknown. For example, a career advisory expert system may require the user to input the age of the applicant using a range of age groups so as to recommend a suitable job for people using age range as one of the criteria. In its original form, the NELONET can only handle input queries with true, false, and unknown values. In developing an expert system shell we may make some enhancement of the NELONET by including statements to declare the input and output attributes as well as the range of each attribute [19]. The following statements should be able to serve such a purpose:

> Input Attribute
>   Inputname($A_1, A_2, \ldots, A_m$);
> Output Attribute
>   Outputname($B_1, B_2, \ldots, B_n$);

Attribute Range:

$A_1(R_{11}, R_{12}, \ldots, R_{1r})$;(*r ranges for A_1^*)

$A_2(R_{21}, R_{22}, \ldots, R_{2s})$;(*s ranges for A_2^*)

.

.

.

$A_m(R_{m1}, R_{m2}, \ldots, R_{mt})$;(*t ranges for A_m^*)

$B_1(R_{11}, R_{12}, \ldots, R_{1r'})$;(*r' ranges for B_1^*)

$B_2(R_{11}, R_{12}, \ldots, R_{1r'})$;(*r' ranges for B_2^*)

.

.

.

$B_n(R_{11}, R_{12}, \ldots, R_{1r'})$;(*r' ranges for B_n^*)

where R_{ij} is the jth range value for attribute A_i or B_i.

Such statements can be converted into three-valued NELONET internal representation. If the sum of all the ranges of all input nodes are given by:

$$i = r + x + \ldots + t$$

and output node ranges similarly sum up to m, then the number of hidden nodes required are k where $4^{m-1} < k \leq 4^m$. The connecting weight pair between pth input node and qth hidden-layer nodes can be generated by:

$$W_{pq} = \begin{cases} 1/i(1, 0) \text{ for } \textit{input node} = (1, 0) \\ 1/i(0, -1) \text{ for } \textit{input node} = (0, 1) \end{cases}$$

Given an input vector, a corresponding output can be computed using the above weightages W_{pq} and rules of activation and propagation given in Section 1.3.

In developing an expert system for a knowledge domain, there may be too many input attributes for input queries, but the answer to a particular query may only require values for a few essential attributes in a proper order of querying. Therefore, a proprocessing program can be built into the shell to extract the essential attributes so as to reduce the number of input nodes for building an expert system. On the other hand, to provide system tolerance for deviations of the users' queries from the standard examples learned by the network, it is necessary to provide redundancy in the network construction. A triplication of the network with different ways to select the essential attributes was proposed and implemented in an expert system shell based on the NELONET as reported in [20].

Since a NELONET can also realize a logical system, rule-based expert sys-

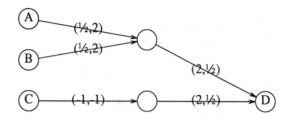

Figure 13.28. Representation of a rule.

tem, and connectionist expert system can be integrated in an expert shell design. A rule such as:

$$\text{IF } (A \text{ and } B) \text{ or } C \text{ then } D$$

can be expressed using a subnet of neural logic network as in Figure 13.28.

4.2. Concept Formation

Concept formation is a kind of inductive inference process to assert that certain objects possess some common properties which are denied for other objects. For example, reptile is a concept which is formed by including some animals which possess the common properties of lizards and crocodiles but deny others which do not have the common properties of lizards and crocodiles.

In this context, NELONET can be used for realizing concept formation. Given a set of common properties for a set of objects so as to define a concept, NELONET can be used to find other objects which also share these common properties. Suppose animals are classified based on a set of properties P_i for $i = 1, \ldots, n$. Now reptile is defined by observing the common properties among the lizards and crocodiles. If biologists are asked to characterize their observation for animals based on the list of properties P_i. They may indicate the presence or absence of such properties for some animals O_s which they have studied. Now we can code the observation from all the sources of observation for various animals. We list the animals O_s at the left-hand side and properties P_i at the right-hand side of a two-layer NELONET. Suppose the types of animals being studied are much less than one hundred. We use a pair of connection weights $(100, 1)$ to link between an animal O_s and a property P_i if this animal possesses property P_i, otherwise the link weight pair is assigned with $(-1, -100)$. Such an assignment is done for all animals to all the properties.

Figure 13.29 is a simple example consisting of a crocodile, a lizard, and two other animals to be classified, where a dashed line represents connection weightage of $(-100, -1)$, and a solid line represents weightage of $(100, 1)$. Thus, A and B are the common properties of a crocodile and a lizard since weightages

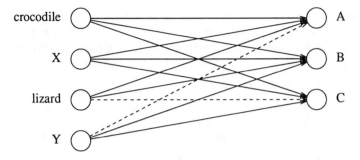

Figure 13.29. Concept formation.

(100, 1) are used to connect A and B to a lizard and a crocodile. Though weightage (100, 1) is connected from C to crocodile it is not the common property of crocodile and lizard because C is connected to lizard by $(-1, -100)$. In general, we can run a large concept formation NELONET forward and backward to reach the stable network state so as to find out all the animals which are considered as reptile. Let us consider the concept of reptile which was defined based on the common properties of lizards and crocodiles. Thus, in the network the lizards and crocodiles are set to true value, that is, (1, 0), and other animals are initialized to unknown values. Also, all the properties P_i of animals are initialized to unknown values. Running the network in the forward direction using the NELONET inferencing mechanism given in Section 1.3 would set all the common properties of the lizards and crocodiles to the true values, but other properties which they do not possess or do not possess in common would set to the false value. For the simple case of Figure 13.29, A and B would set to true value (1, 0) and C would set to a false value (0, 1). These results are the consequence of the way weightages are assigned to the connection between objects and properties so that common properties of the lizards and crocodiles are being enhanced toward true values and their differences are being enhanced towards false values by the NELONET threshold operation. Subsequently, the network is propogating backward from the property nodes to the object nodes then all the objects possess the common properties as the lizards and crocodiles would set to true value and the rest of the animals would set to false value. For the simple case of Figure 13.29, X would set to a true value and Y would set to a false value. In other words, X is classified by the network as reptile but Y is not. At this state, the network is stabalized. Further propagation of the logical values to and fro in the network would not alter the patterns of truth value for the objects and their properties. Thus, all the animals possess the common properties as the lizards and crocodiles are picked up by the network after only one round of forward and backward propagation and such a pair of subsets $(O_c \ P_c)$ taken from object and property sets form a concept of reptile.

Thus, in general, concept formation is realized by first identifying a few objects as the reference objects for concept formation, then running the network forward to obtain their common properties, and next propagating their common properties backward to pick up those objects sharing these common properties. Formally, the concept formation process can be constructed and operated in the following steps:

1.   Network Construction:
    1.   Let $O = \{O_1, \ldots, O_n\}$
       and $P = \{P_1, \ldots, P_m\}$
    2.   Construct a neural logic network with
      O as the input nodes and P as the output nodes.
    3.   For each O_i
    For each P_k
        If O_i possesses property P_k then
           assign $(W, 1)$ as the connection weight pair
             otherwise assign $(-1, -W)$ as the connection weight pair
    $(W \gg 1)$
II.   Concept formation:
    1.   For each concept formation C
    select some prior objects O_p;
       set O_p to $(1,0)$ and $O - O_p$ to $(0,0)$,
    2.   Forward processing:
    Compute the threshold output of P using O as the input;
       For each P_i with logical true value put it in set P_C
    3.   Backward processing:
    Compute the output of O using P as the input;
       For each O_i with logical true value put it in set O_C
    4.   Output (O_C, P_C, C) as a triplet forming a concept C.

Note that this network can also operate in the reverse direction such that properties are regarded as inputs and initialize a subset of properties to logical true values and the rest of the properties to unknown values. Also, objects are initialized to unknown values. Then running the network using properties as inputs would set those objects having this subset of properties into logical true values but other objects not having this complete subset of properties would turn out with logical false values. Knowing the logical values of these objects now the network can reflect back to pick up other common properties which these objects shared. What is obtained from this reversing mode is generally different from the former mode of operation.

4.3. Nonmonotonic Inferencing

In the nonmonotonic inference system, new facts or propositions which contradict the existing facts or properties in a logical system could be added to this system so that classical formal logical inferences have to be withdrawn due to the changes caused by the newly added facts or propositions which are contradicting to what are already in the system. There are several aspects which are considered to have the nonmonotonic effects in the AI logical system. Default reasoning is one aspect which considered "no proof of otherwise" as the acceptable condition in the reasoning processing.

Three aspects of the inference mechanism in NELONET could be considered as some kind of realization of nonmonotonic inferencing.

In the first aspect, let us consider a given set of propositions attached to the nodes of the networks. The logical consequences are different if the directions of the arcs connecting the nodes are reverse. If we allow the directed link between the node to be cut off or reverse or changing the weightage under the influence of the external conditions then this logical system is realizing a kind of construction of nonmonotonic inferencing. The next possible aspect to realize the nonmonotonic inferencing is to make use of the loop oscillating in a NELONET. When there are loops in a NELONET connecting the nodes, the system may not always be able to settle down to a definite final state. However, due to the fact that a NELONET Is a finite network, thus the system would be oscillating among some possible states periodically. If output is obtained from such an oscillating state at a certain instance so that part of the output nodes are having output values matched with some external imposed conditions, then such a logical consequence is considered as nonmonotonic in the sense that it depends on the external requirements for getting the result which could not be inferred in the ordinary way. The last possible aspect is to provide default value to a node through pairs of appropriate weights so that output value from this node would be decided by its default value when inputs connected to this node are having unknown values or the total input values are insignificant as compared with the default value. The default output value in a node would be changed when inputs connected to it are contributing dominately with logical values opposite to the default value of the node.

Note that the logical UNKNOWN is represented as $(0, 0)$ in NELONET, therefore when multiplied with the sypnatical weight it does not influence the threshold decision. On the other hand, if we want to implement a logical system such that UNKNOWN logical value is having a strong influence of a logical consequence, then we should use $(1, 1)$ instead of $(0, 0)$ to represent logical UNKNOWN. In this case, the threshold function only needs to make a slight modification to realize such a representation.

4.4. Temporal Inferencing

Given a set of input patterns which is expected to match a set of output patterns, a NELONET can be constructed to make the exact matching of the input patterns to the output pattern and the sypnastical weight (w_1, w_2) can be computed as given in Section 1.9. If the weightages at different times are constructed based on the available input patterns and the corresponding output patterns are denoted as $(w_1(t_i), w_2(t_i))$ for instances t_i $i = 1, \ldots, n$. Using three-dimensional interpolation polynomial function for $(w_1(t_i), w_2(t_i), t_i)$ with t as the time variable, it is possible to obtain a pair of weights at any instance t within the range of time being considered [21]. Thus, given an input at an instance, the corresponding weight at that instance can be retrieved to compute the output. Such a temporal inferencing system derived from the NELONET may have applications in some knowledge domain.

REFERENCES

[1] J.J. Hopfield, "Neural Networks and Physical Systems with Emergent Collective Computational Abilities," *Proceedings of the National Academy of Sciences,* Vol. 79, 1982, pp. 2554–2558.

[2] G.A. Carpenter and S. Grossberg, "A Massively Parallel Architecture for a Self-Organizing Neural Pattern Recognition Machine," *Computer Vision, Graphics and Image Processing,* Vol. 37, 1987, pp. 54–115.

[3] G.E. Hinton, T.J. Sejnowski, and D.H. Ackley, "Boltzmann Machines: Constraint Satisfaction Networks that Learn," TR-CMU-CS-84-119, Department of Computer Science, Carnegie-Mellon University, Pittsburgh, 1984.

[4] T. Kohonen, "An Introduction to Neural Computing," *Neural Networks,* Vol. 1, 1988, pp. 3–16.

[5] K. Fukushima, "Neocognitron: A Hierarchical Neural Network Capable of Visual Pattern Recognition," *Neural Networks,* Vol. 1, 1988, pp. 119–130.

[6] S.A. Amari, "Neural Theory of Association and Concept Formation," *Biological Cybernetics,* Vol. 26, 1977, pp. 175–185.

[7] S.A. Amari, "A Mathematical Approach to Neural Systems," *Systems Neuroscience,* Academic Press, New York, 1977, pp. 67–117.

[8] D.E. Rumelhart and J.L. McClelland, *Parallel Distributed Processing,* Vol. I & II, MIT Press, Cambridge, MA, 1987.

[9] F. Rosenblatt, "Two Theorems of Statistical Separability in the Perceptron," *Proceedings of Symposium Held at the National Physical Laboratory,* Vol. 1, 1958, London, pp. 421–456.

[10] M. Minsky and S. Papert, *Perceptrons,* MIT Press, Cambridge, MA, 1969.

[11] S.C. Chan, L.S. Hsu, and H.H. Teh, "On Neural Logic Networks," *Neural Networks,* Vol. 1, Suppl. 1, 1988, p. 428.

[12] S.C. Chan, L.S. Hsu, S. Brody, and H.H. Teh, "Neural Three-Valued Logic Networks," *Proceedings of the International Joint Conference on Neural Networks,* Vol. II, Washington DC, June 1989, p. 594.

[13] L.S. Hsu, H.H. Teh, S.C. Chan, and K.F. Loe, "Fuzzy Logic in Connectionists' Expert Systems," *International Joint Conference on Neural Networks,* Vol. 2, Washington DC, Jan 1990, pp. 599–602.

[14] H.H. Teh, S.C. Chan, L.S. Hsu, and K.F. Loe, "Probabilistic Neural-Logic Networks," *Proceedings of the International Joint Conference on Neural Networks,* Vol. 2, Washington DC, June 1989, p. 600.

[15] L.A. Zadeh, "The Role of Fuzzy Logic in the Management of Uncertainty in Expert Systems," *Fuzzy Sets and Systems,* Vol. 11, 1983, pp. 199–227.

[16] L.S. Hsu, H.H. Teh, S.C. Chan, and K.F. Loe, "Multi-Valued Neural Logic Networks," *Proceedings of the Twentieth International Symposium on Multivalued Logic,* Charlotte, NC, May 1990, pp. 426–432.

[17] L.S. Hsu, H.H. Teh, S.C. Chan, and K.F. Loe, "Imprecise Reasoning Using Neural Networks," *Proceedings of the Twenty-Third Annual Hawaii International Conference on System Sciences,* Vol. 4, 1990, pp. 363–368.

[18] R. Turner, *Logics for Artificial Intelligence,* Ellis Horwood, Chichester, England, 1984.

[19] S.C. Chan and Y. Chu, "Introducing a Neural Network Design Language," *Proceedings of the International Joint Conference on Neural Networks,* Vol. 2, Washington DC, 1990, pp. 110–113.

[20] H.H. Teh and A.H. Tan, "Connectionists' Expert Systems—Neural Logic Models Approach," *Interfaculty Seminar on Neural Computing,* National University of Singapore, 1989, pp. 16–32.

[21] H.H. Teh, L.S. Hsu, S.C. Chan, and K.F. Loe, "Temporal Neural Logic Networks," *Proceedings of the 2nd International IEEE Conference on Tools for Artificial Intelligence,* Herndon, VA, 1990, pp. 372–376.

Author Index

Subject Index